ITALY
Trip Planner & Guide

ITALY
Trip Planner & Guide
Leslie and Adrian Gardiner

PASSPORT BOOKS

This first edition published 1994 by
Passport Books,
Trade Imprint of NTC Publishing Group,
4255 West Touhy Avenue,
Lincolnwood (Chicago), Illinois 60646-1975
U.S.A.

Conceived, edited, designed and produced by
Duncan Petersen Publishing Ltd, 54 Milson Road, London W14 0LB
from a concept by Emma Stanford

Typeset by Duncan Petersen Publishing Ltd;
film output by Reprocolor International, Milan

Originated by Reprocolor International, Milan

Printed by GraphyCems, Navarra

ISBN: 0-8442-9219-2

Library of Congress Catalog Card Number: 93-85444

Every reasonable care has been taken to ensure the information in this
guide is accurate, but the publishers and copyright holders can accept
no responsibility for the consequences of errors in the text or in the
maps, particularly those arising from changes taking place after the text
was finalized. The publishers are always pleased to hear from readers
who wish to suggest corrections and improvements.

Editorial director Andrew Duncan
Assistant editors Joshua Dubin, Mary Devine and Laura Harper
Art director Mel Petersen
Design assistants Beverley Stewart, Chris Foley
Maps by Chris Foley and Beverley Stewart
Illustrations by Beverley Stewart

Photographic credits
John Freeman: pp. 15, 19, 22, 23, 25, 30, 31, 39, 46, 47, 54, 55, 70, 78, 79,
87, 95, 102, 103, 106, 111, 114, 131, 135, 143, 147, 159, 170, 191, 199,
206, 207, 209, 214, 219, 226, 227, 246, 258, 263, 270, 275, 282, 286, 287,
294, 295, 297. **Leslie Gardiner:** pp. 38, 63, 86, 94, 166.
Adrian Gardiner: pp. 154, 234, 239.

Adrian Gardiner was born in Edinburgh and attended art college in the same city. He has been writing from an early age: his first article appeared when he was six in the *Edinburgh Evening News*. While a student, he hitch-hiked around Italy and has made many return trips since, including an extensive one specifically for this guide. He has written many travel features on Italy, France and Britain and the Benelux countries, specializing in discovering the undiscovered. His published titles are *Classic Touring Routes in Scotland* (1991) and *Scottish Crafts* (1993).

Leslie Gardiner, father of Adrian Gardiner, has been touring Italy since 1941, when as a fugitive of war he walked from the Alps to Sicily. He has written about 20 books, including Italian biographies, history and travel. Over the years he has picked up numerous literary and travel-writing awards in Italy, including the prestigious Michelangelo Prize of 1976, quincentenary of the artist's birth. In 1982, in recognition of his many articles and broadcasts, he was appointed Commendatore of the Italian Order of Merit, a rare distinction for a foreigner.

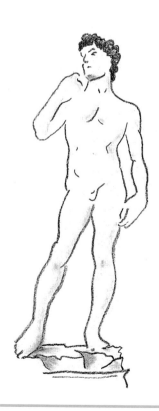

Master contents list

This contents list is for when you need to use the guide in the conventional way: to find out about where you are going, or where you happen to be. The index, pages 310-320, may be just as helpful.

HOWEVER...
There is much more to this guide than the region-by-region approach suggested by the contents list on this page. Turn to page 8; and see also pages 10-11.

Contents

Italy Overall
- *master map*

Italy Overall, pages 26-105, is a traveller's network for taking in the whole country, or large parts of it.

Each 'leg' of the network has a number (ie Italy Overall: 1); you will also find it described as a 'National Route', plus the number.

The term National Route does *not* simply mean a line on a map. Each 'route' features a whole region, and describes many places both on and off the marked route. Think of the National Routes not only as physical trails, but as imaginative ways of connecting all the main centres of Italy, and of describing and making travel sense of the country as whole.

They are designed to be used in these different ways:

1 *Ignore the marked route entirely*: simply use the alphabetically arranged Gazetteer of Sights & Places of Interest, and the map at the start of each 'route', as a guide to what to see and do in the region, not forgetting the hotel and restaurant recommendations.

2 Follow the marked route by public transport (see the transport box) or by car. You can do sections of the route, or all of it; you can follow it in any direction. Link the routes to travel the length and breadth of Italy.

Rome, **Florence** and **Venice** have sections of their own, pages 106-119, 120-127 and 128-137.

Each route has a section to itself, beginning with an introduction and a simplified map. The page number for each such section is shown on this master map.

Always use the simplified maps in conjunction with detailed maps (suggestions are given on the introductory pages).

Some practical hints on how to travel red, blue and green are given in the introductory pages and the simplified maps, including key roads and their numbers. Generally, though, there are no absolute rules for going red, blue or green and you are meant to link the places, using a detailed road map, in whatever way suits you best.

> RED *marks key sights and centres, not to be missed.*
>
> BLUE *marks important places, certainly worth a visit.*
>
> GREEN *places are for those who aren't in a hurry and want to experience the region in some depth.*

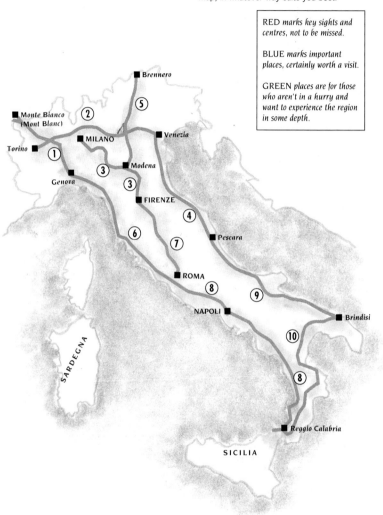

The *Italy Overall* section is ideal for:

■ Planning, and undertaking, tours of the whole country, or parts.

■ Making the journey to or from your eventual destination as interesting and as rewarding as possible.

■ Linking the in-depth explorations of localites provided by the Local Explorations section, pages 138-304.

Contents

The Local Explorations
- master map

The Local Explorations are strategies for exploring all the interesting localities of Italy. Also described as Local Tours, they complement the National Routes, pages 8-9. **They are designed to be used in these different ways:**

1 *Ignore the marked route entirely:* simply use the alphabetically arranged Gazetteer of Sights & Places of Interest, and the map at the start of each Local Exploration, as a guide to what to see and do in the area, not forgetting the hotel and restaurant recommendations.

2 Use the marked route to make a tour by public transport (see the transport box) or by car. You can do sections of the route, or all of it. (In the introduction it tells you how long you might take to cover everything the quickest way, by car.)

If you are driving, you can generally follow the tour in any direction; usually, the route as marked is an attractive and convenient way to link the places of interest; you may well find other ways to drive it. Always use our map in conjunction with a detailed road map (suggestions are given on each introductory page).

Contents

The *Local Explorations* are ideal for:

■ **Planning single-centre holidays**: each Local Exploration encapsulates an area which would make a great holiday. The introductory page to each section is designed to tell you whether the area will suit you: what you can expect; and something of its history, geography, people, customs, food.

■ **Entertaining yourself while you are there**: each section is packed with ideas for things to see and do. The tour, followed in full, can fill several days, and will always make a memorable journey, but most of the the sights and places of interest make fascinating day or part-day trips in their own right, not to mention the detours.

■ **Planning multi-centre holidays**: the map on this page shows you at a glance all the interesting parts of Italy. Combine them at will to experience the different faces of the country; or link them, by means of the national route network.

Rome, **Florence** and **Venice** have sections of their own, pages 106-119, 120-127 and 128-137.

The Local Explorations or Tours, pages 138-304, generally follow each other in a north-south/west-east sequence.

Conventions Used in this Guide

A single *lira* sign – **L** – or several *lire* signs, such as **LLL**, in a hotel or restaurant entry, denote a price band. Its object is to give an indication of what you can expect to pay. Accommodation offered at any one place may well span two or more price bands.

Hotels
Double room with shower:

L	Up to L80,000
LL	L80,000-L160,000
LLL	More than L160,000

In tourist literature, hotels are given stars. Four or five stars corresponds to our LLL; two and three stars to LL; one star to L.

Restaurants
Meal for two, excluding wine:

L	Up to L50,000
LL	L50,000-L100,000
LLL	More than L100,000

Hotels and restaurants in this guide are a selection of personal recommendations – not exhaustive lists. They have been chosen to represent interest and quality, or to satisfy specific needs, at every price level.

Opening times – hotels and restaurants
Where hotel and restaurant opening times are not specifically mentioned in this guide, assume that they follow these general rules:

Most city hotels are open all year round and staffed day and night. In rural areas and purely touristic locations hotels may close between October and Easter. In ski centres some hotels open December to April only. In some mountain spa and 'climatic' resorts you may find a hotel opening in summer only, another nearby opening in winter only. Family-run inns and hotels may close for one month annually – often December, January or February, sometimes August.

Restaurants and *trattorie* open for lunch and dinner; the latter meal is generally available up to 10 or 11 pm. They close one day a week, normally Monday. On one or more other days,

🛏 after a heading in **Sights & Places of Interest** means that there is an accommodation suggestion (or suggestions) for that place in **Recommended Hotels**.

✕ after a heading in **Sights & Places of Interest** means that there is a suggestion (or suggestions) for that place in **Recommended Restaurants**.

only dinner may be served. It depends on location and size of establishment. *Rosticcerie, tavole calde* and *pizzerie* in all towns serve hot and cold snacks and pizzas and keep late hours. Bars are open every day from early am to late pm, serving not only coffee, aperitifs and other drinks but also sandwiches and cakes.

Opening times – museums, galleries, churches, tourist attractions
This guide does not give opening times for every place described: the following *general* rules should enable you to time your visit; if in doubt, enquire at the local tourist office.

State museums, which include major art galleries, national and regional museums and archaeological sites, open 9-2 weekdays except Mon, 9-1 Sun and public holidays. A few popular places open again 4-7 or thereabouts, and special sites such as Pompeii and Herculaneum are open all day in high summer from 9 am to 10 pm.

The Vatican museums have their own routine – Mon to Sat 9-1.45, Easter and Jul-Sep 8.45-4. They also open on the last Sunday in the month (but not Easter Sunday) when admission is free.

Many small churches, being vulnerable to theft, are kept locked – a notice

↗ After a place name on a map means that the sight or place of interest is covered in detail in another part of the book. To find out exactly where, look up the place in the **Sights & Places of Interest** gazetteer which follows the map: a cross-reference is given in every case.

on the door tells you where to find the sacristan. Many more are open to visitors mornings only.

Remember that works of art all over Italy are covered up for five days preceding Easter Sunday.

Mileages for routes and tours
Are approximate. In the case of Italy Overall, they represent the shortest distances you could expect to travel on the route, almost always the 'red' option.

In the case of Local Explorations, they also represent the shortest possible distance you could expect to cover, excluding detours.

Since the routes and tours are designed to be travelled in whole, in part, or indeed not at all, the mileages are given as much for passing interest as for their practical value.

Something for Everyone
Getting the most from your guide

Here is a *small* selection of ideas for enjoying Italy opened up by this guide, aimed at a range of needs and tastes. The list is just a start: the guide offers many, many more ideas for what really matters: suiting *yourself*. You'll find that it takes into account not only your tastes, but how much time you have.

Sun, sand and art
Any resort in Italy Overall: 4 *and* 6; *plus Local Explorations:* 7 *and* 24.

Florence, plus quintessential Italian countryside
Florence city section plus Local Explorations: 9 10 *and* 11.

Renaissance Italy
*Florence plus Local Explorations:*10.

Undiscovered Italy
Local Explorations: 13, 16 *and* 18.

Ancient Italy - the Romans, and before
Rome city section plus Local Explorations: 14 *and* 17.

Lakes and mountains
Local Explorations: 2, 3, 4, 5 *and* 15.

Rugged upland Italy: for walkers
Local Explorations: 4, 12 *and* 15.

Venice plus
Venice city section with Local Explorations: 6.

Unspoilt Mediterranean idyll
Local Explorations: 26.

Sun, sand and sophistication
Local Explorations: 27.

Italy with an extra dimension: Sicily
Local Explorations: 24 *and* 25.

The ideal three-day break: sun, sea, ancient history, island retreats, stunning coastal scenery, close to an international airport.
Local Explorations: 21.

Grand old cities of the north
Italy Overall: 2.

ITALY:
An Introduction

Where to go in Italy? Everywhere if possible; certainly all the long-distance routes and local explorations described in this book. Italy was Europe's premier tourist destination long before she was joined by France. Her very shape recommends her. Nearly the whole country is outstandingly picturesque, the climate is delightful, the grandeur of her ancient monuments, paintings, sculptures and architecture is unmatched in the world. Her Roman remains are the bedrock of western civilization. Her medieval and Renaissance arts alone would make her a great metropolis of the spirit, even if she were not the cradle of the Christian faith.

The Italian landscape is a coloured picture-book. The Adriatic coast is an almost unbroken chain of sandy beach resorts, some over-developed and some not. The western shores are more varied, rocky and shingly. The whole length of the Apennines is wonderful country for touring by car, on foot or in the sturdy diesel-drawn cars of narrow-gauge railways. Skiing is most highly organized at Alpine resorts, but there are also busy slopes in Tuscany, the Abruzzi, Calabria and Sicily. The northern lakes, Italy's oldest tourist destinations, still hold their magic.

The densest concentrations of medieval towns and Renaissance arts are within the Milan-Venice-Rome triangle. Place names such as Florence, Ravenna, Urbino, Perugia, Assisi, Arezzo and Siena are familiar, but scores of places rarely mentioned in guide-books have abundant treasures. (It is easy, and a mistake, to spend all your time in churches, museums and galleries, but remember that a cathedral is a cool place on a hot day.) The ecclesiastical architecture reflects every European style – a legacy of Italy's turbulent history. The Romanesque and Saracenic of the deep south deserve as much attention as the Gothic and Renaissance of the north and centre.

Add to Italy's attractions a population well-disposed towards strangers and tolerant of their foibles. You will rarely encounter deliberate rudeness. The modern Italian has acquired dignity and self-assurance. He is lively and pragmatic, well informed about current events (especially the scandals) in your country. Italian women retain the graceful ways and flattering submissiveness towards men which have served them well down the ages. In all, when you mingle with Italians you cannot help feeling that they have hit on a secret of successful living which has eluded the rest of us.

• *Ponte Vecchio, Florence.*

We cannot force them into a national stereotype. Italy, politically uni-fied since 1870, with a common language little changed since Dante's time is still a collection of regions where about 400 distinct dialects are spoken, incomprehensible to outsiders, let alone foreigners. Turin and Florence were capitals of Italy before Rome. Numerous cities claim pre-eminence in age and cultural achievement. Regional pride is expressed positively in respect for traditions (observe the brilliant organization of small pageants and the explosions of gaiety that attend them) and neg-atively in *campanilismo*, 'attachment to one's own belfry' or parochial-ism. Sometimes you wonder whether Italy's disgrace – streams of garbage down hillsides, atmospheric and river pollution – arises from protests against laws made in Rome.

Family ties are strong in Italy, but the old faith is less tyrannical than formerly. Outlandish cults prosper; pornography on late-night television has to be seen to be believed. The sexes uninhibitedly mingle, the tempo of everyday life increases. But however frenetic the urban scene, there comes a moment when calm descends on the piazza and the citizens, husbands and wives, boys and girls, take their evening promenade, the twilight mart of ideas, reminiscences and hearts.

Landscapes are the picture-book, life is the drama. To board a bus, go shopping, order a meal is to be involved in a small adventure. Food is a big subject and you may feel you know all about it without going to Italy. The cuisine, however, is as versatile as the landscape. Outside cosmopolitan centres it is more than regional. A hill between two vil-lages can separate two philosophies of eating and drinking. And only in Italy, on the spot, can you know the true flavour of pasta sauce, *vino locale* or *espresso* coffee.

Leslie and Adrian Gardiner

BEFORE YOU GO

Climate: when to go, and to which parts

Italy enjoys a wide variety of weather. The northern plains have 'continental' weather, hot summers and cold winters. The middle regions and Adriatic coast enjoy a more temperate climate. The south is sub-tropical, mild in winter and often unpleasantly hot in summer. Inland Sicily has an average daily temperature in August of 35C (95F).

Italy rarely suffers the long overcast spells common in northern Europe. Rain tends towards the dramatic rather than the drizzly. Spectacular thunderstorms clear the air. Freak weather patterns may be produced by seasonal winds: the Balkan *bora* in spring, the *maestrale* (mistral) from southern France, the *scirocco*, hot and sticky from the Sahara and the *föhn*, a fast warm wind from the Alps. The big lakes have their predictable wind patterns, to the delight of wind-surfers. Coasts have refreshing sea and land breezes.

May and September are ideal months for touring in Italy. Inland cities, including Rome and Florence, can be crowded heat-traps in summer. Avoid August if possible: Italy itself is on holiday and many museums and restaurants close for all or part of the month. While fog lingers along the northern lakes and valleys, the high-level resorts are bathed in sunshine.

Clothing

Travel light, even in your own car. Formal clothes are unncessary for an Italian holiday, unless you stay in the grand hotels. If you visit churches or monasteries, respect local feelings and cover up bare flesh. As in most Mediterranean countries, everyone goes hatless nowadays, even to church. Shorts are ridiculed anywhere other than the beach.

While lightweight clothing is *de rigueur*, take a jersey or sweater for evenings. All summer visitors should have a light raincoat, a pair of light, comfortable shoes and of course a sun hat; in winter you need a heavier coat.

Documentation

Citizens of the EC, the U.S.A. and of course other countries require a valid passport (no visa). Drivers need a current licence: if it is not the pink EC type it should be accompanied by a translation in Italian. Travelling in your own car you need the registration document and insurance certificate. A policy extension (in the U.K., a 'green card') to make the cover comprehensive while motoring abroad is also recommended – without it your insurance is only the legal minimum. The 'green card' comes with a standard accident report form. In Italy it is obligatory to fill this in at the time of the accident.

Medical and travel insurance

EC residents should carry the form entitling them to reciprocal health treatment in other EC states. However, the cost of treatment and medication must be paid for at the time and reclaimed later after a long-winded procedure. Other nationalities are recommended to purchase (or to arrange on an existing policy) medical and travel insurance before departure.

If you buy insurance against loss or theft of personal belongings, read the insurer's conditions in the event of a claim *before* you go abroad. They may well require you to report loss or theft to the police in order to validate a claim.

Money

The standard unit is the *lira* (L), plural *lire*. Paper notes are in thousands, 1, 2, 5, 10, 50 and 100. The commonest coins are 50, 100, 200 and 500.

Sterling and dollar travellers cheques are more acceptable than *lire* ones, but if possible avoid travellers cheques because Italian banks are staggeringly slow and inefficient. With Eurocheques, available to EC members, you can cash the equivalent of £150 per day, but it may take half an hour or more, once you have penetrated the metal-detecting, airlock-type door. Much depends on how far off the beaten track you are: in cities and in the north, cash dispensers are increasingly common. Most accept the major international credit cards. With Visa, for example, you can draw £225 a day.

Major credit and cheque cards are accepted without demur in all but the humbler *pensioni* (guest-houses) and *trattorie* (small restaurants) in rural locations. But it is rare to find a petrol station that accepts any card apart from Diners. Motorway service areas are more tolerant. The most common card sign in Italy is Carta Si, a composite which includes Visa, Mastercard and Eurocard.

We strongly advise a money belt or inside zipped pocket for carrying cash, cheques, cards and passports. Some cities, Rome, Naples, Genoa, Palermo and Bari particularly, are notorious for bag-snatchers who often work in pairs. Carry your bag or purse on the side away from the kerb. In cafés and restaurants keep them on your lap; and be especially vigilant on crowded buses and in street markets.

Import duty
The regulations follow general EC rules. Instead of the former duty-free allowances, there are now guidelines for individual import and export of such goods as wines, spirits and tobacco across EC borders. Customs officers still maintain their vigilance, often covertly, against prohibited goods such as drugs and weapons which might assist terrorist activity. Get advice before travelling with pets or citizens' band radios. They are a complicated subject.

Tourist information outside Italy
The Italian State Tourist Office (ENIT) has branches in most capital cities offering a wealth of free tourist literature including lists, updated twice a year, of tour operators, and special interest and self-catering holidays.

ENIT Amsterdam 1054 ES Amsterdam, Stadhoudeskade 6.
ENIT Dublin 47 Merrion Square, Dublin 2.
ENIT Frankfurt 6000 Frankfurt/Main 1, Kaiserstrasse 65 (also in Dusseldorf and Munich).
ENIT London 1 Princes Street, London W1R 8AY.
ENIT New York Suite 1565, 630 Fifth Avenue, New York NY 10111 (also in Chicago, Montreal and San Francisco).
ENIT Paris 23 rue de la Paix, 75002 Paris.

The governing body of Italian travel agencies, which must be licensed, is FIAVET, Via Livenza 7, Rome.

Local customs: what to expect, how to behave
The Italian's day begins early and ends late, frequently after midnight. The siesta after the main meal, which is lunch, lasts an hour or two in the north, all afternoon in the south. Early evening is devoted to a promenade (the *passeggiata*), up and down a main street or square. It fulfills many purposes: gossip, matchmaking, showing off new clothes. Not until 8 or 8.30 do the restaurants start filling up. Theatres, cinemas and the opera begin about then, and go on until midnight.

All but the anarchic young take pride in their personal appearance. Women are extremely fashion-conscious – hence the prevalence of great Italian fashion designers. Since clothes, shoes and jewellery are always stylish, if not always of top quality, men and women manage to look smart even on limited incomes. Leather has an enduring appeal for the Italian.

Be prepared to shake hands on meeting or parting from Italian acquaintances, though you may have met or parted from them an hour earlier. Don't be offended by personal questions. Accept compliments about your clothes, your appearance and (if a woman) your beauty in the spirit in which they are made. They are the Italian's way of being friendly. Don't take outbursts of Latin emotion too seriously and do not try to compete. There is nothing the Italian admires more than the *sang-froid* traditionally associated with the British and other northern Europeans.

Italy in the 1990s remains a patriarchal, separatist society: conscious of the differences between the classes, the sexes, the regions, and not particularly inclined to minimize them.

Petty bureaucracy is rife. You will not reform the system single-handed. Exercise patience, try to smile rather than snarl at the railway booking-office free-for-all and the long queue at the bank which never moves. Having children with you can work wonders in melting bureaucratic indifference.

GETTING THERE

By air
Direct flights from European capitals are operated by major airlines to many Italian destinations. It is a money-saving rule to book through a travel agent or discount flight specialist rather than directly with an airline. Doing so enables you to sift through the various options on a route where competition between operators is intense. Some airlines, including Alitalia, offer cut-price car hire if you book both flight and car rental together.

British travellers, and North American visitors breaking their transatlantic journey in Britain or Ireland, have the choice of flights from all major British and Irish airports to 16 Italian destinations.

By rail
The Eurail Pass, available only to non-European nationals, provides an economic and practical means of unlimited travel throughout Italy (and indeed continental Europe). Certain age groups are eligible for valuable discounts. Enquire at a main railway station.

European nationals can buy similar unlimited travel passes (in the U.K, the Interail Pass) for railway journeys in Europe but outside their own country, again with discounts for certain age groups. Enquire at a main railway station.

The main railway routes into Italy are from Paris to Turin; from Paris along the south coast of France to Ventimiglia; from Basle to Milan and and from Munich south over the Brenner Pass. Rail fares are generally only a little cheaper than the cheapest air fares. You can put a car on express sleeper trains in many northern European cities, for example, Paris-Milan or Düsseldorf-Genoa.

EC (Eurocity) and TEE (Trans Europe Express) luxury trains, first class only, at a special fare with obligatory seat reservation, include: 'Cisalpin' (Geneva-Milan); 'Galilei' (Paris-Milan-Florence); 'Leonardo da Vinci' (Dortmund-Verona-Milan); 'Pablo Casals' (Barcelona-Milan); 'Palatino' (Paris-Rome); 'Rialto' (Paris-Venice) and 'Tiziano' (Hamburg-Milan).

By bus
The cheapest and least comfortable option: it takes between 30 and 40 hours to get from northern Europe to Rome, up to 48 from London.

By car
The main routes into Italy are via the French, Swiss and Austrian Alpine passes, and also along the south coast of France via Nice and Menton to Ventimiglia. The Mont Blanc and Grand St Bernard toll tunnels are open all year, as is the Brenner Pass; the Simplon is closed Nov-Apr. The Mont Blanc tunnel costs from £9 to £18 ($13 to $27) depending on the size of the vehicle, the Grand St Bernard £11 to £37 ($16 to $55).

GETTING AROUND

By rail
Mussolini's memorable achievement was to make the trains run on time. Generally they still do. If a train is more than 29 minutes late, you are entitled to a partial refund of the ticket cost.
Rail fares are based on a sliding scale. The farther you travel the cheaper, proportionately, it becomes. You may get on a train without a ticket, but it will cost more from the conductor. Certain fast long-distance trains are subject to a supplementary charge. Most local commuter trains are second-class only.

For the tourist there is the BTCL, an unlimited-circulation ticket valid for 8, 15, 21 or 30 days.

By car
The motorway system is comprehensive, but except south of Salerno, near Naples, and on sections by-passing cities, you have to pay tolls. The charge varies according to the terrain: Genoa to La Spezia, 100 km of tunnels and viaducts, costs £5 to £8 ($7 to $12); Milan to Brescia, 100 km, flat and dead straight, costs £3 to £4 ($4 to $6). Italy also tops the European league for petrol prices, and cut-price petrol coupons for foreign visitors were phased out in 1992.

Cities and A-class roads are normally very congested. Do not contemplate driving in Rome or Florence unless you have nerves of steel. Florence and

• *Enduring Venice scene.*

Milan are particularly inconvenient cities for drivers. Moreover, the Italian authorities have taken enthusiastically to the concept of tow-away zones, so park with caution. You may find it worth buying a *Disco Orario* from a car accessory shop. In places where parking is restricted to certain time limits, you set the disc to your time of arrival.

Driving regulations: Motoring laws follow European norms. Reflective warning triangles, to be placed 50 m behind your car when broken down, are obligatory. Fines for speeding are severe and may be imposed on the spot. Speed limits are 50 kph in towns, 90 kph in the country and 110 kph on motorways rising to 130 kph for vehicles with an engine capacity more than 1,100 cc.

Off the motorways, petrol stations close for up to three hours at lunchtime, usually Saturday pm and all day Sunday. Lead-free petrol (*senza piombino*) is widely available.

Italian drivers couple skill and panache with excitability and impatience. They are by no means the worst in Europe (that distinction belongs to the Portuguese) but the characteristic they call *far figura* (to make an impression) comes out even in the mildest-mannered when they get behind the wheel. It is not uncommon to be followed for 3 km along a straight road and then to be overtaken on a blind bend.

Right-hand-drive cars are unlikely to be stolen, but auto-theft is a scourge in Italy as elsewhere. Thefts from moving cars is not unknown, so follow the American habit of locking the doors from the inside, at least in cities. Leave nothing visible inside the car. Lock valuables in the boot (trunk) or take them with you. Thefts should be reported to the police; ask for a photocopy of their report if you intend claiming on your insurance.

Taxis
These have a characteristic colour in each city and are metered. Charges vary according to location. Rome is the most expensive, the minimum fare being about £4 ($6) for 3 km or nine minutes.

By air
Rome, the main international and domestic hub, is the principal base of the national airline Alitalia. Milan is the secondary hub, much frequented by the international business community. Venice, Pisa (for Florence) and Catania are largely tourist gateways. In Rome you are never more than an hour from any Italian airport – by air. Domestic flights are cheap and on top of that there are reductions for families and discounts for night flights.

By bus
Despite the comprehensive rail service, there are numerous privately-run bus services, especially in remote areas.

ESSENTIAL PRACTICAL INFORMATION

Accommodation

Italy has a clutch of the world's most expensive hotels, including the Cipriani in Venice, up to L700,000 a night, single room only, in 1993. The Costa Smeralda in Sardinia is also renowned for luxury at a price. Large cities have the big, cosmopolitan hotels such as Sheratons and Hiltons; such places are thin on the ground in southern regions, along the Adriatic coast and in small tourist towns.

More affordable are the numerous *alberghi* and *pensioni*, graded by stars. One star means old-fashioned, basic and cheap; two is usually creaky but comfortable; with three you can expect elevators, car parking and TVs in rooms. Lastly there is the *locanda*, the lodging house typically found in small villages. Here you can expect to pay about L20,000 a night. Displayed on the door of every room in every hotel and *pensione* is the official tariff. If you are charged more, demand an explanation. The tariff should show whether taxes, air-conditioning and breakfast are included. Unlike in France, you are not expected to eat in the hotel restaurant; many hotels do not have one.

In coastal areas there are the tourist villages, a relatively new development for Italy, with inexpensive chalet accommodation. New also is the *agriturismo* scheme: converted farm buildings available for bed-and-breakfast. Many have integral kitchens for self-catering; they are nearly always sound value for money, though not necessarily cheap. Contact a local tourist office or Agriturist, Corso V. Emanuele 101, Rome.

More and more visitors to Italy are staying in furnished villas or apartments. Contact a well-known company with a proven track record.

Banks and currency exchange

Banks open Monday to Friday 8.30-1.30 and 3-4. Currency exchanges (*Cambii*) keep longer hours, proportionate to the size of place in which they are located. You find them at railway stations as well as airports, ferry terminals and town centres.

Breakdowns

Motorways have SOS telephones with two buttons: one for medical assistance and one for breakdowns. On other roads, dial 116 for English-language assistance. Cars with foreign number plates are towed free to the nearest garage.

Drinking and smoking regulations

These generally follow EC norms.

Electricity

As in most of Europe, Italy is 220V, 50 AC. Plugs are two-pronged. Take an adaptor for foreign electrical appliances.

Embassies and consulates

Australia (embassy and consular department) Via Alessandria 215, Rome; tel. 06 832 721.

Canada (embassy) Via GB de Rossi 29, Rome; tel. 06 841 5341. Consulate: Via Zara 30, Rome; tel. 06 440 3028.

France (embassy and consular department) Piazza Farnese 67, Rome; tel. 06 686 011.

Germany (embassy) Via Po 25c, Rome; tel. 06 844 1812. Consulate: Via F. Siacci 2; tel. 06 805 338.

Ireland (embassy) Largo del Nazareno 3, Rome; 06 678 2451.

Netherlands (embassy and consular department) Via Michele Mercati 8, Rome; tel. 06 322 1141.

U.K. (embassy and consular department) Via XX Settembre 80a, Rome; tel. 06 482 5441 or 482 5551.

U.S.A. (embassy and consular department) Via Vittorio Veneto 119-21, Rome; tel. 06 46 741.

Some countries maintain consulates outside Rome in major cities such as Bari, Brindisi, Cagliari, Florence, Genoa, Milan, Naples, Rome, Trieste, Turin and Venice.

Emergencies

Public emergency service: telephone 113 (this number is manned by multilingual operators).

Carabinieri immediate action service (crime and road accidents): telephone 112. Use the above numbers only in real emergencies – vital medical aid, serious personal danger, natural disaster. Otherwise call 116.

Lost property

Foreign visitors should read the instructions which come with their travellers cheques: they explain exactly how to replace them if lost or stolen.

Reports of lost documents such as passports have to be made on stamped legal paper. For a replacement passport, contact your consulate or telephone 116 for advice.

Measurements
Italy operates on the metric system:
One litre = 1.7 pints
(1 imperial gallon = 4.54 litres);
1 U.S. gallon = 3.73 litres.
One kilogramme (1,000 grams) = 2.2 lbs.
One kilometre (1,000 metres) = 0.62 miles.
To convert kilometres to miles multiply by five and divide by eight, and vice-versa.

Medical matters
The Italian National Health Service operates through local health units – see under *Unità Sanitaria Locale* in the telephone directory. EC nationals should show their reciprocal health care form (see under Documentation). Pharmacies are usually open 8.30 to 12.30 and 3.30 until 7.30. They are closed on Sundays and on alternate Wednesdays and Saturdays, but they operate a 24-hour service on a rotating shift basis, details of which are displayed on pharmacy doors and windows.

Medicines are rather expensive, and so is dental treatment, which you have to arrange for yourself.

National holidays
Fall on January 1 and 6; Easter Sunday and Monday; April 25th; May Day (May 1st); August 15th; December 8th, 25th and 26th. Provincial towns additionally celebrate local feast days.

Opening hours
Banks: see above, under Banks and currency exchange.

Museums and tourist attractions: see *Versatile Guide* Conventions, page 12.

Post offices transact business Monday to Friday 8.30 am to 1.30, and 3 to 4; they close around noon on Saturdays. You can buy stamps at tobacconists and news stands.

Shops keep flexible hours, usually 8 am to noon and 4 pm to 7.30 or 8.

Most close on Sundays and one (variable) afternoon per week, but in tourist resorts most shops open all day every day. Cafés and coffee bars open 7 am to 10 pm or later.

Post and telephone
Post offices will hold letters addressed to individuals on the move until collected in person. The envelope should carry the name of the recipient, the words *Fermo Posta* and the name of the locality. The recipient pays a fee to collect the letter.

Phonecards for the latest telephones are sold at post offices and many bars and tobacconists. Older models take 100 or 200 *lira* coins or *gettoni* tokens worth 200 *lire* each. To telephone abroad, go to a bar with a public phone (*a scatti*) or go to a SIP (Società Italiana Posta/Telefoni) office, book a cabin and pay for your call afterwards. Dial 12 for local directory enquiries, 13 for the operator, 113 for the emergency service, 116 for general assistance or information in principal foreign languages.

Rush hours
Between 7.30 and 9 am, and in the evening between 6 and 8. Main thoroughfares in and out of Rome and Naples are particularly congested at these times.

Time
The whole country observes European Standard Time (GMT plus one hour) and is one hour ahead of the U.K. and six hours ahead of U.S. Eastern Standard Time. Summer Time applies from the last weekend in March (advance one hour) to the last weekend in September (retard one hour).

Tipping
Despite what some guide books tell you, tipping is now widely frowned on in Italy. There are a few exceptions: all restaurants and a few bars – you can tell by looking for a saucer of coins near the till – and public WCs. In major museums, signs will warn you not to tip the guides. Taxi drivers, of course, will expect something.

Tourist information
The Italian State Tourist Office or Ente Nazionale per il Turismo (ENIT) oper-

• *Street life, Comiso, Sicily.*

ates information services at the international airports of Rome, Milan and Naples and at the following road frontier crossings:

Imperia: Autostrada dei Fiori-Ventimiglia and Ponte San Ludovico, Ventimiglia.

Como: Ponte Chiasso, Brogeda Autostrada.

Brenner Pass: Brennero Autostrada.

ENIT in Italy provides tourist information through 21 regional tourist boards in the 21 regional capitals and about 100 provincial tourist boards called Enti Provinciali Turismo (EPT) or Aziende Promozione Turistica (APT). The provincial boards operate tourist information offices, indicated by an italic *i* in every place of interest.

Regional and provincial boards do not deal directly with the public. They produce the material which information offices distribute free of charge – maps, street plans, leaflets, hotel lists, timetables, programmes of events.

On the outskirts of cities, usually where motorways join the *tangenziale*, there are enlarged service areas providing tourist information and a hotel booking service. Major tourist attractions are well signposted from motorways, and in many towns there are large yellow plaques headed *Itinerario Turistico*, listing local attractions.

• Pisa.

According to legend, refugees from Troy founded Rome in 753 BC. Historically, the first identifiable inhabitants were Etruscans in the central regions and Greeks in the south.

Rome drove out the Etruscans, destroyed the Greeks, triumphed over the Carthaginian (North African) invaders and by 250 BC dominated the whole peninsula. Civil strife led to civil war until Augustus in 27 BC became head of what was by then the Roman Empire. It reached the zenith of its power soon after AD 100. Assaulted at home and abroad by Goths, Huns, Persians and Franks, the Empire had collapsed by about 450 AD and for the next 1,400 years Italy was nothing but a geographical expression. An Eastern Empire, capital Constantinople (modern Istanbul), continued to dominate the eastern Mediterranean; Lombards made Milan the capital of their own kingdom; then came Saxons, Normans, the German Hohenstaufens, Angevins (French) and Aragonese (Spanish), whose heritage is still evident all over Italy.

The finest flowering of culture in Italy, known as the Renaissance, lasted from about 1300 to 1550. Its centre was Florence and the violent squabbles which impoverished other city states of the peninsula did not obstruct its progress. From this period onward the Church was influential, and a notable patron of arts and literature.

In succeeding centuries, France and Spain battled for Italy. Bonaparte's French army swept through in 1796 and gathered the country into a group of client states. It was, however, the Austrians in the north and the Spanish Bourbons and Papal armies in the south who had to be driven out before Cavour, Prime Minister to the King of Sardinia, could make a bid for a unified Italy. In 1870, with the aid of Garibaldi, the royalists achieved their aims. 'Italy is made,' said Massimo d'Azeglio. 'Now let us make the Italians.'

United Italy embarked on some disastrous colonial adventures. Though she came late into the First World War, she gained Trentino, Alto Adige and Trieste at the peace conference. Mussolini, a newspaper editor, took advantage of labour troubles and political lethargy to establish a Fascist state and ally himself with Germany in the Second World War. His ignoble end and the monarchy's unpopularity brought in a republican government in 1946. It was – and still is – a chaotic arrangement of inter-party alliances which against all odds produced the economic miracle of the 1950s and 1960s. Italy today is a strong member (and beneficiary) of the EC and a formidable power in Europe. Unsteady governments, mafia scandals and corruption in high places make news abroad.

KEY DATES

Early history

Legendary founding of Rome by Romulus	753 BC
Etruscan cities in Italy	750 BC
Greeks settle in south	734 BC

Roman Republic

Roman republic founded	510 BC
Rome extends authority over central Italy	290 BC
Rome expels the Greeks	275 BC
Hannibal the Carthaginian invades Italy	219 BC
End of Punic (Carthaginian) wars	146 BC
Julius Caesar assassinated	44 BC

Roman Empire

Augustus inaugurates Golden Age of culture	27 BC
Persecution of Christians under Nero	AD 64
Vesuvius eruption destroys Pompeii	79
Roman Empire at zenith of its power	117
Empire divided, East and West	395
Sack of Rome by Alaric the Goth	410
Lombards invade Italy	568
Rome becomes centre of Christian world	590
Charlemagne becomes first Holy Roman Emperor	800

Middle Ages

Rise of Venice as sea power	1125
Death of St Francis of Assisi	1226
Massacre of the Normans in Sicily	1282
Death of Dante	1321

Renaissance

Lorenzo de' Medici rules Florence	1469
Birth of Michelangelo	1476
Consecration of St Peter's, Rome	1626
Milan, Naples and other cities ceded to Austria	1715
Spanish Bourbons established in Naples	1734
Bonaparte conquers Italy	1797

Risorgimento

Italy and France at war with Austria	1859
Garibaldi seizes Sicily	1860
Kingdom of Italy established	1870

Modern times

Italy enters the First World War	1915
Mussolini's march on Rome	1922
End of Fascist era	1943
Republic of Italy established	1946

KEY CULTURAL THEMES, PLACES AND TERMS

Pre-history
Nuraghi towers (many sites in Sardinia); *trulli* (beehive-shaped huts, Valle d'Itria, Puglia).

Pre-Roman and Ancient Rome
Etruscan civilization: Lazio region north of Rome; museums of Tarquinia, Volterra, Chiusi, Villa Giulia (Rome).

Magna Graecia: Segesta, Selinunte, Agrigento, Syracuse, Taormina (all in Sicily); Paestum, Metaponto; museums of Naples and Reggio Calabria.

Rome, Ostia Antica, Tivoli, Ercolano, Pompeii, Verona, Turin, Aosta, Brescia, Piazza Armerina (Sicily); national museums of Rome and Naples.

Early churches and monasteries
Rome, Milan, Padua, Stilo (Calabria), towns of Lombardy, Tuscany, Puglia; La Verna (Tuscany), Monte Sant' Angelo (Puglia), Monte Cassino; Ravenna, Monreale for mosaics.

Renaissance painters
Assisi and Arezzo (Cimabue); Arezzo, San Sepolcro, Urbino (Piero della Francesca); Florence (Giotto, Uccello, Botticelli, Fra Filippo Lippi, Ghirlandaio, Leonardo da Vinci, Michelangelo, Raphael); Padua (Giotto); Parma (Correggio); Prato (Lippi); Milan (da Vinci); Mantua (Mantegna); Perugia (Perugino); Venice (Giorgione, Titian, Veronese); Rome (Michelangelo, Raphael, Caravaggio); Naples (Correggio, Caravaggio).

Baroque painters
Venice (Guardi, Canaletto, Tiepolo).

Sculpture and architecture
Pisa (Pisano family); Florence (Ghiberti, Brunelleschi, Donatello, Michelangelo, Cellini); Padua (Donatello); Rome (Michelangelo, Bramante, Bernini); Venice (Verrocchio, Palladio); Vicenza and neighbourhood (Palladio); Monte San Savino (Sansovino).

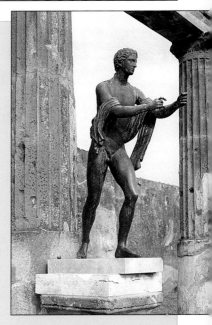

• Statue of Appollo, near the portico of the sacred area, Pompeii.

Art galleries
The world-famous ones are the Uffizi, Pitti and Accademia in Florence; the Brera in Milan; the Accademia in Venice and the Capitoline and Borghese in Rome.

Modern architecture
Turin, Milan, Rome; leading modern art galleries are in Milan, Rome, Florence and Ancona.

Opera
Major venues are La Scala, Milan; La Fenice, Venice; San Carlo, Naples and the opera theatres of Parma, Genoa, Rome, Palermo, Catania, Bologna, Trieste and Bergamo. The season is December to May, but summer opera, al fresco, is performed in Verona, Macerata and Rome.

Drama and music festivals
Are held in summer in many towns, the best being Florence, Ravenna, Rome, Siena, Stresa, Pesaro, Torre del Lago Puccini and Syracuse.

Northern Italy

Between Mont Blanc and Genoa
Italy's North-West Frontier

290 km; map Touring Club Italiano Piemonte e Valle d'Aosta

This is the fast route between the Alps and the Mediterranean. The Alpine end attracts thousands of skiers in winter and spring; the summer scene is better known to Italians than foreign visitors. The latter are usually too busy getting down to the 'real' Italy, or home from their tours, to linger among the rough rocks and scree slopes of the Valle d'Aosta and the rounded hills and plains of rural Piedmont.

Our route follows historic routes by which the Roman legions invaded northern Europe and it looks at the land which gave united Italy her first king and her first capital city, Turin (see Local Explorations: 1). At one end, under Mont Blanc, you are close to the highest Alpine peaks. At the other, in Genoa, you are between two Italian rivieras.

The *autostrada* (red route) speeds through the Valle d'Aosta and Piedmont with only a passing glance at abbeys and castles, long thin valleys, crags shining with glacial armour-plating and small lakes set in national parks. Many areas of Piedmont are sanctuaries for wildlife, visitable, restoring the nature-lover's faith in the planet. Our blue and green routes wander into a country strangely neglected by tourists and find, amid some industry and intensive agriculture, a world of interest with a hard-working, down-to-earth *montagnard* population, speaking French or an impenetrable French-Italian dialect of great antiquity. Artisans of the country districts specialize in pottery, woodwork and metalwork. Numerous small towns have traditions of musical-instrument manufacture: guitars, accordions, harps and bells.

Hot, spicy, nourishing foods, robust diets for robust people, characterize the Valdostana and Piedmontese cuisines. Red wine is sometimes served hot and spiced, perhaps in a wooden loving-cup. Restaurants offer *gnocchi alla fontina* (dumplings in soft cheese), *carbonades* of salted meats with red wine, goat and chamois cutlets, salami, fruits of the earth from mushrooms to honey. Fine wines grow in Piedmont. Among the most palatable are the classic red Barolos and dessert *moscato* produced along the river near St-Vincent. A fiery regional *grappa* helps keep out winter cold. (See also Local Explorations:1.)

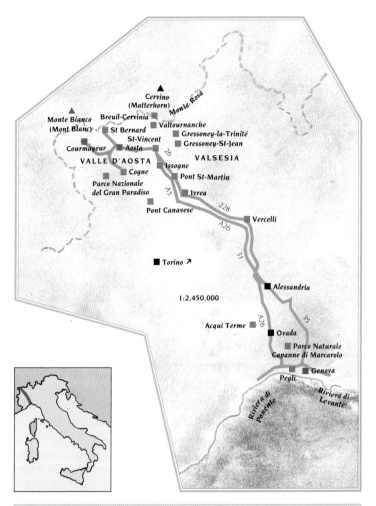

1:2,450,000

TRANSPORT

You may travel by rail all the way from Genoa to the slopes of Mont Blanc, leaving the national rail network (between Genoa and Turin) at Chivasso and proceeding by Ivrea and Aosta to Pré St Didier, or vice versa. The only lines actually penetrating the western and southern Alps are between Turin and Modane and the dramatic '*Treno del Mare*' under the Col di Tenda between Cuneo and Nice. Provincial railways of Piedmont can be picturesque, especially in the south, but you spend a lot of time in tunnels. Far-reaching cableways, funicular railways and comfortable bus excursions make it easy to escape into the mountains from many bases in Piedmont and Valle d'Aosta. Genoa is a major junction of roads and railways. It has excellent connections with the south of France and the rest of Italy.

Leading regional bus companies include: A.M.T., Via Lagaccio, Genoa (for East and West Rivieras); Autostradale, Piazzale Castello 1, Milan (for Riviera and Alpine resorts); Pesci, Corso Perrone 50, Cornigliano, Genoa (Piedmont generally); Sapav, Corso Torino 396, Pinerolo, Turin (Piedmont and Valle d'Aosta); and Savda, Strada Ponte Suaz 6, Aosta (Valle d'Aosta and Turin).

SIGHTS & PLACES OF INTEREST

ACQUI TERME

On Route 30, 35 km S of Alessandria. Not much is to be expected from a place whose name translates as 'Bathwater' but this spa town is thriving without losing its pleasant old-fashioned air. One hot spring, La Bollente ('The Boiler'), is in the town centre. The number of hotels and restaurants reflects an age-old popularity with both invalids and holidaymakers. Roman aqueduct, 11thC castle and cathedral.

AOSTA ⇔ ×

On Routes 26, 27, 45 km E of Mont Blanc. It was originally Augusta, garrison town of Rome's north-west frontier where the legions recovered from, or fortified themselves against, mountain sickness on the St Bernard Pass. Superficially a tourist trap, Aosta has more in it than meets the eye. If you can stay two hours, see the **Arch of Augustus**, built when the city was founded in 25

HOTELS AND RESTAURANTS

Our hotels are up-market ones with proven reputations for comfort, civility and cuisine. The whole route is furnished with venerable provincial and country inns and modern winter-tourist-oriented establishments both simple and elaborate.

Restaurant menus feature food and wine of the country – the former hearty and nourishing, refined in the north with touches of French flair, the latter highly prized at its best even across the border in France.

BC; the **Praetorian Gate**; the **Roman theatre and amphitheatre**; and the slender graceful columns of the cloisters at **Sant' Orso's collegiate church.**

The outlook on all sides proclaims Aosta's strategic importance in Roman times. Northward the tremendous

---

RECOMMENDED HOTELS

AOSTA
Valle d'Aosta, LLL; Corso Ivrea 146; tel. 016 541 845; credit cards, AE, DC, E, MC, V; closed mid-Nov to mid-Dec.

The large modern hotel with garden and car parking is peacefully sited on the edge of town. Large picture windows look out on the mountains.

COURMAYEUR
Palace Bron, LLL; Plan Gorret; tel. 016 584 2545; credit cards, DC, V; hotel closed May, mid-Sep to mid-Dec; log-fire restaurant closed Mon.

In pinewoods on east side of town overlooking mountains and valley, 26 luxurious rooms. Most Courmayeur hotels are seasonal. An exception is:

La Brenva, LL; at Entreves, 4 km N; tel. 016 589 285; credit cards, DC, E, MC, V.

Small, picturesque, quite special.

IVREA
Castello San Giuseppe, LL; at Chiaverano, 5 km N of town; tel. 012 542 4370; credit cards, AE, DC, E, MC, V; restaurant closed Sun.

A 17thC Carmelite monastery, then a Napoleonic fort and now a luxury hotel with a beautiful walled garden shaded by exotic trees. Some rooms have frescoed ceilings, as has the grand dining-room. A lovely place, beautifully maintained. Superior service.

ST-VINCENT
Elena, LL; Piazza Monte Zerbion; tel. 016 651 2140; credit cards, AE, DC, E, MC, V; closed Nov.

Comfortable modern air-conditioned hotel in centre near casino.

Grand Hotel Billia, LLL; Viale Piemonte 18; tel. 016 635 46; credit cards, AE, DC, E, MC, V.

Seriously expensive but it has everything: heated outdoor swimming-pool, tennis, games room, health suite, sauna, two restaurants, night-club and plenty of car parking. Near casino.

Alpine arch curves round – Mont Blanc, the Matterhorn, Monte Rosa. Southward the peaks of the Gran Paradiso stand guard (see Valle d'Aosta, below). Nostalgia trips for motorists who recall the gradients and treacherous gravel of the Alpine crossings are offered by city bus companies. To the **Grand St Bernard** is 34 km. There is now a 7-km tunnel under the worst bits and it attracts much more traffic than in the old days. To the Little St Bernard is 56 km and there is no tunnel here. The route has been drained of its international traffic and is like a country lane.

BREUIL-CERVINIA

See Valle d'Aosta, page 32.

CAPANNE DI MARCAROLA NATIONAL PARK

Off A26, 40 km NW of Genoa, 13 km E of Ovada. Broad-leaved woodland, home to foxes, squirrels, hares, game birds and perhaps a wild boar. In summer several village spires are seen above the level of two artificial lakes. The short road to the lakes is private.

COURMAYEUR ⬓ ✕

See Mont Blanc, page 32.

GENOA ⬓

After a first visit we had a poor opinion of Italy's fifth city and largest port. We recalled the expensive shops in Via XX Settembre, the three caravels of Columbus picked out in flowers which sailed across a green slope, the **Eternal Flame** commemorating the dead of the Second World War and the Avenue of the Partisan Brigades. Genoa, known to some as 'Little Stalingrad', was always proud of its anti-Fascist record. We saw ragged hordes with all their possessions in bundles monopolising the quays – Sicilians waiting for the Palermo boat. We saw how Genoa had turned her palaces into municipal bureaux and shipping offices, overshadowed the Columbus statue with a railway station and allowed an urban race-track to miss by the slightest margin the heroic sculpture at **Quarto dei Mille**, where Garibaldi departed with his Thousand on that 'mad but sublime' adventure of 1860 which brought the Italian south a step nearer Italian unity. No passer-by could direct us to **Mazzini's tomb**,

---

GENOA – ACCESS
Road and rail routes follow the Riviera di Levante (east) and Riviera di Ponente (west). The motorway to Livorno ('Leghorn'), Autostrada dei Fiori ('of Flowers'), swings high above the old Via Aurelia from Rome. At right angles, railways, roads and footways entwine in the narrow ravine which splits Genoa's bowl of hills like a central aisle, leading inland.

Daniel O'Connell's statue (Genoa was a haven of refuge for the 19thC revolutionaries) or to 50 other monuments that would constitute major sights in many towns. The one we were urged to see was the 16thC **Lanterna**, the most powerful lighthouse in the Mediterranean, often visible from seaward before the domes, towers and skyscrapers of the city, climbing back into green uplands, came into view.

Later we learned to admire Genoa. She is La Superba ('The Proud'), both aristocratic and mercantile. Her name goes back to Janus, they tell us, greatgrandson of Noah. Consequently to seek out **Columbus's birthplace** and scour the dirty alleyways where he played as a child is to make a pilgrimage into a fairly recent past, a mere 500 years or so.

To see the house, or rather the house built on the site of one believed to have been owned by the navigator's father, take Vico Dritto di Ponticello ('Straight Alleyway of the Little Bridge') from Piazza Dante, the city centre. The building adjoins Porta Soprana, a massive gatehouse in the 9thC perimeter wall. Fragments are incorporated in Genoa's medieval walls, to which you gain access by brick stairs. You can walk along them.

Here you are in the scrambling network of lanes and *carrugi* (passages) which belonged to the old port and every turning brings a surprise – a fountain, a triangular cloister, an ancient nail-studded door, a statuette in a niche, a grotesque lamp. For detailed exploration, get the free booklet *Genoa the Old City* from the local tourist office. (You need strong legs for Genoa; there are hardly 20 paces of level ground except on the water-front.)

• *Castello Aymavilles.*

Churches abound, ancient and modern, simple and ostentatious. **San Sisto** on Via Prè near the dockyard stands on the site of a church of AD 260 and an inscription relates to the destruction of the 'serpent Basilisk' in AD 580. The cathedral of **San Lorenzo**, striped black and white inside and out, stands near Porta Soprana and the Ducal Palace. Its Saracenic touches recall the Crusaders who brought much wealth to Genoa. They also brought San Lorenzo a cup hollowed out of an enormous emerald, the *tazza di smeralda*, reputedly the Holy Grail from which Christ drank at the Last Supper. The story goes that Bonaparte borrowed it and substituted a goblet of green glass.

Via Garibaldi's palaces and mansions are solid proof of this sea-republic's eminence in trade and war. (When Pisa challenged her supremacy, Genoa sent a fleet to fill up Pisa's harbour with stones.) From Largo Zecca at the west end of Via Garibaldi a **funicular railway** ascends the Righi for a panoramic view of the city. Tourist boats ply round the harbour from the Maritime station. Genoa is a notable shopping centre with hypermarkets, street-markets and chic boutiques; a gastronomic Mecca; a yachting harbour and

ocean terminal. Fiera Congress, a surrealistic trade-fair and exhibitions centre, occupies far too much of the downtown sea front beside Piazzale Kennedy (the old Viale Brigate Partigiane survives alongside). The new **football stadium** is a sensation, the new **Teatro della Corte** rivals the refurbished Carlo Felice opera house in splendour.

For accommodation, see Local Explorations: 7.

GRAN PARADISO NATIONAL PARK

On Routes 26 and 507 (Cogne valley road), 20 km south of Aosta. The oldest national park in Italy is geologically part of the Alps, though separated from them by the Dora Baltea river valley. Some 4,000 peaks, numerous glaciers, monolithic outcrops and on the lower slopes flowery meadows, woods and sparkling streams are accessible to hardy walkers. You may see ibexes duelling on a crag or chamois gathered at a salt-lick. Golden eagles and ptarmigan nest on the heights. The flora is rich, with gentians a speciality and the black orchid (it smells like chocolate), hard to find.

In the Gran Paradiso you lose the

made world. The scattered habitations are connected by footpaths. Hunting is prohibited but, where the occasional motor road penetrates, poaching is rife and litter abundant. At Colle Nivolet cars race over meadows and motor cycles churn up the slopes.

The painless car route to the park's confines is from Aosta, up the Cogne valley. From Ivrea make for **Pont Canavese**, where you have a choice of three roads into the park. It is a 40-km hike across the park from end to end and even then you are nowhere near the Gran Paradiso itself, the culmination of peaks at 4,061 m.

GRESSONEY-LA-TRINITE and GRESSONEY-ST-JEAN
See Ivrea, below.

ISSOGNE
See Valle d'Aosta, page 32.

IVREA 🛏
Off the A5, 50 km N of Turin. Venerable cathedral and medieval castle confirm Ivrea as an old feudal town, a cross-roads and market-centre of northern Piedmont. You would never guess that Ivrea is part of *Tecnocittà*, the Turin-Ivrea-Novara triangle of industry. The huge Olivetti plant exemplifies its hi-tec role.

A small lakeland north of the town offers what Italians call *relax*. Five pools of glacial origin support sailing schools, camping parks, lidos, hotels and conference halls. At weekends people flock from Turin. Hard to believe that 100 years ago Sirio, the largest lake, was the place to which two runaway lovers, Arrigo Boito the composer and Eleanora Duse the actress, fled – sure no one would find them.

West of Ivrea, towards the Gran Paradiso, is the district of **Canavese** where all Italy's itinerant tinkers and chimney-sweeps used to come from.

• *Lago Blu, Valtournanche.*

North from **Pont St-Martin** (17 km), where a single-arched Roman bridge crosses the turbulent river, a minor road strikes up the Lys valley to **Gressoney-la-Trinité** and **Gressoney-St-Jean**, base camps for the ascent of Monte Rosa (4,633 m).

MONT BLANC
On Routes 26 and 26dir, 40 km NW of Aosta. Highest mountain in the Alps (4,807 m), Mont Blanc straddles the Italy-France border but the 11.5-km road tunnel denies motorists more than a distant view. Meadows and forests clothe the lower ground and **Courmayeur** at 1,224 m is both a summer and a winter resort.

This village of cobbled streets, like its neighbours, is saturated with trinket shops and supermarkets. Trains go to Aosta (37 km), luxury coaches take you to the **Grand St Bernard** and **Valtournanche** and a cable-car rides spectacularly over the Mont Blanc glacier.

PEGLI
On Route 1, 10 km W of Genoa. Riviera beaches near Genoa are mostly rocky, pebbly and steeply shelving. Pegli is worth pausing at for its museum of (mainly Genoese) maritime history, the water-park and Oriental garden of Villa Pallavicini and the luxuriant flora of Villa Doria, both open to the public.

PONT CANAVESE
See Gran Paradiso National Park, page 30.

PONT ST-MARTIN
See Ivrea, page 31.

ST BERNARD
See Aosta and Mont Blanc, pages 28 and this page.

ST-VINCENT ⇌ ✕
On Route 26, 30 km E of Aosta. Sheltered by pines and chestnut forests, the resort has capitalized on its mild climate and its hill-top Fons Salutis, a bicarbonate spring (cable-car). Although not a major ski centre, there are clay-pigeon shoots, tennis tournaments and an Olympic swimming-pool in a clean and stylish setting. Energetic walkers can follow well-marked trails along Alpine foothills towards the glaciers of Rutor.

VALLE D'AOSTA
E and W of Aosta. Winter sports sustain the economy of this wild enclave between the high Alps and the Gran Paradiso, whence come the valleys with the evocative names – Valpelline, Valsavaranche, Valtournanche and the rest – to tumble their freezing streams into the Dora Baltea river. The stony slopes and snowy uplands criss-crossed with ski-tows and chairlifts to the high runs look better in winter than summer. After Courmayeur (see Mont Blanc, this page) the popular resort is **Breuil-Cervinia** under the Matterhorn, which Italians call Monte Cervino (4,478 m). Much exploited for tourism, the resort is the terminus of an expensive cable-car trip from Zermatt in Switzerland.

East of Aosta, where *autostrada* and Dora Baltea (now a foaming destructive river) run parallel, several impressive *quattrocento* (15thC) castles survey the valley. See **Fénis**, a fortified stately home near Chambaye, and **Issogne**, a beautiful castle 17 km south of St-Vincent.

VALSESIA
On Routes 26 and 505, 45 km N of Ivrea. In northern Piedmont the wall of the Alps comes down from Monte Rosa in moraine valleys and rocky outcrops. Almost every formation which geology associates with glaciers is found here. Throughout the countryside there is almost no farming, except for sheep, and scarcely any industry from the Swiss border to Lake Maggiore, except for tourism.

Some Valsesia areas are designated natural parks, where chamois, marmots, blue hares and other endangered species are protected. A feature of the torrent valleys are the *caldaie del Sesia* – potholes.

On the **Sacro Monte** near Varallo, amid thick woodland of chestnut and pine, stands the 'New Jerusalem', a church with 45 chapels dedicated to scenes of Christ's life. It was begun in 1431 by the monk Caimi in memory of the holy places he had visited on a pilgrimage to Palestine. Over the centuries most of Piedmont's prominent artists, including Ferrari, Morazzone and Tanzio da Varallo, have contributed to its decoration, which at the last count amounted to 740 statues and

4,000 frescoed figures – the greatest religious complex of its kind.

You reach the Sacro Monte from the Aosta-Genoa motorway by turning north to the A26 at Santhia or Vercelli and north-west up the Sesia valley at Romagnano.

VALTOURNANCHE

See *Valle d'Aosta and Mont Blanc, page 32.*

VERCELLI

On A26, 47 *km* E *of Ivrea*. Like many Piedmont towns it consists of a medieval nucleus with walls or traces of walls around it. Traffic goes by on the ring road, but there is plenty of commercial activity in the town. If you are ticking off the holy places, visit the 12thC basilica of **Sant' Andrea** and see the florid frescos of Gaudenzio Ferrari (he is hardly known outside the region) at San Cristoforo.

The chief interest of Vercelli lies in the landscape. This is the rice metropolis of Piedmont and south of the town, in spring, you could be among the paddy fields of the Orient. Piedmont's economic salvation was a gridiron of canals, forming a complete irrigation scheme, laid down by Camille Cavour, Prime Minister to the King of Sardinia in the 1850s and an architect of the modern Italian state. The long-distance Cavour canal, which connects the infant Po river and the Ticino river, crosses the Aosta-Genoa *autostrada* near Santhia, 16 km west of Vercelli. About the same distance north, on either side of the A26 *autostrada*, are two little enclaves for bird-watchers: from Vercelli, a continuation of the road through Borgo Vercelli takes you into the Casalbeltrame marshes, famous for native and migratory aquatic birds; and west to Oldenico brings you to the wooded isles, sands and shingle banks of the River Sesia, home to egrets, several kinds of heron and many species of duck; and a stopover for long-distance migratory wildfowl.

RECOMMENDED RESTAURANTS

AOSTA
Piemonte, LL; Via Porta Pretoria 13; *tel.* 016 540 111; *credit cards*, E, MC, V; *closed Sun, Nov.*

Close to Roman amphitheatre and tourist office. Cosy rustic-style trattoria much frequented by lovers of local delicacies such as *bace Valdostana* (pasta with cheese of the region).

CASALE MONFERRATO
Castello di San Giorgio, LLL; San Giorgio, W of Casale on Route 457; tel. 014 280 6203; *credit cards*, AE, DC, E, MC, V; *closed Mon.*

Pink 16thC mansion enshrines a stylish restaurant with fine antiques and porcelain. Regional specialities (try *agnolotti alla monferrina*, a succulent lamb dish) and famed local Barbaresco wine. A few superior rooms are available (**LL**) except first two weeks in Jun and first three in Aug.

CHATILLON (ST-VINCENT)
Parisien, LLL; Regione Panorama 1; *tel.* 016 637 053; *credit cards*, AE, DC, E, MC, V; *closed Thur, mid-Jun.*

Very popular, so book ahead. Some recherché dishes include *trotta alla fiamma* (trout) and *filetto con salsa al dragoncello* (roast beef in tarragon sauce), accomplished as never before. Impressive wine list.

COURMAYEUR
Maison de Filippo, LL; at Entreves, 4 km N; *tel.* 016 589 968; *credit cards*, V; *closed Tues, Jun 1 to mid-Jul, Nov.*

Typical Valdostana country inn, antique furnishings, stunning views. Meals al fresco in summer. Our spaghetti with bacon and salami and the cheese *tortellini* with local *fontina* cheese were exceptionally good. Crowded with locals at weekends.

ST-VINCENT
Nuovo Batezar da Renato, LLL; Via Marconi 1; *tel.* 016 631 64; *credit cards*, AE, DC, E, MC, V; *closed Wed, weekday lunch, and in winter.*

A small, elegant, formal restaurant considered among Italy's best. Menu strong on fish (we drank a memorable pinot nero) and regional dishes like *gnocchi con rucola e fonduta*, small cheesy dumplings with greens.

Between Turin and Venice
The Lombardy Plain

430 km; maps Touring Club Italiano Piemonte e Val d'Aosta, Lombardia and Veneto e Friuli – Venezia – Giulia

Our route travels the 'waveless plain' which was anciently Cisalpine Gaul, cockpit of wars which shaped the modern world. On this plain Caesar founded the Roman Empire, the Goths and Huns overthrew it and the Emperor Charlemagne re-established it. Here, 2,000 years after the Romans, Italy achieved unification.

The land rises to the Alps in the north, the more abrupt Apennines to the south. To right and left are great cultural complexes – you could spend a week in any one of half a dozen cities and not see everything. These same places are the nation's industrial and commercial strength. Right-wing separatists, the Lombard League, campaign to shake off Rome and the south and become independent.

Our red route is the *autostrada*, La Serenissima (named for the title of Venice), an ironic name for a motorway with an alarming accident rate. It runs straight, level and featureless and if you can stay awake you may travel from the French frontier to the Balkans in eight hours. Our blue route detours to the grand old cities which remain aloof, though your opera at Bergamo or al fresco drama at Verona may be disturbed by the wail of an ambulance or throb of a police helicopter, racing out to the *autostrada*.

Don't let suburban ugliness deter you from entering the cities. They are the epitome of old Italy: at their hearts you will find the Roman plan and medieval nucleus of broad piazza, cathedral and other dignified buildings adjoining, all gathered in a terracotta basket woven with the tracery of arcades. The last are always 7 Lombard feet (2.67 m) high, to allow horsemen to pass through.

The easterly cities, in the Veneto, produced great art and architecture which Lombardy, having few great artists of her own, collected for her churches and galleries. To the west the genius was for music and literature: Virgil, Catullus and Pliny in Roman times, the Stradivari, Amati and Guarneri in the 1600s and 1700s, the composers Ponchielli and Monteverdi, and the most admired 19thC Italian novelists. Verdi and Donizetti built up the reputation of La Scala Milan and, especially in towns such as Parma and Bergamo, inspired an attitude to opera and opera singers which is both passionate and fiercely critical.

(See also Local Explorations: 2, 3, 5, 6 and 8.)

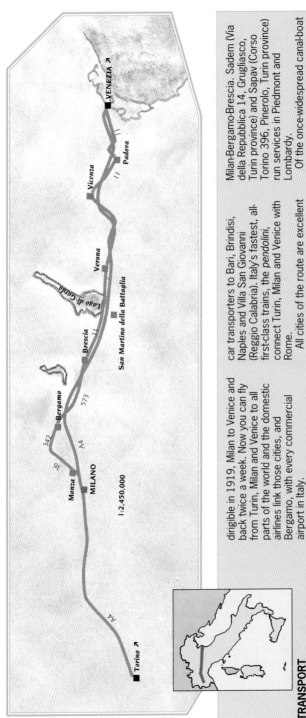

TRANSPORT

The world's first fare-paying airline passengers drifted across the Lombardy plain in a war-surplus dirigible in 1919, Milan to Venice and back twice a week. Now you can fly from Turin, Milan and Venice to all parts of the world and the domestic airlines link those cities, and Bergamo, with every commercial airport in Italy.

Rail services are fast and frequent. Milan's motorail terminal serves many northern European stations; both Milan and Turin have car transporters to Bari, Brindisi, Naples and Villa San Giovanni (Reggio Calabria). Italy's fastest, all-first-class trains, the *pendolini*, connect Turin, Milan and Venice with Rome.

All cities of the route are excellent centres for bus services and tours, local or long-distance. Autostradale (Piazzale Castello 1, Milan) is the major bus operator on routes Turin-

Milan-Bergamo-Brescia. Sadem (Via della Repubblica 14, Grugliasco, Turin province) and Sapav (Corso Torino 396, Pinerolo, Turin province) run services in Piedmont and Lombardy.

Of the once-widespread canal-boat passenger network only the quaint *Burchiello* on the Brenta Canal (Padua-Venice) survives. See page 41.

1:2,450,000

SIGHTS & PLACES OF INTEREST

BERGAMO ✕

Off the A4, 50 km E of Milan. The city of two halves, High Town and Low, is a stepping-stone from the Lombardy plain to the Alps. Parts of the Bergamasque hills, behind the High Town, are inviting but a stern test for the occasional walker.

High Town (Città Alta), lofty and girdled with walls, has narrow winding ways lined with *palazzi* and a virile old tower rising above blue domes and arches. There are three art galleries, one with a Botticelli. Add the shady ramparts, breezy piazzas, views of high hills and wide swathes of the 'waveless plain' and you may agree with Stendhal: 'The prettiest place I have ever seen'.

Looking down over the Città Bassa you seem to gaze on a town of a thousand churches. A few are early Renaissance, but there is nothing remarkable about most of them nor in general about this half of Bergamo. One pleasant feature is the **Sentierone** ('Big Path'), a chestnut avenue which fills up with life and colour during the evening *passeggiata*.

Bergamo invented the *commedia dell' arte*, from which Punch and Judy is derived. In the plays and puppet shows, Harlequin is said to be modelled on the witty fool of local peasant lore.

The native celebrity is Gaetano Donizetti (1797-1848), the operatic composer. Bergamo's opera theatre is important and annually on the composer's birthday in September a Donizetti festival is held.

BRESCIA ⇌ ✕

Off A4 on Route 45bis, 48 km E of Bergamo. A bronze *Victory*, 2 m tall, and

RECOMMENDED HOTELS

BRESCIA
La Mongolfiera, LLL; *Bellavista, Erbusco; tel.* 030 726 8451; *credit cards, none.*

Not a hotel, but an *agriturismo*, a very up-market one. Take the Rovato exit from the A4 into the beautiful rolling countryside of maples and chestnuts of the Franciacorta area (see Local Explorations: 3). Six suites comprise living area, bedrooms and bathrooms. Main shared dining-room has open fire and traditional cuisine. Car parking, porter and laundry service; antique furnishings, a home from home. Fitness centre nearby.

MILAN
Gritti, LL-LLL; *Piazza Santa Maria Beltrade 4; tel.* 028 010 56; *credit cards*, AE, DC, E, MC, V.

Just off Via Torino which runs south-west from piazza in front of Duomo. (You can see the gold Madonna on the Duomo from upper-floor rooms.) Bustling modern place, fair value for city centre. Hall decorated with 'original' old and new masters. No restaurant; many nearby.

Manzoni, LL; *Via Santo Spirito 20; tel.*

027 600 5700; *credit cards, none.*

Five hundred metres north of Duomo in one of the city's smart shopping areas. No restaurant; basement bar and some garage space. Top of its price bracket, and nothing outstanding, but adequate and conveniently situated.

PADUA
Donatello, LL; *Piazza del Santo; tel.* 049 875 0634; *credit cards*, AE, DC, E, MC, V; *hotel closed mid-Dec to mid-Jan; restaurant closed Wed, Dec, Jan.*

Medium-sized modern hotel; large bedrooms with air-conditioning and TV. Adjacent Sant' Antonio restaurant offers al fresco dining on pavement terrace in summer, overlooking St Anthony's Basilica. At top end of price bracket.

TURIN
Turin Palace, LLL; *Via Sacchi 8; tel.* 011 562 5511; *credit cards*, AE, DC, E, MC, V.

Top of city's hotels: expensive, elegant with a successful blend of antique and modern furnishings. Garage. In city centre opposite station, close to shopping and tourist information.

Genio, LL-LLL; *Corso V. Emanuele II,*

other classical treasures in the **civic museum** confirm this industrial city's Roman origins. In the same street, Via dei Musei, another building displays Dark Age finds. Marble is the monumental building material, a snow-white variety. A mayor of Brescia persuaded the Italian government to use Brescia marble for the flamboyant Victor Emmanuel monument in Rome, which ensured full employment and the mayor's re-election for life. See the **Loggia**, a Renaissance palace, and the **Rotonda**, a 12thC *duomo* with 8thC crypt. The 13thC Torre del Popolo soars above it. Enjoy the stimulus of a busy swarming city while wandering at random from old church to old church, admiring local schools of painting.

MILAN 🛏 ✕

Mediolanum to the Romans, Mailand to the Germans: 'May Land'. They felt a burst of spring when they came out of the northern winter. It is a phoenix of a city, sacked by Goths in AD 539 and risen again; destroyed by the Emperor Frederick Barbarossa in 1162 and risen again; lost and won by the Visconti and other regional despots; ruined by the French, rebuilt by the Spanish, pillaged by the Austrians and rescued in 1859 by the makers of modern Italy. Milan then rose to be the nation's banking, commercial and cultural capital, disdainful of Rome.

Start south of Piazza del Duomo in the **Ticino** quarter, the oldest part of the city, where they speak the true Milanese dialect. Here the Naviglio Grande ('Grand Canal') streams in from Lake Maggiore, executes a sharp turn at the dock and flows on again, as the Naviglio Pavese, to join the River Ticino at Pavia. Bars and *trattorie* sit over its meandering offshoots (one of which went underground to Piazza del Duomo with stone to build Milan cathedral).

54; *tel.* 011 650 5771; *credit cards*, AE, DC, E, MC, V.

Just east of main station, Porta Nuova. Nineteenth-century building houses modern hotel, airy and bright. Bar; plenty of restaurants in vicinity.

Villa Sassi, LLL; *Strada al Traforo del Pino 47; tel.* 010 890 556; *credit cards,* AE, DC, E, MC, V; *closed* Aug; *restaurant closed Sun.*

Just off Strada di Superga, leading to the basilica on east edge of city. Private house atmosphere predominates in this 17thC villa set in parkland. Just 15 rooms. The restaurant, El Toula, is one of Piedmont's best and only the freshest seasonal ingredients are used. Menu is strong on roast meats and the wine list substantial. Ample car parking. *Very* expensive, but your visit will be unforgettable.

VERONA

Due Torri Baglioni, LLL; *Piazza Sant' Anastasia 4; tel.* 045 595 044; *credit cards,* AE, DC, E, MC, V.

The height of luxury in the city centre, west of the river near Castel San Pietro. Bedrooms have every facility and public rooms, furnished with antique furniture and fine procelain, give the sensation of stepping back in time. Restaurant and some car parking. *Very* pricey.

Il Torcolo, L-LL; *Vicolo Listone 3; tel.* 045 800 7512; *credit cards, none.*

Just 19 rooms so worth booking ahead. Central location 100 m from Arena and close to other main sites. Rather drab exterior conceals smart interior furnished in rustic style with antiques. Terrace; no restaurant but plenty nearby.

Ciopeta, L; *Vicolo Teatro Filarmonico 2; tel.* 045 800 6843; *credit cards, none; closed mid-Dec to mid-Jan; restaurant closed Fri eve, Sat except during Jul and Aug.*

West of Arena near Ponte Scaligero. Really a restaurant with rooms (just 5) and an attractive terrace. Half-board decent value.

VICENZA

Campo Marzio, LLL; *Viale Roma 21; tel.* 044 454 5700; *credit cards,* AE, DC, E, MC, V; *restaurant closed Sat lunch, Sun, Aug.*

Just 500 m west of city centre in quiet location on edge of the Campo (public park). Large, cheerful, modern: the most up-market in the city. Car parking.

Many such canals network the Piedmont and Lombardy plains, connecting lakes and rivers, unobstructed by locks, bringing currents of fresh green water into dusty towns. Barge traffic dwindles – one day these canals may be waterways for leisure craft.

In the same Ticino quarter, near Porta Ticinese, 16 white columns stand in mid-street. They are relics of 3rdC baths, or maybe a marble Roman palace. Milan's oldest churches are here, sunk in small piazzas. At **Sant' Eustorgio**, about AD 330, the first Christian emperor, Constantine, deposited the supposed bones of the Three Magi, but they were afterwards sent to Cologne, where they remain. There are wonderful little shrines and chapels in this church, the work of Balduccio and Michelozzo.

San Lorenzo's church is the jewel of Milan, unmistakably Roman, with carvings and mosaics both pagan and Christian and the heavy tomb of Ataulphus the Goth, who married the Byzantine princess Galla Placidia (see Ravenna, Italy Overall: 4).

Next is **Sant' Ambrogio**, basilica of St Ambrose (born AD 340), bright light of the Dark Ages, spiritual father of Milan and one of the four Doctors of the Roman Catholic Church. We recommend these dim little ecclesiastical gems even to tourists who do not normally collect churches. (We are all bemused by the numbers of them in Italy – how refreshing at times to see the sign CHIESA CHIUSA, 'Church Closed'.)

Two blocks from Sant' Ambrogio is **Santa Maria delle Grazie**, on whose refectory wall Leonardo da Vinci painted the world's second most famous picture: *The Last Supper*. (Italians know it as *Il Cenacolo*, and that is the sign you should follow.) Try to see it early in the day, before the crowds arrive and when the first pale sunlight filters in.

That leaves the obligatory **duomo** with its 135 Gothic spires and 2,245 exterior statues, which took 500 years to build. An elevator takes you to the roof, where you feel you are walking among stalactites or among the angels.

Conveniently gathered in the web of streets above Piazza del Duomo are the **Brera**, a top art gallery famed for its Tuscan and Venetian masters; the

• *Prato della Valle, Padua.*

four-square **Castello Sforzesco**, with gardens, lakes and museum of antiquities; the **public gardens** with modern art gallery and Zoo; and the **Scala** theatre, now rebuilt with a museum of the theatre attached.

Before you leave the Piazza del Duomo, walk through the **Galleria**, a spacious arcade of cafés and merchandise which is Milan's talking-shop, and the smaller *galleria* of boutiques which runs underground across the piazza.

MONZA
On Route 36, 15 km N of Milan. Few head for Monza except to see motor-racing at the Autodrome in the leafy surroundings of Villa Reale. The town is now virtually a suburb of Milan, but of equal antiquity. Its barbarian palaces have long vanished but its enormous church, on a 6thC foundation, remains. Here the iron crown of Lombardy, said to contain a nail from the Crucifixion, was placed on the heads of Holy Roman Emperors-elect, starting with Charlemagne. And here it is still kept in a side-chapel in the **duomo**. This cathedral, mostly 14thC, has serpentine columns, many florid relics and the painted tomb of Queen Theodolinda of the Lombards, patroness of Monza, along with the silver hens and chickens and other bizarre gifts with which she endowed the church in AD 590.

PADUA ⚓ ✕
Off the A4, 32 km W of Venice. Galileo lectured at its university, Palladio the architect was born here, even the city walls were designed by scholars. **Giotto's frescos** in the **Scrovegni chapel** (it was donated by a sort of medieval scrap-metal millionnaire; Scrovegni – 'Scruffy' – was his nickname) and Donatello's ponderous **equestrian statue** outside the Duomo are the supreme treasures of this 'City of the Saint' (Anthony, patron of all Italy).

Padua's busy traffic weaves round the chalk-white statuary of the Prato della Valle, over old bridges and subterranean canals, down cobbled porticoed lanes, past smart dress shops and piazzettas of small trades, especially shoemaking, the traditional occupation.

There are industrial estates too, and at night the neon signs of Alfa-Romeo,

• Statue of Andrea Palladio, Vicenza.

Lanerossi, Bira Peroni and Pirelli compete with the floodlighting on the Duomo's clustering domes and the **Torre Orologio**. The latter contains a clock so ingeniously constructed that the city fathers put its inventor to death to keep it exclusive. On the pretext of making a final adjustment before they hanged him, he climbed the Tower and twiddled a screw and the clock never chimed again.

SAN MARTINO DELLA BATTAGLIA
Off the A4, 8 km S of Lake Garda. Take 'S. Martino' slip-road from motorway. The great tower commemorates the battle of Solferino (a village 9 km S) of 1859 in which 30,000 Piedmontese corpses paved the way for Italian unity. On the crest of the hill behind Solferino is a monument with tablets for 77 countries, each inscribed in the countries' own script. It commemorates the founding of the International Red Cross by Henry Dunant, a Swiss and an accidental observer of the battle, shocked by what he saw. The tablets honour the signatories to the Geneva Convention.

TURIN ⚐ ✕

See Local Explorations: 1.

VENICE

See pages 128-137.

VERONA ⚐ ✕

Off the A4, 120 km W of Venice. You may see a menagerie of lions and camels, cart-loads of palmettos and cardboard sphinxes entering town – props for *Aida*, which they give every summer at the **Arena**. The other open-air Roman theatre across the river does classical drama and Shakespeare before a more genteel audience. On the chalky *gradine* (stone benches) you read chiselled inscriptions: 'Catullus sits here'; 'This is Milo's chair'. In Verona the Roman past is an everyday experience. The Arena is the third largest and most complete of Roman amphitheatres in Italy and it seats 22,000.

The city, coloured with its many buildings in soft red Verona marble, lies in a curve of the navigable Adige river, here a smooth-flowing, honey-coloured water. Long years of Austrian domination (they relinquished the Adige's east bank only in 1866) and of Venice's rule (note the Lion of St Mark on its pillar at the end of Piazza delle Erbe) have left their mark, but Verona's chief tourist attraction is the bogus **'Juliet's balcony'**. See it, but see also **Ponte Scaligero**, a dignified old bridge named for Verona's ruling family over earlier centuries, and the **Castelvecchio** adjacent to it, the Scaliger seat of government. Count Ciano, son-in-law of Mussolini, was tried and executed here on the ex-Duce's orders in 1944. The building is now a museum and art gallery with some fine Venetian and Veronese paintings and 14th-18thC sculpture.

RECOMMENDED RESTAURANTS

BERGAMO
Gourmet, LLL; Via San Vigiolo 1; tel. 035 256 110; credit cards, AE, DC, E, MC, V; closed Tue, first half of Jan.

There are also a few comfortable rooms in this excellent eatery in the città alta, overlooking the modern city. Meals served in shady garden in summer; car parking.

BRESCIA
Risorgimento, L; Via Trumplina, Stocchetta; tel. 030 200 8304; credit cards, AE, DC, E, MC, V.

Busy (chaotic when we arrived for Sunday lunch) place in north suburb of city. Specializes in fish, but it's also a popular pizzeria. Car parking. Albergo above has a few rooms (**L**), basic but comfortable if you don't mind some traffic noise.

MILAN
Boeucc, LLL; Piazza Belgioso 2; tel. 027 602 0224; credit cards, AE; closed Sat, Sun lunch, New Year, Christmas, Aug.

The name, in Milanese dialect, means 'hole': the city's oldest restaurant was once a dark basement. It's now a chic place with chandeliers and a garden terrace. The veal (*cotoletta alla Milanese*) must be the best in a city where food standards are high, and the chestnut ice-cream (*gelato di castagne*) made a memorable dessert. 400 m north of Duomo. Booking advised.

Don Lisander, LLL; Via Manzoni 12a; tel. 027 602 0130; credit cards, AE, DC, E, MC, V; closed Sat eve, Sun.

Named after 19thC novelist Alessandro Manzoni who lived nearby. Six hundred metres north of Duomo; highly-contemporary decoration. The branzino con funghi (sea bass with mushrooms) were an interesting combination; the menu tends towards traditional favourites. Fairly formal and reservations advised. Outdoor service in summer.

Savini, LLL; Galleria V. Emanuele; tel. 027 200 3433; credit cards, AE, DC, E, MC, V; closed Sun, Christmas, New Year, second week Aug.

Seriously expensive; booking essential. One of Italy's most famous restaurants, the place to see and be seen (you could find yourself sitting next to the prime minister or Pavarotti).

PADUA
Le Calandre, LL-LLL; Sarmeola near Rubano; tel. 049 630 303; **hotel** of

Piazza delle Erbe, a general rendezvous with fruit and vegetable stalls and cafés under striped canopies, is at hand; so is the **Lamberti** tower, a viewpoint. Some distance away but worth the walk is **San Zeno's cathedral** with exotically-decorated bronze doors.

VICENZA ⊭
Off A4 on Route 11, 66 km W of Venice. Inseparable from the name of **Andrea Palladio** and elegantly endowed with the buildings which established that architect's reputation worldwide. See especially the palaces of Porto Festa, Thiene and Chieracati (Venetian pictures inside), the Loggia del Capitanato and Palladio's last work (1580), the delightful little **Olimpico** theatre with its permanent audience of marble statues around the stage and the gallery.

The neighbouring countryside is dotted with aristocratic villas. Palladio's **Rotonda**, 3 km south, is the supreme example. About 50 more are within easy reach, and a free booklet from the local Ente Turismo explains how to get to them.

BRENTA CANAL
Connects Padua and Venice. More than 70 Palladian villas line the Brenta Canal among willows and magnolias. Under the Tiepolo ceiling of Villa Pisani, Hitler first met Mussolini (1934). You can drive the route (51 km) or sail in the *Burchiello* passage-boat, with a bus-link from either terminal; April to October. Book through Siamic Express, 42 Via Trieste, Padua (tel. 049 660944).

BUDGET OPTION – **MILAN**
Try the **Rigolo, LL**; *Via Solferino 11 (corner of Largo Treves); tel. 028 646 322; credit cards,* AE, DC, E, MC, V; *closed Mon, Aug.*

Sensible cooking and sensible prices. About 1 km north of city centre.

---

same name, **LL**; *tel.* 049 635 200; *credit cards,* AE, DC, E, MC, V; *closed Christmas, New Year; restaurant closed Mon, two weeks mid-Aug.*

Off the *autostrada* west of Padua. High standards attract discerning gourmets for such regional specialities as *mazzancolle con radicchio* (king prawns with chicory). Hotel has 35 rooms, car parking.

TURIN
Due Lampioni da Carlo, LLL; *Via Carlo Alberto 45; tel.* 011 839 7409; *credit cards,* AE, V; *closed Sun, Aug.*

Non-smoking, a rarity in Italy, and equally surprising was the trout risotto cooked in champagne (*risotto alla trotta e Champenoise*). Menu strong on truffles (seasonal, autumn) and fine wine list. North-east of Porta Nuova station.

Taverna della Rose, LL; *Via Massena 24; tel.* 011 545 275; *credit cards,* AE, DC, E, MC, V; *closed Sat lunch, Sun, Aug.*

Traditional restaurant a few blocks west of station with Piedmont dishes such as *pasta e fagioli* (pasta and bean soup), and veal or lamb cooked in Barolo wine.

VERONA
12 Apostoli, LLL; *Corticella San Marco 3; tel.* 045 596 999; *credit cards,* AE, DC, V; *closed Sun eve, Mon, first week Jan, mid-Jun to early Jul.*

One of the city's top restaurants, built on foundations of Roman temple. Medieval atmosphere, vaulted ceiling. The *sogliola alle ulive* (sole with olives) was one of several interesting house specialities, and the wine list included a brisk Soave.

BUDGET OPTION – **VERONA**
Tired of eternal pasta and grilled lamb? For a change try the **Hong Kong, L**; *Via Cattaneo 25; tel.* 045 803 0544; *credit cards,* E, MC, V; *closed Tues.*

Great value Chinese restaurant, just west of the Arena.

<u>Northern Italy</u>

Between Milan and Florence
The Northern Apennines

330 km; maps Touring Club Italiano Lombardia and Emilia Romagna

Half the journey is as flat as an inland sea, the other half mountainous. One half traverses the Po plain or *pianura padana*. The other half rides the forest fleece of Apennine, a mountainland concertinaed into awesome folds and canyons where beech, chestnut and pine are anchored on jumbled peaks, cliffs and ravines. The Autostrada del Sole (red route), in these regions one of Italy's busiest motorways, takes the Apennines in a series of high viaducts and tunnels. Alongside it through the plain goes the Via Emilia, a Roman military highway. The towns strung along it, the capital cities of extinct duchies, are not large or heavily industrialized but each is a nexus of routes, drawing much cross-country traffic. (The situation may improve when the *autocamionale*, a motorway for trucks, is completed – perhaps in 1994 – between La Spezia and the Brenner Pass.)

These towns are amazing. The urban plan took shape in the Middle Ages when radial streets, piercing perimeter walls, were superimposed on square-built Roman stations. Rosy brickwork, the soft Roman brick that cats love to snooze on, and yellow or beige plasterwork give them an unassailable antiquity. Striated façades and copper domes of churches, weathered to green, add eye-catching chromatic touches. On our blue and green routes you will find them throughout Lombardy, Emilia and in Florence's bowl of hills. They typify the authentic Italian city, where the inhabitants live in the heart of it, where the principal piazza is 'del Duomo' or 'della Repubblica' and the main road south is 'Via Roma' – where country people coming in to market are distinguished by their black clothes and patriarchal looks. Maybe the place is now surrounded by cheap high-rise *case populari* (council tenements) and arc-welding shops, maybe a haze of petroleum or chemical smoke hangs over rice meadow and maize crop... but still the towns survive.

Do not expect too much of the River Po, Italy's longest river. It proceeds in shallows, amid sandy islands. In summer the bridges look ridiculous, 20 times too long for that feeble trickle. The best stretch for canoes is downstream from Castelvetro near Piacenza to Boretto near Parma. You find small boatyards and gravelly beaches there.

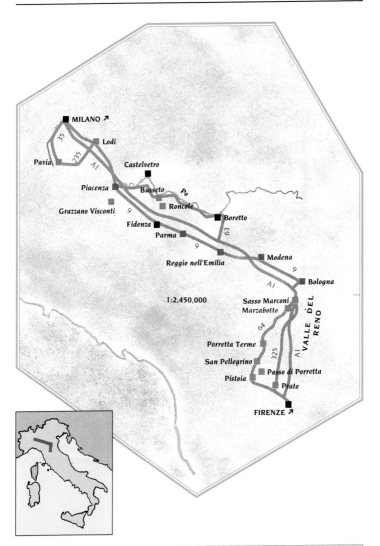

TRANSPORT

Airports: Bologna, Reggio, Parma, Milan.

Companies operating express buses between major towns include Autostradale, Piazza Castello 1, Milan; Lazzi, Via Mercadante 2, Florence; and SITA, Viale dei Cadorna 105, Florence. Towns and villages of the Po plain and Apennines are served from all large towns. Motorists can avoid the Cisa Pass (1,040 m) by putting cars on the train between Pontremoli and Borgo Taro.

Milan-Bologna-Florence is a major rail route and the high-speed trains make short work of the arduous Bologna-Florence section. Branch railways from Emilian cities cross the Po on lengthy bridges, linking the Apennine foothills with those of the Alps. A slow but exceptionally picturesque line through the Apennines is Parma-Sarzana.

A boat service, mainly patronized by tourists, operates in summer along the Po from Boretto, north-east of Parma. The intention is to extend it to other river towns.

SIGHTS & PLACES OF INTEREST

BOLOGNA ⊨ ✕
On the A1 or Route 64, 90 km N of Florence. Founded in 189 BC, it boasts two leaning towers, square and bricked like factory chimneys. The taller, the Asinelli, has the city at its feet and from its top (498 steps) you can imagine the sort of place Bologna once was, a forest of towers, all inhabited by warring families. Away from Piazza Maggiore the wynds and alcoves seem expressly designed for ambush and furtive plot. You feel like buying a black cloak to fling over your shoulder in the medieval manner.

A major sight is the university, the oldest in Europe (founded AD 1088). Law and medicine are the senior faculties but there is scientific emphasis too. Here Galvani pioneered electricity with experiments on frogs' legs.

Visit **Piazza Nettuno** to see Giambologna's fountain and statue of Neptune (1566); admire the Gothic and Renaissance palaces close by, most of them now serving administrative purposes for the city. **Piazza Mercanzia** has small old shops with their original signs. Of the churches, **San Domenico** has important frescos and bas-reliefs, a statue of the saint and three statuettes by Michelangelo. Along Via Maggiore, south-east of centre, you find the **Santo Stefano** group of antique churches and **Santa Maria dei Servi** which houses a Cimabue Madonna.

Bologna is a compact city inside its ring road and there are gastronomic restaurants (*mortadella* and salami the specialities) along its big, rectilinear, arcaded streets. Feasts of music, often avant-garde, are guaranteed at the **Opera** theatre.

BUSSETO
On Route 9, 15 km from Fidenza. The lethargic country town dreams of past greatness. A dilapidated castle recalls the Pallavicini lords who in the 1100s claimed all the territory between the Apennines and the Po. On the outskirts stands **Sant' Agata**, the modest country house of Giuseppe Verdi, and at **Villa Pallavicini**, the civic museum, are Verdi memorabilia. This composer, who aroused such fervour in 19thC

RENO VALLEY
Between Bologna and the Porretta Pass. Before the *autostrada* came bounding over the torrents on concrete stilts the smooth-flowing Reno (Italian for 'Rhine') provided southbound travellers with a dramatic introduction to the high Apennines. The old road winds but is nowhere steep. You pass through small spa townships, hardly known to the world. Here is **San Pellegrino** and, across the watershed, Porretta Terme (see below), a climatic station with wells. Ten km south of Bologna the spread of yellow farm-like buildings is **Sasso Marconi**, where the inventor of wireless telegraphy was born. The next village going south is **Marzabotto**, where the discovery of an Etruscan necropolis is transforming scholars' ideas about that enigmatic race.

Italy – the nationalist movement keeping step with his rise to fame – was born in 1813 at **Roncole**, 6 km down the road to Parma. The Italian custom is to add a great celebrity's name to his birthplace, as in Sasso Marconi, Caprese Michelangelo, Torre del Lago Puccini – so Roncole is now Roncole Verdi. Villagers take the honour calmly. We have been three times to the Verdi cottage-museum and three times found it closed.

FLORENCE
See pages 120-127.

GRAZZANO VISCONTI
See Piacenza, page 47.

LODI
On Route 9, 35 km SE of Milan. The **duomo** is in the old Lombard style, with Lombard lions supporting the porch. Both here and at **San Francesco's church** you see very old frescos and reliefs. The octagonal **Incoronata church** (15thC), by Battagio, a pupil of Bramante, is a marvellous building, inside and out.

Lodi is where Napoleon, opening his Italian campaign in 1796, inflicted a crushing defeat on the Austrians and was hailed by his grenadiers as their

RECOMMENDED HOTELS

BOLOGNA
Lu King, LL; *Via Emilia Ponente 65; tel. 051 734 273; credit cards, AE, DC, E, MC, V.*

On Route 9 at Anzola Emilia, just north-west of Bologna and 5 km from the *autostrada*. Modern building furnished in oriental style with large car-park in front. Non-smoking rooms.

Corona d'Oro 1890, LLL; *Via Oberdan 12; tel. 051 236 456; credit cards, AE, DC, E, MC, V; closed Christmas, New Year, Aug.*

In city centre, close to Palazzo Communale, it's been a hotel for a century – but long before that the building was a printer's workshop. 1930s decoration and modern pastel shades combine with antique features. No restaurant but plenty in vicinity.

Orologio, LL; *Via IV Novembre 10; tel. 051 231 253; credit cards, AE, DC, E, MC, V.*

City centre, in a quiet pedestrianized zone. Views of Duomo from top floor. Rooms recently refurbished to a high standard. No restaurant.

FIESOLE
Bencista, LL; *San Domenico between Fiesole and Florence; tel. 055 591 63; credit cards, none.*

Fiesole is desirable, trendy and expensive and boasts some of the best hotels in Italy. The Bencista is more affordable than some, but don't turn up on spec – you'll be disappointed. This former monastery has 40 beautiful rooms and, set on a hillside with memorable views of Florence below, is surrounded by olive groves. Runs like a country club with half or full-board only. Non-smoking restaurant; ample car parking.

MODENA
Canalgrande, LLL; *Corso Canal Grande 6; tel. 059 217 160; credit cards, AE, DC, E, MC, V; restaurant closed Tues, first three weeks Aug.*

In city centre, 300 m south of Duomo, this 17thC Duke's palace has large bright rooms with all facilities. Shady garden; has restaurant.

PARMA
Torino, LL; *Borgo Mazza 7; tel. 052 128 1047; credit cards, AE, DC, E, MC, V; closed Aug and last week Dec.*

Just west of Duomo close by the museum. Garage car parking. Furnishings fairly plain, but hotel runs like clockwork with cheerful staff. No restaurant, but Parma offers many.

PISTOIA
Il Convento, LL; *Ponte Nuovo, E of Pistoia on minor road to Montale; tel. 057 345 2651; credit cards, E, MC, V; restaurant closed Mon, mid-Jan to Easter.*

No prizes for guessing the original purpose of this place, set on a hillside with wonderful views over the city. The former monks' cells have been converted and incorporated into the dining-room, in a concept like the Victorian English 'snug'. Set in shady parkland with swimming-pool and car parking.

PORRETTA TERME
Santoli, LL; *Via Roma 3; tel. 053 423 206; credit cards, AE, DC, E, MC, V; open all year; restaurant closed Mon.*

This spa town, on the slow Route 64 between Bologna and Pistoia, is seasonal; but the Santoli is open all year. It offers 48 comfortable rooms, a relaxing garden and hydrotherapy. Half-board gives value for money.

SAN BENEDETTO VAL DI SAMBRO
Musolesi, L; *Madonna dei Fornelli, 4 km S of San Benedetto; tel. 053 494 100; credit cards, E, V; restaurant closed Mon.*

High in the hills, midway between Florence and Bologna, about 13 km from the nearest *autostrada* exit. Restaurant serves fine food at modest prices. The best value for miles around. Car parking.

'Little Corporal' – the title, he always claimed, of which he was most proud

MARZABOTTO
See Reno Valley, page 44.

MILAN
See Italy Overall: 2.

MODENA 🛏 ✕
On Route 9, 40 km NW of Bologna. At the ducal court of Modena, a walled town of stormy history, Bonnie Prince Charlie learned some of his bad habits. His mother was the Duke's daughter.

The largest cathedral in the Po plain and some undistinguished churches round about may be inspected for their examples of the Modenese painting school, especially the touching and amusing primitives. The Ghirlandina bell-tower is unusual. For all its tumultuous past, Modena is a fresh-looking, smiling town with elegant shops. It was early into automobilism: it had one of the first Grand Prix race tracks and is the proud base of Enzo Ferrari's factory.

PARMA 🛏 ✕
On Route 9, 60 km NW of Modena. If you

46

• Bologna, Piazza Maggiore.

can explore only one city of the Po plain, make it Parma, city of edible violets, hams and cheeses. These days the hams and cheeses are made in factories lower down the plain and stacked in rustic, thermostatically-controlled warehouses.

Parma's history, like that of its Via Emilia neighbours, begins with the Roman garrison established around 180 BC. It continues with the struggles of acquisitive barons – Visconti of Milan, Cangrande della Scala (or Scaliger) of Verona, Gonzaga of Mantua and Este of Ferrara. Her medieval overlords were King Louis of Bavaria, blind King John of Bohemia and finally the Farnese dynasty. Alexander Farnese, son of a Pope, built the extraordinary **Farnese Theatre**, made entirely of wood. Though damaged in the Second World War it is still in business. The same Farnese when Duke of Parma conceived the vast **Pilotta Palace** (it spread over a courtyard where *pilotta*, the game of pelota, was played). The palace of splendid facings, high stucco ceilings and mosaic-tiled floors houses a **national** (that is regional) **gallery** with works by Tiepolo, Van Dyck, Holbein and especially Parma's own painter, Correggio, along with specialist museums of various kinds. **Palazzo Farnese**, the Duke's own elaborate mansion, stands opposite.

Parma is a city of spacious piazzas. **Piazza del Duomo** has the Lombard-styled cathedral with red marble lions, the huge square campanile and the octagonal baptistery in grey and red Verona marble. Coloured marble and Roman brick are the trademarks of this well-preserved and restored ducal capital.

Piazza Garibaldi, also very large, is the place for cafés, evening promenades and as often as not political demonstrations. The Duomo has a renowned work of art in its dome: Correggio's *Assumption*, a daring flight of fancy in which the Virgin appears to lift off with radiant power. His contemporaries called this fresco a 'hash of frogs' legs'.

There are many music shops. Parma produced Arturo Toscanini (he played in the theatre orchestra) and more than its share of great operatic tenors and divas. The **Teatro Regio**, notorious for its harsh and unforgiving audiences, has been the graveyard of many a young singer's hopes.

The city is very dry in summer. Its fountains expire and even the sizeable River Parma contributes nothing to the Po, 24 km away, which needs all the water it can get. But the public gardens have shady walks and meadows bloom in the neighbourhood, under the Apennine walls.

PAVIA ✕

On Route 35, 36 km S of Milan. The mark of a true river-city, a covered bridge (partly destroyed in the Second World War, rebuilt in the old manner), beautifies a town strategically placed on the Ticino, just above its confluence with the Po. The old Naviglio Pavese (see Milan, page 37) runs dead-straight into Pavia, the highway from Milan accompanying it.

Pavia was once a royal Lombard seat and there is still something majestic about it. Outstanding monuments include the Romanesque church of **San Pietro in Ciel d'Oro**, where the tomb

of St Augustine (not the English saint) finally came to rest. The art gallery, the inevitable Visconti fortress and six domestic towers (500 years ago there were hundreds) add dignity. Bramante designed the Duomo (1488), Leonardo da Vinci did the dome and interior.

Where Pavia now stands Hannibal crossed the Ticino and marshalled his elephants for the opening skirmish of the second Punic War (219 BC). Pavia was Charlemagne's Italian power-base and some insist that he founded the University (in 774). It is certain that Boethius, the philosopher, and Lanfranc, Archbishop of Canterbury in William the Conqueror's time, wrote and lectured there, and that Petrarch was a student; it is less certain that Columbus enrolled as a student in 1447.

Out of town on the canal bank is the **Certosa** or Charterhouse of Pavia, a flamboyant 14thC monastery with lavish ceilings and a façade of polychromatic marble, more like a fortified complex of ballrooms than a religious house.

PIACENZA ✕

Off the A1 on Route 9, 68 km SE of Milan. Hannibal fought Scipio at Piacenza and

• *Arcade, via Santo Stefano, Bologna.*

decimated the garrison of a town which then marked the northern limits of the Roman republic. Though long in the forefront of Lombard quarrels, Piacenza had a useful situation on the Trebbia and near the Po and was among the first places to enjoy a revival of commerce in the Middle Ages. Its cattle fair was once the largest in Europe. Open piazzas and terracotta brick give the town its charm. On the broad Piazza dei Cavalli the **Palazzo del Commune** and its prancing equestrian statues – huge horses, insignificant men – suggest a scene from a drama of chivalry. On the minor road to Bettola, 14 km south, the village of Grazzano Visconti is restored to its 14thC innocence with working craftsmen and artisans, an unusual 'heritage' ploy for Italy. On official holidays they wear traditional costume. Wood, pottery, metalwork and other craft items are for sale at somewhat inflated prices.

PISTOIA ⊨ ✕

On the A11, 33 km NW of Florence. A delightful town of winding streets, flower and fruit markets, neat houses and several churches brightened with della Robbia medallions and friezes in polychrome terracotta. All this and the striped green-and-white façade of **San Giovanni Fuorcivitas** give Pistoia brilliance in art and colour.

PORRETTA TERME ⊨

On Route 64, 32 km N of Pistoia. Perched on the crest of Apennine the small town has long attracted a discerning clientele to its hotels and restaurants. The invalid element is concerned with gastric, rheumatic, diabetic and nervous complaints but the very air is a tonic and healthy people come long distances to take deep breaths and saunter among gardens and cool woods. There are splendid views north and south from the Porretta pass, 21 km to the south.

RECOMMENDED RESTAURANTS

BOLOGNA

San Domenico, LLL; Via Sacchi 1, Imola; tel. 054 229 000; cards, AE, DC, V; closed Mon, first half Jan, most of Aua

A 33 km detour south-east down Route 9, but we have to include one of Italy's best restaurants. Elegant and formal. You may have to choose between the roast duck cooked with black olive sauce and the pigeon in garlic (piccione arrostito profumato all'aglio). The Trebbiano was one of several highlights of the wine list. Such quality is costly, and advance booking is essential.

Ruggero, LL; Via degli Usberti 6; tel. 051 236 056; credit cards, AE, DC, V; closed Sat lunch, Sun, last week Jul, first three weeks Aug.

Worth booking ahead for this trattoria, just north of Piazza Maggiore in the city's heart, for it has a loyal local clientele. Mainly meat: grills and roasts, and the bolliti (stews) are more interesting than the menu makes them sound.

Notai, LLL; Via de'Pignattari 1; tel. 051 228 694; credit cards, AE, DC, E, MC, V; closed Sun.

A few metres south of Piazza Maggiore, and booking advised here too. Places like this have earned the city the title of gastronomic capital of Italy. Try the tortelli di ricotta tricolori, a famous local speciality. Decent wine list; outdoor service in summer.

Rosteria Luciano, LL-LLL; Via Nazario Sauro 19; tel. 051 231 249; credit cards, AE, DC, E, MC, V; closed Tues eve, Wed, Christmas, New Year, Aug.

Another of the best. Menu changes daily and is strong in the dessert department. Booking essential.

MODENA

Villa Fontana, LL; Via S. Onofrio, Lesignana; tel. 059 849 293; credit cards, AE, DC, E, MC, V; closed Mon.

It's hard to find – we stumbled on it accidentally – but worth persevering. Take the Carpi road off the Modena tangenziale and before Ganaceto look for the villa on the right. The fine building is fronted by a double staircase and fountain. Winner of the coveted Golden Fork Award. Fairly formal; great food, lengthy wine list.

PARMA

Parizzi, LL; Strada della Repubblica 71; tel. 052 128 5952; credit cards, AE, DC, E, MC, V.

PRATO ✕

On *Route 325, 20 km NW of Florence*. The artists and academics know it well but it is overshadowed by the great art centres of Florence and Pistoia, and many people find it by accident. Judging by its considerable array of historic buildings and art treasures, Prato was not always in the shade. The **town art gallery** and 13thC **Emperor's castle** (Holy Roman Emperor) are worth looking at, but the green-and-white-striped **cathedral** is the top attraction. Donatello designed the exterior pulpit. Inside, Fra Filippo Lippi frescoed one of his greatest works, *Herod's Feast*. Contemporaries were disapproving of this holy man's frank portrayal of Salome and outraged when he eloped with a local nun.

REGGIO NELL'EMILIA

On *Route 9, 25 km NW of Modena*. Least-visited of the ancient towns along the Via Emilia, it has a layout as pleasing as any, some fine statues and bronzes in the Piazza del Duomo, a very good civic theatre built in 1857 and an art gallery, the **Parmeggiani**, which displays jewellery, silks and weapons of different lands as well as pictures. Its prize exhibit is El Greco's painting of Christ. Most agreeable in Reggio is to find a town centre which really looks its medieval part, having few foreign visitors, and to study paintings without having to look over people's shoulders.

RONCOLE
See *Busseto, page 44*.

SAN PELLEGRINO
See *Reno Valley, page 44*.

SASSO MARCONI
See *Reno Valley, page 44*.

The Strada bisects the city; the Parizzi is 1 km east of the river. Try any of the pasta dishes with *parmigiano* (cheese) or *burro tartufo* (truffle butter). Fine wines; booking advised.

Parma Rotta, LL; Via *Langhirano* 158; *tel. 052 158 1323; credit cards*, AE, DC, E, MC, V; *closed Sun in summer, Mon rest of the year*.

South of city centre, this long-established trattoria will appeal to non-smokers. Car parking; summer service under pergola. Spit-roasted meats and other typical Lombardy dishes. Home-made *grappa*, if you like that sort of thing.

PAVIA
Locanda Vecchia Pavia, LLL; Via *Cardinal Riboldi 2; tel. 038 230 4132; credit cards*, AE, DC, V; *closed Mon, Wed lunch, Aug*.

Booking is advised for this popular place just south of the Duomo. The *pappardelle* (ribbon pasta) was home-made and came with a succulent squid and clam sauce. Excellent wine list.

PIACENZA
Antica Osteria del Teatro, LLL; Via *Verdi 16; tel. 052 323 777; credit cards*, AE, DC, E, MC, V; *closed Sun eve, Mon, first half Jan, Aug*.

The best in town: booking advised. The *tortelli dei Farnese* is worth investigating and the marinated lamb (*costolette d'agnello presale*) delicious.

PISTOIA
Antica Trattoria, L-LL; Via *Ponte dei Bini 93, San Piero Agliana; tel. 057 471 0872; credit cards*, E, MC, V; *closed Wed*.

Hidden away in vineyards south of the main Pistoia to Prato road, but signposted from it. Popular with locals; chef is a perfectionist and menu changes daily. Everything freshly cooked. Strong on meat dishes such as wild boar, rabbit. Car parking.

PRATO
Gli Alberi, LL; *Carraia, Calenzano; tel. 055 881 9912; credit cards*, AE, DC, E, MC, V; *closed Sun lunch*.

On minor road west of and parallel to A1 *autostrada*, north of Prato. Ample car parking opposite. Menu changes daily and often features T-bone steak and other hearty dishes. It's an excellent place for *tiramisu*, the liqueur-soaked chocolate-based dessert which is almost becoming an Italian institution.

Between Venice and Pescara
The Northern Adriatic Shore

490 km; maps Touring Club Italiano Emilia Romagna and Umbria Marche

This is another 'road to Rome' – the Via Romea, the long haul down the Adriatic shore by which pilgrims from eastern and central Europe travelled to the Eternal City. In the north, Venice and Ravenna always attracted pilgrims of their own but the rest of the coast was poor and backward, its broad ribbons of soft sand useless and a mere hindrance to fishermen. Then the tour operators discovered it and struck gold. A town where the word 'hotel' was unknown gave the language a new verb: *riminizzare*, to make like Rimini, to ravage with concrete, asphalt and high-rise buildings. From the Po Delta to the mountains of the Abruzzi the place-names now read like one big fat holiday brochure. They call it the Grande Spiaggia d'Europa: Europe's Grand Plage.

Our red route, the *autostrada* betwen Rimini and Pescara, pursues a foothill line, clear of coastal congestion. For long stretches it is not even within sight of the sea. The blue route is the historic one, hugging the shore, heavily trafficked at the northern end and passing through main streets and along promenades of resorts which are full of carefree holidaymakers in July and August. It would take years to sample these hundreds of resorts. You make your own discoveries and perhaps find little to choose between them, except in size. Sandy beaches abound in the north, turning to shingle and rock as you move south, though Pescara's 8-km beach is sandy. Some resorts are new and their sub-tropical plantations struggle to establish themselves. Most are 30 to 40 years old, unashamedly 'family' with carefully-raked sands, striped umbrellas, beach beds and bathing huts lined up with military precision and the squares of hotels geometrically laid out.

We draw attention to those places which offer a little more than sun, sea and sand. Our green offshoots go inland to pick up sites of special interest – not too far inland, because our Local Explorations: 8, 12 and 13 cover the Romagna, Marche and Abruzzi hinterland.

The northern section crosses our old friend the *pianura padana* or Po plain, flat and fen-like, the sight lines limited by thick woodlands. South of Rimini the Apennines begin to close in. Around Pescara the high hills billow down to within a stone's-throw of the coast.

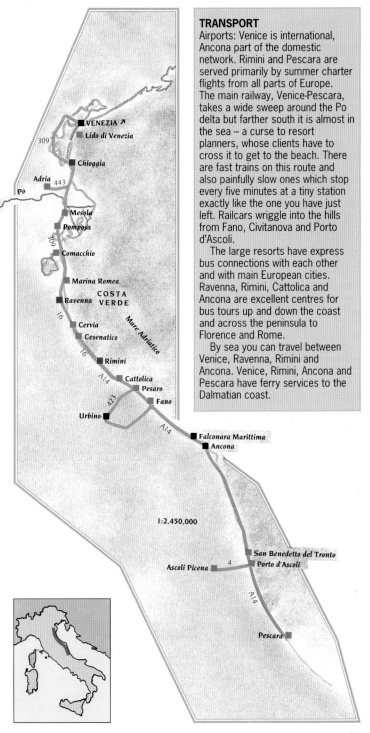

TRANSPORT

Airports: Venice is international, Ancona part of the domestic network. Rimini and Pescara are served primarily by summer charter flights from all parts of Europe. The main railway, Venice-Pescara, takes a wide sweep around the Po delta but farther south it is almost in the sea – a curse to resort planners, whose clients have to cross it to get to the beach. There are fast trains on this route and also painfully slow ones which stop every five minutes at a tiny station exactly like the one you have just left. Railcars wriggle into the hills from Fano, Civitanova and Porto d'Ascoli.

The large resorts have express bus connections with each other and with main European cities. Ravenna, Rimini, Cattolica and Ancona are excellent centres for bus tours up and down the coast and across the peninsula to Florence and Rome.

By sea you can travel between Venice, Ravenna, Rimini and Ancona. Venice, Rimini, Ancona and Pescara have ferry services to the Dalmatian coast.

51

SIGHTS & PLACES OF INTEREST

ADRIA
On Routes 309 and 443, 65 km SW of Venice. Here you stand on the site of a Graeco-Roman city which gave its name to the Adriatic Sea. The town is in no way remarkable except for its interesting **archaeological museum** containing chariot-wheels and two equine skeletons. East and south are plainlands of silt carried down by the mighty Po and other important rivers – Reno of Bologna, Adige of Bolzano and Brenta of Padua, all winding to the sea within a short distance of each other. The silt-choked Adria's harbour and the small town is now 22 km inland.

ANCONA ⌨ ✕
See Local Explorations: 13.

ASCOLI PICENO
Half an hour from San Benedetto del Tronto by road or rail takes you to this provincial capital – see Local Explorations: 13 – and the rugged country of the central Apennines.

CATTOLICA ⌨
On Route 16, 25 km S of Rimini. Southernmost of the Romagna resorts, It claims the most agreeable climate – warm sea, temperate air. **Gradara**, its castle, housed Francesca da Rimini, tragic figure immortalized by Dante. Just south is **Riccione**, picturesque and pop, staging art shows and regattas in summer and a plethora of down-market entertainment from spring to autumn.

CERVIA ⌨
See Costa Verde, this page.

CESENATICO ⌨
On Route 16, 21 km N of Rimini. Long straight monotonous boulevards are dedicated entirely to tourism – then you locate the canal port with pink-roofed houses and innumerable bars and cantinas under blue sunblinds which form a canopied corridor along the waterfront; and its yellow-sailed *bragozzi* (fishing craft), the subject of 1,000 water-colours. Cesenatico has water sports and night life in full measure. In summer at nearby Cesena there are trotting races.

HOTELS AND RESTAURANTS
There are more hotels per kilometre on this route than on any other. This part of the Adriatic coastline is one unbroken string of resorts. Most hotels are of a type and, while looking for accommodation in Rimini, Pesaro, San Benedetto, Senigallia and other important seaside towns is not a problem, there is little variety and most places are open only for four months in summer. A compensation, with so many establishments competing for business, is reasonable prices. There are hardly any reasonable areas in coastal Italy to compare with them. We list places as far as possible which are open all year round.

A similar lack of variety extends to the restaurants. Seafood fans will be in their element for, apart from any intriguing novelties, even the humble *zuppa di pesce* (fish soup) can be something of an art form. *Pizzerie* and *tavole calde* (snack bars) reflect the cosmopolitan clientele of the resorts with bacon sandwiches, steak and chips, frankfurters, paella and suchlike 'national' specialities, and Chinese and Indian take-aways are not unknown.

In search of variety or even a *filetto* you may be tempted to turn inland: see Local Explorations: 10, 13 and 16.

CHIOGGIA ✕
On Route 309, 58 km S of Venice. It is the poor person's Venice and, on account of its compact streets, canals and bridges, historic market hall and coloured fishing boats, preferred by many artists and discerning tourists. Beyond the pine trees at the harbour entrance is a beach called **Sottomarina** which shows signs of becoming another Lido.

COMACCHIO ✕
See Costa Verde, below.

COSTA VERDE
N and S of Ravenna. The Adriatic has retreated and orchards cover the roadstead where Caesar's galleys lay at

anchor. For 32 km on either side of the city's ship canal, belts of umbrella pines have sprung up. On the footpaths and riding tracks you might be in a forest, though you hear the sea lapping a sandy shore. The *pineta* (pinewood) has lizards, doves and nightingales, the air is sweet with juniper, acacia, robinia and honeysuckle. Dante and Byron meditated in these green aisles of the Ravenna coast.

The chief resorts are **Cervia**, a 17thC planned town, and **Milano Marittimo** next door, arrived at by avenues through the *pineta*, much frequented by Italians for its sailing, motor-boating, water-skiing, riding and a lively night life. Northward, the **Marina di Ravenna** and **Marina Romea** are backed by a denser *pineta* with peaceful riding trails. The latter, one of the most exclusive resorts, has an open-air theatre and is gradually transforming its chain of small lakes into a grand sailing area.

More exclusive still is **Lido di Spina**, a complex of seaside cottages individually styled and designed for those with money to spend. On this stretch of the Green Coast Garibaldi waded ashore in 1849 with his dying wife and unborn child in his arms and the Austrians combing the woods for him. **Porto Garibaldi**, named for him, destroyed in the Second World War, blooms again as a resort. Behind it are the **Valli di Comacchio**, a wilderness of sandy causeways, rectilinear lagoons and canals. The reeds harbour wildlife, especially cranes, despite the continual hum of dynamos at the pumping stations. **Comacchio** is a battle honour of the Royal Marines, who fought desperate actions here in 1944. The town has mini-canals along its little streets and is an eel-curing centre – September is the month when immense draughts of them are hauled from the netted sea gate. Sunk in the mud nearby is the Etruscan necropolis of Spina.

FANO ⬀

On Route 16, 12 km SE of Pesaro. It has its Augustan arch, its Malatesta palace and a 12thC loggia; also two beaches, one sandy and one shingly, with all the usual amenities and a yacht harbour. Rail connection with Urbino inland (see Local Explorations: 13) on a steep, slow but outstandingly scenic route.

LIDO DI VENEZIA

6 km SE of Venice. From the 12thC onwards the Doge of Venice was rowed out to the Lido in his barge to cast a ring into the Adriatic and symbolically cement the union between sea and city. 'I shall force him to consummate the marriage', said the Sultan of Turkey, but he never did.

The Lido and its tawny 5-km sandbar was built up to protect Venice from the sea but it might have been designed for a pleasure ground. It accommodates every facility from golf to roller-skating. Every known and a few unknown water-sports are practised. Shady avenues, made for easy strolling, give shifting cameos of the domes and ceaseless boat traffic of La Serenissima (Venice). Ultra-modern hotels and apartment blocks, staid villas, restaurants and stylish (and expensive) shops are planted in woodland, shrubbery and flowers whose extravagant growth takes the breath away. You can play tennis, gamble, marvel at the latest outrageous beach fashions and visit the theatre. You can even go horse-riding – we say 'even' because in the 18thC in the city of canals and gondolas a traveller saw Venetians paying good money to see a stuffed horse.

The Venice Film Festival is held here. It seems miraculous that one attenuated sand-strip should accommodate so many features and such diverse peoples and activities. Yet the Lido, which gave its name to lidos worldwide, rarely feels stuffy or overcrowded.

MARINA ROMEA

See Costa Verde, page 52.

MESOLA

See Pomposa, page 54.

PESARO ⬀

On Route 16, 40 km SE of Rimini. Touristic developments spread inland from a shallow sea to a town of historic *palazzi* and stately churches. The **Rocca Costanza**, a 15thC fort in the town walls, is now a prison. The **ducal palace** and **Piazza del Popolo** are major sights. Pesaro was a majolica centre and its **civic museum** has a lavish collection of mosaics and ceramics. The house of Rossini and an annual opera festival (August) pay homage to the illustrious *bel canto* citizen.

• *Basilica of Sant' Apollinare Nuovo, Ravenna.*

PESCARA

On Route 16, 150 km S of Ancona. The busiest Abruzzi resort with the longest beach on the Adriatic, it is a canal port with much local colour and space for yachts. Mountains and a string of hopeful seaside developments – we liked Roseto degli Abruzzi – cover its approaches. **Gabriele d'Annunzio** (1863-1938), poet and patriot, was born on Piazza Garibaldi, near the port area. The house is visitable.

POMPOSA

On Route 309, 45 km S of Chioggia. This Benedictine abbey, deserted by its monks, remained unregarded for two centuries. Now the touring buses bring crowds to stand in silent awe before wonderful frescos and mosaics by Emilian disciples of Giotto. The 11thC campanile is 55 km high. Ten kilometres into the Po delta the circular village of **Mesola** hangs to the skirts of an Estensi (Este family) hunting-lodge – another wonder of this little lost world.

PORTO D'ASCOLI

See San Benedetto del Tronto, page 55.

RAVENNA ⇌ ✕

On Route 309, 146 km S of Venice. The most brilliant of Byzantine mosaics draw visitors to this pink city of flat wide streets, once capital of the western Roman empire. Mosaics of the 5thC **Galla Placidia mausoleum** (she who married the Barbarian chieftain, see Milan, page 37), under a low barrel-roof which is seemingly clothed in blue velvet and golden sequins, are best seen in the early morning. The mosaic patterns of the **baptistery**, newly restored for the first time in 1,500 years, of 6thC **San Vitale**, of **Sant' Apollinare Nuovo** in the city and **Sant' Apollinare in Classe**, 8 km away in meadows beside the shore (it was a Roman anchorage – *classis* is 'fleet') – these works attain a standard of texture and technique almost sublime. Without pomp or exaggeration, after 14 centuries, they still convey the glory of the Byzantine tradition.

The **tomb of Dante** under its loggia was the haunt of drug-pushers and their clients when we were last there. The **cathedral's** exotic cylindrical belltower stands aloof. The **Accademia gallery** has the crusader Guidarello Guidarelli, a knight of Imola (died 1501). Hardly anything is known about him but his recumbent effigy has captured the affections of so many women that they have had to put him behind a rope in a side room. Even so, his white marble torso and phallic sword bear traces of lipstick and amorous *graffiti* and he receives floral tributes from all over the world. Local girls say his sympathetic looks can mend broken hearts.

Though Ravenna's streets have a dusty, washed-up look and in forgotten corners and courtyards shrubs and flowers run wild, this is a city to linger in. All-pedestrian **Piazza del Popolo** in the centre has Venetian colonnades – Venice ruled the roost in the 15thC. Old-style coffee-houses have brass urns and *napoletana* percolators. Ravenna is still a port, though 6 km from the sea. Up the ship canal comes Italy's imported semola, the raw material of pasta. All around, encroaching on the *pineta* and the monuments of antiquity, are the lattice tanks and towers of the petro-chemicals industries and the villas of the spaghetti millionaires.

RIMINI ✉

On Route 16, 50 km SE of Ravenna. As the 'Sun Coast' metropolis, oldest and most advanced of resorts with nine beaches all in line, it hardly needs an introduction. Don't overlook the art treasures and antiquities: behind its juke-box din, slot-machine arcades, British-style pubs and general vulgarity, Rimini is older than Rome. The **Augustan arch** and **bridge of Tiberius** are as distinctively ancient-Roman as anything in Rome herself.

The **Malatesta castle** recalls the city's involvement with Renaissance warlords. The **Malatesta temple**, by Renaissance architect Alberti, is a picture gallery of major works by Giotto, Duccio and Piero della Francesca. There are comprehensive vacational

• *Near Cervia.*

activities on land and sea all year round, and first-class opera in summer.

SAN BENEDETTO DEL TRONTO ✉

On Route 16, 68 km NW of Pescara. Not quite the largest fishing port on the Adriatic shore, it has the largest and oldest fishmarket. It is worth getting up early to see it in action. The town is nevertheless clean and odourless – faintly scented, in fact, with the broad avenues of mature pines. Though undeveloped, the beach brings fair numbers of holidaymakers.

Two kilometres of firm sands lead you south to the highly respectable small resort of **Porto d'Ascoli**, which is well-furnished with modern hotels and shops (including excellent grocery stores for picnic ingredients) and free of noisy entertainments by day and night. This place is a typical example of the small, genteel resorts which you may come across, sandwiched between more popular places, on the Marche and Abruzzi coasts.

VENICE
See pages 128-137.

RECOMMENDED HOTELS

ANCONA
See also Local Explorations: 13.

Emilia, LL; *on coast road, 2 km W of Portonovo, 12 km S of Ancona; tel. 071 801 145; credit cards, MC, V; closed Dec-Feb.*

Above the sea in the foothills of Monte Conero, the hotel has a unique feature: a vast collection of paintings by artists who paid for their board and lodging in kind (the proprietor now has enough of them). Rooms and furnishings are studiedly 'contemporary' with modern fabrics and all facilities. Shady terrace for al fresco dining (**LL-LLL**). Swimming-pool, tennis, ample car parking.

Grand Hotel Palace, LLL; *Lungomare Vanvitelli 24; tel. 071 201 813; credit cards, AE, DC, E, MC, V; restaurant closed lunch daily.*

In the tradition of grand hotels – opulent, old-fashioned, with old-fashioned high standards. In the port area near Duomo with garage and restaurant for residents only.

CATTOLICA
Europa Monetti, LL; *Via Curiel 39; tel. 054 195 4195; credit cards, none; closed mid-Sep to mid-May.*

Of several dozen hotels here the Europa offers best value. Swimming-pool, secure car parking, restaurant (**L**) for residents only.

CERVIA
Cinzia, LL; *Viale Italia 252, Pinavella, 2 km S of resort; tel. 054 498 7241; credit cards, MC, V; closed Oct-Apr.*

A medium-sized seaside hotel with its own heated swimming-pool on a pleasant terrace. Restaurant is for residents only. Car parking.

CESENATICO
Park Hotel Grilli, LLL; *Viale Torricelli 12, Villamarina, 3 km S of Cesenatico; tel. 054 787 174; credit cards, AE, DC, E, MC, V; restaurant closed in winter.*

Elite establishment with swimming-pool and health complex. Tennis, shady garden. Non-smoking restaurant. Half-board is most economical here.

FANO
Corallo, LL; *Via L. da Vinci 3; tel. 072 180 4200; credit cards, AE, DC, E, MC, V.*

Close to seafront, just around corner from tourist office. Rooms are bright with all amenities. Restaurant.

MARTINSICURO
Maxim's, LL; *Lungomare Italia 12, Villa Rosa; tel. 086 171 2620; credit cards, none; closed Oct-Apr.*

Large amorphous resort hotel, public rooms a little like public halls, but offering many indoor and outdoor entertainments. Best feature is the restaurant, excellent food at moderate prices.

MILANO MARITTIMA
Miami, LLL; *Traversa 31; tel. 054 499 1628; credit cards, AE, DC, E, MC, V; closed Dec-Feb.*

Useful for the out-of-season traveller – unlike most, this hotel opens in spring and autumn, when you may negotiate **LL** rates. Beach, heated swimming-pool, neat garden. Car parking.

PESARO
Des Bains, LL; *Viale Trieste 221; tel. 072 133 665; credit cards, AE, DC, E, MC, V; closed Christmas, New Year; restaurant closed Sun in winter.*

Very close to seafront by Piazza della Libertà, it has 66 rooms and some luxurious suites (**LLL**). The restaurant (residents only) maintains high cosmopolitan standards.

RAVENNA
Argentario, LL; *Via di Roma 45; tel. 054 435 555; credit cards, AE, DC, E, MC, V.*

Full marks for situation near public park and art gallery, 500 m southeast of town centre. Unpretentious, but fully deserves the plaudits of regulars.

Central Byron, LL; *Via 4 Novembre 45; tel. 054 422 225; credit cards, AE, DC, E, MC, V.*

A versatile family and business

hotel. No restaurant but see **Tre Spade**, this page.

Da Giovanni, L; *Cotignola, off* A14dir, *25 km W of Ravenna; tel. 054 540 138; credit cards,* AE, MC, V; *restaurant closed Sat, mid-Aug.*

It is well away from the *brouhaha* of the coast but quickly reached along the *autostrada*. Ten pleasant rooms, so best to book; though you could go along for a meal in its prestigious restaurant (**LL**) while inspecting it.

RIMINI

Grand Hotel, LLL; *Piazzale Indipendenza 2; tel. 054 156 000; credit cards,* AE, DC, E, MC, V.

The best in town, as name and location suggest – and there is plenty of competition. Amenities include heated swimming-pool in a garden shaded by subtropical shrubs and flora, tennis, private beach, nightclub, restaurant. Spacious rooms, an atmosphere of restrained elegance. *Riminesi* come to the restaurant on special occasions.

SAN BENEDETTO DEL TRONTO

O Viv, L-LL; *at Acquaviva Picena, 9 km W of San Benedetto; tel. 073 576 4649; credit cards,* AE, E, MC, V.

Few foreign visitors find this 12-roomed foothills hotel in quiet countryside – and it is a find. Bright furnishings give renovated old *palazzo* a new look. Intimate cosy restaurant (**LL**).

SENIGALLIA

Ritz, LL; *Lungomare Dante Alighieri 142; tel. 071 635 63; credit cards,* AE, DC, E, MC, V; *closed from third week Sep to mid-May.*

Large hotel with air of grandeur, vines, terraces, swimming-pool – style at reasonable cost. Restaurant. Closed when the town is dead.

A rare all-year hotel is **Eden, L**; *Via Podesti; tel. 071 792 6802; credit cards,* AE, DC, E, MC, V; *open all year; restaurant closed Sat.*

Fragrant garden, inexpensive restaurant.

RECOMMENDED RESTAURANTS

ANCONA

Villa Amalia, L-LL; *Via degli Spagnoli 4, Falconara Marittima, 13 km N of Ancona; tel. 071 916 0550; credit cards,* DC, V; *closed Tues.*

Fascinating menu leans towards fish – we had sea bass with oysters (*spigola con zabaione di ostriche*). Nice garden and a few rooms (**LL**).

CARTOCETO

Symposium, LL-LLL; *15 km SW of Fano; tel. 072 189 8320; credit cards, none; closed Mon, parts of Jan and Jun.*

Pretty garden for summer dining. Seasonal menus, some challenging dishes, such as eel and bacon salad. Best to book.

CHIOGGIA

Al Bragosso, LL; *Sant' Anna di Chioggia, on Route 309, 8 km S of Chioggia; tel. 041 495 0395; credit cards, none; closed Wed, Jan.*

Renowned seafood. People come from Venice. Admirable presentation.

COMACCHIO

Il Sambuco, LLL; *Via Caduti del Mare 30, Porto Garibaldi; tel. 053 332 7478; credit cards,* AE, DC, E, MC, V; *closed Mon, two weeks Jan, Nov.*

Balcony meals on warm evenings. Mainly seafood (try scampi with hot artichoke salad) and a fine white Sauvignon to go with them.

RAVENNA

Tre Spade, LL-LLL; *Via Rasponi 37; tel. 054 432 382; credit cards,* AE, DC, E, MC, V; *closed Mon, most of Jul, Sun eve in winter.*

Converted mill in city centre where gourmets come to eat. We have had roast pheasant and pigeon, also *millefoglie di branzino e salmone* (layers of bass and salmon discreetly flavoured with ginger). Superior wines.

Between Modena and the Brenner
Po Plain and Austrian Alps

330 km; maps Touring Club Italiano Trentino Alto Adige and Emilia Romagna

If you ask which is the most beautiful motorway journey in Italy, some will say Verona to the Brenner Pass, others the Brenner Pass to Verona. That, together with a more humdrum stretch of motorway between Verona and Modena, is our red route. If you have the option, south to north is the more spectacular way to travel: a steady climb on an imperceptible gradient, crossing and re-crossing the ice-blue Adige river from the wide plain of the Po towards the peaks and pinnacles of the Brenta and Dolomite massifs. That way you have the mountains ahead of you and the sun on them, reflecting unearthly colours. Several times you approach an impasse. Each time the crags open up and allow the road to slip through.

For our blue route between Trento and Vipiteno you will need more time. The road is sound and mostly it follows the narrow valleys of riverine lakes and torrents, but there are tortuous sections across the saddles of the watersheds. You rise to about 700 m and are hardly aware of it, the naked cliffs (too steep for snow to lie on them) to right and left being more than twice that height. The one difficult pass with many hairpin bends, well-guarded but calling for careful driving, is that of Monte Giovo or Jaufen at 2,094 m. It is not recommended for caravans and is closed between November and mid-June. Many ski resorts, castles, old towns and sensational views are packed into the Trentino and Alto Adige regions. The latter, still a debatable land, is known to the Austrians as Sud Tirol. Every town, village and hill has both a German and an Italian name; we use the Italian, but acknowledge the combination of Teutonic efficiency and Latin gaiety which gives these regions their agreeable atmosphere.

The red route is a painless way of getting in or out of Italy. The Brenner motorway sweeps on to Innsbruck and the Munich-Salzburg-Vienna autobahn network. The Brenner Pass at 1,371 m is simplicity itself for the motorist.

At the south end of the route our green alternative wanders off among some historic monuments of the Emilian and Lombardy countryside. If you feel like lingering around Bolzano, Trentino and Mantua, have a look at Local Explorations: 3 and 4 (Dolomites), 5 (Lake Garda) and 8 (Po Plain).

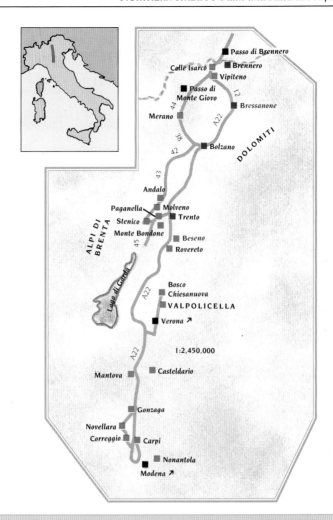

TRANSPORT

Between the Brenner Pass and Verona the main railway line between Austria and Italy accompanies the motorway and the Adige river. At Trento a branch line struggles through the Val Sugana to Bassano del Grappa and ends up in Venice. At Bolzano a branch line goes west to Merano. The electric trains which used to thread the high valleys to the ski resorts are no more and it is wearisome travelling by bus - everyone goes to the winter sports grounds by car, then cable-car. But there are reliable bus services along major routes and all the country towns round Merano, Bolzano, Trento, Verona, Mantua and Modena are adequately served. Autostradale (Piazzale Castello 1, Milan) run buses to Mantua, Molveno and the Garda; SAD (Via Conciapelli 60, Bolzano) runs services and tours in the Dolomites.

A dense network of ski-tows, ski-lifts and cable cars of modern construction gives another dimension to mountain travel. Cable cars and chairlifts can carry 4,000 people an hour to the summits near Trento. The world's first cable-car was installed at Bolzano in 1908.

SIGHTS & PLACES OF INTEREST

ANDALO ⚐

On Route 45bis 38 km NW of Trento. An Alpine township on a lake, transformed but not spoiled by the tourist boom. Mountain lifts take you to the **Paganella** summit at 2,103 m, an aerial platform overlooking one of the most celebrated views of the Alps. Andalo is also a base-camp for mountaineers. Skating rinks at the hotels and a bus service to Trento and the Garda.

BESENO

See Trentino Castles, this page.

BOLZANO ⚐ ✕

On the A22, 102 km S of the Brenner Pass. The regional capital is a market centre with a busy piazza, an arcaded main street and attractive narrow streets leading off it, lined with high-gabled houses and plenty of window boxes and wrought iron. A sheltered situation on the Adige river, exceptionally attractive surroundings, a strong Austrian flavour to the cuisine. The centre for the Alto Adige castles (see Alto Adige Castles, page 61).

BOSCO CHIESANUOVA

On a minor road via Montorio, 31 km N of Verona. A pretty town at 1,104 m easily reached by car or bus from Verona. The cool climate and fresh air make it popular in summer. Roads and chairlifts rise to skiing heights.

BRESSANONE ⚐ ✕

On the A22, 40 km N of Bolzano. A small-

TRENTINO CASTLES

Size and intricacy are the features of the scores of castles distributed over this region. Lofty defences, great frescoed chambers and galleries – all are different, all occupy majestic sites. **Beseno** near Rovereto is the largest, **Stenico** (see page 64) the most impressive.

The Trentino castles have had real money lavished on them and now they work for tourism as the *mises-en-scène* for drama, ballet and medieval banquets. From Trento in summer special trains with costumed guides and piped madrigals run the castles routes: Fridays into Valsugana east of Trento; Saturdays along the Vallagarina by Rovereto; Sundays up the Valle di Non north of Trento. If you have a chance of seeing a fireworks display or *son et lumière* at a Trentino castle, grab it. An unforgettable experience.

er, cosier Bolzano with similar riverside parks and an arcaded shopping centre. Cathedral cloisters and Renaissance frescos make it an important centre of history and art. Delightful walks in the neighbourhood to the vineyards and ruined abbey of Novacella, to 13thC Chiusa and the Sabbiona monastery.

CARPI

Off the A22 on Route 413, 16 km N of Modena. Its **Giulio Ferrara civic museum** exhibits the often under-

HOTELS AND RESTAURANTS

The establishments we recommend below are confined to the northern half of our route. For the southern half, see Verona (Italy Overall: 2), Modena (Italy Overall: 3), and Local Explorations: 4, 5 and 8.

Our listing has a higher-than-usual percentage of **LLL** places. Several are converted medieval castles with every possible luxury. Along our route there are also dozens of inexpensive châlet-type inns, smothered in geraniums, particularly away from the major

centres of Merano, Bolzano and Trento. Andalo and Molveno have such places. Opening times are seasonal in such mountain resorts.

At the north end of our route, anticipate Austrian emphasis to the cuisine: stews and spiced meats – and beer. Try to visit a *stube*, the Tyrolean version of a *bierkeller*. As we come south the cooking becomes more Italian. Polenta appears on menus. Pasta becomes more varied. Olive oil consumption increases. But north or south, you will not go hungry.

rated Emilian artists of the 16thC. The **Sagra church** is worth a visit but the showplace is the **Del Pio castle** with its 'long portico' bordering a spacious piazza.

CASTELDARIO
See Mantua, this page.

COLLE ISARCO
On the A22, 10 km S of the Brenner Pass. The nearest resort to the Brenner. Not a bad place to stay for your first or last night in Italy – cinema, hotels, *pensioni*, swimming-pools and the inevitable skating rink. Five kilometres from Terme Brenner, which has ski-tows to the high ground.

CORREGGIO
Off the A22 on Route 468, 20 km NW of Modena. An old city of the plain, a small replica of Mantua. The **Palazzo dei Principi** has Mantegna's *Redeemer* and some elaborate Flemish tapestries.

GONZAGA
Off the A22 at Pegognaga, 23 km S of Mantua. Around a ruined castle and a decrepit mansion you muse on the fates of dynasties and the mutability of human affairs. The insignificant village recalls a nobody who split warring factions and seized Mantua in 1328; his descendants who enjoyed power and glory for four centuries, during which they patronized Petrarch, Boccaccio, Ariosto and Mantegna; and the last inglorious Gonzaga who threw it all away and died disgraced.

MANTUA
Off the A22, 67 km N of Modena. By way of boulevards, banks and other places of commerce you enter the city of Virgil (he was born 8 km to the south, near modern Pietole), a ducal capital long renowned, her silvery *campanili* shining, her tiny *rii* (canals) trickling under tottering walls, her lakes and lagoons spreading to purple hills. On Piazza Sordello the **ducal palace** is a complex of 500 stately rooms and about 50 courtyards, each a statement of Gonzaga extravagance. There are scaled-down apartments for dwarves, a staircase for horses, a hall of mirrors, a maze-puzzle ceiling.
Castello San Giorgio just around

the corner has the Mantegna masterpiece, the walls of the bridal chamber, covered with scenes of courtly life on which, from the painted dome, impudent *putti* (naked babies) peer down in ingenious perspective. In the same group of buildings, known as the Reggia, are the cathedral, the Bonacolsi palace, the domed basilica of Sant' Andrea, the 13thC Ragione palace next to a tower with a large 15thC astronomical clock – and the so-called house of Rigoletto.

Take all Rigoletto associations – Gilda in Sant' Andrea, peeping at the Duke, the Maddalena tavern on the marshes – with a pinch of salt. For political reasons Verdi transferred the opera's setting from its real location,

---

ALTO ADIGE CASTLES
Chains of fortresses grimace at each other across Isarco, Adige and Talvera, the south-running streams of the Alps. To judge by the frescos in their banqueting halls – Tristan, Siegfried, King Arthur and even Julius Caesar rub shoulders – they castellated this region long before the age of chivalry. Unlike Trentino castles they are domesticated, with slender towers, square or conical red caps and toy portcullises, like nursery forts. Few have had a defensive role since the pugnacious Counts of Tyrol retired beyond the Brenner in 1420. They keep a benevolent eye on romantic landscapes and are museums of pictures, arms and armour. Pearl of the region is **Coira**, west of Merano, home of the Trapps since 1504, rich in arabesques and weapons. **Maretsch** has Biblical frescos, **Castel Guardia** pinewood panelling, **Tirolo** a stone bestiary, **Sant' Erasmo** an antique painted chapel. Some 120 castles are visitable, all within comfortable reach of Bolzano and Merano by excursion bus. The castle **Roncolo** (1237) stands guard over Bolzano itself. Last century a canny mayor presented the ruin to Emperor Franz Joseph of Austria, who restored it beautifully and handed it back.

Paris. Likewise a fiction is Romeo 'standing at the rusty gate of stagnant Mantua' – he was never there.

Walk (15 minutes) or drive south to the Gonzaga summer retreat, **Palazzo Tè**, another flamboyant showcase of painted horses, giants and Bacchanalia (the latter explicit even to modern eyes). The place is decrepit and deprived of its lake, but long-term renovation is taking place. On the way to it you pass **Mantegna's house**, another Renaissance gem (1476).

A bronze **bust of Tazio Nuvolari**, possibly the greatest racing motorist in history, is in the public garden on Viale Nuvolari, near the railway station. His tomb is at **Casteldario** outside the city. The inscription says: 'Now he travels still faster on the highways of Heaven'.

MERANO 🛌 ✕

On Route 38, 26 km NW of Bolzano. The little old river town has become a garden city, thanks to its popularity with German and Austrian visitors. They came for the wine-cure, then for hill-walking; now every car has skis on its roof. Shady avenues on the riverbank are labelled 'winter' and 'summer', at the bandstand an orchestra plays –

RECOMMENDED RESTAURANTS

BOLZANO

Grifone, LLL; *Piazza Walther 7; tel. 047 197 7056; credit cards*, AE, DC, E, MC, V.

Attached to hotel of same name with tables on main piazza for summer dining. Versatile menu includes *weinsuppe* (cinnamon-flavoured wine soup) and vegetarians should try *spinatspaetzli*, parmesan-coated spinach dumplings.

Abramo, LL; *Piazza Gries 16; tel. 047 128 0141; credit cards*, AE, E, MC, V; *closed Sun, last three weeks Jun.*

A substantial wine cellar supports this fine out-of-town establishment. Elegant atmosphere, silver and crystal table-settings. Non-smoking. Strong on vegetarian dishes and fish: salmon with champagne sauce was delicious. Outdoor service in summer.

BRESSANONE

Fink, LL; *Via Portici Minori 4; tel. 047 234 883; credit cards*, V; *closed Wed, first three weeks Jul.*

In town centre just north of Palazzo Vescovile. Rustic-style trattoria very popular with locals. Wide-ranging menu does not disdain country staples such as *castrato alla paesana*, a hearty beef stew.

MERANO

Flora, LLL; *Via Portici 75; tel. 047 331 484; credit cards*, AE, DC, E, MC, V; *closed lunch, Sun, mid-Jan to end Feb.*

Reservation necessary for this tiny candle-lit place within the arcades near Duomo. Perfectionist chef creates many gastronomic treats including an appetizing smoked salmon garnished with fennel (*carpaccio di salmone*). Wines include a red Montalcino.

Andrea, LLL; *Via Galilei 44; tel. 047 337 400; credit cards*, AE, DC, E, MC, V; *closed Mon, most of Feb.*

Near Monte Benedetto funicular, north of city centre, this stylish restaurant is famous for desserts. Its *crema bavarese* (strawberries and cream) is a triumph. Wines are not bad either.

TRENTO

Chiesa, LLL; *Via San Marco 64; tel. 046 123 8766; credit cards*, AE, DC, E, MC, V; *closed Sun, Wed eve, two weeks mid-Aug.*

In a 15thC building in the shadow of the Castello, this is the best restaurant in town yet not extortionately expensive. Menus change regularly and offer refined versions of venerable regional dishes. Try *tonco del Pontesel*, a traditional stew.

VIPITENO

Pretzhof, LL; *at Tulve, 8 km E of Vipiteno; tel. 047 276 4455; credit cards, none; closed Mon, Tues lunch, third week Dec, Jan, second half Jun.*

This attractive place with its terrace and magnificent views is worth the detour on its own account and a quite exceptional Tyrolean cuisine is the bonus.

there are beer gardens and wine bars everywhere. The old town, compressed between stream and mountain, consists of little more than the long arcaded Via dei Portici, a corridor of gift shops.

MODENA

See Italy Overall: 3.

MOLVENO

On Route 45bis, off Route 237 to route 421, 45 km NW of Trento and near Andalo. Sheltered by the Brenta cliffs, in a paradise of woods and meadows thick with wild fruits and flowers (you may pick only certain kinds on certain days), Molveno sits by a lake where once you could bathe all year round. The hydro board has now let in glacial streams. Ski-tows rise to the Paganella area. The hilly little town has superior hotels and offers farmhouse holidays.

MONTE BONDONE

See Trento, page 64.

NONANTOLA

On Route 255, 11 km E of Modena. The abbey has a treasury and archive of documents signed by Charlemagne, Frederick Barbarossa, Countess Matil-

• *Brenta uplands*

da and other potentates of the Middle Ages.

NOVELLARA

Off the A22, 34 km NW of Modena. Here and at Guastalla, 14 km north, are two typical palace-forts of the Gonzagas, part of the Mantuan defensive system. Novellara also has two Gonzaga villas, Casino di Sopra and Casino di Sotto.

PAGANELLA

Mountain: see Andalo, page 60.

ROVERETO

Off the A22, 24 km S of Trento. Motorists in transit curse its narrow streets, pedestrians its flights of steps. Vineyards come down to the triangular walls and bastions of a Venetian castle which houses the Italian **First World War museum**. The town, an interchange of lake traffic, tempts the passing trade with an Olympic swimming-pool, riding schools, bowling, tennis, clay-pigeon shoots, athletic tracks and *son et lumière*. The neighbourhood produces classic wines, including the red Marzemino prescribed by Mozart in the last act of *Don Giovanni*.

STENICO

On Routes 45bis and 237, 30 km W of Trento. A pretty village on a tough road (before 1918, under the Austrians, there was no road at all), it lies at a junction of valleys with the Brenta massif above – the point at which, travelling north, you stare wide-eyed at such heights and colours. Balconies overflow with geraniums, orchards march down near-vertical slopes. A short stiff climb takes you to a great 10th-14thC fortress.

TRENTO 🚩 ✕

On the A22, 60 km S of Bolzano. The regional capital, a clean and unassuming town, has faded frescos on house façades, restored frescos at **Castello Buonconsiglio** (the name recalls an ecclesiastical milestone, the Council of Trent of 1545), a spotless **piazza**, **cathedral** and fountain group, a **bishop's palace** and a clock-tower decorated with fish-tail battlements. Open-air theatre and concerts on the piazza. Pavement cafés with fine ice-cream and delectable *macedonie* of the soft fruits which grow abundantly round about. (Even lemons and oranges thrive in Trentino's valleys.)

The skyline is a tumbled chaos of peaks, slashed with snow like the foam of a stormy sea. Trento's own moun-

---

RECOMMENDED HOTELS

ANDALO

Piccolo, LL; *tel. 046 158 5710; credit cards, AE, DC, E, MC, V; closed late spring, autumn.*

Best-situated of village's numerous hotels, with fine views of the Brenta mountain range. Good inexpensive restaurant. Nearby is the **Maria, LL**; *tel. 046 158 5828; credit cards, AE, DC, E, MC, V; open all year.* At both places half-board is a bargain.

APPIANO

Schloss Korb, LLL; *at Missiano, 4 km N of Appiano; tel. 047 163 6000; credit cards, none.*

By the Wine Route (Strada del Vino) and 10 km west of Bolzano, the Korb is a medieval castle set in a valley of terraced vineyards, with sauna and indoor and outdoor swimming-pools. Rooms furnished Tyrolean style with antiques and woodcarvings. Car parking; restaurant. Lower end of price category.

BOLZANO

Park, LLL; *Via Laurino 4; tel. 047 198 0500; credit cards, AE, DC, E, MC, V; restaurant closed Sun.*

Centrally situated near the station and Duomo. Up-market with stylish art-nouveau opulence. Large lush garden with heated swimming-pool. Notable restaurant **Belle Epoque, LL-LLL**; furnished in period style. Car parking.

Grifone, LLL; *Piazza Walther 7; tel. 047 197 7056; credit cards, AE, DC, E, MC, V.*

In the pedestrianized town centre, a long-established, comfortable and elegant hotel. Some rooms have balconies with views of town and surrounding mountains; others are furnished with Tyrolean antiques. Car parking.

See also Recommended Restaurants, page 62.

BRESSANONE

Dominik, LL-LLL; *Via Terzo di Sotto 13; tel. 047 230 144; credit cards, AE, E, MC, V; closed Nov-Easter; restaurant closed Tues.*

Modern building overlooking the river, 500 m east of town centre in a pleasant quiet garden. Swimming-pool, sauna, health suite, car parking. Restaurant with summer service under pergola; locally-caught trout a seasonal speciality.

Elefante, LLL; *Via Rio Bianco 4; tel. 047 232 750; credit cards, none; closed most of winter; restaurant closed Mon except Aug-Oct.*

Famous historic inn, named after an incident in the 16thC, when it stabled a gift for Ferdinand, Emperor of Austria. Large park with heated swimming-pool. Close to Route 12. Beautifully furnished rooms, plenty of carved wood, Tyrolean antiques and chandeliers. Car parking. Renowned restaurant (**LLL**) where menus change according to availability of produce – from hotel farm.

tain, **Bondone** (2,000 m), is at the end of a zigzag 14-km road. Long favoured by hill-walkers, it claims to have seen the launch of winter sports in the 1930s. Chairlifts ascend to a panoramic glass restaurant on a neighbouring summit at 2,100 m.

VALPOLICELLA
On Route 12, NW of Verona. Undulating hills, clothed with vines, slope to the Adige river. Here the well-known tipple tastes better than that sent to the supermarket by tanker. A famous Paris street is named for the village and castle of **Rivoli** on its plateau above the river. Here in 1797 the French army under its new general Bonaparte met the Austrians for the third time and made it three victories out of three.

VERONA
See Italy Overall: 2.

VIPITENO ✕
On the A22, 15 km S of the Brenner pass. One of the best-looking of Tyrolean towns on the Isarco riverside with a quaint main street, coloured houses, old shop signs and a historic gatehouse. Skiing and walking on four neighbouring mountains. A popular tourist stopover. In summer the hotels may not be adequate to the demand.

GARGAZZONE
Alle Torre, L; *in small village on Route 38 between Merano and Bolzano; tel. 047 329 2325; credit cards, MC; closed Feb; restaurant closed Thur.*
It boasts an orchard with heated swimming-pool and reasonable restaurant. Half-board is a bargain: only 11 rooms, so best to book.

MERANO
Palace Hotel, LLL; *Via Cavour 2; tel. 047 334 734; credit cards, AE, DC, E, MC, V; closed early spring, late autumn; restaurant closed Tues lunch mid-Jun to mid-Jul.*
Expensive, luxurious, close to river among trees, with swimming-pool. Highest standards of comfort and service. Health suite offers sauna, massage and other spa treatment, and a fountain dispenses spa water. Car parking. Restaurant, the **Schloss Maur**, is formal; adjoining grill room less so. Art-nouveau decoration with stained glass and wood panelling.

Castel Rundegg, LLL; *Via Scena 2; tel. 047 334 100; credit cards, AE, DC, E, MC, V; closed last three weeks Jan.*
Also with spa facilities and in parkland, east of town centre. Original tower of the 12thC castle contains turret room with 360° views. Restaurant (residents only) is intimate; food faultless.

Castel Freiburg, LLL; *Freiburg, 8 km SE of Merano; tel. 047 324 4196; credit cards, AE, DC, E, MC, V; closed Nov-Easter.*
Modernized 14thC castle on hilltop above Merano, with glorious mountain views. Indoor and outdoor swimming-pools; sauna and tennis. Beautiful garden; wood-panelled restaurant; antiques and armour. Car parking.

TRENTO
Accademia, LLL; *Vicolo Colico 4; tel. 046 123 3600; credit cards, AE, DC, E, MC, V.*
Ancient building in historic heart of city among painted façades. Bedrooms are bright and modern. Public rooms retain medieval character. Notable restaurant (must book if not resident – tel. 046 198 1580) leans toward nouvelle cuisine and is formal.

Castel Pergine, L; *Pergine Valsugana, 12 km E of Trento; tel. 046 153 1158; credit cards, none; closed mid-Oct to Apr; restaurant closed Mon.*
Tenth-century hilltop fortress with beautiful walled garden. Excellent baronial-style restaurant (**LL**). Hotel is near top of price bracket.

VILPIANO
Sparerhof, L-LL; *Via Nalles 2; tel. 047 167 8671; credit cards, E, MC, V; restaurant closed Sun, Mon lunch and in winter.*
Small comfortable place on Route 38 between Merano and Bolzano. Garden, sauna, heated swimming-pool. The owners have built up an impressive collection of modern art.

Central Italy

Between Genoa and Rome
The Tyrrhenian Coast

330 km; maps Touring Club Italiano Liguria, Toscana and Lazio

The sea is always a presence, though you cannot always see it. The middle section of this journey is the 240-km Tuscan littoral between Marina di Carrara and Ansedonia – soft deep sands and, south of Livorno (Leghorn), a stretch of precipitous rocks. A virtually unbroken series of lidos and marinas with belts of umbrella pines, holiday bungalows, camp sites and caravan parks decorates the shoreline. This road gives the best access to the great art centres of Lucca, Pisa and Siena, which we cover in Local Explorations: 9 and 11.

North and south of that section are the Ligurian coast and Rome's Lazio coast. Along the former, in every rocky cove, fishing villages have hollowed out their lairs. The hoary pastel-painted tenements, their back walls pinned against cliffs, look like pasteboard houses and, despite over-enthusiastic road-building, it is still hard to get at some of them.

The Lazio coast is more recently developed (within living memory it was fatally malarial), with square blocks of hotels laid out on geometrical street-plans. New-looking resorts draw a tentative clientele from Rome. Paradoxically they adjoin the heartland of Etruria, a country of high culture when Rome was a collection of mud huts.

Our red route is mostly the Autostrada dei Fiori ('Flowers'), so-named for the luxuriant foliage of the Ligurian coast and the flowers grown there for the spring markets. In 1993 the *autostrada* was complete between Genoa and Livorno and between Rome and Civitavecchia, with some unfinished sections in between.

TRANSPORT

The limited-stop express is the train for this route. Otherwise it is a tedious journey. The only attractive section, between Genoa and La Spezia, with one tunnel after another, gives brief, tantalizing glimpses to seaward.

Change at Sarzana for two exciting lines, one through the Lunigiana gorges to Parma or Milan, the other through the marble mountains of the Apuan Alps (see page 68) to Lucca. Change at Viareggio or Livorno for Pisa or Florence. Change trains at Grosseto for Siena.

Car ferries connect Genoa with Corsica (12 hours), Sardinia (13 hours) and Sicily (22 hours). Livorno serves the same islands and also those of the Tuscan Archipelago (see below). Campiglia Marittima is the station for Piombino, the port for Elba. Civitavecchia-Olbia is the short sea route to Sardinia.

Bus companies offering long-distance services on the Genoa-Rome routes include: SITA (Florence), Pesci (Cornigliano and Genoa), Europabus (Rome) and (from Britain) National Express Eurolines, (Victoria Coach Station, London).

The blue route is that of the Via Aurelia, ancient Rome's Highway 1, first of the 'consular' routes (named after the Roman consuls) which fanned out from the Eternal City and ensured that 'all roads led to Rome'. The green route weaves from side to side of that important artery, giving access to gnarled old forts and watch-towers and places known and unknown, including islands of the Tuscan archipelago which are at present only pencilled in on the map of tourist Italy. For all that the coastal road to Rome has been travelled for centuries, there is still undiscovered country along it.

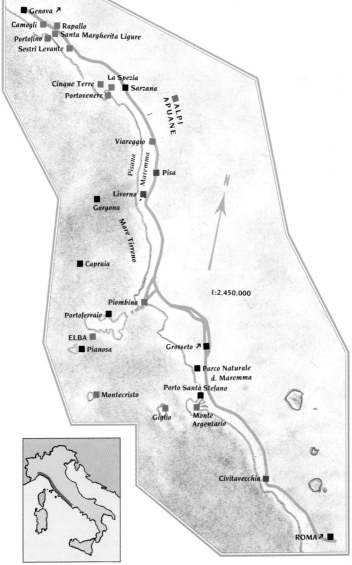

SIGHTS & PLACES OF INTEREST

APUAN ALPS

Off Route 1, 16 km SE of La Spezia. Pure white marble, a freak of geology, they break above the Tuscan shore and make a foamy backdrop to the sunny resorts and pinewoods of Marina di Carrara, Marina di Massa, Forte dei

---

HOTELS AND RESTAURANTS

Our route follows the coastline from Genoa to Rome and restaurants are heavily fish-orientated. (Many say 'Fish Dishes Only'.) Away from the ubiquitous *pizzerie* seafood predominates, from the humble sardine through cod and mullet to the more exotic cuttlefish and squid. At many villages near our route you can watch your meal being landed. With pasta dishes on the Ligurian coast you are likely to be offered *pesto*, a sauce of basil, pine nuts, garlic and *pecorino* or parmesan cheese. Culinary experts insist that the sweetest basil in Europe grows on the hill terraces above Genoa. Travelling south, you leave the Ligurian shores for the so-called Estruscan Riviera. The cuisine is Tuscan. Menus are shorter on fish and longer on grilled meats. There is never any shortage of places to stay. Several towns, such as Cecina Mare and Marina di Massa, are nothing but settlements of hotels which jostle for the best positions along the strand. Some resorts have conjoined to the extent that you may drive through half a dozen without knowing which is which. A few places – Portofino and the Monte Argentario promontory are the best examples – are chic, trendy and expensive. Most resorts (anything with Mare, Lido or Marittimo after its name) go determinedly for the package-tour or camp/caravan markets. Such places are noisy in the season, rather forlorn at other times. The hotels and restaurants we list here are outstanding in terms of quality and value for money. See also Local Explorations: 9, 11 and 14. For Genoa, see Local Explorations: 7; for Rome, see page 106.

Marmi and Pietrasanta. For 300 years Italy has exported these mountains all over the world, chiefly for prestigious public buildings. In Massa and Carrara, where dust settles like snow, homely items like bedsteads and babies' teething rings are made of marble.

Drive to the quarries behind Massa and Carrara into a white world of crevices, dust-heaps and marble litter. Sounds are muffled except for the steady whirr of the saws. Souvenir marble is sold on site.

Michelangelo spent seven years at Pietrasanta choosing one marble block. Some say it was a woman, not the marble, that kept him there.

CAMOGLI

Off Route 1, 20 km E of Genoa. Sea-eggs on the rocks, baby octopi on the fish-monger's slab, aquarium and naval museum – typical of a dozen Riviera fishing villages, Camogli was also a cradle of sea-captains. In sailing-ship days you heard the Camogli dialect in the bars of Cape Town and Buenos Aires. It is also the village of gargantu-an frying-pans, brought out for a grand banquet at the May feast of San Fortunato. **Tombs of the Dorias**, poten-tates of Genoa, lie in the San Fruttuoso monastery next door. Newly-arrived skin-divers in the bay rush ashore to report the discovery of a submerged statue. It is **Christ of the Abyss**, visible from above, casualty of a shipwreck long ago.

CINQUE TERRE

Off Route 1, 10 km W of La Spezia. The 'Five Lands' are five villages, crushed into coves below and above vine terraces which the Romans planted, forming one geographical entity. **Monterosso** at the west end has now joined the world: it has a beach, hotels, parasols and even a road. The church appears to be putting out to sea. Old-time smugglers, hauling in contraband on a rope, acted stupid and persuaded the revenue officers they were trying to turn the church to face the shore. **Vernazza's church** also rises from the harbour. Legend says an octopus tolls the bell from the crypt.

Cornigia's vines grow so steeply from the sea that men need ropes and ladders to tend them. Shale, not soil, nourishes Cinque Terre wines, the famous pale amber *vernaccia* and *sci-achettrà* (it means 'chatterer') in their fish net wrappers.

Manarola is precariously heaped around the outfall of a torrent which descends 760 m in 3 km. A cliff walk, the Via dell' Amore (but lovers must have good heads for heights), goes to **Riomaggiore**, easternmost of the Cinque Terre, terminus of a road from La Spezia (6.5 km). No cars in the villages, no souvenir stalls, no accommodation but the simple *locanda* (lodging-house). Skimpy black-sand beaches. Access from Genoa or La Spezia by rail. A coastal highway is projected.

CIVITAVECCHIA

Off the A12, *72 km* NW *of Rome.* An old port, of less importance now than formerly. Ferries sail for Olbia and other Sardinian ports (7 to 12 hours). The 17thC **Fort Michelangelo** presides over a workaday town. Pebbly beaches and small-boat harbours are scattered around, notably at **Santa Marinella**, 10 km south on a coastline which bristles with old forts. Local buses serve the peaceful Etruscan hinterland.

ELBA 🛏

A mere 20 minutes in the hovercraft from Piombino, Elba's virgin crown of *macchia* – buckthorn, bramble and rosemary – overlooks gulfs which bite deep into the land, giving a long coastline of sand strips and impregnable cliffs. The sea is inviting, the sub-aqua work fascinating if you can get down to it. Best accessible beaches are at **Porto Azzurro**, **Lacona** and **Marina di Campo**; also next door to your landing-place, **Portoferraio**. The way into this chief town, among tiers of houses, is through the Porta a Mare, a massive

---

RECOMMENDED RESTAURANTS

CECINA
Scacciapensieri, LLL; *Via* Verdi 22; *tel.* 058 668 0900; *credit cards,* AE, DC, V; *closed* Mon.

Corso Matteoti divides the downtown area and Via Verdi is three blocks east. *Tagliolini alle triglie* (ribbon pasta with red mullet) is a speciality and the *scampi marsigliesi* looked delicious. An interesting wine list included a distinguished *brunello*. It is wise to book a table.

MONTEROSSO
Il Gigante, LL; *tel.* 018 781 7401; *credit cards,* AE, DC, E, MC, V; *closed* Tues *except in high season, and in winter.*

This trattoria on the shore of a resort which has recently resigned from the secret world of the Cinque Terre (see page 68) and joined the real world is a mecca for seafood fans. Menus change daily but you can rely on a delicious *zuppa di pesce* (fish soup) and perhaps spaghetti *con salsa di polipi* (sauce of baby octopi). The Gigante attracts plenty of custom at weekends.

PORTOFINO
Il Pitosforo, LLL; *tel.* 018 526 9020; *credit cards,* AE, DC, E, MC, V; *closed* Tues, Wed lunch, two months in winter.

A charming waterfront building with terrace and portico, much frequented by jet-setting yachtspersons who can moor almost alongside. Excels in seafood. Our *stocco accomodou* (the menu is in dialect but our waiter spoke English) turned out to be cod delicately grilled with sauce of pine nuts and tomatoes. Everything costs the earth on and around the Portofino promontory, but this restaurant is not a rip-off. It also excludes yobbos, however rich.

SANTA MARGHERITA
Trattoria Cesarina, LLL; *Via* Mameli 2c; *tel.* 018 528 6059; *credit cards,* DC, V; *closed* Wed.

Seafood-rich menu varies according to day's catch. Stuffed and baked fish are specialities, the marinated salmon is worth waiting for (drink with local Pigato dry white).

VIAREGGIO
Romano, LLL; *Via* Mazzini 120; *tel.* 058 431 382; *credit cards,* AE, DC, E, MC, V; *closed* Mon, *most of* Jan.

Top-of-the-range seafood, notable *calamaretti ripieni* (stuffed baby squid). Exquisite *bronzino al forno* (oven-baked bass).

time-worn gateway. Inland, beyond the high town, are the abandoned furnaces and quarries of old 'Iron Town'.

All roads on Elba are attractive but savage twists and gradients make them hard going. The Portoferraio dwelling of the isle's most distinguished visitor, Bonaparte, exiled here 1814-15, is not inspiring. Better value, if only for views and lush greenery, is his former summer residence at San Martino, 10 km into the hills.

GENOA
See Italy Overall: 1.

GIGLIO
See Tuscan Archipelago, page 73.

GROSSETO
See Box: Maremma National Park.

LA SPEZIA
Off the A12, 100 km SE of Genoa. Italian sailors throng the steep streets of the old quarter, contributing to the rich warm humming life of a typical Mediterranean seaport. The naval barracks and dockyard are in the harbour area, with a first-class **naval museum** in the old gun factory. Along a spacious promenade run terraces of pink and

• *Vernazza, Cinque Terre.*

primrose mansions, set in extravagant layouts of palms, oleanders and rhododendrons. Here everything is post-1945 – La Spezia underwent a three-month wartime bombardment which left only stumps of palm-trees on her waterfront.

On the heights, from the Isolabella and Castellazzo gates in the city walls (you can drive to them), you have views of the soft blue Spezia gulf. You can see **Lerici**, where Shelley set up house with a complex menage and Byron swam over from Portovenere (5 km) to meet him. Shelley drowned in a sailing accident but other celebrities colonized Lerici, Fiascherino, Tellaro and San Terenzo: D.H. Lawrence wrote about the problems of getting Frieda's piano down the cliffs.

Excursion boats and buses from La Spezia visit every corner of this populous gulf of which the jewel is Portovenere (see page 71).

MONTECRISTO
See Tuscan Archipelago, page 73.

MONTE ARGENTARIO
Off Route 1, 46 km S of Grosseto. Three

causeways attach the promontory to the mainland. On one stands **Orbetello**, ringed with Spanish walls. See beside its lagoon a florid monument to Italo Balbo, the long-distance aviator of the 1930s and a hero of Fascist Italy. The hangar at Orbetello is one of the architectural gems of that era.

Monte Argentario has a fashionable yacht harbour at **Porto San Stefano**, a pretty little harbour (but no beach) at **Porto Ercole**, also three Spanish forts and two Saracen towers. Expensive hotels have commandeered the best coves for bathing, the sea swell deters swimming from the exposed rocks and the promontory seems vulnerable to forest fires, which spoil the thyme-scented high ground. There are ferries from Porto San Stefano to Giglio and Giannutri (1 hour).

PISA
See Local Explorations: 9.

PORTOFINO 🛏 ✕
Off Route 1, 30 km E of Genoa, 5 km S of Rapallo. Bars, boutiques, night-clubs, a fashion-plate piazza, lace-making a prestige industry – Portofino complements St Tropez on the other Riviera and is the smartest resort in Italy outside the Costa Smeralda (see Local Explorations: 26). Fishing craft share the toy harbour with luxury yachts. Walk to the Peak (610 m) or to Santa Margherita (see this page) or San Fruttuoso (see Camogli, page 68).

PORTOVENERE
On Route 530, 12 km S of La Spezia, Gulf of Spezia. Tightly-packed medieval houses and sea front ramparts which were part of Genoa's defensive system resist the ravages of tourism. Coves, grottoes and the sea bed attract explorers. The miniscule **Grotto Arpaia**, or 'Byron's Grotto', inspired the poet's *Corsair* and a few years later Wagner wrote part of *Das Rheingold* on the same spot. Many boatloads of visitors from La Spezia (12 km) in summer, quiet at night and out of season.

RAPALLO
On Route 1, 22 km SE of Genoa. The rock-bound coast draws apart to admit Rapallo and its conical terraced hill. The English writer Max Beerbohm discovered it, the 1920s were its golden

---

DETOUR – **MAREMMA NATURAL PARK**
Off Route 1, 18 km S of Grosseto. Coastal area betwen Grosseto and Tarquinia. 'Natural park' in Italy often means a wilderness and most of the Maremma is just that: dry marsh, a sparsely-populated coastal plain of some interest to botanists and slaughterers of wild game. Buffaloes produce mozzarella cheese and wild boar provide the aromatic but greasy Maremma ham. Maremma herdsmen, ugly brutes, generally ride the horses in that vicious free-for-all, the Palio of Siena.

Saltwater fauna and sand-loving plants predominate, with belts of pinewood in the hilly Monte dell' Uccellina district, a protected area south of Grosseto. Up-and-coming beach resorts on the mainland north and south of Elba are banded together under the bogus sign of 'Costa Maremmana'.

---

years, but it is host to thousands still and is fully equipped with hotels, bars and palm-court-type saloons. Historic monuments are **Hannibal's Bridge**, the **Civic Towers** and the **Salines Gate**. Past the hilltop castle a cable-car travels to **Montallegro** on higher hills, a huge ornate sanctuary, viewpoint and market for religious trinkets. From its courtyard fascinating little footpaths descend to distant valleys. The signposts are paint-splashes on jutting rocks; study the coded plan before you start.

ROME
See pages 106-119.

SANTA MARGHERITA LIGURE ✕
Off Route 1, 3 km S of Rapallo. The tourist industry considers Rapallo (above) up-market, Santa Margherita thinks it vulgar. Edwardian-style hotels testify to Santa Margherita's seniority as a holiday destination for the well-heeled. You pay to use a lovely sandy well-kept beach, the rest is shingle. Immaculate gardens and walks, an air of decayed gentility about the small town behind the promenade, whose buildings are in the authentic Ligurian style. **Paraggi**,

RECOMMENDED HOTELS

CASTAGNETO CARDUCCI
La Torre, LL; *in countryside 6 km SW of Castagneto, which is 58 km S of Livorno; tel. 056 577 5268; credit cards, MC, V; restaurant closed Mon.*

The building of mellow stone near the tower of Donoratico has just 11 rooms and, 7 km from the coast, has an atmosphere of tranquillity. The restaurant (**LL**) specializes in country cuisine using home-made pâtés and home-produced beef.

CECINA
Il Palazzaccio, LL; *Via Aurelia Sud 300; tel. 058 668 2510; credit cards, none; open all year.*

Neat little place on south side of town about 1 km from the razzmatazz of the resort of Cecina Mare. Thirty fully-equipped rooms with bath; TV lounge and ample car parking.

CECINA MARE
Lido, L-LL; *Largo Cairoli 7; tel. 058 662 0669; credit cards, AE, DC, E, MC, V.*

We chose it from 100 hotels in this resort for its clean modern looks and air of comfort and were not disappointed. It is about 30 m from the beach. Twenty-four adequately furnished rooms, TV lounge, lively bar and ice-cream counter. Restaurant serves fresh fish and Tuscan dishes. Rates vary according to the season.

DONORATICO
Bambolo, LL; *Via del Bambolo 31 (about 20 km S of Cecina); tel. 056 577 5206; credit cards, AE, DC, V; closed in winter, also mid-Jan to mid-Feb.*

Built in the 17thC as a hunting lodge for a noble Pisan family, it is now a haven of luxury with an impressive range of amenities. Rooms, with TV, telephone and minibar, are furnished with exceptional taste. Swimming, sauna, sun-bathing in solarium, table tennis. Hotel will organize horse-riding and bicycle hire. Restaurant has arches and a pleasing decorative style.

ELBA
Hermitage, LL-LLL; *Biodola, 9 km from Portoferraio; tel. 056 596 9932; credit cards, E, MC, V; closed in winter.*

A development of small select apartments in pinewoods close to a sandy beach. Heated swimming-pools, tennis, private bathing, garden and ample car parking. Busy in the season – not many Elba beaches are as accessible as this one, and various entertainments are laid on; you are also a mere stone's throw from Napoleon's villa, which attracts its own crowds. Half-board obligatory.

PORTO ERCOLE
Il Pellicano, LLL; *Cala dei Santi, 4 km from Porto Ercole on Monte Argentario; tel. 056 483 3801; credit cards, AE, DC, MC, V; closed Nov-Easter.*

The rambling Tuscan villa in beautiful gardens overlooking a smart yacht-haven and fishing port has its own beach on the rocky crescent of shore. Heated swimming-pool. Tennis, riding and water-skiing available. Rooms have all civilized amenities, restaurant is noted for seafood and you may eat on the terrace in summer. A Scottish hotelier launched this luxury pad with well-heeled British and Americans in mind. The Grahams have now moved on, but the Italian management maintains exclusive standards.

PORTOFINO
Eden, LL; *Vico Dritto 18; tel. 018 526 9091; credit cards, AE, DC, E, MC, V; closed first three weeks Dec; restaurant closed Dec-Mar.*

Only nine rooms, so book if possible. Bedrooms reflect atmosphere of stylish simplicity. Garden and shaded terrace for drinks and meals in summer. Portofino standards are high and so are prices, but this small hotel aims at top quality without charging top prices.

PUNTA ALA
Piccolo Hotel Alleluja, LLL; *Via del Porto; tel. 056 492 2050; credit cards, AE, DC, E, MC, V.*

Near Grosseto and convenient for a day trip to Elba, but it was accessibility to rich Romans which made this notable establishment's reputation. Close to beach, golf course and yacht marina. The desert coast has really been made to smile in the Piccolo's carefully-manicured gardens which are a botanical wonderland of exotic shrubs and aromatic herbs. Outdoor restaurant.

SAN VINCENZO
I Lecci, LLL; *Via della Principessa* 116; *tel.* 056 570 4111; *credit cards*, AE, DC, E, MC, V.

An oak forest conceals this grand oasis, 27 km south of Cecina, a few minutes' walk from its private beach on the Tuscan shore. Luxurious bedrooms and public rooms, satellite TV and private terraces to all 74 rooms. Two swimming-pools and health suite with gymnasium and sauna. Two restaurants nearby.

SESTRI LEVANTE
Helvetia, LL; *Via Cappuccini* 43; *tel.* 018 541 175; *credit cards*, E, MC, V; *closed* Nov-Feb.

Close to the 'blue Spezzian gulf' on the Baia di Silenzio. The rooms are extremely comfortable but the real charm is in situation (the terrace bar overlooks colour-washed houses of an old fishing-port) and atmosphere, more that of an exclusive club than a hotel. No restaurant, but breakfasts are lavish (served outdoors in summer).

a tiny resort susceptible to gross overcrowding, is in the next small bay. It has a historical museum inside a grim old fortress. Tennis, bowls and sailing at Santa Margherita – all the conventional activities.

VIAREGGIO ✕
On Route 1, 24 *km* N *of Pisa*. One of Italy's most successful seaside resorts, planted on a 32-km ribbon of gritty orange sand which shelves gently into the Tyrrhenian Sea. A 3-km promenade separates beach from pine-woods, hotels and shops. High charges are levied for deck chairs and the like. Families pay up and look pleasant, observing that the sands are well-manicured, tidy and safe for children. Eight kilometres south is **Torre del Lago Puccini**, the late composer's villa and gardens, embracing Puccini's tomb and museum and a theatre where summer opera is performed.

THE TUSCAN ARCHIPELAGO
Some are plainly visible from the Tuscan shore, others are dim shapes. Ferries serve them from Livorno, Portoferraio (Elba) and Porto San Stefano. They are islets of pale limestone and tangled scrub, cacti and olives, with rudimentary harbours and a handful of inhabited dwellings. They have a common history: the ancient Romans and the princes of the Church retired to them; monks established hermitages; the Italian government used them as penal settlements.

At **Gorgona** and **Capraia** fishermen gather for the annual assault on the anchovy. **Pianosa** is more developed, attracting skin divers. (It may once again become a penal colony within the next few years.) Prehistoric bones have been recovered from its seashore caverns.

Giglio, closest to the coast, is most visited. There is a hotel and a campsite and the small port is exceptionally pretty.

If time allows only one trip, choose **Giannutri**. In Roman times it was almost covered by a splendid villa. Slender columns rise in unexpected spots and the excavations have not ruined the forlorn beauty of the site. Sixty-four km from the mainland lies the rough dark rock of **Montecristo**. Once a royal game preserve and a menagerie, it has a ruined monastery whose 19thC custodian gave Dumas the idea for his best-known novel. You have to make your own arrangements for visiting Montecristo. The trip can be bumpy and landing is often difficult.

Central Italy

Between Florence and Rome
The Heart of Italy

290 km; maps Touring Club Italiano Umbria Marche and Lazio

Tuscany, Umbria, Lazio...central Italy is the picture-book land of cypress, terraced vineyard, hill-top citadel, of bullock-carts (more likely now to be tractor-trailers) with huge vats of red wine, of an archetypal peasantry (these days in the driving seats of combine harvesters). The area is saturated by memories of the Etruscans, Romans and medieval wars. Places enshrined in Dante's *Divine Comedy* may disappoint you because light industry and promiscuous housing have dealt harshly with their outskirts. Penetrate the districts to which the yellow signs *Quartiere Medioevale* or *Quartiere Storico* beckon and you are in a web of little streets which look much as they did when Dante and Boccaccio were boys.

This is the shortest 'road to Rome' of several. When you detour from main roads the routes are mountainous – Croce di Pratomagno touches 1,593 m – but our red and blue routes go along the valleys. They are the lines followed long ago by armies, pilgrims and Grand Tourists and more recently by railway and *autostrada* builders. The red route is all *autostrada*: subject to congestion at both ends, Florence and Rome.

Warm springs persuaded northern Europeans to linger on the Florence-Rome axis but the major attraction was a wealth of fine arts. (How often artistic achievement goes with the turbulence of civil war.) The Tuscan country south of Florence, as much as Florence herself, was the cradle of Renaissance art. Within an hour's drive of the Casentino (see below) you can see the birthplaces of Piero della Francesca, Masaccio, Paolo Uccello, Giotto, Fra Angelico, Michelangelo, Vasari, Luca Signorelli, Perugino and the architect Sansovino. Unobtrusive municipal museums and country chapels still contain those artists' master-works.

In Italy the heritage industry is almost unknown because the heritage is central to everyday life. Tuscan and Umbrian towns are renowned for their elaborate parades, jousts, games and races, dazzling spectacles of immemorial local victories and rivalries. In summer many a village has its weekend *sagra* or feast – of the ducklings, of the mushrooms, of the moustachioes. We stumbled on a *sagra dei grassi* ('of the fat'), visitors welcome, special dishes and prizes for those weighing 140 kilos or more.

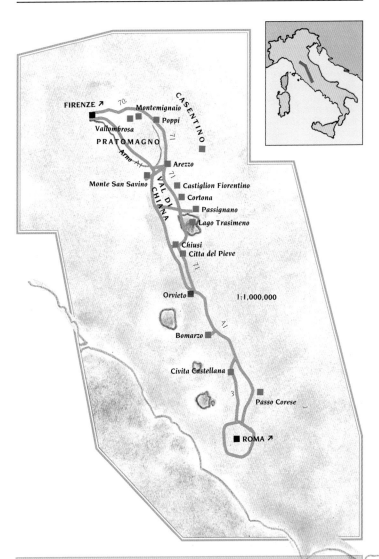

TRANSPORT

The Florence-Rome railway is busy with domestic and international trains. At Terentola, on Lake Trasimene's N shore, the main line connects with a slow, more appealing route to Rome via Perugia, Foligno and Terni. Change at Orte for a trans-Apennine route eastward and a less-stimulating loop around Lake Bracciano. Change at Arezzo for the leisurely railcars through the Casentino and Val di Chiana.

The principal inter-city bus operators are: Appian Line (Via Barberini 109, Rome), Lazzi (Via Mercadante 2, Florence) and SITA (Viale dei Cadorna 105, Florence). Among Apennine villages journeys may take time. We have spent a day, and changed four times, travelling between two townships 32 km apart.

Summer bus services are extended to include monasteries and historic places in the hills and also some Tyrrhenian and Adriatic resorts.

SIGHTS & PLACES OF INTEREST

AREZZO 🚗 ✕
Off the A1 or on Route 69, 90 km SE of Florence. Drive through or come out of the railway station and you see a modern town with a few expensive curio shops. Climb Via Guido Monaco (the monk who invented our musical notation) and cross Via Petrarca, where both Petrarch and Vasari were born, and you ascend to the Middle Ages, a wonderful old place of historic buildings and art treasures where all the façades have sockets for displaying banners on days of pageantry - which are frequent. Arezzo, of Etruscan origin, was for centuries in conflict with Florence and old antagonisms die hard. 'See how the Arno turns away from Arezzo in disgust', say the Florentines, indicating the river's U-turn outside the town.

Romanesque churches of great dignity are grouped near the oddly-shaped sloping Piazza Grande. The **cathedral** houses Piero della Francesca's sullen, sultry *Maddalena*. **San Domenico's church** has Cimabue's *Crucifixion*. Round the barn-like interior of **San Francesco's church** on Via Madonna del Prato is the series of frescos illustrating the *Legend of the Cross*, which many consider Piero's greatest work. Indeed, whole books have been written about it.

RECOMMENDED HOTELS

AREZZO
Continental, LL; *Piazza Guido Monaco 7; tel.* 057 520 251; *credit cards,* AE, DC, E, MC, V; *restaurant closed Sun eve, first half Aug.*

City centre, 200 m from church of San Francesco. Large bright rooms with all facilities. Restaurant: Tuscan cuisine. Arezzo has car parking problems: try west end of Via Petrarca, off Piazza Guido.

CHIANCIANO TERME
Michelangelo, LL; *Via delle Piane 146; tel.* 057 864 004; *credit cards,* AE, DC, E, MC, V; *restaurant closed Nov-Easter except Christmas period.*

Serenely secluded in spa town (season is Apr-Oct) beside a shady park. Heated swimming-pool, tennis, car parking. Restaurant.

FABRO
La Bettola del Buttero, LL; *tel.* 076 382 063; *restaurant tel.* 076 382 446; *credit cards,* AE, DC, E, MC, V; *closed Sat eve, Sun, mid-Aug, mid-winter.*

A stone's throw from the *autostrada*, Fabro exit, 20 km north of Orvieto. Shady terrace for outdoor dining. Ample car parking.

GAIOLE IN CHIANTI
Castello di Spaltenna, LLL; *tel.* 057 774 9483; *credit cards,* AE, DC, E, MC, V; *closed mid-Jan to Feb.*

Quietly sited in tiny village (on Route 408, south-west towards Siena from A1 at Montevarchi). Medieval castle has been turned into small hotel (21 rooms) and popular restaurant (**LL**) set in great hall with minstrels' gallery. Booking advised. Swimming-pool, car parking.

GREVE IN CHIANTI
Villa le Barone, LL; *1 km E of Panzano, 6 km S of Greve; tel.* 055 852 621; *credit cards,* AE, E, MC, V; *closed Nov Easter.*

Based around an old Tuscan country dwelling, with swimming-pool and car parking. The restaurant is residents only, and hotel offers half-board only, giving it the ambience of a private club. Greve was the birthplace of Amerigo Vespucci, who gave his name to continents.

INCISA IN VALDARNO
Galileo, LL; *tel.* 055 863 341; *credit cards,* AE, DC, E, MC, V.

Very convenient stopover for long-distance travellers: just turn off for Regello services and follow signs. Swimming-pool, tennis, car parking, restaurant (**L-LL**).

LUCIGNANO
Da Toto, L; *Piazza del Tribunale 6; tel.* 057 583 6988; *credit cards,* AE, E, MC, V; *closed Nov; restaurant closed Tues.*

Medieval walled town south of Monte San Savino, 6 km from the *autostrada*. Lucignano exudes charm and so does the hotel, right in the historic centre with some rooms over-

Local Renaissance painters, Signorelli and Vasari among them, are represented in the **Gallery of Medieval and Modern Art**. Near an incomplete Roman theatre, close to the railway station, the **archaeological museum** has very old red glazed vases called *corallini*, rare examples of a technique devised in this town.

Walking the streets and gardens of the high town you can see ordinary citizens involved in medieval tennis and other curious pastimes. The *balestrieri* (crossbowmen) and *sbandieratori* (flag-wavers) may be out, practising for a manifestation or deadly serious contest with some rival Tuscan town. The annual crowd-puller is the Saracen Joust, first Sunday in September, when horsemen in the battledress of chivalry attack a swivelling target.

BOMARZO

Off the A1 at Attigliano, 35 km SE of Orvieto. The very name expresses open-mouthed astonishment. Below the village and its towering fortress lies the Park of the Monsters in a demesne of rough limestone and scrub. Casually scattered are follies and grotesqueries which Count Orsini in 1552 sculpted *in situ* from boulders. You can walk into the gaping granite mouth of the Mascherone (Great Mask) and take a seat at the dining-table – its stone tongue. Stone giants wrestle, ele-

---

looking the piazza and others the Val di Chiana. Rooms furnished rustic style; pergola garden (where meals are served in summer), swimming-pool and car parking. Restaurant (**LL**). Early booking essential for last half of May, when town celebrates Maggiolata, floral feast.

MONTE SAN SAVINO

Sangallo, LL; *Piazza Vittorio Veneto; tel.* 057 581 0042; *credit cards,* AE, DC, E, MC, V.

An historic hilltop town in Chianti country, and close to the *autostrada*. This 3-star hotel is just outside the city walls. Rooms are small but neat with TV, phone and shower. Attractive ground floor bar/lounge. No restaurant (but visit the one next door; see page 81). Some car parking.

ORVIETO

La Badia, LLL; *La Badia, on Route 71, 5 km S of Orvieto; tel.* 076 390 359; *credit cards,* AE, MC, V; *closed Jan, Feb; restaurant closed Wed.*

Benedictine monastery of the 13thC, set in parkland with wide panoramas. Rooms are modern and comfortable. Swimming-pool, tennis, car parking, restaurant. Well-established, so booking is advised.

POPPI

Parc Hotel, LL; *Via Roma 214; tel.* 057 552 101; *credit cards,* AE, DC, E, MC, V.

Not one to consider if you're batting down the motorway in a hurry. It is some distance away, reached by fair roads through pretty Casentino countryside. A bright modern palace of luxury at the foot of the hill in the new town. Some reserved car parking. Rooms, in shades of pink, are air-conditioned. Restaurant, also strongly pink, specializes in Tuscan cuisine and overlooks 12thC Guidi castle. Swimming-pool, garden, arrangement with local golf club.

SINALUNGA

Locanda dell'Amorosa, LLL; *tel.* 057 767 9497; *credit cards,* AE, DC, E, MC, V; *restaurant closed Mon, Tues lunch, mid-Jan to end of Feb.*

Two kilometres south of Sinalunga, based in old Tuscan farm buildings around a courtyard. Tower and Renaissance villa contain just ten rooms furnished rustic-style and with every facility. Car parking; restaurant.

TRASIMENO

Villalago, L; *Sant' Arcangelo di Magione; tel.* 075 848 078; *credit cards,* DC; *closed Dec, Jan.*

Brand new building of old rustic stone in its own grounds 1 km south of lake. Quiet and peaceful with ample car parking. 13 rooms: simple and elegant. No restaurant, but the varied attractions of Castiglione are near.

Sauro, L; *Isola Maggiore; tel.* 075 826 168; *credit cards,* AE, DC, E, MC, V; *closed mid-Jan to mid-Feb.*

Reached by ferry from Passignano. Small (ten rooms) and peaceful. Beach nearby. Restaurant (**LL**).

• Carved figures, door of Orvieto's duomo.

phants maul enormous Roman soldiers, an opulent Venus wears a plant-pot hat, a granite oak-tree is dwarfed by granite acorns, the fountain will not hold water, the Doric temple is a crazy house.

Was this laborious exercise in disproportion Orsini's protest against the mannerism of his age? Did a hopeless passion for his neighbour Julia Farnese unhinge his mind? His own words, inscribed at the entrance, tell us the monsters are there for fun. Those with tight lips and raised eyebrows, he says, should stay away.

CASENTINO

Area to N of Arezzo. Locked on the north by mountains where Arno and Tiber rise, on the west by the Pratomagno (see page 81) and on the east by the thronging masses of Apennine, the Casentino is insulated from main lines of communication. It is the valley of green slopes and cooling streams which tantalized tormented souls in Dante's *Inferno.* The red-and-brown rail-car trundles up the infant Arno almost to its source, a stopping trip of 48 km through chapters of Tuscan history. At Campaldino in 1289 Dante took part in the last battle of the civil wars, Guelph against Ghibelline. At Pratovecchio the 'first scientific painter' Paolo Uccello was born.

Slim angular towers and decayed abbeys dot the route. Romena has a place in the *Divine Comedy.* The **Camaldoli monastery** and **hermitage** (where monks live in isolated cells), enclosed in woodland and flowering vine, is a popular excursion from Bibbiena.

CASTIGLION FIORENTINO

On Route 71, 20 km S of Arezzo. The rising ground opens out views of the Chianti hills and Val di Chiana. The tall tower gives panoramas of Tuscany and Umbria - all the mutinous lands it commanded when Castiglion was a Florentine outpost. In the township heaped around it you can see Signorelli's *Deposition from the Cross* and a good-looking loggia in the central piazza.

CHIUSI

On Routes 71 and 146, 16 km SW of Lake Trasimene. The Clusium of Lars Porsena the Etruscan king in Macaulay's poem about Horatio, it 'closes' (*occludere*) the long thin valley of Chiana, once swampland, now irrigated and fertile. Chiusi at first glance is merely a railway junction. You have to hunt among rocks and scrub for the Etruscan tombs, whose contents are displayed in the town museum.

CITTA DEL PIEVE

On Route 71, 8 km S of Chiusi. A hill town at a junction of routes, birthplace of Perugino. Some of his paintings, distinguished by his luminous 'Perugino blue' of which the composition remained a secret, are in the Duomo and the oratory of Santa Maria dei Bianchi.

CIVITA CASTELLANA

On Route 3, 53 km N of Rome. The town is industrial now but it has an impressive pedigree. The Falerians, a Bronze Age people, built it and established a ceramics tradition which flourishes today, judging by the numbers of pottery shops and workshops along the approach roads. The Romans destroyed the place in AD 241 and rebuilt it 700 years later, calling it Falerii Novi. That medieval 'New Town' is a picturesque ruin today but its triangular walls and nine gateways are intact and the **Rocca**, designed by Sangallo, the chief military architect of the 16thC, is still a solid fortress, housing pre-Roman ceramics. The mosaics of the **cathedral** pavement and portico were crafted by the Cosmati, famous 13thC marble workers. Inside the Roman wall, among alleys and stairways, are several churches including the tiny ancient **Santa Chiara**.

CORTONA

On Route 71, 32 km S of Arezzo. Etruscan tombs are dotted about the neighbourhood in tumuli affectionately known as *meloni* ('melons'). In the town antique tower-blocks give vertical space to a citadel compressed in walls. Precipitous streets lead to the **upper church**, to Fra Angelico's *Annunciation* and works by native artist Luca Signorelli. Cortona continues to honour

• *Orvieto.*

HOTELS AND RESTAURANTS
This route is relatively short. You could breakfast in Florence and lunch in Rome without breaking the speed limit. Most of our route is through Tuscany and it is never hard to find food and accommodation at short notice.

We list more hotels than restaurants because many of our recommended hotels *have* fine restaurants. Most of our choices are in country locations: hilltop villages, converted farmhouses and monasteries. Note that **LLL** in this section means upmarket rather than outrageously expensive.

If we were driving this route again tomorrow, we should make for the wonderful medieval towns of Lucignano or Monte San Savino ... in preference to another encounter with the surly traffic wardens of Arezzo. But Arezzo has its charms, including a lively night-life.

the arts with frequent exhibitions and an antiques market in a fine natural setting under Monte Sant' Egidio (1,056 m). In the beautiful Palazzo Pretorio is the much-respected **Museum of the Etruscan Academy**.

FLORENCE
See pages 120-127.

LAKE TRASIMENO ⌂
On Route 71, 16 *km W of Perugia.* Broad, shallow, muddy at the edges and surrounded by low hills, it is not the most spectacular of Italian lakes. Here in 217 BC the consul Flaminius tried to turn back Hannibal. He failed and lost his life but his name lives on in Via Flaminia, the old road north from Rome, while the invaders are remembered only in vague ruins on Isola Maggiore in the lake, derisively dubbed the 'Carthaginian palace'. The lakeside towns – Castiglione, **Passignano** – have ferries, excursion boats, windsurfers and water-skiers and a beach. There is a hotel on Isola Maggiore.

MONTEMIGNAIO
See Pratomagno, page 81.

MONTE SAN SAVINO ⌂ ✕
32 *km SW of Arezzo (by road or branch railway).* This small town sits on a balcony of the Chianti hills. It has dignity as well as serenity. Some churches, loggias and palaces are the work of the citizen Sansovino (1460-1529), pioneer of a graceful architectural style. Among them you find little country shops, *trattorie* and crafts workshops pursuing a range of traditional trades such as broom-making, birdcage-making and ceramic painting.

In a tiny sanctuary overlooking the *autostrada* sits the **Madonna delle Vertighe**, now known as the Virgin of the Motorways, protectress of all who travel fast by road. Her lantern was donated by the *autostrada* contractors.

ORVIETO ⌂ ✕
Off the A1 on Route 71, 104 *km N of Rome.* Orvieto is still a lofty fortress town, though the volcanic plateau on which she sits is wearing away. Your footsteps ring on the cobbles of the silent streets as you make your way between Renaissance façades to a Gothic **cathedral** which took 300 architects and 300 years to complete. Signorelli's finest frescos are inside, also works by Gentile da Fabriano and Lorenzo Maitani. The latter fashioned the extraordinary mosaics on the façade, illustrating Bible stories. See also the priceless reliquary of Ugolino di Vieri in its marble tabernacle. Sip the dry white Orvieto wine, the perfect accompaniment to Umbria's river and lake fish, while admiring the view from the 12thC **Piazza del Popolo**. Descend **St Patrick's Well**, the city's 16thC water supply, a curious hole in the ground with two concentric spiral staircases.

PASSIGNANO
See Lake Trasimeno, this page.

PASSO CORESE
Off the A1 on Route 4dir, 32 *km N of Rome.* A former cavalry school and centre of equestrianism. Its 'cemetery of champions' has the graves of animals fondly remembered in the world of horse trials, dressage and show-jumping. The **Hall of the Lances** in the main building is a museum and

armoury. Outside occasional public events, Passo Corese is a working establishment but you may visit by prior arrangement with the Colonel-in-Charge, Equitation School.

POPPI ⌘

Off Route 70, 50 km E of Florence. Most complete and authentic of the Casentino towns. On peaceful streets of flagged pavements citizens move with a smooth drowsy motion, like fish in an aquarium. Poppi has the best-kept stronghold in Tuscany, a fort of the Guidi warlords. Citizens have a strong family likeness to the frescoed saints, peasants and soldiers of the Gothic painters in this most Renaissance of towns. Etruscan figurines and ear-rings have been turned up by the Rotavators in the vineyards.

PRATOMAGNO

E of the A1, between Florence and Arezzo. The 'Great Meadow' is the watershed between two courses of the Arno, north of the river's U-bend. Terraced and wooded below, bare on top, its undulating hummocks remind you of a procession of tonsured monks. For some years the green forest was a wilderness and a paradise for huntsmen and mushroom-gatherers. New roads have opened access from foothill villages but the ridge still provides a splendid lonely walk of 22 km with views across southern Tuscany. Approach the north end via **Montemignaio** or **Vallombrosa**, where the poet Milton played the organ and found a line for *Paradise Lost*: 'Thick as autumnal leaves that strow the brooks / In Vallombrosa'.

The only man-made object in your path from the *rifugio* (refuge hut supplying drinks and snacks to hunters) above Montemignaio to the minor road down to the Valdarno at the southern end is the lattice pylon of the **Croce di Pratomagno** (1,593 m) and beside it a memorial stone, commemorating Bert Hinkler. The Australian aviator crashed his single-engined Puss Moth there in January 1933 on the first leg of an attempt to lower his own record for a solo England-Australia flight. His body, dragged away and half-eaten by foxes, was found three months later when the snows melted.

ROME

See pages 106-119.

VALLOMBROSA

See Pratomagno, this page.

RESTAURANTS

AREZZO
Tastevin, L; *Via de'Cenci 9; tel. 057 528 304; credit cards, AE, DC, E, MC, V; closed Mon, most of Aug.*
Town centre, 100 m south of church of San Francesco. Popular trattoria spread across three rooms with a café annexe and piano player. Try the *risotto tastevin*, a truffle and rice dish. Inexpensive local wines.

MONTE SAN SAVINO
La Terrasse, LL; *Via G. di Vittorio 2; tel. 057 584 4111; credit cards, AE, E, MC, V; closed Mon.*
Don't be misled by the sign 'American Bar'. Roberto Lodovichi's restaurant has a typically Tuscan interior of exposed brick and vaulted whitewashed ceilings. Presentation is immaculate, service brisk. Menu strong on desserts. Some detest muzak but we enjoyed an unobtrusive programme of classical/modern jazz. Thirty metres from Hotel Sangallo (see page 77).

ORVIETO
Le Grotte del Funaro, LL; *Via Ripa di Serancia 41; tel. 076 343 276; credit cards, AE, DC, E, MC, V; closed Mon.*
In the old quarter, in caves beneath the volcanic rock the town is built on. Umbrian specialities (see Local Explorations: 12) form the menu. A wide selection of wine.

Villa Ciconia, LL; *near Orvieto Scalo; tel. 076 390 677; credit cards, AE, DC, E, MC, V; closed Mon.*
Close to the *autostrada*, a beautiful 15thC villa set in mature parkland. Tuscan/Umbrian cuisine: prepared with imagination and presented with flair. Car parking. Also a few rooms (**LL**).

Southern Italy

Between Rome and Reggio Calabria
The Deep South

800 km; maps Touring Club Italiano Lazio, Campania – Basilicata and Calabria

Italy's capital defect, said Bonaparte, was her shape – too long for her breadth. Travellers are made aware of it when they head for the deep south. You imagine that you will cross the great north-south divide somewhere around Rome. In fact you cross it 240 km farther on, somewhere around Naples. From Rome to Reggio in the train takes eight hours.

On the *autostrada*, our red route, you can do the trip comfortably in the day. There is something to be said for adopting that approach: much of the country across which the *autostrada* leaps is stony and arid with awe-inspiring mountains, bordered by a lonely, inhospitable coastline – a landscape to be admired in passing, not to penetrate. And on that long journey there is no obvious half-way house. Except for a small vacation-land on the coast around Maratea there are few places to eat or sleep at between the Salerno-Paestum district and Cosenza in Calabria.

The blue route (around the coast) and the green route (through the mountains) follow roads which have been greatly improved in the past 30 years. Traffic on them is not heavy, but you should allow two-and-a-half days for travelling, plus whatever time you decide to spend in places of interest. Several villages on the shore, neglected for centuries, are beginning to see a future for themselves in sub-aqua, water skiing and sailing. You have opportunities, in other villages where perhaps they have not seen foreigners before, of staking out your own private holiday resort.

The mountain route, though shorter, takes longer to drive than the coastal route.

This is a journey through an archaic Italy. On the shores of the Bay of Naples, classical and modern worlds join hands (see Local Explorations: 21). Relics of Greek civilization, hardly disturbed, lie in the regions of Calabria and Lucania which they call Magna Graecia, a 2,700-year-old settlement of emigrés from the Hellenic homeland. One such relic is Sybaris, but life in the deep south for the past few centuries has been anything but sybaritic. The cuisine is basic, the wines are indifferent, promising chefs escape to the north as soon as they can.

All in all, though, this route opens a new perspective on Italy. That said, press on. As Bismarck said to the Prince of Wied when he offered him the throne of Albania: 'It will always have been an experience.'

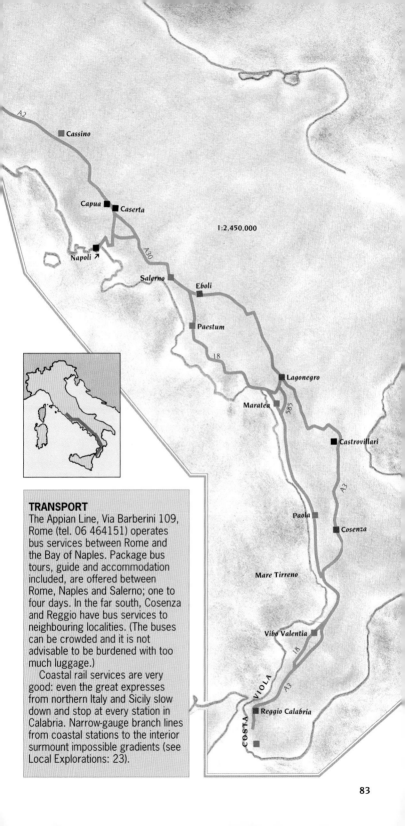

1:2,450,000

TRANSPORT
The Appian Line, Via Barberini 109, Rome (tel. 06 464151) operates bus services between Rome and the Bay of Naples. Package bus tours, guide and accommodation included, are offered between Rome, Naples and Salerno; one to four days. In the far south, Cosenza and Reggio have bus services to neighbouring localities. (The buses can be crowded and it is not advisable to be burdened with too much luggage.)

Coastal rail services are very good: even the great expresses from northern Italy and Sicily slow down and stop at every station in Calabria. Narrow-gauge branch lines from coastal stations to the interior surmount impossible gradients (see Local Explorations: 23).

SIGHTS & PLACES OF INTEREST

CAPUA and CASERTA
See Local Explorations: 18.

CASSINO 🚃
Off A2, 120 km SE of Rome. The unremarkable town lies under **Monte Cassino** (460 m), site of the 6thC monastery whose Benedictine friars carried Christianity throughout pagan Europe. The building, twice destroyed (earthquake 1349, a three-month battle 1944) and twice rebuilt is a place of solemn pilgrimage and meditation, not a tourist attraction. It has a valuable collection of illuminated manuscripts. The panoramas are breathtaking.

Military cemeteries on Monte

RECOMMENDED HOTELS

ALTOMONTE
Barbieri, L-LL; *Via San Nicola 30; tel.* 098 194 8072; *credit cards*, AE, DC, MC, V.

Peaceful location in old-fashioned township south of Castrovillari and 20 km from *autostrada*. Garden terrace, lovely views, excellent restaurant (**LL**) by Calabrian standards.

AVELLINO
Jolly, LLL; *Via Tuoro Cappuccini 97a; tel.* 082 525 922; *credit cards*, AE, DC, E, MC, V.

A short detour east along the A16 motorway brings you here, a hotel of the reliable chain of Jolly. Comprehensive facilities and restaurant (**LL**). At lower end of price band.

CARPINETO
Il Faggio, L; *Via Rerum Novarum; tel.* 069 790 31; *credit cards, none; restaurant closed Mon.*

Though 22 km from the *autostrada* (Anagni junction, 40 km south-east of Rome), it is a beautiful drive and, climbing steeply from the attractive town of Carpineto Romana, you are rewarded with panoramic views. A favourite of Italian ski clubs, this place is thronged in winter but at other seasons, except August, you may have the place to yourself. Restaurant (**L**) is recommended.

CASSINO
Rocca, L; *Via Sferracavallo 105; tel.* 077 631 1212; *credit cards*, AE, DC, MC, V.

Best value of the town's hotels, 9 km from the famous monastery and museum. Swimming-pool, tennis, restaurant, *some* car parking available.

CETRARO
Grand Hotel San Michele, LLL; *on Route 18, 6 km N of town; tel.* 098 291 012; *credit cards*, AE, DC, E, MC, V; *closed Nov.*

Occupies former monastery with all amenities of a grand hotel including swimming-pool on terrace overlooking coast. Own beach. Tennis, 9-hole golf course. Orchard and vineyard (latter supplies wine for restaurant). Some self-catering apartments available.

DIAMANTE
Solemare, LL; *tel.* 098 587 550; *credit cards*, AE, DC, V; *closed Oct.*

On the precipitous north Calabrian coastline, north of Cetraro, it has 16 rooms (so book in high season), a terrace, sub-tropical garden and stunning views. Restaurant (**LL**) is worth noting if you are only passing through.

DRAPIA
Maddalena, L; *tel.* 096 367 025; *credit cards*, V.

Small hotel in peaceful setting amid agreeable scenery 5 km inland from picturesque Tropea. Tennis, swimming-pool, shaded terrace, restaurant.

FIUGGI FONTE
Fiuggi Terme, LL; *Via Prenestina 9; tel.* 077 555 212; *credit cards*, AE, DC, E, MC, V.

Airy modern hotel in attractive spa town, 750 m above sea level in Ernici hills, 72 km south-east of Rome. A lovely situation. Swimming-pool, tennis, ample car parking. Decent restaurant (**LL**) competes with several others in the vicinity.

Villa Medici, L; *Via Valiccelle 6; tel.* 077 555 547; *credit cards, none.*

Cassino's slopes contain the dead, predominantly Polish troops, who battled for the strongpoint at lethal cost in Second World War.

CASTROVILLARI
See Local Explorations 23.

COSENZA
Off A3, 180 km N of Reggio. Provincial capital and gateway to the Sila highlands (see Local Explorations: 22). Opposite a wilderness of apartment blocks and dusty piazzas in the flat new town, the dingy old town climbs on ever-narrowing lanes to a **ruined castle**. Views from its ramparts, round the bowl of hills in which Cosenza lies, reward you for undergoing the torture of a thousand steps.

This family-run *pensione* with restaurant is a real find. Attractive decoration, garden and delightful little terrace, bath or shower to every room – all come amazingly cheaply. Close to Bonifacio VIII spring.

MARATEA
Villa Cheta Elite, LL; *on Acquafredda road, 8 km N of Maratea; tel. 097 387 8134; credit cards, AE, DC, E, MC, V; closed in winter.*

A building of character on the picturesque Basilica corniche, set in gardens with a floral terrace above sea cliffs. Garden service in summer. Restaurant.

PALESTRINA
Stella, L; *Piazza della Liberazione 3; tel. 077 555 212; credit cards, AE, DC, V.*

For a busy historic town, Palestrina has astonishingly few facilities for visitors. This hotel in a hilly old part of town has pleasant views of Alban hills and Giustino Coccia's restaurant (**LL**) adjoining makes it a stay worthwhile.

PAOLA
L'Ostrica, LL; *tel. 098 261 0009; credit cards, AE, MC.*

This useful overnight stop west of Cosenza on a coast road poorly provided with hotels is close to a beach of sorts (across the railway). Some train noise at night. Has a reasonable restaurant (**L**). This place is the best of a poor bunch.

PIEDIMONTE SAN GERMANO
San Germano, L; *tel. 077 640 4652; credit cards, AE, DC, E, MC, V.*

Terrace and beautiful gardens surround this hotel with its popular restaurant (**LL**) close to the *autostrada* midway between Rome and Naples (turn north at Cassino junction and left on Route 6).

PIZZO
Marinella, LL; *Riviera Prangi; tel. 096 326 4060; cards, AE, DC, E, MC, V.*

On the coast midway between Cosenza and Reggio, where both our routes come together. Its standards of service and comfort are above average for the region, the terrace garden is attractive and there is a more-than-adequate restaurant (**LL**).

REGGIO CALABRIA
Grand Hotel Excelsior, LLL; *tel. 096 581 2211; cards AE, DC, E, MC, V.*

A luxury hotel in deprived Calabria has to be special, and this hotel sets a fine example in style and sophistication. Well-equipped public rooms, sensibly-furnished bedrooms (not very large). One of the best restaurants in town. It stands directly opposite the National Museum, 0.5 km from Stazione Marittima and ferry harbour.

SCALEA
Grand Hotel de Rose, LL; *Lungomare Agnella; tel. 098 520 273; credit cards, AE, DC, V; closed mid-Dec to mid-Jan.*

Exotic terraced gardens distinguish this cut-above-the-average place south of Maratea. Beach, tennis, water-sports, salt water swimming-pool. Restaurant (**LL**).

TROPEA
Baia Paraelios, LL; *tel. 096 360 0004; credit cards, AE, DC, V; closed in winter.*

Just north of Tropea and west of Parghelia, it consists of 70 peaceful self-contained villas above sparkling white sands. Swimming-pool, terrace, waterfront dining area. Full board only, rates varying with season.

• *Cosenza.*

Two rivers, Busento and Crati, meet in the new town. The Goths temporarily diverted the former to make a secret burial place in its bed for their leader Alaric and the spoils of Rome (AD 410). The grave still defies discovery.

COSTA VIOLA

On Route 106, 21 km S of Reggio. Not flowers but rainbow effects of sun and sky give the Violet Coast its name. Tricks of light provide the **fata mor-gana**, a legendary optical illusion over the Messina Strait. A shimmering city – presumably Messina – hangs upside down above the water. More people claim to have seen it than have actually done so and no photograph has been produced. Your best chance, they say, is at dawn, from Reggio's promenade, after a night of thunderstorms.

On the 64-km stretch of rockbound coast do not miss **Palmi**, where the palm-trees which gave the place its name grow to extraordinary heights, tossing their plumes and straining against stout hawsers in the breeze. The upper town is a shrine to the memory of Francesco Cilea, locally-revered composer of *Adriana Lecouvreur* (1902) and some less-well-known operas. The museum devoted to this shy musician is charming; the sculpted wall-monument which protects his tomb illustrates the story of Orpheus and Eurydice.

Palmi stands at the end of a pretty road, lined with orange groves, which climbs to Aspromonte and the mountain villages.

Bagnara is the next town south. Instead of automobiles it has boats, all parked anyhow on streets which, with their low-built cottages and cobbles, would not seem out of place in Devon. Look seaward between mid-April and June and you will see the *pescespada* (sword-fish) fleet of small boats with disproportionately high masts and low bowsprits drifting aimlessly until the shriek of a lookout brings them to full alert. Swordfish, delicate as salmon, are on Bagnara restaurant menus all summer in steaks or *en croûte*.

Scilla, next town south, is the Scylla of Homer's *Odyssey*. An Aragonese castle, now a youth hostel, sits like a crown on the mythical rock above orange gardens. Local people identify offshore patches of disturbed water with Charybdis the whirlpool, but the navigational chart says nothing about it. Beneath the castle a row of antique cottages, some tastefully modernized, called La Chianalea, is strung along the shore.

EBOLI

Off A3, 30 km E of Salerno. Cristo si è fermato a Eboli ('Christ stopped at Eboli'), a proverb meaning that here you step out of civilized Italy, was the title of a popular novel by Carlo Levi about political exile under the 1930s Fascist regime. The town is remarkable for nothing else, but 49 km north is Caposele, where Mussolini harnessed the headwaters of rivers to serve the thirsty land of Puglia. The water is carried by the Apulian Aqueduct, 240 km long with many branches, and ends under a monument at the tip of Italy's heel (see Cape Santa Maria di Leuca, Local Explorations: 22).

LAGONEGRO

On A3, 140 km SE of Salerno. Inscriptions on a blackened tomb in the ill-lit 10thC **San Nicola church** seem to read 'Donna Lisa... del Giocondo'. Though art historians insist that Mona Lisa was a young Florentine matron, Lagonegro likes to think she was a

• *Salerno.*

local girl and points out that the rocks among which she sits in da Vinci's painting are typical of local scenery. You will not otherwise want to linger here, unless to undertake the strenuous walk to **Monte del Papa** (2,000 m) for a view of two seas, Ionian and Tyrrhenian, and the whole breadth of Lucania.

MARATEA 🛏

On Route 18, 20 km S of Lagonegro. A well-kept secret for years, the pink and white houses on low cliffs, surrounding a small-boat harbour, are being 'improved' with up-market tourist developments. The old quarter above the port has naive paintings by local artists in the medieval **Rosario** and **Santa Maria Maggiore churches**. The grotto of **Marina di Maratea** has stalactites and stalagmites. A big new hotel-and-restaurant complex is centred on a de luxe hotel which was once the most expensive in Italy.

NAPLES

See Local Explorations: 21.

PAESTUM

Off Route 18, 25 km S of Eboli. The Greek **Temple of Poseidon** with its 35 fluted columns stands amid ruins where sluggish streams wind through the marshes to the sea. It is the biggest and best of Magna Graecian remains on the mainland of Italy and was until recently among the least visited. The Paestum shore is now cluttered with hotels and campsites and under the headland to the south several small coastal places – notably Agropoli and Acciaroli – are gaining reputations for sea bathing and sub-aqua exploration.

PAOLA 🛏

On Route 18, 30 km W of Cosenza. The only sizeable seaside town on some 110 km of Calabrian coastline, Paola is a sleepy place with a sandy beach, not too clean, divided from the community (as is nearly always the case in Calabria) by the mainline railway. The blue and yellow pantiles of San Francesco's sanctuary smile down from the head of a short steep valley choked with bamboos. This Calabrian San Francis performed many miracles. Short of the boat fare to Sicily, he spread his gown at Paola and floated over for free.

At Paola the 1,500-m Apennine chain stops short on the edge of the sea and one of Italy's steepest railways takes a formidable route inland to Cosenza.

REGGIO CALABRIA 🚢

S *terminus of A3, on the toe of mainland Italy.* Not to be confused with Reggio Emilia in the north. Gabriele d'Annunzio called its sea front the most beautiful kilometre in Italy – it is actually 10 km long, and on the railway which runs parallel with it there are no fewer than six stations. The most northerly is Villa San Giovanni, the train-ferry terminal for Messina in Sicily.

Reggio's promenade, lined with tropical flora, has a tremendous outlook across the strait to the vast snowy bulk of Mount Etna (here known as Mongibello or 'beautiful mountain'). The city is rightly proud of its **national museum**, where Calabria's pre-history and the relics of Magna Graecia are imaginatively and immaculately displayed. Two gigantic Greek statues, recovered from the sea and brought to the museum in 1981, are dated to 450 BC.

The **botanical gardens** contain rubber, pepper, camphor and other unusual trees. A private garden at the south end of the town has aromatic shrubs and herbs. Here stands the **Experimental Station for Essences**, visitable by appointment. In its laboratories the essential oils of citrus fruits and jasmines yield up their secrets. Unique among them is the bergamot, a hybrid fruit of indeterminate origin, a mongrel intruder in the orange and lemon orchards of old-time peasant farmers (probably a mixed marriage between a lime and an orange). It is now scientifically cultivated and is a big currency earner, its rind supplying the zest which 'fixes' all the best perfumes. Many lands, most recently Japan and the Ivory Coast, have tried to set up rival bergamot gardens, but the fruit will flourish nowhere in the world outside a few miles of the Reggio shore.

ROME

See pages 106-119.

SALERNO

Off A3, 55 km SE of Naples. Partly rebuilt since the bombardments of 1943, when Allied armies invaded the beaches and fought for their lives against Panzer grenadiers, Salerno is a bustling city at all seasons with much yachting and tourist activity in summer. Behind a beautiful broad promenade

---

THE CASTELLI ROMANI

The *castelli*, which are not castles but small towns, lie between Rome's old road (Via Appia) and her new (Autostrada del Sole). They are draped on the shoulders of the volcanic Alban hills around the crater lakes of Albano and Nemi. Frascati, only 25 minutes in the suburban train from Rome Termini station, is synonymous with refined dry white wines. Well-preserved houses in woodland and shady avenues named for twinned towns (including Maidenhead in England) are ranged on a 300-m balcony of the hills overlooking Rome. Spacious villas (parks) of the cardinal princes and Roman nobles cluster round Frascati. **Villa Aldobrandini** is rich in statuary, fountains and grottoes. Bus excursions to classical Tuscolo.

Best-known of the *castelli* is **Castel Gandolfo**, perched on the rim of Lake Albano. A narrow street ascends to the Pope's summer palace, past a fountain by Bernini (in Piazza del Plebiscito). With a permit from the Prefettura della Casa Pontifica, Vatican City, you may visit **Villa Barberini**, the papal observatory. Funicular railways shuttle back and forth to the lake and on the streets you run a gauntlet of sacred memento stalls and their vociferous owners. Castle Gandolfo always has a holiday air.

A one-day tour: leave the *autostrada* at San Cesareo, follow Route 216 to Grottaferrata (frescos and catacombs), 297 to Castle Gandolfo and Albano Laziale (Roman gate, tombs and amphitheatre), 7 to Genzano (views), north on minor lakeside road to Ariccia and Nemi, 217 'Via Laghi' to Rocca di Papa and its airy bluff (funicular in three minutes from Valle Violata), 218 to Frascati.

HOTELS AND RESTAURANTS

Rome to Reggio: from the cradle of civilization to the land that time forgot. You cross Italy's north-south divide somewhere south of Naples. North of the line places to sleep and eat are plentiful; south they are rare. Nearly half this journey is in Calabria, a region some guide-books ignore.

On the coast there is seasonal accommodation in the various lidos which have sprung up in the past 30 years. Hotels inland cater more for the business traveller.

Our restaurant listing is short, but most of our listed hotels have acclaimed restaurants. See also Local Tours: 17, 21 and 23.

---

which looks across to the Sorrentine peninsula is an old town of steep alleyways and a Norman cathedral with massive bronze doors.

VIBO VALENTIA

On Route 18, 100 km NE of Reggio.
Briefly it was the precarious capital of the Kingdom of Naples after Bonaparte had chased the Bourbons away and put his brother-in-law Joachim Murat on the throne. 'Give me 100 Neapolitan bravoes and I will conquer Europe', said Murat – but his bravoes turned on him and escorted him to his execution by firing squad on the terrace of Pizzo castle (1814). **Pizzo**, 6 km north of Vibo Valentia, has excellent safe bathing on a 2-km strip of sand which links it with Vibo Marina. The latter was a naval base in Roman times, then a struggling commercial port. It is now coming forward as a yachting harbour and holiday cottage centre.

Vibo Valentia, 3 km inland, has also awakened from a long sleep. It adjoins Hipponion, an important city of Magna Graecia, and it displays the archaeological finds in its museum at **Palazzo Gagliardi** on Piazza Garibaldi. Remains of 2,500-year-old Doric Temples are visible.

RECOMMENDED RESTAURANTS

CECCANO
Delle Rose, L; *Piazza Mancini 14; tel. 077 560 0050; credit cards, none; closed Tues, Aug.*
On Route 156, about 8 km south of the Frosinone junction on the *autostrada*. A trattoria with reliable food at modest prices. Tasty grills.

FIUGGI
Tak Tic, L; *Via Prenestina 35, Serrone; tel. 077 552 4110; credit cards, E, MC, V.*
On Route 155 between Fiuggi and Palestrina. Ample car parking. Roman cuisine. We liked the *abbacchio alla Scottadito* (charcoal-roasted lamb) and the house *fettucine alla Tak Tic* (mushroom pasta). Wood-fired pizza and sound, inexpensive local wines are also offered.

GENZANO DI ROMA
Trattoria da Titto, L-LL; *Via F. Cervi 1; tel. 069 398 450; credit cards DC, E, MC, V.*
Genuine Roman cuisine characterizes this family-run place in back-street with terrace looking down on Lake Nemi. Generous portions. Well-known Genzano dry white wine available here.

GIZZERIA LIDO
Pesce Fresco, LL; *tel. 096 846 6200; credit cards, AE, DC, E, MC, V.*
On Route 18, 2 km north of the Lido, close to Lamezia Terme airport and *autostrada* junction. Menu alters with the day's catch of always-appetizing fish. Half-board at Pesce Fresco's adjacent lodging (**L**) is excellent value.

ZAGAROLO
Trattoria Giardino, LL; *Corso V. Emanuele 5; tel. 069 524 015; credit cards, AE, DC; closed Tues.*
Two brothers, Tancredi and Giancarlo, run this immaculate restaurant clinging to the slope under the *centro storico*. Fine views across vineyards. Typical *cucina romana*, emphasis on charcoal grills.

Southern Italy

Between Pescara and Brindisi
The Southern Adriatic

450 km; maps Touring Club Italiano Abruzzo Molise and Puglia

H ere is a view of a land which is distinct from cliché Italy – a land most Italians are unfamiliar with. Here the Abruzzo, Molise and Puglia regions narrow down to the heel of Italy's boot, the Apennines fade away and an undulating agricultural country replaces them. The heel has a kick in it, in the form of generous wines, noted for strength if not always for quality. Most of Italy's olives are grown in Puglia.

Urban architecture reinforces the foreign look. It is the legacy of a fascinating mixture of foreign overlords down the ages – Goths and Byzantines and Normans (the last made themselves at home on Italy's heel about the time their brothers were conquering England in 1066); the Swabian Hohenstaufens, leaving the most indelible marks; Saracens, Greeks, French again and Aragonese, coming and going. For long periods this Adriatic coast looked towards Athens and the eastern Mediterranean rather than Rome or Florence and that gives the seaport towns and the thickly-limewashed hill cities a character all their own.

You could sum up the extraordinarily rich ecclesiastical heritage in the phrase 'simple faith and Norman blood'. In the mountainous Abruzzi you come across many a sacred grotto and lonely sanctuary, often cut out of living rock, with legends of miracles attached to them. In Puglia, where important churches abound, religion was a more stern and stately business. This is the region of the clinical, austere style called Apulian Romanesque. To compensate for the strict geometry, the medieval architects let themselves go in the matter of gargoyles and carved beasts – some of the stone monsters are terrifying.

The beach resorts of our blue route, the old Adriatic highway, are less regimented than the great holiday places farther north. Sand is left *au naturel*, not raked and sifted every day. Puglia's olive woods stop short of the coast and the sun blazes down on treeless, flat tongues of rock which Nature designed for skin divers. Add to that a market-gardening tableland, some *bijou* fishing harbours, two big cities, red earth, dazzling white limestone and green swathes of vegetation and you have the topography of the route.

The red route is mostly *autostrada*, one of Italy's latest and least congested. Our green route probes undiscovered landscapes, of which there are many in these regions. (See also Local Explorations: 19, 20.)

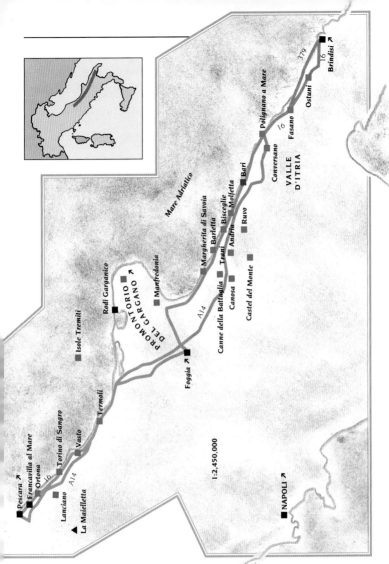

1:2,450,000

TRANSPORT

Airports: Bari (international and domestic), Foggia and Brindisi (both domestic) serve the air traveller. The main railway is the coastal Ancona-Lecce line, which has a branch going inland from Pescara (the rest of Abruzzo being virtually trainless) and branches from the big railway junction of Foggia in Puglia to the Gargano promontory.

The national highway Venice-Brindisi is the route for express buses through the regions. Local bus services in Molise and the Abruzzi are useful but, away from the coast, they take roundabout routes. In Puglia they are first-class and so are the country roads. The principal operators are SITA (Foggia, Bari, Brindisi) and the road services of Sud-Est and Calabro-Lucane railways.

Bari and Brindisi have boat services along and across the Adriatic. Ortona, Vasto, Termoli and Rodi Garganico have hydrofoil and/or ferry-boat links with the Tremiti isles (45 mins to 2 hrs). From Manfredonia you can sail round the Gargano promontory, a whole-day trip.

SIGHTS & PLACES OF INTEREST

TREMITI ISLANDS 🛏

Tremiti is a corruption of Diomede. The Greek hero came home from Troy to find his wife unfaithful. He wandered away with two companions; the gods took pity and changed them into seabirds. Alighting, they became islands. This is one version of the Tremiti group's origins. The limestone trio, 33 km from the Gargano promontory (see Local Explorations: 19), comprise **San Nicola** with its castellated abbey, **San Domino** with pinewoods and steep cliffs and **Caprara** with sea caves remarkable for their rainbow tints. Their waters yield excellent mullet, lobster and sea trout, said to feed on sea-bed carpets of violets. Sub-aqua championships are held, the hydrofoils and ferries come and go from Ortona, Vasto, Termoli and the Gargano, but for much of the year two of the isles are oases of silence. On San Domino there are hotels, a campsite and a tourist village.

BARI 🛏

On Route 16, 114 km NW of Brindisi. First a Japanese film crew was mugged in broad daylight. Next we bought a phial of holy manna at the San Nicola festival and found we had paid a large sum for a teaspoonful of olive oil. If it were Naples one might expect it, but Bari's boulevards and blocks of palm trees, the planned 19thC layout, look so well-organized, like the prestige capital of a tropical land.

Towards the waterfront the old city of tunnels and lanes remains intact. Prominent among its Romanesque churches is that of **San Nicola**, the original Santa Claus, built on the spot where sailors of Bari landed his bones in 1087. These bones exude the manna, retailed as a panacea, and every May the saint's out-sized statue, glittering with precious stones and cloth-of-gold vestments, goes for an airing in the streets and a trip across the harbour.

Bari, largest city and busiest port in the SE, has a Byzantine castle, a promenade 8 km long (but only a modest beach) and a huge multi-faculty university which turns out a high proportion of Italy's lawyers and politicians. The **archaeological museum** is important – ancient Greeks and Romans trod this coastline. Art gallery collections reflect the lack of a strong native tradition but in spring Bari hosts a big international arts festival. The most interesting buildings are at the seaward end of **Corso Vittore Emanuele II**: they include the attractive art-nouveau Margherita theatre .

The city's costly modernization provides the most impressive sights: the **World Cup football stadium** of 1990, dropped from outer space; the town-within-a-town of the **Fiera di Levante**, the south's answer to the Trade Fair of Milan; palatial hotels and business parks. In the city centre there are scores of discos, pubs and night spots. From the airport you can fly to many European capitals, including London. Ferries and shipping services link the port with a dozen Adriatic and Ionian destinations. Chemical and metallurgical plants do nothing for the environment. (Barium was discovered here.) Bari manufactures Italy's best-selling drink, Birra Peroni. There are more than 100 grain-milling and pasta-producing establishments and others for fish processing and canning. The fishing industry, on which Bari's prosperity was founded, continues to thrive.

BARLETTA ✕

On Route 16, 55 km NW of Bari. You can sit in the cantina (cellar tavern) where, in a prickly post-mortem on a battle of 1503, a French officer taunted his Italian ally with cowardice. The upshot was a duel between 13 Italians and 13 Frenchmen, the event passed into history and a hill-top monument called the **Disfida** (challenge) **of Barletta**, 16 km south, commemorates it. The Italian captain's apt name was Fieramosca ('Proud Fly').

This ancient port has its Swabian castle and several churches in the local Apulian-Romanesque style. Its most wonderful antiquity is a gigantic **bronze statue**, green with age, recovered from a shipwreck, said to be of a

Roman emperor, now glowering down on a main shopping street.

Towards Bari smaller ports are evenly spaced out on low tongues of bleached rock, introverted little communities, each disdainful of its neighbour. **Trani, Bisceglie** and **Molfetta** are tucked into natural inlets with *bijou* harbours and tar-scented streets where you are quite likely to meet a new fishing-boat on rollers, built in someone's backyard, being coaxed with seaman-like ingenuity towards a slipway. Trani's rose-pink **cathedral** (1097-1197) is the perfection of ruler-and-compasses Romanesque austerity, all the more impressive for standing on a patch of waste ground.

BISCEGLIE

See Barletta, page 92.

BRINDISI

See *Italy Overall*: 10.

CANNE DELLA BATTAGLIA

Off Route 93, 10 km S of Barletta. With an outflanking movement unparalleled in classical warfare, Hannibal crushed the Romans yet again and yet again failed to follow up his advantage. Canne's serene site above the arid bed of the Ofanto river is cut with many trenches – the graves, not entirely of casualties of the battle of 216 BC, but mainly of victims of 11thC genocide by the Normans. Helpful diagrams, reconstructions and a museum bring the battleground to life without spoiling the atmosphere. The whole layout, unlike that of many battlefields, acts as a spur to the imagination.

RECOMMENDED HOTELS

BARI
Sheraton, LLL; *Via Rosalba 27 (on outskirts near ring road on Route 16); tel.* 080 521 6551; *credit cards,* AE, DC, E, MC, V.

Lavish standards of Sheratons around the world. Swimming-pool, sauna, car parking. When we stayed the computer system controlling the lifts went down, causing some annoyance to those with rooms on the 14th floor. But it was brand new and the builders will by now have sorted out the teething troubles. Cool marble floors in public areas. Breakfast is a more serious affair than the coffee and pastries usual in Italy.

FASANO
Sierra Silvana, LL; *Selva di Fasano, 5 km W of Fasano; tel.* 080 933 1322; *credit cards,* AE, DC, E, MC, V; *closed in winter.*

On a wooded ridge just off midpoint of Bari-Brindisi journey. Attractive garden and terrace for al fresco dining, residents only. (There was a fashion show laid on.) Air-conditioned rooms, swimming-pool.

POLIGNANO A MARE
Grotta Palazzese, LL; *Via Narciso 59; tel.* 080 740 677; *credit cards,* AE, DC, E, MC, V.

Exterior is nothing wild but interior is carved out of rock on cliff edge. Restaurant (**LLL**) in its natural grotto is spectacularly floodlit at night. It serves succulent seafood and charcoal-grilled fish. A definite experience.

RUVO
Pineta, L-LL; *Via Carlo Marx 5; tel.* 080 811 578; *credit cards,* AE, MC; *restaurant closed Fri.*

Convenient stopover on Route 98 about 10 km inland from *autostrada.* Tranquillity reigns. Restaurant (**LL**).

TREMITI ISLANDS
Gabbiano, LL; *San Domino island; tel.* 088 266 3044; *credit cards,* AE, DC, E, MC, V; *open all year.*

Best value of islands' hotels, beside sea and sheltered by pinewoods. Tennis. A panoramic terrace for drinks and meals.

VASTO
Villa Vignola, LLL; *at Vignola, 6 km N of Vasto; tel.* 087 331 0050; *credit cards,* AE, E, MC, V.

Only five rooms attached to a superior restaurant, so you should book ahead. Beautiful surroundings with outdoor dining area (indoor restaurant is non-smoking). A genuine oasis of luxury at lower end of price bracket and very handy for both *autostrada* and coastal highway.

• In the Abruzzi.

CANOSA

On Route 93, 22 km SW of Barletta. Prominent on maps as a junction of motorways, Canosa has a few Roman remains, a ruined medieval castle and a cluster of funeral chambers from the 4thC BC; but what you will remember best is the sombre **mausoleum of Bohemund**, casting its shadow over town-centre streets. The massive granite slab was obviously designed to ensure that this hero of the First Crusade (died 1111) would never rise again.

CASTEL DEL MONTE

On Route 107dir, 29 km S of Barletta. 'The most perfect castle in Italy' it is said – the most perfect geometrically, that is. It was built as a mere hunting-lodge but no building could more decisively express the power and authority of the Swabian Emperor Frederick II (known as Stupor Mundi, the 'wonder of the world' for his restless ambitions, intelligence and enormous building programmes).

The Castel presides over a smiling landscape of meadows and olive woods, a refreshing scene after the treeless, waterless rock-bound coast. Its symmetry – eight sides and eight towers, each with eight walls, all fitted into a precise circle – gives it a strict severity, not as disagreeable as that of

some Puglian churches because it is of pale stone and seems to be lightly poised on a hillock which might have been made for it. Closer inspection reveals a fascinating mixture of classical, Gothic and Moorish styles. All is open to the public, but the interior is quite bare. The mound around it is a deservedly popular picnic spot.

CONVERSANO

On Route 634, 30 km SE of Bari. The greatest excitement is probably a car-boot sale of agricultural implements, but among the permanent attractions are a 10thC monastery, an 11thC cathedral and a 12thC castle. You can walk up to the cyclopean walls which enclose the town – they border the ring-road. Note the immense size of the boulders with which they are constructed. They are of incalculable age and unique.

FASANO ⇆ ✕

On Route 16, 61 km NW of Brindisi. The coastline runs on, stony and bleak under a pitiless summer sun, but if you detour to Fasano's selva, a forested hill with dwarf oaks and assorted Mediterranean flora, you may take off the dark glasses. Summer cottages, restaurants, fashion shows and motor-cycle races are destroying this hill's rustic charms. At one time visitors came only to look at its **stalactite caves** and at the pre-Roman city of **Gnathia** (Egnatia to the Romans) 6 km towards the shore. There the excavations are well laid-out and a modern museum, called Antiquarium, displays precious finds. Two kilometres from Fasano is a safari zoo where exotic animals roam semi-wild in woodlands of olive, almond and florid shrubbery – a novelty for the south of Italy.

FOGGIA

See Local Explorations: 19.

FRANCAVILLA AL MARE

On Route 16, 8 km S of Pescara. It is 'Frenchtown' not 'Freetown', two towns in fact, the old piled up on a rock, compact and isolated, the new a line of hotels, a promenade and an attractive sandy beach partly sheltered by green hills. The upper town has an agreeable

• Opposite: Bari.

situation with the sea at its feet, low fertile hills on either side and much sub-tropical greenery. Nearly all the town's medieval detail and ornament are gone but the narrow bustling ways still climb among small loggias, piazzas and peepholes, giving surprising views of the coast. Francavilla once had 12 towers but you see only the stumps of them.

The town remembers a local beauty called Domenica Catena, who was snatched in a Saracen raid and placed in the Turkish sultan's harem. There she acquired such influence over him that she not only became mother of a sultan (Selim II) but was allowed to return to Italy and end her days in a convent.

F.P. Michetti, a 19thC genre painter, lived in an old convent on Francavilla's sloping vineyards and two of his broad canvases of Abruzzo life are displayed in the municipal buildings. He is greatly revered and has inspired an annual painting competition at Francavilla.

GARGANO PROMONTORY
See Local Explorations: 19.

LANCIANO
On Route 84, 40 km SE of Pescara. People of the Abruzzo hinterland believe in miracles. Lanciano, a market centre on the coastal plain, has its **eucharistic miracle** in San Francesco's church: five drops of Christ's blood and a wafer of his flesh. Together and separately they weigh 20 grams. That was established in the 15thC, says the priest; they have not since been out of the reliquary. Do they work miracles? 'They cure scepticism', says the priest.

New roads from Lanciano take you on a roller-coaster ride to the snow-fields and winter sports of the Maielletta (1,995 m).

MANFREDONIA
Departure point for boat excursions around the Gargano coastline. See Transport, page 91.

MARGHERITA DI SAVOIA
On Routes 16 and 159, 14 km NW of Barletta. No stereotype of an Adriatic resort, this clean quiet town of drowsy harbour and coloured boats sits among angular causeways, saltpans and glistening mounds of salt. There

are 500 salt cisterns round about. Salt's normal concomitant, curative waters, is not in evidence but one hotel does offer brine baths and the town is officially described as a spa.

MOLFETTA
See Barletta, page 92.

NAPLES
See Local Explorations: 21.

ORTONA
On Route 16, 22 *km SE of Pescara.* A pathetic-looking town and harbour, infested with idlers, has since our first visit ribboned out north and south, like its neighbours. (There is no natural obstacle to stop them until they meet.) On twin beaches, **Lido Riccio** and **Lido Saraceni**, newly-planted hotels, shrubs, roses, beach cabins, drinks stands and pedalos are formed up like defences against a sea-borne invasion. A formerly down-at-heel boatyard builds yachts. The town, unremarkable except for the customary cathedral, *palazzo* and Aragonese fort, is a shopping centre. (Roman department stores have branches in Adriatic resorts – for some reason people come to the coast to buy new and antique furniture.)

Tosti, adored composer in Victorian Britain (he wrote *Adieu* and not much else), is honoured in his native Ortona with a May festival called Maggiolata. Hydrofoils run frequently in summer to the Tremiti islands (2 hours). South of town is a large Canadian military cemetery (Italian campaign of 1943-44).

OSTUNI ×
On Route 16, 35 *km NW of Brindisi.* It looks Oriental, or at least Spanish: a staring snow-white wedding-cake of a city with blank walls, meagre little black window-slits, thickly lime-washed streets. Cathedral dome and belfry, bishop's palace and castle ruins surmount the fortified acropolis. To enter buildings you first penetrate mysterious winding passages and internal courtyards, as in a Turkish town. Ostuni is a vision from afar and itself provides two visions: on one side the scalloped rocky coast and cobalt Adriatic; on the other the Italian national colours with green market gardens, white-washed *trulli* (stone beehive huts, see

Local Explorations: 20) and terracotta ploughland of the Valle d'Itria.

The town was a defensive site of classical times and is mentioned by Pliny and Ptolemy, but of the earlier Illyrian stronghold (which flourished around 1,000 BC) no trace remains.

PESCARA
See Italy Overall: 4.

POLIGNANO A MARE 🏨
On Route 16, 35 *km SE of Bari.* Its view from seaward is reproduced on many a picture postcard of Puglia and you hurry to get one last snap before the dilapidated houses collapse into the wedge-shaped gorges which are pitted with caves like slabs of Emmental cheese. But Polignano has trembled on this brink for centuries. The criss-crossing alleyways, knobbled court-yards and massive 12thC bell-tower of the Chiesa Madre are safe enough. There are a few restaurants, a camp-site and a lido. Outside the town on the Adriatic highway is a tourist village with sports facilities.

RUVO 🏨
On Route 98, 34 *km W of Bari.* A town of significance until the Middle Ages, Ruvo marks time with fortifications of various eras. The Romanesque **cathedral** is gracefully proportioned and distinguished by its fine rose window. Ruvo's pride is the **Jatta Museum** of ceramics, some of the pots and amphorae dating back to 500 BC.

TERMOLI 🏨
See Local Explorations: 18.

TORINO DI SANGRO
On Route 16, 45 *km SE of Pescara.* Veterans of the Second World War may know the Sangro river of bloody memory. Torino at its mouth is a shingly mini-resort, generally quiet. A ten-minute walk takes you to the British war cemetery on the hill.

TRANI
See Barletta, page 92.

VASTO 🏨
Embarkation point for the Tremiti Islands, page 92.

Southern Italy

Between Brindisi and Reggio Calabria
The Ionian Shore

730 km; maps Touring Club Italiano Puglia, Campania – Basilicata and Calabria

Tracing the instep of Italy, between heel and toe, is a journey for the traveller rather than the tourist. In these parts the word 'marina' means a little hill town's access to the sea, not a harbour crammed with yachts. Between Taranto and Reggio the road runs close to the shore, crossing the outfalls of gravelly torrent beds, the mouths of destructive watercourses which descend from the Apennines more in the manner of cataracts than rivers. No large towns interrupt the line of the route. When you stop you can sit or walk on a deserted beach and know how Robinson Crusoe felt. Round Cape Spartivento ('Scatterer of Winds') the sea breaks on wrack and dune and a platelayer's hut on the railway line only accentuates the solitude. The narrow ribbon of sand goes on for ever, mighty Aspromonte – the Apennines' last fling – rears up from the water's edge, an abrupt climax to the peninsular backbone. An Italian writer, Giustino Fortunato, calls it 'a geological wreck sticking out of the sea'. This is the route which a few discriminating foreign authors, the British travellers George Gissing and Norman Douglas among them, found peculiarly exhilarating.

The inland section of our route between Taranto and Brindisi crosses chessboard layouts of cultivation. It is fast, breezy and busy at times. On this highway the charioteers and despatch riders of Rome preceded us – it is none other than the Via Appia, part of the vital link between Rome, capital of the Western Empire, and Constantinople, capital of the Eastern.

If you have planned the full round trip of Italy, down one side and up the other, this route joins both ends of Italy Overall: 8 and 9 and completes the circuit. The main road of ragged-edged tarmac is at least level all the way; beware potholes in villages. This is our red suggestion – there is really no alternative.

A few green options are included. Add to them at your discretion. You see a village tumbling down the near-vertical face of Aspromonte and feel you must find out what kind of strange people choose that inaccessible spot to live in (often they are of Greek origin). When tempted into a foray to the interior, remember that you may find nothing to eat, little to drink and inhabitants struck dumb at the sight of a stranger; and that you will probably have to return by the same contorted road with tremendous seascapes for consolation.

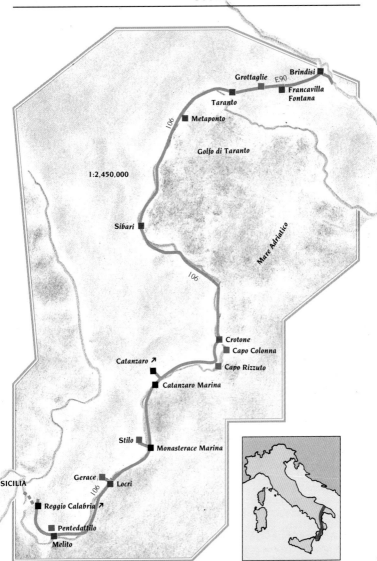

TRANSPORT

Brindisi and Reggio Calabria have domestic air services and are also on main railway lines to Naples, Bari, Lecce and Taranto. The provincial Sud-Est line connects inland towns of Puglia and Basilicata with main-line stations at Francavilla Fontana and Metaponto (for Bari/Lecce and Potenza/Naples respectively).

Brindisi, Taranto, Reggio Calabria and Crotone are useful bases for renting automobiles at no great expense, either self-drive or chauffeured; SITA, Ciccimarra and ACTP are the principal bus operators. The private railway companies, Sud-Est and FCL, run buses from their stations to surrounding villages and along the routes of closed lines. There is a fast catamaran service between Brindisi and Otranto (it goes on to Corfu and Igoumenitsa), operated by Misano Alto Adriatico Navigazione, Via Tunisi 10, Brindisi (tel. 0831 562043).

SIGHTS & PLACES OF INTEREST

BRINDISI 🚢 ✕

On Routes 16 and 379, 114 km SE of Bari.
From two arms of the sea the city looks east. At the **Tancred Fountain** Crusaders watered their horses before embarking for the Holy Land. The low hills to the north are the 'Balcony of the Orient'. After the Suez Canal was built (1869) Brindisi dispatched the Indian mails from Europe and from that, or from the amount of packing and unpacking that went on along the waterfront, geography books called Brindisi the 'Suitcase of the Indies'. In Mussolini's time the long-haul flying-boats from Karachi put down here and their passengers crossed Italy by rail.

The 19-m **stone column**, long supposed to be Roman and now known to be Byzantine, which stands on a noble flight of steps above the sea front not only marks the end of the Appian Way; it is psychologically the end of western Europe. (Virgil, poet of the *Aeneid*, died at Brindisi but the tablet on the house beside the monument should not be taken seriously.)

Follow the long slope to the ferry port and you come to a Greek enclave – shops, smells, food, taverns and signboards. Brindisi has a cheerfully cosmopolitan air, as befits a town which has been Roman, Saracen, Lombard, Gothic, Byzantine, Norman, Swabian and of course Greek, ancient and modern. For once you do not feel oppressed by the ecclesiastical style. The sturdy little 'round' church of **San Giovanni al Sepolcro**, built by Knights Templar, now sunk into its pavement and impressively forlorn, and **San Benedetto** on Via Marconi with its crumbling square cloister where children play football are friendly and inviting.

Il Timone, ('The Rudder', that being its shape) is the prominent sight – the naval memorial stone, rising gallantly from the sea's edge to 53 m and lit with an eternal flame. Here is the Italian naval college. The cadets occupy both the city's castles: the Swabian (1227), now maritime HQ, and the more unusual Castello Alfonsino (1445), leaning out over the water with its landing-stage *inside* the ramparts.

The beach, not a brilliant one, stretches along the southern arm of the harbour. Among aquatic events regularly staged are sailing, rowing and motor-boat races.

CAPO COLONNA

See Crotone, page 101.

CAPO RIZZUTO

See Crotone, page 101.

HOTELS AND RESTAURANTS
Along our route through the depopulated south hotels and restaurants are relatively scarce. Even the major cities – Brindisi, Taranto and Reggio – are not over-endowed with places to eat and sleep at. It is some compensation that such places as there are usually represent good value for money and with few exceptions are never really crowded, even in August, the Italian holiday month. Car parking is easier too, for land is cheap. You may be disturbed by the unhygienic appearance of certain old-style hotels and restaurants. Their kitchens, however, are usually spotless.

Fruit and vegetables thrive in this subtropical climate of the south. Aubergines, olives, peppers, garlic and several varieties of onion are abundant. Along our route, never far from the coast, fish will predominate in *trattorie*: tuna, sardines and swordfish – this last as common and delicious as is reindeer steak among Laplanders. There are robust country cheeses: *pecorino, ricotto, scamorze* and *mozzarello*. Salami and various hot spicy sausages – *morsello* is one – complement lamb and pork dishes.

Years ago it was alleged you couldn't get a drinkable bottle of wine south of Naples. Fearing theft, it was said, farmers harvested their vines too early and the result was thin and acidic wine. Things have changed. Names to look for (mostly reds) are Cirò, Pellaro, Lamezia and Savuto. Some have an aftertaste of almonds, a characteristic of Ionian wine, and most are of higher-than-average strength.

See also Local Explorations: 20 and 23.

RECOMMENDED RESTAURANTS

BOVALINO MARINA
Villa Franca, L-LL; *just off Route 106, 12 km S of Locri; tel.* 096 461 402; *credit cards*, AE, DC, E, MC, V.

Attractive terrace for summer dining; inside it's non-smoking. Tasty local specialities, with emphasis on fish.

BRINDISI
Il Cantinone, L; *Via da Leo 4; tel.* 083 156 2122; *credit cards*, E, MC, V; *closed Tues, two weeks mid-Aug.*

Atmospheric and authentic interior, and much valued by locals. Just off Piazza San Teresa in city centre, close to the Duomo. Car parking nearby.

MASSAFRA
La Ruota, L-LL; *Via Barulli* 28; *tel.* 099 687 710; *credit cards*, DC, E, MC, V; *closed Sun eve, Mon, first half Aug.*

A short detour north from our route (see Local Explorations: 20). Popular restaurant with numerous regional specialities.

TARANTO
Al Gambero, LL; *Vico del Ponte* 4; *tel.* 099 471 1190; *credit cards*, AE, DC, V; *closed Mon, Nov.*

Close to the station, overlooking Mare Piccolo and the Città Vecchia, with car parking (once you have negotiated the city's confusing one-way system). Attractive area for outdoor dining.

CATANZARO, CATANZARO MARINA
See Local Explorations: 23.

CROTONE ⌖
On Route 106, 73 km NE of Catanzaro. A featureless town on a flat promontory where industry, notably Montecatini Chemicals, has obliterated the classical heritage. Hard to believe that Milo, the strong man of Greek legend, was born here (he died trapped in the fork of a tree he was splitting with his bare hands) or that Pythagoras, mathematician and philosopher, lectured in a Crotone temple to the esoterics ('inside the curtain') and the exoterics ('outside the curtain') – the semi-soundproof curtain excluding the riff-raff from too much dangerous learning.

The sea is clear on a smooth curving gulf with gently-shelving sand. On the stony headland of **Capo Colonna**, 11 km south, the last surviving column of a gigantic Greek temple points a weathered finger at the sky. Round the corner on the so-called 'Isle' of **Capo Rizzuto** you drop into a time-warp of Arcadian innocence. You meet herds of ribboned goats, kerchiefed toddlers in charge of them, farmers in broad-brimmed hats on high-wheeled carts. Crimson clover and yellow marguerites cover the pastures and the paintwork of small dwellings repeats the colour scheme. The 'Isle' is edged with firm sands across which you walk to the shell of a great sandspit fortress, a relic of an Aragonese early-warning system. You might suppose that its builders were the last people to disturb Capo Rizzuto's idyll. The inhabitants' manners match their life-style. After we had persuaded some young girls to be photographed one of them whispered: 'Do we have to pay anything?'

FRANCAVILLA FONTANA
On Route 7, 33 km W of Brindisi. 'Free-town Fountain' – a creation of Angevin governors (1364), endowed with generous civic privileges. It became a crossroads and market town and is today a centre from which to explore the countryside by slow train. The **Palazzo Imperiale**, a 15thC castle as grand as its name, is a masterpiece of decorative masonry in sandstone and local red *carparo*.

GERACE
6 km inland from Locri, 100 *km E of Reggio.* The green, yellow and white marble for the largest and most appalling cathedral in Calabria (*circa* 1100) was pillaged from Greek temples on the shore below. Once a 'perfectly delicious' township according to 19thC artist and versifier Edward Lear, it is now depopulated, sunbathing the years away, overflowing with gardens of unkempt palms, bamboos and hybrid fruits.

Down on the shore is **Locri**, with **Locri Epizefiri** ('Locri-in-the-West') 3 km south, oldest of Magna Graecian cities in Italy. The stub of a fluted column stands amid the rubble of considerable temples – not evocative, handy if you are looking for somewhere to sit.

GROTTAGLIE

On Route 7, 24 km E of Taranto. When invaded by the Goths in the 5thC AD the inhabitants scurried into the karst caves and ravines round about and did not emerge for five centuries. Then they built a town which in due course their feudal masters walled and castled. Agriculture and the making of strong wines built up Grottaglie's economy and a ceramics industry made it famous. Those Ali Baba oil-jars you see set out to dry on the flat roofs are

• *Artisan tradition, Grottaglie.*

exported nationwide. Although the potters work in an artisan tradition they have aroused artistic interest both in Italy and abroad. Visitors are always welcomed to the workshops, the kilns and the roof-tops.

LOCRI

See Gerace, page 101.

MELITO

On Route 106, 31 km S of Reggio. After rain the sea is a scummy brown from two *fiumare* (short sharp torrents). Melito in between them marks the end of the bergamot strip (see Italy Overall: 8) and the start of the Jasmine Riviera. The white blossom is cropped in May and used in the manufacture of perfumes. For the rest of the year the jasmine fields look like potato allotments. Balanced on the mountain ledge above Melito is another village. One of Nature's jokes, a five-fingered granite

• *La Cattolica, Stilo.*

outcrop 61-m high, gives the place its Greek name: **Pentedattilo** ('Five Fingers'). There is more to the story than that. In a complex Calabrian drama of sex and vendetta the families of two rival barons were wiped out and in a chamber of the ruined castle (you can still see it) a dying woman left her imprimatur of five bloody fingers.

METAPONTO ⌘

Off Route 106, 54 km SW of Taranto. This small seaside town has the best of both worlds, ancient and modern. The superb **archaeological park** comprises four temples, a market-place, a potters' quarter, a Roman camp and a set of tall pillars known as the Palatine Tables, where Pythagoras lived and taught. The **museum of ancient history** is probably the best in southern Italy, outside Naples and Reggio. Metaponto's **lido**, only a step from the ruins, is a dream of pale sand and solitude but the neighbourhood is menaced by camping parks which threaten to wake it up in the not-too-distant future.

PENTE-DATTILO
See Melito, page 102.

REGGIO CALABRIA
See Italy Overall: 8.

SIBARI
On Route 106, 130 km SW of Taranto. It used to be Sybaris, founded by Greeks and notorious for luxury and loose living. Archaeologists have unearthed a Greek town on the mudflats of an estuary, underneath a Roman settlement already excavated. The broad but feeble Crati river must have been navigable then – the material brought to light suggests that Sybaris was an entrepôt port along a trading corridor between Greece and the cities of Etruria. The uninformed visitor finds the site extensive but exhausting. Some fragments of pots and statues have been put on display in the Parco dei Tori beside the main road; others are housed next door to the railway station. A proper museum has been a long time a-building, and is short of funds.

STILO
15 km inland from Monasterace Marina. The ascent is a cat's cradle of loops and twists, the village is glued to a cliff above a *fiumara* outfall, a wilderness of boulders and ridged gravel. A five-minute scramble above the village discloses **La Cattolica** and, once you set eyes on it, you see why the path is well-trodden and the visitors' book full of exotic names and addresses. The building is a toy church in orange brick, with five cupolas the size of dustbin lids

– an ancient doll's house of a church, one of the Greek Orthodox tradition's most marvellous bequests. Wear anti-mendicant spray or carry a lot of small change: Stilo babies learn to beg at their mothers' knees. One hanger-on brushes the acanthus leaves aside, another lifts the barbed wire, a third unlocks the gate, a fourth opens the church, a fifth takes a familiar grip of your arm and pours inaccurate history into your ear. Ten centuries have given the locals ample time to bring the art of exploiting La Cattolica to perfection. Obstructed with fat little pillars, the interior would hold a congregation of nine. The annual service that was once held is held no longer.

TARANTO ⇔ ✕

On Route 7, 68 km W of Brindisi. The battle of 272 BC gave us the expression 'Pyrrhic victory'. Latin poets sang of Tarentum's honey, scallops, olives, wool and purple dyes. Now they call the eastern suburbs Magna Graecia, but anything less reminiscent of the glory that was Greece can hardly be imagined. Over the western approaches, illuminating a well-preserved Roman aqueduct, the names of heavy industry glare in neon: Finsider, Finmare, Italsider, Fiat, Italciment – foundries, car factories, cement works, steel strip and rolling mills. The Pope came to say Mass at Italsider's stainless steel altar. Whichever way you enter, prepare for traffic jams. Old Town and New meet at an islet with two swing bridges over which all must pass. New Town is garish and ill-paved, Old Town a maze of *pendii* (alleys) and *postierli* (little squares) with strange names. Stick Alley and Turtle Square are ankle-deep in fish heads, toddlers crawl like maggots (even in the south of Italy a Taranto fisherman's philoprogenitive instincts are proverbial), the suffocat-

---

RECOMMENDED HOTELS

BIANCO
Vittoria, L; *19 km S of Locri (on the coast); tel.* 096 491 1014; *credit cards,* AE, DC, E, MC, V.
A beach hotel with ample car parking, and a restaurant which serves decent food at modest prices.

BRINDISI
Majestic, LL-LLL; *Corso Umberto I, 151; tel.* 083 122 2941; *credit cards,* AE, DC, E, MC, V; *restaurant closed Fri.*
On edge of public park, close to station and with car parking. Clean and comfortable with air-conditioned rooms. Restaurant (**LL**).

Mediterraneo, LL; *Viale Aldo Moro 70; tel.* 083 182 811; *credit cards,* AE, DC, E, MC, V.
Aldo Moro is the continuation of Route 7 into the city centre. Air-conditioned rooms, many with balconies. Car parking.

CASTELLANETA MARINA
Golf Hotel, LLL; *at Riva dei Tessali, 8 km S of Castellaneta; tel.* 099 643 9251; *credit cards,* AE, DC, E, MC, V; *restaurant closed Oct-May.*
The most prestigious establish-ment for miles around, set in a huge park adjoining the beach. Eighteen- and 9-hole golf courses. Swimming-pool, tennis, car parking. Restaurant with shady terrace for dining.

CIRO MARINA
Il Gabbiano, LL; *2 km N of marina; tel.* 096 231 338; *credit cards,* AE, E, MC, V.
Peacefully located, with its own beach and vista of beautiful unspoiled coastline. Car parking. Restaurant with outdoor service in summer.

CROTONE
Tortorelli, L; *Viale Gramsci; tel.* 096 229 930; *credit cards,* V; *restaurant open only Jul, Aug.*
Useful overnight stop between Taranto and Reggio, though Crotone is not the most attractive town. The reason to linger here is the excellent restaurant (**L**), but it is residents only (and note opening, above). Just 16 rooms, with air-conditioning, so safer to book in summer.

LIDO SILVANA
Eden Park, LL; *on Gulf of Taranto, just E of Pulsano; tel.* 099 633 091; *credit cards,* AE, DC, E, MC, V.
Own beach and swimming-pool. Car parking; all rooms with TV and phone. Garden and terrace for sum-

ing tenements prop each other up and to knock at a door is to dislodge a picture of baby Jesus two floors above... but warmth and *allegrezza* redeem the Old Town, filthy but happy, welcoming to strangers, free of crime. The main street, Via Duomo, wide enough for one vehicle, was once Taranto's principal thoroughfare along which a dubious nobility rolled in crested carriages.

Taranto boasts two seas. In Mar Piccolo, above the swing bridges, lie coloured fishing boats and the missile destroyers of the Italian Navy, stern to the jetty under Judas trees, a pretty haven for men-o'-war. Near the fishmarket you can eat through a menu of a dozen seafood dishes at any one of a dozen restaurants, while drinking the robust wines of Roccafortezza, 16 per cent alcohol.

Mar Grande is a bay, decorated with black bicycle tyres, the half-submerged rings to which mussels attach themselves. On white sands the tourist cabins proliferate, newly-planted belts of pines hold the beaches together and boat races and regattas are a regular entertainment.

Taranto's red-letter day is Good Friday, when the hooded penitents sway through Old and New Towns, inching forward at a few steps per hour to the haunting *marcia funebre* of a silver band. Only in Seville, where this snail-like procession originated, can you see anything similar. Those not involved crowd the restaurants for fish banquets.

There are no outstanding churches, no noted painters, only one worthwhile museum: the **Museo Nazionale**, exhibiting delicate golden ornaments which Greek colonists' wives wore in Taranto 2,500 years ago.

mer dining (**LL**). A peaceful alternative to staying in Taranto.

MASSAFRA
Appia Palace, LL; *2 km N where Route 7 becomes* autostrada A14; *tel.* 099 881 501; *credit cards*, AE, DC, E, MC, V; *open all year.*

Tennis-court, health suite, air-conditioned rooms, restaurant. Car parking no problem.

MESAGNE
Duepi, L; *on Route 603, 13 km W of Brindisi; tel.* 083 173 4096; *credit cards*, DC, E, MC, V; *restaurant closed Fri.*

Just 14 rooms. Car parking. Locally-renowned restaurant (**L**).

METAPONTO
Turismo, L; *at the Lido, 5 km E of main highway; tel.* 083 575 010; *credit cards*, none; *closed mid-Oct to Mar.*

Close to the Roman site of Metapontum, and by the beach with an attractive terrace for dining.

ROSSANO
Murano, L-LL; *Lido Sant' Angelo, 2 km N of Rossano; tel.* 098 321 788; *credit cards*, AE, DC, E, MC, V; *restaurant closed Fri.*

Attractive situation by beach, with terrace for dining al fresco. Restau-

rant. Car parking. Conveniently located for visiting *Codex Purpureus*, renowned early-Christian illuminated book (Diocesan museum, 9 km south).

SIDERNO
Grand Hotel President, LL; *on Route 106, 2 km S of Siderno; tel.* 096 434 3191; *credit cards*, AE, DC, E, MC, V; *open all year.*

Modern seaside hotel with 120 air-conditioned rooms. Own swimming-pool, tennis-court, car parking, restaurant. At top of its price bracket.

TARANTO
Park Hotel, LLL; *Viale Virgilio 90; tel.* 099 330 861; *credit cards*, AE, DC, E, MC, V; *open all year.*

Running along the seafront, Viale Virgilio is Route 7, the Lecce and Brindisi road. The Park has a swimming-pool and air-conditioned rooms with TV and phone. Restaurant (**LL**). Car parking.

TREBISACCE
Stellato, L-LL; *mid-way between Taranto and Crotone; tel.* 098 151 546; *credit cards*, none.

In 'arch' of Italy's 'foot'. Small hotel by beach, with inexpensive restaurant. Car parking. A welcome oasis in an area where hotels are few.

Rome:
introduction

Prick the soil with a needle, said the poet, and you uncover the bones of heroes. Rome has inherited such wealth from its millennial history that you will find traces of far-off events and civilizations in every street and square, underlying the bustle and brio which are the hallmarks of modern urban Italy. The very manhole covers in the pavements bear the letters SPQR – the 'Senate and Populace of Rome' of the history books. You see what Romans think of themselves when you look at car number plates. Two letters, MI for Milan, GE for Genoa and so on, identify the licensing city. Vehicles of Rome have ROMA spelled out in full. For little more than a century Rome has been Italy's capital, but for 20 centuries and more it was the capital of western civilizations, arts, laws and religious faiths. It was never a productive city but it gathered in the talents and products of other cities and lands. It does so today, as a glance at the fashion, silk, leather and antiques shops along this walk will show you, especially in the Corso and Piazza di Spagna areas.

Rome rises among seven hills (the growth of the city has made them less conspicuous) and across seven architectural strata from scores of ancient temples and 100 km of early Christian catacombs to the imperious Fascist monuments of this century. Each layer is decked with the adornments of its era in stone, glass and paintwork. One large book on the palaces, fountains or churches would have to be a mere catalogue of names. Our walks can only help you to sample the flavour and sharpen your appetite for deeper explorations. Ask not why they call it the Eternal City. The French traveller Ampère said you might get superficially acquainted with Rome in ten years, but twenty would be better.

USING THIS SECTION

It is a cliché that walking is the best way to experience the life and character of a city, and it is nowhere more true than in Rome. Additionally, Rome is not a pleasant place to drive in, city centre parking is limited and expensive, tow-away trucks are remorseless. Many areas are pedestrianized, temporarily or permanently, and to get close to the finest monuments, churches and fountains you have to be on foot.

Our three Rome walks explore three areas which the first-time visitor cannot afford to ignore. They do more than link up major sights – they are designed to give you flavours of the city. For those who already know the main attractions, they offer opportunities for looking behind the scenes. The first walk takes you north-west of the Termini station to pick up the geographical heart of the city, the principal public palaces and the imperial and modern delights of the Villa Borghese.

The second explores the ancient monuments of the original city, touching at five of the 'seven hills' on which Rome was built. The third takes you west of the Tiber, from St Peter's basilica to the Trastevere quarter where, they say, the genuine uncorrupted Romans live.

Do the walks in either direction. For some they will be too much if it is a hot day – do them in part or allow two days. You will never be more than a few minutes from a bus stop or Metro station. The important thing is not to wear yourself out trying to cram in too many sights. You might easily, for example, decide that you want to spend the whole day in the Vatican museums or Villa Borghese.

Alternatively, the information in each of the three walks can just as well be absorbed in an armchair to get to grips with the city in its various different aspects; and of course, the hotel and restaurant recommendations at the end of this section can be consulted as and when needed.

The restaurant recommendations are on page 119.

• Vatican.

ACCOMMODATION GUIDELINES

'In any rented room, sleep is impossible; it costs money to rest in Rome' – Juvenal, about AD 100. In some parts of Rome, and especially in the area coverd by our Villa Borghese walk, the best hotels tend to be expensive, claustrophobic, electrically lit all day, subject to background noises and short on parking space. In our selection, we try to avoid some of these disadvantages.

There are accommodation booking services at the main *autostrada* exits Roma Nord and Roma Sud; also at Termini, the railway station. If you prefer to stay centrally, the district around Via del Corso has a fair range of hotels. The station area and Via Veneto are something of a gamble: some very seedy places are mixed in with some very elegant (and expensive) ones. Parking is almost impossible and the streets can be noisy day and night.

The Aventine area, some distance from the city centre, has quieter, roomier modern hotels on the slopes of the most southerly of the seven hills. Also a sound choice for modern hotels in quiet locations is the suburban area north and west of the Vatican. The Metro (Linea A) runs out to Ottaviano through this district, so you can be in central Rome within minutes.

ARRIVING

By air: Leonardo da Vinci airport, or Fiumicino (30 km W of city centre) caters for international flights. It is linked to Termini station by bus and, every 15 minutes from 5.30 am to 1 am, by train. In the airport main building you will find a tourist information office, a *bureau de change*, a post office and all the major car rental desks. Ciampino airport (18 km SE) handles charter and domestic flights.

By rail: Termini station in the centre of Rome is, as the name suggests, the end of the line for national and international trains from all directions. It has a tourist information office. Tiburtina station, a junction between north and south Italian lines, is where you may arrive if using the motorail services. Ostiense station serves Ostia, Viterbo and Naples via the Pontine route. Roma Nord station serves Viterbo. Prenestina station serves Avezzano and Pescara.

By road: You will probably enter Rome from the Autostrada del Sole (A1), which goes down the length of Italy from Milan to Reggio Calabria. On the outskirts of Rome it joins the main ring road (Grande Raccordo Anulare). Taking your car into Rome is not advised: the central car-parks are expensive and usually full; street parking, even in spaces set aside near hotels, exposes the vehicle to damage from auto-thieves. Tourist information offices at the *autostrada* exits can often book you into central hotels with garages, but these are the most expensive places and space is at a premium in summer.

PUBLIC TRANSPORT

City buses are orange-coloured. Buy tickets, about 1,000 *lire* (1994), or books of tickets at news kiosks or tobacconists. They are valid for 90 minutes and you time-stamp them in a machine on board. An eight-day ticket costs about 7,000 *lire* (1994). Most services start from and terminate at Termini station: signposting at bus stops is very clear and easy to understand. An electric minibus, No. 119, serves the central area.

The Metro or underground railway is fast and efficient but not too popular with foreign visitors – you see little of the city as you travel, of course. Its geography is simple, a T with one line (Linea A) crossing the city west-east from the Vatican to the Appian Way and the other (Linea B) going SW from Termini station to the EUR zone on the way to Ostia lido. The two lines join at Termini station.

City Transport (A.T.A.C.) bus No. 110 does a three-hour tour from Piazza dei Cinquecento (in front of Termini station), rounding up all the regular sights for 6,000 lire (1992, probably 7,000 in 1994). Daily in summer, 3.30 pm; weekends in winter, 2.30 pm.

NEIGHBOURHOODS TO AVOID

Rome is not the world's safest city. Many inhabitants live on their wits. Where tourists gather there also are the touts and hawkers offering everything from street plans to shoeshines, from plaster saints to young girls 'very fresh, very clean'. Best have nothing to do with them – while one is telling you how much he admires the British/Americans/Dutch his accomplice may be slitting your back pocket. Pickpockets and bagsnatchers follow the flow of newly-arrived strangers. In places well-populated by tourists, however, there is always a high-profile police presence.

Both sides of the Tiber near the Isola Tiberina, the west bank of the Tiber in Trastevere and ill-lit streets all over the city should be approached with caution after dark. You should avoid walking alone. The 64 bus (between Termini station and St Peter's Square) and the Sunday morning market at Porta Portese are said to be hazardous for tourists. There is much to be said for getting up at six and sightseeing until mid-morning, when the air is fresh and the undesirables have not yet surfaced.

Villa Borghese and the Corso

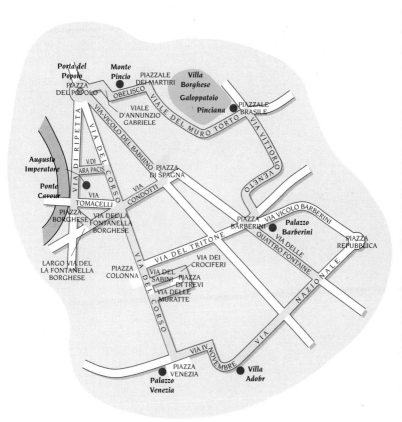

Introduction Villa Borghese, which occupies such a broad area of green on the street map of Rome, is mostly open common land with sparse grass. You could spend all day here, nevertheless. It has attractions for all ages and all seasons (described below) and is very popular with Romans. Outside it, beyond the historic perimeter walls, you find Rome's smartest street (Via Veneto), two of its major tourist attractions (Trevi fountain and Piazza di Spagna) and one of its most impressive squares (Piazza del Popolo). Our walk covers all this and more. The distance is 8 km and, to give sights proper attention, you should allow six hours for it preferably spread out over two days, perhaps more.

Start Villa Borghese – see map. Start this walk at **Villa Borghese**, the broad area of grassland, paths and avenues lined with statues, 1 km north of Rome's Termini railway station. Exit by **Porta Pinciana**, whose two great towers strengthened the Aurelian Walls against 6thC Gothic invasions. Proceed along fashionable **Via Veneto**, admiring stylish clothes and elegant shops but avoiding bars and restaurants if the budget is limited. Cross **Piazza Barberini**, where Bernini's Triton spouts water from his thrown-back head. He is one of Rome's favourite fountain gods and the first of those you will study with appreciation on these walks among some of the renowned fountain groups of Rome.

You might spend 40 minutes in the **Barberini Gallery** with 13th-18thC old masters and rich furnishings before continuing along Via Quattro Fontane to **Via Nazionale** and the Modern Art and Aurora Pallavicini galleries. The next big square is **Piazza Venezia** with the palace balcony from which Mussolini used to harangue the citizens. **Palazzo Venezia**, considered the geographical centre of Rome, is now a museum of tapestries and crafts. In the piazza, beside the ostentatious Vittoriale or national altar, Italy's Unknown Soldier is buried.

Turn north to the **Corso** and beware hurtling traffic. The **Doria Pamphili Gallery** (left) is rich in European paintings, notably Correggio and Caravaggio. Before you reach Piazza Colonna turn right on to the Via delle Muratte for the **Trevi Fountain**, a major sight for the visitor to Rome. Tossing in a coin is a recent custom. (During the night they gather up many kilos of coins of all the nations; certain Tuesdays, at dawn, you hear the roaring waters hushed and see the basin emptied and men in waterproofs brooming up the coins which have escaped the vacuum hoses.)

Back on the Corso turn right to **Piazza Colonna**, named for the tall pillar decorated with battle scenes which Emperor Marcus Aurelius put up in AD 179 to celebrate a decisive victory over the barbarians. The palazzi, north side, are **Montecitorio**, seat of the Italian Parliament's chamber of deputies, and **Chigi**, where the prime minister lives. Continuing along the Corso, turn left for the **Mausoleum of Emperor Augustus** and family (closed at the time of writing) and in Via Ripetta the **Ara Pacis** ('Altar of Peace') set up by Augustus about 20 BC to mark the total pacification, as he thought, of Rome's enemies. Retrace your steps to the Corso, or return through the piazza and street called **Fontanella Borghese** where a busy market in old prints is held every am except Sunday. Cross the Corso to Via Condotti, noted for its expensive shops, and into **Piazza di Spagna**. The house where John Keats the poet died is a museum. Babington's tearooms, opposite, are another breath of 19thC England. Everyone photographs the beautiful old fountain which represents in stone a waterlogged sailing ship: the **Barcaccia**, meaning 'rotten old boat'. The blaze of colour between the piazza and the church of Trinità dei Monte above is caused by flower-beds and the overflowing baskets of the flower-sellers on the **Scalinata**, known to British and Americans (but hardly anyone else) as the Spanish Steps. The ascent, being conducive to the provocative pose, has long been the haunt of artists' models and movie hopefuls. Street-traders and dubious touts also congregate there but when you have run that gauntlet you are on the **Trinità Heights** with a classic view of Rome, roof-tops, bell-

SIGHTS OF THE VILLA BORGHESE

Another time, try to see these: its curious **fountains**, its **zoo** (open all year), the **lake** where children row boats under their Roman fathers' stern gaze, the best **modern art gallery** in Italy, the international show-jumping arena, the **Piazza di Siena** (annual event in May). **Villa Giulia** in the north-west corner is the repository of Etruscan marvels, including a complete chambered tomb and the Apollo of Veio, a statue so exquisite that it had to be torn from the embrace of the peasant who unearthed it.

At the end of Viale Museo is the **Galleria Borghese** with paintings by Raphael, Botticelli, Titian, Carpaccio and others, and sculptures including Canova's *Venus*, for which Napoleon's sister Pauline Borghese sat. Here and all over Rome, galleries, monuments and museums generally open am daily except Monday; sometimes also pm Tuesday and Thursday.

Admission on public holidays is often free, otherwise expect to pay L1,500 to L2,500. At specialist museums you may have to apply in advance to Rome's Antiquities and Fine Art Directorate. The Aurelian Walls, mentioned above, are accessible from Porta Pinciana and Porta del Popolo. Pay L2,000 to walk on them am daily (not Monday), also pm Tuesday and Thursday.

towers, the Trastevere ('across the Tiber') quarter and the wooded Giani-colo (Janiculum) slope in front of you.

Head now for **Piazza del Popolo** along narrow streets where antiques buffs lose all sense of time. **Via Babuino** takes its name from an old battered fountain statue set against a wall. It probably portrayed Silenus, but Rome likes to think it is a baboon. The exits from these narrow lanes to Piaz-za del Popolo are framed by three beautiful churches, one of which, **Santa Maria del Popolo**, is a gallery of frescos, pictures and carvings by such masters as Pinturicchio, Sansovi-

• *Trevi Fountain, Rome landmark.*

no, Caravaggio and Raphael. The **obelisk** in mid-piazza, dominating it for all the square's broad dimensions, was brought from Egypt by Emperor Augus-tus and is more than 3,000 years old.

From this square you return to Villa Borghese by way of Viale dell' Obelis-co, entering by **Porta del Popolo**, another gap in the Aurelian Walls which leads back to your starting-point at Porta Pinciana. That is probably enough for one hot day in Rome – and Rome in summer can be extremely hot and airless.

The Heart of the City

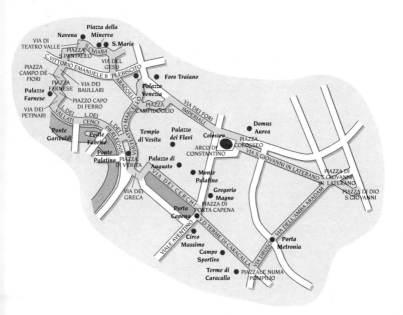

Introduction This is the walk of five hills, Capitoline to Palatine and between Caelian, Esquiline and Aventine. No steep gradients: except for the Janiculum across the Tiber (see page 115 [Walk 3]), the hills of Rome are the gentlest of mounds.

Start Begin on the Campidoglio, just south of Piazza Venezia and the grandiose marble monument, impressive in its snowy *floridezza*, to Victor Emmanuel the first King of united Italy (reigned 1860-78). Whatever you think of it as a work of architecture, it makes a magnificent landmark for the traveller in Rome.

The **Campidoglio** on Capitol Hill is the sacred hub of Rome. It challenges the Palatine as the city's legendary nucleus. Here, traditionally, the she-wolf suckled the abandoned twins Romulus and Remus. The sculpture of the incident, familiar on coins, stamps and emblems of Italy, is right here in the **Capitoline Museum**, along with other world-renowned works of antiquity including the *Dying Gaul*. The *She-Wolf* statue dates to 500 BC, but the thirsty twins were added later.

Myth and legend brood over this hill. Here and hereabouts was the Tarpeian rock (north-west side) where traitors were hurled to their deaths; the enclosure for the sacred geese, whose cackling saved Rome; the temple of trophies and of the Roman warriors' spears, which waved of their own accord when danger threatened the city. A stairway of 122 steps rises to the 4thC church of **Ara Coeli** ('Altar of Heaven') on the Capitoline summit. On its site the Sibyl had earlier appeared to Emperor Augustus, predicting the birth of Christ. There are choice paintings in this church but its most revered treasure is an olive-wood effigy of the Holy Child, said to have come from a tree in the Garden of Gethsemane, said also to have miraculous healing powers.

Michelangelo designed the Campidoglio we see today, the open piazza embedded in museums and palaces with graceful ramps and flights of steps leading up and down. The centrepiece is an equestrian statue of Emperor **Marcus Aurelius** in gilded bronze, wonderfully lifelike. Popular fancy has it that the horse is turning to gold and that, when the transformation is complete, he will sing to announce the end of the world. (He has recently spent a few years under restoration, and now looks as though that day is not far off.) Descend from the Campidoglio gardens on to **Via dei Fori Imperiali**, with the Forum on your right and behind it the Palatine Hill on which Romulus is said to have marked out the city limits when the city was a few caves and huts. Take the route slowly: it is all hallowed ground. The granite columns, arches and ruined temples of the **Roman Forum** are an evocation of pagan grandeur – thanks to Mussolini, who cleared all the slums in the 1930s and opened out the classical scene. Among at least 50 important monuments are the supposed **tomb of Romulus**; the **Via Sacra** and remains of the sanctuaries which lined it; and a score of little temples and basilicas over which the imagination runs wild. Observe that hole in the ground, for example, with a stone base and part of an arch across the way from it: that is **the house of the Vestal Virgins** and the hearth of the sacred flame which they tended. The girls, symbols of purity, were taken very young from patrician homes, kept in seclusion and trained in all the virtues. Once a year they had an airing in a closed chariot to a shuttered private box at the Colosseum. For misdemeanours such as letting their eyes wander they were flogged, sometimes starved to death. None the less Nature found a way and numerous pregnancies were recorded.

At the far end of the Forum relief maps in coloured stone put some flesh on the bones of the bare pillars and broken masonry, sunk below modern street level. On the right is the three-faced **Arch of Constantine**; on the left Nero's **Golden House**, whose ornamental waters the Colosseum eventually enclosed; in front, the **Colosseum** itself, like a 2,000-year-old multi-storey car-park. A cat population, tawny and well-fed with tourist titbits, basks on the tiers of this 50,000-seater stadium where, they say, gladiatorial combats did not normally take place; only mock sea fights and suchlike. (The place for the blood-and-thunder of a Roman holiday was the Circus Maximus, to which we shall come beyond the Palatine hill. It seated 385,000, two-thirds of ancient Rome's population.) Note the secretive little alcoves round the Colosseum at ground level, handy for casual sex. Their name, *fornices*, put a word into modern languages.

Go straight ahead now to **San Giovanni in Laterano**, cathedral and parish church of Rome, with a stern 17thC façade and the foundations of a 4thC chapel behind it. It is of this, not of St Peter's, that the Pope is bishop and vicar. Pious visitors go behind this church to ascend on their knees the dim narrow Scala Santa ('Holy Staircase') of 28 marble steps encased in wood. Some believe that this was originally the staircase of Pontius Pilate's house in Jerusalem.

Return to Piazza San Giovanni in Laterano and walk south beside Villa Celimontana and the Caelian Hill, to the **Terme di Caracalla** of AD 217, the largest of Roman baths. The popular al fresco summer opera has lately been suspended for fear of damage to the fabric.

Heading west on Via Terme di Caracalla you have the **Aventine** on the left, the **Palatine** on the right. If you feel energetic, explore the Farnesian garden, the site of Emperor Tiberius's villa on the Palatine. Continuing west, the long rectangle of dry grass is the **Circus Maximus** and beyond it on Via Greca you come to **Piazza Bocca della Verità** and two delightful little pagan temples, also the church of Santa Maria in Cosmedin. In its porch you will find the 'Mouth of Truth': a Roman drain outlet in the form of a grotesque mask. Tell a lie with your hand in its mouth, says the legend, and you get it bitten off. (Last century the English traveller Augustus Hare actually saw someone bitten – by a scorpion

• *Piazza Navona, Rome.*

nesting inside the mask.)

From the Bocca it is only a short step back by Via Teatro di Marcello to your starting-point on the Campidoglio. Gluttons for punishment can extend the walk 3 km by taking to the Tiber bank and walking upstream. Except in time of flood, or after spate when the walkway is muddy, you can stroll at the water's edge, and there are steps to the riverside road at every bridge. Pass **Ponte Fabricio** and **Ponte Garibaldi** with the Tiber island, **Isola Tiberina**, and the landing-stage for up-river excursion boats in between. Next is **Ponte Sisto**, the ancient Aurelian bridge with its *occhialone* or 'big eye' in the stonework, an old-time flood gauge.

Just off the **Lungotevere** ('along the Tiber' road) at this point stand two palaces. The **Spada** is now an art gallery. The **Farnese**, begun by Sangallo in 1515 and continued by Michelangelo, is elegant inside and out, generally reckoned Rome's most beautiful building. Its lines may be familiar to you – many stately buildings including London's Reform Club on Pall Mall have been modelled on it.

Across the Farnese piazza the Via Baullari takes you past the **Baracco museum** (Egyptian, Assyrian and Greek sculptures) to **Piazza Navona**, a great Roman rendezvous on account of its three huge and intricate fountain groups. On Bernini's **Four Rivers** fountain the Nile hides her eyes – her source was unknown in 1601. Elaborate and proportionately costly ice-creams are served at piazza cafés, notably the Tre Scalini. At the south end of Piazza Navona try to find time for **Palazzo Braschi**, the museum of Rome. This place is full of curiosities, including the highly decorative but never-used coaches of the papal railway train. From an upper window you have a stirring view of the piazza and the three great fountains in line. Usual Rome hours: open am daily except Mon, also pm Tues and Thur; free admission on Sun am.

Now walk east to Piazza della Rotonda and the **Pantheon** of Rome, built 27 BC, enlarged 150 years later by Emperor Hadrian. Great size and noble proportions are its features. Raphael is buried here and so are the kings of reunited Italy. Take Via del Gesù, Piazza del Gesù and Via Aracoeli to return in 10 minutes to the Campidoglio.

Among the hotel and restaurant recommendations, pages 118-119, you will find some convenient staging posts along this route. They are generally tourist-orientated and expensive.

Across the Tiber

Introduction An exploration of the area west of the Tiber, between St Peter's and the Trastevere quarter. On this walk you are for a while detached from the main tourist stream as you cross the Gianicolo (Janiculum) Hill and marvel at the panorama of Rome spread below.

Start St Peter's – see map. Begin on the roof of **St Peter's basilica** and get to it by climbing the stairs or taking the lift/elevator on the right inside the central nave. Do this early (the basilica opens at 7 am) before the queues build up and from the great terraces round the dome you will see Rome awaken. Up there you can drink coffee, shop for souvenirs and use the WCs. Climb higher to the gallery and look down inside the dome. People and huge statues on the floor of the nave, more than 100 m down, are pigmies. No statistics give such a vivid idea of the tremendous scale on which this building was conceived and realized. If a choir is singing below the sounds are funnelled up in an overwhelming diapason of harmony.

You can even climb a narrow stair to the lantern balcony under the orb and cross which put the finishing touches to the labours of Bramante and Michelangelo in 1589 and completed 1,200 years of St Peter's history. The panorama of Rome expands around you, Vatican City and its gardens are at your feet.

Descend, cross St Peter's Square and walk down **Via della Conciliazione** to the Tiber bank. The stately avenue commemorates the pact which re-united Pope and city in 1929 after decades of hostility. Mussolini achieved that, and built the road, and to him we owe the modern view of St Peter's Square, where Bernini's perfectly proportioned columns, 380 of them with half as many statues, curve out from the basilica in welcome, embracing the world.

At the Tiber end of Via della Conciliazione you pass the round fort of **Castel Sant' Angelo**, as seen on Rome's best-selling picture-postcard. Emperor

Hadrian built it for his mausoleum AD 135-39. When the barbarians came to Rome they raked out his ashes and dumped them in the Tiber. The Castel is now a picture gallery and armoury.

Instead of crossing the Tiber, follow the river downstream. You are heading for the **Trastevere** quarter and there are two options: walk straight down Via della Lungara or bear right where that street begins and take the **Passeggiata del Gianicolo** or 'Janiculum Walk'. It crosses that celebrated hill and Piazza Garibaldi and descends on Via di Porta San Pancrazio. There you cross Via Garibaldi and enter **Piazza Santa Maria in Trastevere**. Several lanes and streets hereabouts are confusingly named for Garibaldi. Here the fiercest fighting took place when in 1849 the papal troops and their French allies drove the 'Liberator' and his freedom fighters from Rome. (A useful book is G.M.Trevelyan's *Garibaldi's Defence of the Roman Republic*.) All along the Janiculum you pass busts of Garibaldi, his wife and comrades-in-arms, nowadays targets for spray-gunners and graffiti artists. There is even a memorial lighthouse, donated by Garibaldi's sometime homeland, Argentina. During the week the Passeggiata is a quiet shady walk, frequented chiefly by nuns and convent children. You have uninterrupted views of central Rome. At weekends the route tends to be burned up by adolescents on motor-bikes.

You arrive at **Santa Maria in Trastevere**, one of Rome's most distinguished churches, perhaps its oldest ecclesiastical foundation. Tradition says that Saint Callixtus established it about AD 220 and that it was the first 'St Mary's Church' in history. When you have examined the mosaics on the façade, go inside and feast your eyes on a more elaborate pictorial series of mosaics. They are by Cavallini and, like the church which now stands here, are of the 12thC.

Then sit a while on the piazza and absorb the Trastevere scene. You may see black-eyed children playing venera-

ST PETER'S AND THE VATICAN

Time presses on the traveller in Rome, but spare a few hours for the spiritual side. March boldly into St Peter's, pausing only to observe, far right and high up, the stove-pipe from which on the election of a Pope a puff of white smoke tells the world 'Habeamus Papam' – and far left the sentries of the Pope's Swiss Guard. Their slashed coloured breeches recall a ragged regiment which stumbled in defeat through Tuscan gorges – figures of fun to all beholders. News of their heroic last stand followed them, and the tattered breeches became the papal guards' badge of honour.

In the central nave see at least Michelangelo's *Pietà* (Virgin and dead Christ) in its chapel near the entrance; Bernini's bronze *baldacchino* or canopy over the central throne; the blackened 12thC statue of St Peter near a central pier, his big toe worn away by millions of devout kisses; and behind him the steps to the **crypt**, with the Vatican grottoes beyond it, containing 2,000 years of civil and religious monuments, among them a tomb lately uncovered which is probably that of St Peter himself.

Beyond the north side of St Peter's façade are the Vatican museums, 27 of them – most visitors try to see Michelangelo's **Sistine Chapel** (properly 'Sixtine' for Pope Sixtus), the **Raphael rooms** and the **Pinacoteca** or art gallery. Behind them are the Vatican gardens with some amusing fountains – formerly rarely seen, but now open daily in summer except Wednesday.

Entrance near Piazza Risorgimento or you can take the hourly bus right into the gardens from the Vatican Information Office in St Peter's Square. Vatican City is crammed with bizarre things, including all the mini-panoply of a sovereign state and the Pope's own railway station.

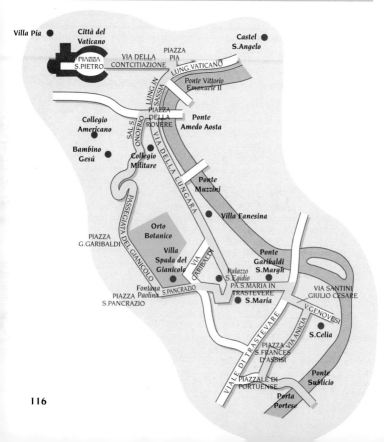

ble street games against a fountain which is portrayed in one of the Santa Maria mosaics: the spot where they say oil gushed out at the moment of the Nativity in Bethlehem. You see washing strung high above the skeins of alleyways. Round the corner in **Piazza San Callisto** there may be one or two workmen, sprawling on the steps in their dinner break, a raw onion in one hand, a hunk of bread in another and a flask of *vino brusco* at their feet, eating and drinking from each in turn.

Not even mass tourism, which equates the Trastevere with Local Colour, can ruin the character of a village-within-a-city whose inhabitants think little of imperial Rome and whose very shop signs and restaurant menus proclaim their own dubious dialect. The word Trastevere itself – 'beyond the Tiber' – implies detachment. But the tourist buses roll in and the spuriously atmospheric bars and *trattorie* proliferate. Gipsy flower-girls, all smiles, can turn nasty when rebuffed. We are assured that mugging is unknown; bag-snatching is not.

Trastevere churches are of all periods, some of them built on the cells of saints with almost forgotten names. For an education in the legendary saints, popular poets and customs and beliefs of the district, look in at the **folklore museum** on Piazza Sant' Egidio, which forms the third of an interlocking trio of piazzas with Santa Maria and San Callisto. Then walk down Via Lungaretta to **Piazza Belli** near Ponte Garibaldi on the Tiber bank. (Gioacchino Belli, 19thC vernacular poet, celebrated the earthy side of Roman life.) Take the main artery, Via Trastevere, and turn left for the cloister and garden of **San Giovanni dei Genovesi** and the charming little fountain in the garden of **Santa Cecilia**, a church of 5thC origins with an important Guido Reni painting inside.

In nearby **Piazza dei Mercanti** there are tourist restaurants and at the end of Via Anicia, going south, you come to the baroque church of **San Francesco a Ripa** ('Saint Francis on the riverbank'). It holds one of Bernini's last statues and in the adjacent convent the cell of Saint Francis of Assisi is preserved.

Now it is just a step to Via Ascianghi and **Porta Portese**, the flea market of Rome – mostly old clothes and bric-à-brac with occasionally some unusual antiques on the stalls which are set up every Sunday morning on the square and in the side-roads leading off it. Another step takes you to **Ponte Sublicio**, formerly Ponte Aventino, Rome's oldest river crossing whose wooden bridge Horatio defended in Macaulay's well-known poem; and to the Lungotevere bus routes under the Aventine Hill.

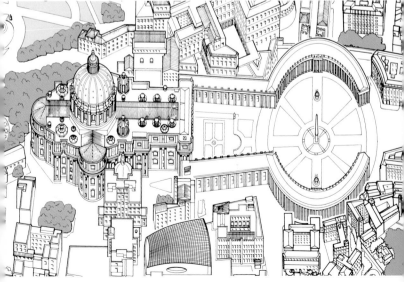

RECOMMENDED HOTELS

Telephone numbers: prefix with the area code 06 if you are dialling from outside Rome.

Ariston, LL; Via Turati 16; tel. 4465399; credit cards, AE, DC, E, MC, V.

Just south of Termini station. Rates include breakfast but air-conditioning is extra.

Atlante Star, LLL; Via Vitelleschi 34; tel. 6879558; credit cards, AE, DC, E, MC, V.

Superb views of St Peter's from roof-top restaurant Les Etoiles. Luxurious. Non-smoking areas. Half-board a better deal than overnight, so this helps if you are a few days in Rome.

Columbus, LLL; Via della Conciliazione 33; tel. 6865435; credit cards, AE, DC, MC, V.

A 15thC cardinal's palazzo, a stone's roll from St Peter's. Many original features retained during conversion, including frescoed gallery. Walled garden, some parking.

Della Conciliazione, LL; Borgo Pio 165; tel. 6875400; credit cards, AE, DC, E, MC, V.

Midway between St Peter's and Sant' Angelo.

Del Sole al Pantheon, LLL; Piazza della Rotonda 63; tel. 6780441; credit cards, AE, DC, E, MC, V.

Prices reflect the historic location. The 15thC building was sensitively refurbished a few years ago; 26 spacious bedrooms have TV and direct telephone.

Duca d'Alba, LL; Via Leonina 12; tel. 484471; credit cards, AE, DC, E, MC, V.

N of Colosseum.

Eden, LLL; Via Ludovisi 49; tel. 4743551; credit cards, AE, DC, E, MC, V.

Large modern palazzo at junction of two boulevards near Via Veneto. Decoration includes Etruscan pottery. Top floor restaurant has fine view of Rome. Despite its size, the Eden has a reputation for cheerful efficiency. Popular with American visitors.

Excelsior, LLL; Via Veneto 125; tel. 4708; credit cards, AE, DC, E, MC, V.

Among Rome's most opulent hotels, still with some of the furnishing which backed the action in Fellini's La Dolce Vita. It was running to seed, but as flagship of a large group is now blooming again.

Gerber, LL; Via degli Scipioni 241; tel. 3216485; credit cards, AE, DC, MC, V.

Quiet residential area north of St Peter's near Lepanto station (Metro). Small garden, roof terrace.

Nord Nuova Roma, LL; Via Amendola 3; tel. 4885441; credit cards, AE, DC, E, MC, V.

Near Piazza Repubblica and Rome Tourist Office; small but well-designed rooms; bar, breakfast room.

Panama, LL; Via Salaria 336; tel. 8552558; credit cards, AE, DC, E, MC, V.

Suburban villa with garden and open aspect; attentive service. Room charge includes breakfast.

Portoghese, LL; Via dei Portoghesi 1; tel. 6864231; credit cards, E, MC, V.

Plenty of single rooms. The hotel is officially in Portuguese territory.

Quirinale, LLL; Via Nazionale 7; tel. 4707; credit cards, AE, DC, E, MC, V.

Useful location near station and main bus routes. A large efficient establishment with garden restaurant and facilities for the disabled.

Sant' Anselmo, LLL; Piazza Sant' Anselmo 2; tel. 5743547; cards, MC, V.

In the up-market residential Aventine district. The public rooms have marble floors; bedrooms are attractive. Parts reserved for non-smokers. Bar/breakfast room opens on to terrace and garden with fountains. No restaurant, but trattoria at hand.

If full, try **Villa San Pio, LLL**; Via di Sant' Anselmo 19; tel. 5755231.

Trevi, LL; Vicolo del Babuccio 20; tel. 6789563; credit cards, AE, DC, E, MC, V.

Unpretentious, cosy, pretty bedrooms; in earshot of Trevi Fountain.

RECOMMENDED RESTAURANTS

Among Rome's thousands of restaurants, *trattorie, pizzerie* and *osterie con cucina* you find every regional cuisine as well as that of Rome, which is distinguished for casseroles, oven-roasted meats, complicated sauces and many vegetables, notably artichokes. Ribbons of pasta are not tagliatelle but *fettucine*. *Gnocchi* are made with semolina. Top of the wine league are the Castelli Romani whites – Frascati, Colle Albani, Grottaferrata – and the red Cesanese.

Al Moro, L; *Vicolo delle Bollette 13; tel. 6783495; credit cards, none; closed Sun and throughout Aug.*
Huge mounds of pasta, *carbonara* and country-style *saltimbocca, frittate* (stuffed pancakes), pecorino cheese, the classic heavy Roman diet.

Al Pompière, LL; *Via Santa Maria dei Calderai 38; tel. 6868377; credit cards, none; closed Sun and throughout Aug.*
Favoured dishes are duck in orange sauce, globe artichokes and *ricotta*-stuffed ravioli. Close to river.

Arco di San Callisto, L-LL; *in street of same name, off Piazza Santa Maria in Trastevere; tel. 5818323; credit cards, none.*
Cavernous, roomy restaurant under arches, genuine family cuisine, no frills but top-quality food and service. Wayward opening hours – best to book.

Charly's Saucière, LL; *Via di San Giovanni in Laterano 270; tel. 736666; credit cards, AE, E, MC, V; closed Sun and throughout Aug.*
French cuisine and *fondues*; stays open late for theatre crowd; air-conditioned, often crowded, booking essential.

Checcino dal 1887, L-LL; *Via Monte Testaccio 30; tel. 5746318; credit cards, AE, DC, MC, V; closed Aug, restricted hours Mon and Sun during rest of summer.*
Historic building, typical Roman cuisine including braised oxtail and artichoke hearts; fine wine list; seating outdoors; must book.

Checco er Carrettiere, LL; *Via Benedetta 10; tel. 5817018; credit cards, AE, DC, V; closed Sun evening, Mon and from 10th Aug to 10th Sept.*
Traditional Roman cuisine, fresh fish and lamb, tables outdoors.

Da Giggetto, LL; *Via del Portico d'Ottavia 21a; tel. 6861105; credit cards, AE; closed Mon and Jul.*
Traditional trattoria with some outside tables. Roman specialities and fresh fish.

Dal Bolognese, LLL; *Piazza del Popolo 1; tel. 3611426; credit cards, AE, DC, E, MC, V, closed Mon.*
Elaborate regional dishes, excellent minestrone and cutlets *bolognese*.

Pastarellaro, LL; *Via di San Crisogno 33; tel. 5810871; credit cards, AE, DC, E, MC, V; closed Tues and all Aug.*
Many specialities include hare in red wine sauce and veal Severino.

Patrizia e Roberto del Pianeta Terra, LLL; *Via dell' Arco del Monte 95; tel. 6869893; credit cards, AE, DC, E, MC, V; closed lunchtime, Mon and all Aug.*
Renowned for lamb in fragrant sauce and for patisseries. Don't expect change from L200,000-L300,000 for two for a memorable evening. Essential to book.

Ranier, LL; *Via Mario de' Fiori 26; tel. 6791592; credit cards, AE, DC, E, MC, V; closed Sun.*
Ranier crêpes are famous but menu ranges eclectically from *gnochetti alla parigina* to chicken *Giorgio V.*

Sabatini, LLL; *two branches: Vicolo Santa Maria in Trastevere 18; tel.* 5818307 (closed Wed); *and Piazza Santa Maria in Trastevere 13; tel.* 5812026; *credit cards, AE, DC, E, MC, V.*
Superior fish and Roman cuisine, some outdoor tables.

For a light meal or a snack with drinks, try **Babington's** on Piazza di Spagna. **Caffè Greco** in Via Condotti, one of the last of the old Italian coffee houses where poets gathered and political plots were hatched; and the **Pantheon** on Piazza della Rotonda for sitting outside and watching the world go by.

Florence:
introduction

There was plenty of domestic strife in medieval Florence but little inter-ference from foreign invaders. The Florentines were therefore able to develop an economy based on silk and wool manufacture and a stable banking system. They flourished while Rome and the cities of Lombardy were tearing themselves apart. They resisted the tyranny of both Pope and Holy Roman Emperor and they enjoyed the nearest thing to a democracy that any city state had known since ancient times. An enlightened business class built itself airy palaces with inner courtyards instead of fortifying their dwellings, setting an example for the graceful urban plan of subsequent ages. Under its leader Cosimo de' Medici (1389-1464), a banker and the father of a line of energetic administrators, Florence recovered the classical virtues and managed to reconcile Christian dogma with pagan wisdom and the natural sciences. Look down on Florence from the surrounding hills and you see, side by side, the two pivots of the citizen's existence: the political centre of Piazza della Signoria and the Palazzo Vecchio; and the religious centre round the green-and-white-marbled Giotto tower and Baptistery and Brunelleschi's pink-and-grey cathedral dome, the most beautiful in the world, spread like an immense umbrella to protect the spiritual values of the people, as the city walls protected their persons. (The walls of Florence were demolished when she briefly became capital of Italy, 1865-1871, but there are a couple of surviving gateways.)

Cosimo de' Medici and his grandson Lorenzo ('Il Magnifico') encouraged the phenomenon we call Renaissance Man: the intellectual all-rounder. Florence ushered in the Renaissance, an unprecedented and never-to-be-repeated upsurge of painting, sculpture, architecture, literature and intellectual enquiry. The Old Masters whom we revere today were considered surrealistic or downright pornographic during their working lives. Donatello got into trouble for restoring classical nudity to sculpture – see his *David* in the Bargello museum. The key to Botticelli's symbolism is his ingenious dovetailing of pagan and Biblical themes – see his *Annunciation*, *Primavera* and *Birth of Venus* in the Uffizi gallery (page 000). In the earliest Florentine painters, those we call Gothic – Mabuse, Cimabue, Giotto, Duccio – there are hints of geometrical study. Paolo Uccello, whose amazing battle-piece *The Rout of San Romano* was kept in Lorenzo's bedchamber and a section of which is also in the Uffizi, dabbled in perspective. Piero della Francesca, Masaccio and Leonardo da Vinci carried 'scientific painting' to the major art centres of Italy, Donatello and Verrocchio advanced sculptural techniques, and they all learned their trades in Florence.

It was not only art that this city, one-tenth the size of Rome, gave to the world. The financiers of Florence taught Europe banking and invented the florin, the first stable

USING THIS SECTION
As with all the itineraries in this guide, there is no compulsion to follow them from beginning to end; and indeed, you don't have to follow them at all. The information in both of the walks can just as well be absorbed in an armchair to get to grips with the city in its various different aspects; and of course, the hotel and restaurant recommendations on pages 126-127 can be consulted as and when needed.

currency. Her physicians turned alchemy into chemistry and biology. (Artists like Leonardo and Michelangelo profited from their anatomical discoveries.) She was the metropolis of mathematics and astronomy: Amerigo Vespucci, who gave his name to continents, was Florentine; Columbus in 1492 carried a chart drawn up by a Florentine which would have told him, had he examined it, that the Atlantic Ocean was only 2,500 miles wide. She was the cradle of Italian literature: Dante, Petrarch, Boccaccio. Centuries later, the language of Italy is basically the language of Florence.

Even if history leaves you cold, you can hardly fail to discover that this city, spread across a bowl in the Tuscan hills, with its slanting prospects from every eminence, was designed, as the Italians say, to 'clutch the throat'.

ACCOMMODATION GUIDELINES

Hotel booking services are at Santa Maria Novella railway station and at exits into the city from the motorways. In central Florence there is a wide range of accommodation. Prices are high and, despite the traffic-restricted 'blue zone', the city is noisy around the clock. In summer months and in November (international fashion fair) it is unwise to arrive without pre-booked accommodation. Some travellers, scandalized by hotel prices, stay in the neighbouring towns of Prato and Pistoia (see Italy Overall: 5) and commute by frequent fast train to the centre. Fiesole too (8 km away) is a popular tourist dormitory but here you depend on buses.

ARRIVING

By car: coming by *autostrada* from north or west, exit for Florence at Firenze Nord; from the south and south-east, exit at Firenze Certosa *not* Firenze Sud. The city has car parking problems and a large area of the centre is all-pedestrian. The underground car park at the main railway station is inexpensive – if you can find a space. Farther out of town to the north-east, at Fortezza da Basso, is a large car-park linked to the city centre by a free bus service. Another solution is to book a hotel with garage space (see Accommodation Guidelines, above).

By train: local, national and international trains terminate at Santa Maria Novella station, the city's transport hub.

By air: although Florence has a small airport (Peretola), most visitors fly into Pisa, 85 km away, linked by a fast shuttle train with the Air Terminal at Santa Maria Novella.

PUBLIC TRANSPORT

Florence is served by six bus companies, the main one being A.T.A.F. with an information office at Piazza del Duomo 57. Ticket sales as for Rome (see pages 106-119): you have to buy them at tobacconists' or other authorized agencies. Most services terminate at the Duomo or Santa Maria Novella. No. 7 buses link Santa Maria Novella and Fiesole; No. 13 the Duomo, Santa Maria Novella and Piazzale Michelangelo south of the river. The tourist information office at Santa Maria Novella distributes free maps with route details.

Information on a programme of morning and afternoon city bus tours is provided by local travel agents, who also accept bookings.

NEIGHBOURHOODS TO AVOID

Florence is a safe city compared with Rome or Naples, but do not relax all guard. Wherever tourists are found *en masse*, there too are pickpockets and bag-snatchers. Trouble is most likely to occur at the main railway station and Piazza Santa Maria Novella around it, mainly after dark when the pushers and prostitutes are at work. The notorious serial killer who patrolled suburban hills, preying on campers and courting couples, was reported to have been arrested in January 1993.

South of the Arno

Introduction Our first walk introduces you to the city with a succession of breath-stopping views from the southern slopes of the Oltrarno ('beyond the Arno') district. Entering the city for the first time by road (the nearest practical airport is Pisa, 85 km away), you may well find this southern approach the best. Come off the *autostrada* at Firenze Certosa and 6 km towards the city bear right in Piazza Porta Romana. In a few moments the famous Pitti Palace is beside you, and the Ponte Vecchio, the Arno's covered bridge, the only one not destroyed in the Second World War, is down the slope ahead of you.

Central Florence is pedestrianized and main routes around it, especially the Lungarno or riverside drives, are congested even outside the tourist season. The city, of course, is eminently a place for strolling in, but you are advised to use the car-parks south of the river or north of the historic centre.

In the area covered by this walk there are numerous hotels and *pensioni* in the middle range.

Museums and monuments abound, every church contains treasured pictures, statues, mosaics or relics. The State museums open am daily except Mon. Other opening times vary: the Azienda Turistica Firenze at Via Manzoni 16 provides current timetables.

Start Lungarno Serristori – see map. From here walk or take the bus to Piazza Poggi and Porta San Niccolo (14thC gate-tower, restored) and up the ramp or zigzag road to **Piazzale Michelangelo**, a renowned viewpoint. The monument incorporates replicas in bronze of five of the Michelangelo originals. About 1 km above the *piazzale* stands the 11th-13thC Romanesque gem of **San Miniato al Monte** with its beautiful green-and-white façade and some important della Robbia terracottas inside.

Hearty walkers can take the skyline route from here, west along Viale Galileo and Viale Machiavelli to **Porta Romana**, rejoining the walk at the Boboli gardens; it is also a bus route (5 km). The shorter way, panoramic in parts, is down Via del Monte to **Porta San Miniato**, another gate in the old city wall, and left on Via di Belvedere to a third gate, **Porta San Giorgio**, and the big star-shaped fortress of **Belvedere**. Its outlook does not belie its name, but the fort's main function nowadays is to be an exhibition centre – contemporary arts, antiques, Italian fashions, science and engineering.

A gate beside Forte di Belvedere admits you to the **Boboli Gardens**, Florence's principal public park. They are a series of more or less formal gardens, lined by winding paths, with statuary, fountains, lakes and grottoes extensive and well-maintained but always looking at least to British eyes as though they need a few days under the sprinkler. You may picnic here. One exit takes you into the 15thC **Pitti Palace**, a royal residence 1866-1871, now one of Italy's great art galleries, especially for portraits, silver, tapestries and plasterwork. Old Masters are represented too and there is a large modern art collection.

Coming out of the Pitti you could descend Via de' Guicciardini and end your walk at the **Ponte Vecchio**. A worthwhile extension, however, is at hand. Cross Piazza dei Pitti and follow Strucciolo dei Pitti to **Santo Spirito**. The church was one of Brunelleschi's last works but finished by another hand (1444) and inside it has Fra Filippo Lippi's *Madonna*. Press on by Via Sant' Agostino and Via Santa Monaca to the **Carmine church** which contains in its Brancacci chapel the movingly near-primitive frescos of Masolino and Masaccio (1425-1428), pioneers of the Renaissance. The latter, a country boy from the upper Arno region, afterwards the *enfant terrible* of artistic Florence, died in mysterious circumstances soon after leaving Florence with this job unfinished. He was only 27.

Cross Piazza del Carmine (it has one of the city's few capacious car parks; see also restaurant recommendations, page 127) and turn right on to Borgo San Frediano to Via di Santo Spirito and Borgo San Jacopo, streets lined with handsome old *palazzi*. Just ahead of you is Ponte Vecchio and the inner city.

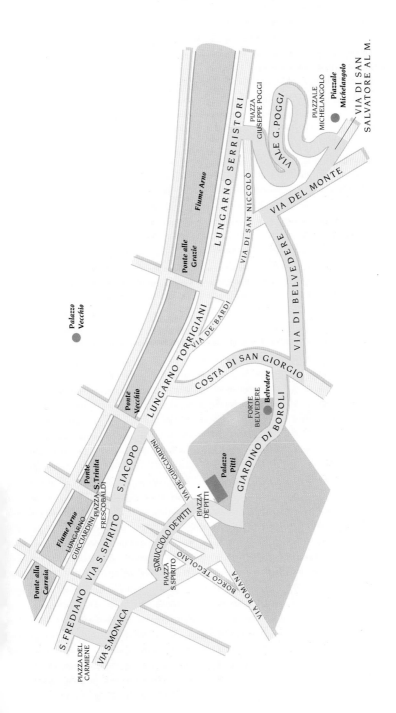

North of the Arno

Introduction This expedition penetrates the historic nucleus of Florence among palaces and churches where the spoils of the Renaissance are gathered. In distance it is not long: you could stride around the course in an hour or so. Eight or nine absolutely unmissable sights are dotted along the route, however, not to mention a few of the best and busiest shopping streets. Even if you merely admire the architecture from the outside and only look at the open-air statuary, you will have to add on the time you spend staring in stupefaction before unchallengeable genius.

In one day's walk you will not give more than perhaps two places the attention they deserve – our choice would be the Uffizi gallery and the Santa Maria Novella church – but you will surely resolve to come back again and again until you are properly acquainted with the rest. This sort of walk can turn a strident philistine into an arts fanatic in the course of an afternoon.

Start in Piazza Santa Croce on the east side of the city centre – see map. It is a square of sensible proportions, the venue over seven centuries for Florence's outdoor entertainments. The famous Calcio, the 16thC football game in fancy dress in which the rules were flexible enough to permit the paying-off of old scores and sometimes kicking your opponent to death, has always been played here. (St John's week, around June 24th, sees one game here, one in Piazza Signoria and one in the Boboli gardens.)

With the large piazza goes the great Gothic church of **Santa Croce**, not in the top flight for artistic riches (though the Giotto frescos, done when the place was new in about 1300, are important enough) but visited because

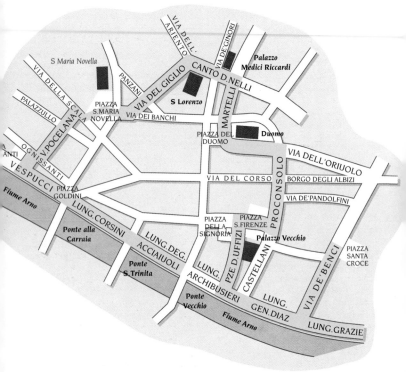

it is a shrine of celebrities. Ghiberti, Michelangelo and Machiavelli are buried here; also Galileo, who had to wait a century for Christian burial on account of his heretical tendencies. Visit the Museo, between two cloisters, to see a marvellous work of restoration: Cimabue's *Crucifixion*, rescued from almost total ruin in the Arno floods of 1966.

Via dei Benci takes you to the Arno bank, where you turn right for the **Uffizi**, headquarters of an enormous medieval bureaucracy (the word means 'offices') and the first public picture gallery of modern times. The last of the Medici bequeathed the building and its collections to the citizens in 1737. In international prestige it runs second only to the Louvre in Paris.

If you haven't walked on the **Ponte Vecchio**, now is the time. An arcade on the riverbank, rebuilt after the 1966 floods like the houses around it, makes a covered way from the Uffizi. The 'Old Bridge' of Florence was much knocked about in flood and war but is now restored to its 14thC shape. The jewellers who work in shops jutting out over the river from both sides of the walkway are the heirs of those from whom Ghiberti and Donatello learned their trades. A **bust**, half way across the bridge, commemorates Benvenuto Cellini, most famous of them.

Retracing your footsteps from Ponte Vecchio, turn into the Uffizi. (By the time you read this there may be a different entrance from that which fronts the river.) The vast picture gallery is of course too much for one day. We suggest you look in for an hour and concentrate on your favourite Old Masters – they are all here, divided into their schools. Of the 45 rooms, the first eight are devoted to Gothic and early Renaissance painters; the section 10-14, usually the most crowded one, is mainly Botticelli. The Uffizi is open 9 am-7 pm on weekdays, 9 am-1 pm Sun; closed Mon.

Emerging on the north side, pausing under the arcades to rummage for souvenirs, trinkets, art works and picture postcards, you enter the renowned medieval square, **Piazza della Signoria**, flanked by the **Palazzo Vecchio**, 13thC parliament hall of Florence, and the beautiful **Loggia dei Lanzi**. (Signoria is government; the Lanzi were the Medici's personal bodyguards.) Both Loggia and Piazza display open-air sculptures of great beauty and technical interest, Cellini's bronze **Perseus** among them; but it is Michelangelo's **David** which rivets the eye. Florence commissioned this 4-m marble statue in 1501 and with it Michelangelo declared his genius. 'The nose is too long,' a councillor objected. The artist obediently went up the scaffold with a chisel and a handful of marble dust. As he pretended to chip, he let the dust trickle down. 'Perfect,' said the *gonfaloniere*, 'you have given it life.'

Not all are aware that this *David* is a copy; the original is in the fine arts museum of the Accademia on Via Ricasoli, north of the Duomo, along with six other remarkable but unfinished statues by Michelangelo.

Ammanati's fountain group on the piazza is no accomplishment of genius, but Florence has its own opinions about art: Neptune, nicknamed Il Biancone ('the big white guy'), is a popular figure.

Turn right along **Palazzo Vecchio** (much art and history inside, if only you had time) and left into Piazza San Firenze. The stern battlemented fort of the Bargello blocks your path. It is the **national museum**, a repository of sculptures as priceless as the Uffizi paintings, the best place in the world for studying Donatello, Verrocchio and the della Robbias. Opposite is the slim tower of the abbey church of Florence, the **Badia**, with decorative porticoes, loggia and 'cloister of the oranges' worth inspecting, though it is many a long year since fruit was grown there.

Continuing north on Via del Proconsolo you approach **Piazza del Duomo** and there before you is Brunelleschi's dome, as unmistakable as the Taj Mahal. Dedicated to Santa Maria del Fiore, this cathedral took 140 years to build (1296-1436). Brunelleschi's crowning glory, the terracotta and coloured marble cupola, bigger and brighter than anything seen before, was said to 'shelter all the people of Tuscany'. As you enter the piazza, another marvel takes shape on the left – **Giotto's** box-like **bell-tower**, jazz-striped in green and white marble. The two apparently incongruous buildings form a miracle of harmony. Stamp Florence on your mind for ever by climbing the Duomo (463 steps) or the campanile (414 steps) and gazing on the rusty old city inside the blue girdle of the Florentine hills. At ground level, remember to look at Ghiberti's bronze doors to the Baptistery, especially the east door (1452) which Michelangelo likened to the gateway to Paradise.

Continue north on Via Martelli to the Medici **Riccardi Palace**, a noble building by Michelozzo and probably Michelangelo too. Its great treasure is Benozzo Gozzoli's well-known *Journey of the Magi* (1459), frescoed on the first-floor chapel walls. Between this palace and San Lorenzo's church, on Piazza San Lorenzo, is the antidote to cultural indigestion, a bustling street-market for clothes, handbags, woven bags, jewellery and leather boxes, open early am to late pm daily except on Sat in summer and Mon in winter. North of here on Piazza San Marco, beyond the Accademia, is another lively rendezvous, cheerful with students from the nearby University.

Turn west on to Via Giglio for **Santa Maria Novella** and its green marbled monumental cloisters with Paolo Uccello's quaint frescos. Returning to the Arno bank on Via Porcellana you may just have time to slip into the **Ognissanti church** to see works by Ghirlandaio and Botticelli. The latter is buried here.

Return to the river on Lungarno Vespucci, walk upstream along Lungarno Corsini (**Palazzo Corsin**i, open 12 pm-1 pm Sat only, has a fine private art collection) and return to the Ponte Vecchio. The gridiron of narrow streets on the left is the smart shopping district. **Via Tornabuoni** and its intersections, especially Via Vigna Nuova, are the axis; all-pedestrian, always crowded between Easter and September.

Refined taste and careful workmanship are the hallmarks of Florentine goods. Straw, skins, silks, gold, silver and semi-precious stones are typical raw materials. Glassware, filigree, embroidered lingerie and ready-to-wear clothes are sought after for their fine detail and stylishness.

RECOMMENDED HOTELS

There are more than 600 hotels and eating places in the area covered by the North of the Arno route alone: so although each of the recommendations that follow deserves its place in the guide for the reasons given, the selection cannot be representative. Calling from outside the city, prefix telephone numbers with 055.

Pitti Palace, LL; *Via Barbadori 2; tel. 282257; credit cards*, AE, V.

Handy for Ponte Vecchio and centre; rooms towards river can be noisy at night. Roof terrace, attractive lounge and breakfast room. Reception desk runs a busy multilingual information service, which is a mixed blessing.

Silla, LL; *Via dei Renai 5; tel. 2342888; credit cards*, A, AE, DC, E, V.

Tastefully furnished old *palazzo* with partial view of the Arno one block north. Inner courtyard and spacious bricked terrace for summer breakfasts. Long a haven for travellers in Florence, the Silla has held prices down when other establishments with less justification have raised them.

Splendor, LL; *Via San Gallo 30; tel. 50129; credit cards*, E, MC, V.

Quiet situation near University and lively Piazza San Marco. The former *palazzo* was never grand, but it makes a comfortable small hotel. You will travel farther and fare worse.

Villa Belvedere, LLL; *Via Benedetto Castelli 3; tel. 222501; credit cards*, AE, DC, MC, V.

Fairly small and select in a serene situation above the Boboli gardens. We liked this place on our first short visit and were impressed, arriving a second time in the car park, to see the receptionist thumbing back through the register so that he could greet us by name when we entered.

Villa Medici, LLL; *Via del Prato 42; tel. 261331; credit cards*, AE, DC, E,

MC, V.

Our first hotel in Florence and a useful choice on account of the central but peaceful location and a dining-terrace view of which one never tired. Public rooms and bedrooms (100-odd, all with bath and full air-conditioning) have dignified furnishings and old engravings of the city. Sizeable garden with heated swimming-pool, tree-lined avenues all around.

FIESOLE
Villa San Michele, LLL; *Via Doccia 4, Fiesole; tel. 50104; credit cards,* AE, DC, E, V; *closed in winter.*

A former convent, some bedrooms converted cells, and the showplace of the historic little town which looks down on Florence 8 km away. Nothing ostentatious: simple luxury and old-fashioned courtesy are the keynotes. Civilized but unadventurous cuisine. View of the hills from the loggia-restaurant makes eating irrelevant.

ALSO RECOMMENDED

On the south side of the Arno are:
Park Palace, LL; *Piazza Galileo;*
Bandini, L *(pensione); Piazza San Spirito 9;* and **Boboli, L** *(pensione); Via Romana 63.*

RECOMMENDED RESTAURANTS

La Loggia, LL; *Piazzale Michelangelo 1; tel. 287032; credit cards,* AE, DC, MC, V.

Panoramic. Prides itself on the classic Tuscan cuisine – simple, refined, well-balanced meals in which the natural flavours of foods are preserved. Home-made bread takes the place of pasta. Wholesome minestrones, great variety of roasts, lean meats without trimmings, grilled fish. A popular rendezvous, especially busy at weekends with visitors to San Miniato, so early booking is advised.

La Sostanza, LL; *Via Porcellana 25; tel. 212691; credit cards, none.*

Not much room and you are not encouraged to linger, but a great place for *bistecca fiorentine*, charcoal-grilled, unadorned, and for a vegetarian cornucopia.

Harry's Bar, *Lungarno Vespucci 22; tel. 296700,* and **Doney**, *Via Tornabuoni 46; tel. 214348; both* **LLL**; *credit cards,* AE, DC, E, MC, V.

Both are smart places for foreigners; smart prices too.

Pinchiorri, LLL; *Via Ghibellina 87; tel. 242777; credit cards, AE, DC, E, MC, V.*

More seriously gastronomic than Harry's Bar; book in advance and expect unhurried service.

For reliability, unpretentiousness and adequate cooking, try the following *trattorie*:

Giannino, LL; *Borgo San Lorenzo 35.*

Full service or (much cheaper) self-service available.

Tito, L; *Via San Gallo 112.*

Antico Barile, L; *Via dei Cerchi 40 (off Piazza Signoria).*

Often crowded.

As you pass through Piazza del Carmine towards the end of the South of the Arno walk, you can eat al fresco at the respected **Trattoria del Carmine, LL**. Still nearer the end of the walk on Via Santo Spirito are **Angiolino** and **Cantinone del Gallo Nero**; *tel.* 218898, both **L**, two traditional *trattorie* with authentic atmosphere. Nearer still, quite close to Ponte Vecchio, are **Mamma Gina, LL**, and **Cammillo, L**, both on Borgo San Jacopo, informal, reliable *trattorie* enthusiastically patronized by tourists. **Mamma Gina**; *tel.* 296009, boasts a French cuisine and risks becoming fashionable; advisable to book.

Venice:
introduction

Some people fall helplessly and permanently for Venice at first glance. Others find it disagreeable: over-priced, overcrowded, over-praised by its worshippers. (Books about Venice, like cookbooks, always do well.) Whatever your initial response, you end up enchanted. Venice is the Babylon or Persepolis of our times. You do not feel obliged, as in Rome or Florence, to study monuments and works of art, though the churches and palaces are stuffed with them. Just to be afloat with that festive pink-and-grey gâteau of a city around you is enough. It is too much for some. The Vorticists wanted to flatten the place and fill up the canals with the rubble of the buildings.

Refugees from the mainland founded Venice in the 5thC AD. Accidentally they hit on a fulcrum of Old World economy. The marshy haven became the trading post and mart of western Europe and the Middle East. Greeks, Byzantines, Goths, Tuscans, Lombards, Moors and Franks stamped their architectural trademarks on the city. Venice provided transport for the Crusades, conquered and planted colonies over the eastern Mediterranean, turned back the Sultan and fought the Moors and mediated between Rome and Constantinople. The city was La Serenissima, Queen of the Adriatic, Mistress of the Seas, most powerful of maritime republics – until Columbus discovered America and economic strategy took a new direction. Even so, Venice remained an independent state until the end of the 18thC.

Venice is not an island. It is 117 islands, separated by 45 km of canals and *rii* (branch canals) which average only 4 m in width and vary from 1 m to 2 m in depth, according to the tide. The Grand Canal is about 4 m deep. One canal goes under a church (Santo Stefano). When you look over Venice from the campanile in St Mark's Square you see no canals – the buildings hide them – but plenty of sandbanks all over the lagoon. The great *palazzi* and churches of Venice rest on sandbanks like those, on millions of wooden piles, driven 6 m down into hard blue clay. Floodwater and rising damp have made many ground floors unusable, but the buildings stand firm. Palaces galore, many nowadays museums or hotels, embroider the waterways with their fretted alcoves and the frivolous masonry of interlocking arcs and circles and intricate armorial devices under which smart motor launches tie up in the spaces formerly reserved for gondolas.

You walk the canals on footways and cross them on high-arched bridges, rather tiring to the legs. St Mark's Square is the only piazza but in front of churches you will often come across a *campo* ('field') like a small piazza.

Reclaimed land on the east and west extremities gives Venice horizontal space – on the west for the big railway terminus and the quays for ocean liners, on the east for the football stadium, the naval dockyard and the gardens of the Biennale art exhibitions.

USING THIS SECTION

As with all the itineraries in this guide, there is no compulsion to follow them from beginning to end; and indeed, you don't have to follow them at all. The information in both walks can just as well be absorbed in an armchair to get to grips with the city in its various different aspects; and of course, the hotel and restaurant recommendations at the end of this section, can be consulted as and when needed.

ACCOMMODATION GUIDELINES

Hotel prices in Venice are almost everywhere way over the top. The mere location doubles what you would reasonably expect to pay and it is only a general rule, with many exceptions, that the farther you retreat from the Grand Canal the cheaper it becomes. In July and August and Carnival Week (before Lent) accommodation is virtually unobtainable for the casual arrival.

Venice is also a surprisingly noisy city. Budget travellers should consider accommodation at a distance. It is easy to make full day-trips from Treviso, Padua and even Vicenza.

NEIGHBOURHOODS TO AVOID

Venice benefits from its island situation. Violent crime is rare because escape is difficult. Surreptitious pilfering – pickpocketing and the like – goes on here as elsewhere.

ARRIVING

By car: you have the choice of parking at Mestre, the inland end of the Venice causeway, and taking a five-minute train ride; or crossing the causeway to the car park at Isola del Tronchetto (fairly expensive, a short walk from railway station) or the car park in Piazzale Roma (very expensive, opposite the railway station across the Grand Canal).

By train: the railway station for Mestre and the mainland world is Santa Lucia at the west end of the Grand Canal. From there it is only a step to the quays where boats (see Venice Transport, below) go to all parts of the city.

By air: Marco Polo airport is on the mainland 8 km NE of Mestre. The airport bus brings you to the railway station. Fast motor-boats (*motoscafi*) plying between the airport and San Marco, east end of the Grand Canal, are expensive: in 1993 about £50 for four people. The Air Terminal is on Riva degli Schiavoni, next door to Piazza San Marco.

VENICE TRANSPORT

The motive power in Venice, apart from your own two feet, is aquatic: the *vaporetto* ('steamer' or waterbus), the *motoscafo* (hired launch) and the gondola. Gondolas are expensive. Trips work out at about 2,000 *lire* (1993) a minute and there is an extortionate minimum fare.

The only cheap gondola experience is the *traghetto* or ferry, across the Grand Canal for about 500 *lire* (1993). On this main artery there are four *traghetto* stations and seven ordinary gondola pick-up points. Soon there may be fewer, for the gondolas (like the barber's-pole mooring posts, heraldically striped) are disappearing: 350 at the last count, compared with 10,000 in the 18thC.

Motoscafi can be hailed or hired by telephone. They are fast, extremely expensive, up to 40,000 *lire* (1993) minimum fare, and environmentally unfriendly.

Vaporetti are organized in 12 *linee*, 17 in summer. Linea 1 plies the Grand Canal, stopping at 19 stages and crossing to the Lido. Linea 5 goes round the city in both directions and also visits islands in the lagoon. Linea 28 goes non-stop up and down the Grand Canal.

Buy tickets on the landing-stage, singly or in cut-price books of ten; or pay a higher fare on board. End to end of the Grand Canal (3 km) costs about L2,000.

WALKING

You are sure to get lost. Street sign-posting is in dialect and house numberings are illogical; but you do not go far without seeing the yellow arrow '*Al vaporetto*'. Relax in picturesque angles at intersections of *rii* without apprehension. Harassment is rare and Venice, self-contained and proud of it, claims to be the safest of major Italian cities.

Arsenal to the Ghetto

Introduction There is no such thing as 'unknown' Venice – the city is a compact whole, is comprehensively explored by all who stay there for more than a few days and has been more written about and talked about than any other city on earth. But you can escape from the area of most intense tourist pressure. This walk takes you as far as possible from the Grand Canal, among the *rii* (small canals) and *campi* (small piazzas) where you recover something of the original simplicity of Venice and see, in busy little streets and unfashionable *palazzi* and churches, reflections of the city's magical encounters with the Byzantines, the Arabs and the Orient. Here is not the showy Venice of the picture-books. Here is the underlying strength of a city once renowned as the secure port, the centre of a fabulously rich economy and the base for daring enterprises.

Start The Arsenale – see map. Take the unromantic and ever-available *vaporetto* from any station on the Grand Canal to the **Arsenale**, two stops east of St Mark's. Follow the Rio dell' Arsenale into the **dockyard**. This is where Venice, in her halcyon era, built the galleys which subdued the Adriatic and spread her influence throughout the East. In the great warehouse, now the **naval museum**, you see the ornate barges of La Serenissima's governors and vessels of many ages and lands, including a Chinese junk. Four stone lions of uncertain provenance (like the famous bronze horses of St Mark's) guard the museum's Renaissance gate.

Go west on Rio di San Francesco, sparing a few minutes for the church of **San Francesco della Vigna**, a clinically pure structure by Sansovino (1534), and continue across Rio di Santa Giustina for $1/2$ km to **Campo Santi Giovanni e Paolo** – in local dialect 'San Zanipolo'. The church, a brick building, not pleasing to the eye, is the last resting-place of the Doges, rulers of Venice, and it has a fine frescoed ceiling by Veronese.

On this same *campo* stands a notable work of art, Verrocchio's equestrian statue of **Bartolomeo Colleoni** (1488). Colleoni, a freebooter and mercenary leader of Venetian armies, left a fortune to the state on condition that his statue should be erected in St Mark's Square. The notoriously devious city fathers stuck to the letter of the bargain: they installed it at a remote St Mark's, a *scuola grande* or charitable foundation of that name. You might look into this *scuola grande*, one of several in the city, as you cross Rio dei Mendicanti or 'Beggars' Canal' and head west again to the pretty and fashionable little church of **Santa Maria dei Miracoli**. Its lovely inlaid marble façade covers a cosy pink and grey interior loaded with saintly images and paintings, a perfect summary of the style they call Venetian Renaissance.

Two blocks west, pick up the Rio di Santi Apostoli and in 300 m you are on the lagoon embankments, the **Fondamente Nuove**, at a crossroads of navigation. If you have had enough for one day, the Linea 5 *vaporetto* will take you east, back through the Arsenale canal and along the **Giudecca canal** (actually an arm of the sea), calling at various stations on Giudecca island and along the **Dorsoduro** ('Hard Shoulder') between the Grand Canal and the Giudecca strait. (This district is covered in the second Venice walk, page 134.)

Or you may take the westbound *vaporetto* to the main railway station, down part of the Grand Canal and across to the Giudecca again, thus completing the circuit of Venice. Or you may travel, as all Linea 5 *vaporetti* do, from the Fondamente Nuove to the isles of San Michele, Murano, Burano, Torcello and Sant' Erasmo. The last three are too much on top of a walking day, but the first two need not take more than an hour. On **San Michele**, five minutes from the Fondamente, 20thC celebrities are buried, including Diaghilev, Stravinsky and Ezra Pound. **Murano**, another five minutes in the boat, is a microcosm of Venice with its

own mini-canals and toy bridges. The isle is entirely preoccupied with glass – glass-blowers' workshops, glass museums and glass retailers adept at the glassy hard sell.

When you return from the islands, continue west in the Linea 5 *sinistra* or anti-clockwise boat (some go one way, some another) to the next stop, **Madonna dell' Orto**. This out-of-the-way church, aggressively Gothic with a domed campanile, contains the tomb of Tintoretto. No artist covered a greater acreage of wall and ceiling in Venice and he is well-represented here. The church was half-ruined in the 1966 floods. Britain, responding more generously than any other nation to Venice's despairing cries, rescued the church and devoted part of its Venice in Peril funds to a handsome restoration.

On leaving the church turn right along the *rio* and left over its wooden bridge. **Corte del Cavallo** ('Horse Courtyard') on the right before you cross is where Verrocchio had his workshop and where the horse of the Bartolomeo Colleoni statue was cast in

• *Side canal, near San Marco.*

bronze.

An attractive route back to the Grand Canal by the banks of the **Misericordia** and **San Felice Canals** and several little churches and *campi* worth looking at would take 20 minutes or so. A more interesting return is by **Calle della Malvasia** and **Campo del Ghetto** to the **Guglie Bridge** on the Cannaregio Canal. This takes you through the old Jewish quarter, the original *ghetto*, where you still find a synagogue and at least one kosher restaurant.

You come out beside **Palazzo Labia**, notable for its Tiepolo frescos and summer concerts, on the Grand Canal. The waterbus stop, 200 m to the east, is close to **Palazzo Vendramin-Calergi**, where Wagner lived and died. It is now the winter casino. The stop after that is **Ca' d'Oro** (Casa d'Oro, 'Golden House'), reputedly Venice's most beautiful *palazzo*, with Mantegnas, Carpaccios, Titians and Giorgiones in its picture gallery. It dates from 1530.

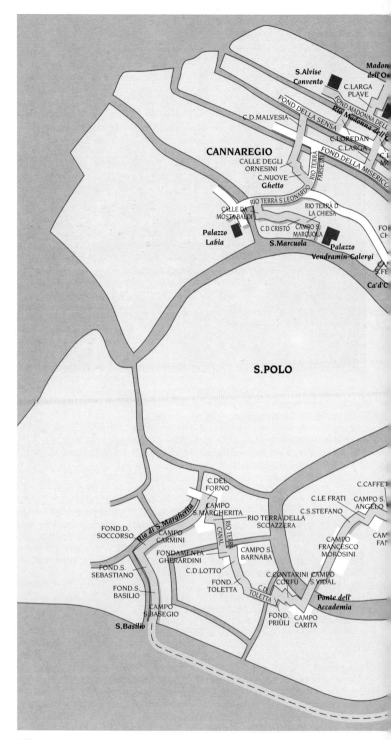

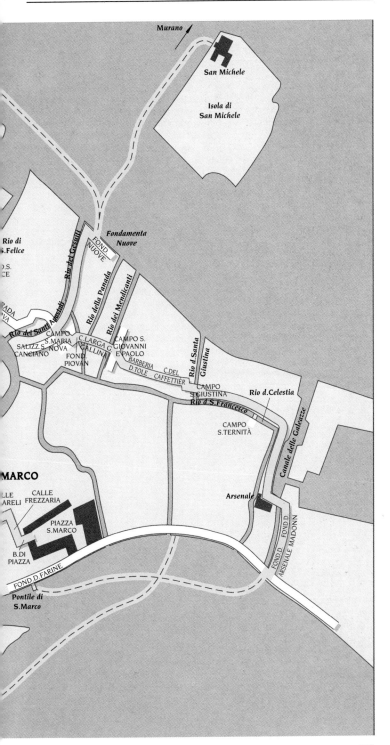

Murano

San Michele

Isola di
San Michele

Fondamenta
Nuove

Rio di
S.Felice

FOND.
NUOVE

Rio dei Gesuiti

Rio della Panada

Rio dei Mendicanti

O.S.
CE

RADA
OVA

Rio dei Santi Apostoli

CAMPO
S.MARIA
NOVA

SALIZZ.
CANCIANO

C.LARGA G.
GALLINA

FOND.
PIOVAN

CAMPO S.
GIOVANNI
E PAOLO

BARBERIA
D.TOLE

C.DEL
CAFFETTIÈR

Rio d.Santa

Giustina

CAMPO
S.GIUSTINA

Rio d.Celestia

Rio d.S.Francesco

Canale delle Galeazze

CAMPO
S.TERNITÀ

MARCO

LLE
ARELI

CALLE
FREZZARIA

PIAZZA
S.MARCO

B.DI
PIAZZA

Arsenale

FOND.D.
ARSENALE MADONN

FOND.D.

FOND.D.FARINE

Pontile di
S.Marco

St Mark's and Dorsoduro

Introduction A stroll through St Mark's Square and a trip along the Grand Canal are for most the first priorities in the Venice experience. Rightly so. Our walk covers much of that ground – you can combine it with the *vaporetto* schedules at various points. Art enthusiasts will not get very far: there are multitudes of famous paintings strewn along the route. Try at least to get to the Dorsoduro, the area between the Grand Canal and the Giudecca. There is much life and colour here, hidden from those who pass by in the *vaporetti*. You can see the boatyard where gondolas are made.

Start St Mark's Square – see map. From the west side of St Mark's Square, behind the Correr museum, turn right into the **Frezzeria**. This street, and **Calle Larga 22 Marzo** at right-angles to it, have Venice's most exclusive shops and galleries (glass, jewellery, fashion, toys, carnival masks, lace and furnishing fabrics).

Calle dei Fabbri and **Mercerie**, streets immediately north, dog-legged links between St Mark's and the Rialto bridge, are the tourists' shopping mecca: narrow, crowded, loaded with souvenir items and tripe à la mode.

At the head of Frezzeria bear left for Campo San Fantin and the **Fenice** opera theatre; one of Italy's best-looking. You can do the full tour of this building; including a glimpse of a horrifically plush royal box.

Continue past San Fantin's *scuola grande* into **Campo Sant' Angelo**, where open-air movies draw big crowds on summer evenings. Bearing left again into the broad **Campo Santo Stefano** you could sit for a while admiring the intricate stonework of the old *palazzi* which enclose the square. Have a look, too, for the canal which goes under the church – visible from the bridge on the south side – and

• *The Grand Canal.*

• *The Doge's Palace.*

ST MARK'S SQUARE

It is the only piazza in Venice, not a square but a distorted rectangle with a *piazzetta* debouching on the south entrance to the Grand Canal. It is thronged with tourists and pigeons. Even when a spring tide floods the pavement, people splash about in rubber boots and the pigeons forage on flotsam.

Five mandatory sights are grouped around it. First, **St Mark's Basilica** – crazy, incredible, dazzling, an Arabian Nights fantasy with six domes over the façade and five huge ones farther back. The door and stairs on the right at the entrance take you to a gallery, level with the four famous bronze horses, copies of which step out proudly on the façade. Here, under the main domes, you can study an acre of 12th-15thC mosaics and, in the **Marciana Museum**, look at eight centuries of ecclesiastical loot.

Second, the 90-m **campanile**. Take the lift/elevator for a fabulous view of Venice and the lagoon, the Alps too on a clear day.

Third, the **Correr Museum**. It contains engraved maps and views of old Venice (you can buy copies), a room devoted to the sculptor Canova (1757-1822), a room commemorating the city's bid for freedom from Austrian rule in 1848 and a popular Carpaccio painting, *Two Venetian Ladies*.

Fourth, the **public library** (1545-1582), named Libreria Sansoviniana

for the architect who did much to revive the glory of Venice. Palladio pronounced it the best work of the Christian era.

Fifth, the **Doge's Palace**, the epitome of boastful splendour. Sansovino's Scala dei Giganti ascends from the courtyard, flanked by enormous statues of Mars and Neptune, war and the sea, the guiding elements in the Republic's prosperity. The Great Council chamber, which seated 3,000 at a banquet, is adorned with the biggest painting in art history, Tintoretto's *Paradiso*, 25 m by 10 m. Guided tours visit the secret apartments and, across the marbled box-bridge of **Sighs**, the noxious dungeons reserved for enemies of the state. The Doges (*duces*, leaders) were prisoners too. They ruled Venice and her empire for 1,000 years and we remember the names of none of them. This palace was their golden cage, from which they exercised purely ceremonial power. They merely rubber-stamped the diktats of a ruthless, all-powerful Council.

Round the piazza, cafés occupy the ground floors of old departmental palaces. Florian and Quadri, more than 250 years in business, maintain the *caffè* (coffee-house) tradition of old Italy. You pay about eight times the going rate for coffee or an *aperitivo*, but you have formal service and music.

135

observe the listing church tower.

Walk south and cross the **Accademia Bridge** on the Grand Canal. From its apex look east towards St Mark's. The array of canalside *palazzi* reinforces the tourist board's claim that 19 in every 20 Venetian buildings are national monuments. Many that you see here are associated with those 19thC travellers and expatriates who launched the city's tourist industry: Byron, Shelley, Ruskin, Browning, Dickens, Henry James, Wagner, Hans Andersen and the rest.

This is also the vantage point for days of pomp and celebration: Carnival (week before Lent); Feast of the Redeemer (July); historical regatta (September); and procession and bridge of boats (November). Venice enthusiastically exploits the Grand Canal's unique potential for pageantry.

The important building facing you across the bridge is the **Accademia**, the principal art gallery and a showcase of the High Renaissance – ambitious themes, strong tones, brilliant colour combinations and an amplitude of feminine voluptuousness – by Giorgione, Bellini, Carpaccio, Titian, Veronese, Tiepolo, Canaletto, Guardi and others. The **Peggy Guggenheim Modern Art Museum** 1/2 km east in the Nonfinito ('never finished') palace is the antithesis of all that – Picasso, Mondrian, Dali, de Chirico around the walls, Brancusi and Henry Moore in the garden. Mrs Guggenheim's admission charges are high, but entrance is free on Saturday evenings.

This southern promontory, between Grand Canal and Giudecca strait, is called **Dorsoduro** ('Hard Shoulder') and west from the Accademia along the Calle di Toletta native Venetians outnumber tourists. You cross Rio di San Trovaso near the boatyard where gondolas are made – a declining trade, kept alive chiefly with orders from fun parks in America.

The Calle now leads into **Campo San Barnaba** and its *rio* with a picturesque floating fruit and vegetable market; and to the long rectangle of **Campo Santa Margherita**, chief market centre of the district. Seafood and lagoon fish predominate. Complain about prices, here or anywhere else, and shopkeepers put the blame squarely on Venice's peculiar transport difficulties. There are grand churches and *scuole* to be admired in this quarter, and do not overlook the characteristic medieval cottages between the Campo and Rio Santa Margherita.

If this is enough for one day, the Linea 2 *vaporetto* will take you from

RECOMMENDED HOTELS

Cipriani, LLL; *Giudecca* 10; *tel.* 5207744; *credit cards*, AE, DC, E, MC, V.

World-renowned. It has the only swimming-pool (salt water, heated) and tennis-court in Venice. Majestic decoration, carefully-tended gardens, own health centre, own yacht basin with private launch always on call for the 'mainland' of Venice (the hotel is on the east tip of the Giudecca, across the water from St Mark's). Staff outnumber guests. Fine views of lagoon, none of Venice. Not a wholly exclusive retreat: it takes package tours, and many visitors come over just to have a drink. Giuseppe Cipriani founded the equally renowned **Harry's Bar** on St Mark's waterfront, which has the same cuisine; also **Locanda Cipriani** on Torcello (see Restaurants, page 137).

Flora, LLL; *Calle Bergamaschi* 2283a; *tel.* 5205844; *credit cards*, AE, DC, E, MC, V.

Though central, just off the smart shopping street of Calle Larga 22 Marzo, it has what most Venetian houses cannot aspire to: a quiet leafy situation, a garden with wrought-iron chairs and a fountain. Pleasant sitting-rooms, diminutive bedrooms, a dignified atmosphere. Only *just* in the expensive category and long a home-from-home for British and Americans. Early booking essential.

Star Hotel Splendid-Suisse, LLL; *Mercerie* 760; *tel.* 5200755; *credit cards*, AE, DC, E, MC, V.

This old *palazzo* rose phoenix-like as a modern, expertly-managed hotel with ample room in living spaces. Trendy furnishings, restaurant, American bar, serve-yourself

Rio di Ca' Foscari to stations on the Grand Canal. If you care instead to walk down Rio di Santa Margherita to Campo San Basegio near the Stazione Marittima (about .75 km) you may end the day with a cruise in the Linea 5 *vaporetto*, crossing to the Giudecca and **San Giorgio** (a cultural enclave under Cini Foundation patronage – music, drama and architectural studies, crafts workshops, open-air theatre) before returning to the Venice 'mainland' on Riva degli Schiavoni, close to St Mark's.

breakfast. Overlooks main shopping street between St Mark's and the Rialto, the rackety heart of tourist Venice, but rooms are efficiently sound-proofed and air-conditioned. Alitalia uses this place for its upmarket 'Intermezzo' package tours.

Santo Stefano, L-LL; *Campo Santo Stefano; tel. 5200166; credit cards, MC, E, V.*

Immaculate canopy and flower boxes proclaim the owners' pride in this bijou 12-bedroomed hotelette on the *campo* with the leaning tower and sub-church canal. Everything toylike, from courtyard to lift/elevator, but limited space cleverly managed. Breakfast, but no other meals, no bar.

Marconi, L-LL; *Riva del Vin; tel. 5222068; credit cards, none.*

A 15thC *palazzo* on the Grand Canal near Rialto, admirably restored and period-furnished. As is usual with canal-side properties, stairs are steep and there is no lift/elevator.

Al Gambero, L; *Calle dei Fabbri 4687; tel. 5224384; credit cards, none.*

Unpretentious little hotel, cheap and friendly, not many bathrooms but otherwise reasonable amenities including restaurant, bar and facilities for disabled.

RECOMMENDED RESTAURANTS

Locanda Cipriani, LLL; *Piazza San Fosca, Torcello; tel. 730757; credit cards, AE, DC, E, MC, V; closed in winter.*

Ruskin called Venice and isle of Torcello 'mother and daughter' and this stylish *locanda* is the offspring of the Cipriani (see Hotels, page 136). Private motor launch shuttles link Cipriani, Harry's Bar and Locanda, a 40-minute trip; *vaporetto* also serves Torcello. The Locanda takes a few guests (**LL**) but is mostly visited for superb cuisine and the quiet good taste with which food is presented. As an excursion venue it can be frantically busy at lunch, deserted in evening.

Antico Martini, LLL; *Campo San Fantin; tel. 5224121; credit cards, AE, DC, E, MC, V; closed Tues, lunch Wed, and all Dec and Feb.*

Near Fenice theatre. Regarded by many as best in Venice, certainly among most formal and venerable. Pink interior, neo-classical pillars, garden terrace for summer, intimate panelled rooms for winter. Food is taken seriously, from traditional Venetian soups and *risi e bisi* (rice and peas) to elaborate liver, kidney, squid, sole, turbot concoctions. Table d'hôte is an excellent budget alternative (**LL**) or eat at the **Vino Vino** annexe next door (**L**), much the same menu for half the price, open till 1 am.

Fiaschetteria Toscana, LL; *Campo San Giovanni Crisostomo; tel. 5285281; credit cards, AE, DC, E, MC, V.*

Not Venetian, but the Venetians come in droves for traditional *ombra* (dry white wine aperitif) and intriguing *carte* of shellfish and molluscs, freshwater and Adriatic.

You can eat local delicacies at **La Colomba, LL**, off the Frezzeria (entrance hung with dove-theme menu cards) and at **Da Nane Mora** (at Salizzada San Giovanni Crisostomo), **Do Forni, Al Conte Pescaor** and **Città di Milano** (all in the San Zulian-Santa Maria Formosa district north of St Mark's, all **L-LL**).

Sea pie, fried stockfish, seafood with spaghetti, game and poultry with Venetian sauces are among many specialities. What you pay depends on whether you order plain dishes (very reasonable) or elaborate ones (very expensive).

<u>Northern Italy</u>

Piedmont

410 km; map Touring Club *Italiano* Piemonte e Valle d'Aosta

'Italy of the Italians' – the expression is apt because from this region between the western Alps and the coastal fringe of Liguria came the Italian nation. Piedmont's Prime Minister Cavour was the architect of the Risorgimento, the rising up of modern Italy; and the King of Piedmont became the first King of Italy.

In another sense it is 'Italy of the Italians' because it attracts few foreign tourists. Although ski resorts are numerous in the mountains, motorists in summer and autumn will have long verdant valleys and Alpine panoramas all to themselves.

Hill-top fortresses are the landmarks of a turbulent history. To take one of many examples, the Susa valley strongholds recall the Waldenses whose relentless opposition to a corrupt papacy paved the way for the spread of Protestantism in northern Europe. To take another, the Savoy dynasty's grandiose hunting lodge at Stupinigi (see page 142), taken over by Bonaparte on his way to Milan to be crowned emperor, was subsequently added to his list of country retreats.

Our tour is a circuit with Turin at 12 o'clock. We take you through some of the least developed and least touristy parts of mainland Italy; if you're going all round it, allow three days. The only busy section is west of Turin, where commercial traffic struggles up to the Fréjus road tunnel on the French border. To the south we cross the infant River Po and, traversing fruitful plains, follow the River Tanaro through vineyards around Asti and Alba (see Wine Routes, page 142). Asti is celebrated for its rather cloying *spumante*, the poor person's champagne. Turin is home to the best vermouths: Cinzano, Martini red and white, Carpano and Gancia. This venerable aperitif (from German *wermut*, wormwood) is a fortified wine flavoured (they say) with as many as 59 aromatic and bitter herbs. Among internationally acclaimed Piedmontese red wines are Barolo (but insist on *vecchio*, at least three years old), Grignolino, Nebbiolo and the sturdy country Barbera.

This is definitely gourmet country, the cuisine a happy marriage between French and Italian. Expect to find *fontina*, a buttery cheese and ingredient of *fonduta* (*fondue*); and *robiola*, made from goats' milk. White truffles (actually dirty brown) enhance many dishes. Hare cooked in Barbera wine is a regional favourite, as are *bollito* (*pot-au-feu*, meat broth) and *gianduia*, a cold chocolate pudding. (See also Italy Overall: 1.)

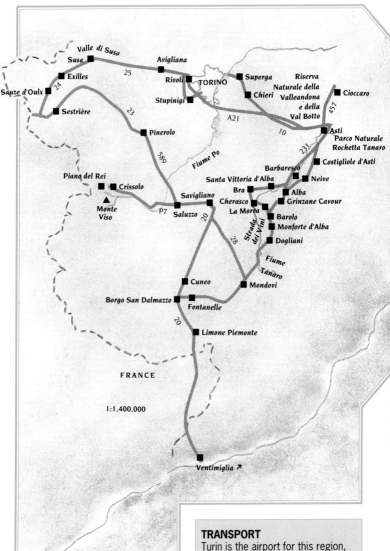

Valle di Susa
Susa
Exilles
Sauze d'Oulx
Sestrière
Pinerolo
Piano del Rei
Crissolo
Monte Viso
Saluzzo
Savigliano
Cuneo
Borgo San Dalmazzo
Fontanelle
Limone Piemonte
FRANCE
1:1,400,000
Ventimiglia ↗

Avigliana
Rivoli
TORINO
Stupinigi
Fiume Po
Superga
Chieri
Riserva Naturale della Valleandona e della Val Botto
Cioccaro
Asti
Parco Naturale Rochetta Tanaro
Costigliole d'Asti
Barbaresco
Santa Vittoria d'Alba
Bra
Cherasco
La Morra
Neive
Alba
Grinzane Cavour
Barolo
Monforte d'Alba
Dogliani
Strada dei Vini
Fiume Tanaro
Mondovi
A21
A21
10
231
457
25
24
23
589
P7
20
28
20

TRANSPORT

Turin is the airport for this region, international and domestic.

A useful network of rail branch lines fills the Turin-Alessandria-Genoa-Cuneo quadrilateral. Some routes are spectacular with many tunnels and viaducts.

The principal bus company, with services to all regional towns and communities and to Genoa and Liguria in coastal towns, is SAPAV, at Corso Torino 396, Pinerolo, Turin. For city buses there is a one-price fare, average L1,000.

SIGHTS & PLACES OF INTEREST

ALBA ⇔
Market town in middle of truffle and wine-growing area. **Roman remains**, **medieval buildings**, a **cathedral** whose pride is its 15thC choir stalls richly *intagliate* (inlaid with woods of different colours).

ASTI ⇔ ×
Off the A21, 55 km E of Turin. Synonymous with *spumante* (sparkling wine) but also noted for full-bodied reds. The **cathedral**, with florid 18thC frescos, is one of the grandest buildings in Piedmont.

Count Vittorio Alfieri, poet and dramatist, was born at Asti. He earned a place in history by eloping with Princess Louise of Stolberg, otherwise known as Mrs Bonnie Prince Charlie.

Near the town are two natural parks: **Rocchetta Tanaro** to the south-east, with remnants of an antediluvian oak forest; and **Valleandona e Val Botto** to the north-west, an important fossil site.

AVIGLIANA ×
The old hill town on the edge of two lakes (watersports) is now part of Turin's stockbroker belt. Towers, arcades, medieval houses and a ruined 17thC castle survive, but the main attraction is the nearby **Sacra di San Michele**. The 10thC fortified abbey

---

DETOUR – **LIMONE PIEMONTE**
From Mondovi take the secondary road south-west to Borgo San Dalmazzo and Route 20 to Limone Piemonte (55 km). Almost on the French border, this long-established hill resort was until recently a well-kept secret. It is now a popular excursion venue. If you feel like continuing south, a dramatic road follows the Roya valley by the cliff-hanging village of Saorge in France, returning to Italian soil above Ventimiglia (see Local Explorations: 7). This adds 64 km to the one-way journey. In the French section (which has been French only since a referendum among inhabitants in 1947) Route 20 becomes Route N204.

---

clings to a rock 500 m up, guarding the approach to the Susa Valley. Note the frescos, carvings and, on the Scalone dei Morti ('stair of the dead'), the zodiac door. The wide-ranging views from the terrace are a bonus.

BARBARESCO
See The Wine Route, page 142.

BAROLO
See The Wine Route, page 142.

BORGO SAN DALMAZZO
See Detour – Limone Piemonte, this page.

CHIERI
A small town with a huge **cathedral** of the 14thC. A few km south is the village of **Santena** with the tomb of Camille Cavour, a founder of the Italian state.

CRISSOLO
A resort on the slopes of Monte Viso (3,841 m). A road, short but with a serious gradient, leads to Piano del Rei, the nearest village to the source of the Po. High above is the **Col de la Traversette** through which Ludovico II, 15thC local potentate, dug one of the earliest Alpine tunnels. (See Saluzzo, page 141.)

DOGLIANI
See The Wine Route, page 142.

EXILLES
See Susa Valley, page 142.

GRINZANE CAVOUR
See The Wine Route, page 142.

LA MORRA
See The Wine Route, page 142.

MONDOVI
Deep in chestnut forests, the town is on two levels linked by cable-car. In the older, upper part of Mondovi Piazza are a **baroque cathedral** and the church of **La Missione**, with important *trompe-l'oeil* paintings. There are **caverns** with stalactites in the neighbourhood.

NEIVE ×
See The Wine Route, page 142.

PIANO DEL REI
See Crissolo, page 140.

RIVOLI
Having no connection with the Rivoli of Parisian fame, it is nevertheless known as the Versailles of Piedmont. It was the largest palace ever built for the palatially-preoccupied Savoy family. The architect was Filippo Juvarra, a name to conjure with in Piedmont (he also did important work in Turin). Fine views.

ROCCHETTA TANARO NATURAL PARK
See Asti, page 140.

SALUZZO
The French Gothic **church of San Giovanni** houses the tomb of Ludovico II (see Crissolo, page 140), one of a long line of marquesses who ruled independent Saluzzo through the Middle Ages. Another notable resident was Giambattista Bodoni, 18thC printer to the Duke of Mantua. This is a good-looking town with cobbled streets separating buildings of mellow brick. **Casa Cavassa**, a Renaissance palace, is beautifully preserved.

SAUZE D'OULX ⌂
See Susa Valley, page 142.

RECOMMENDED HOTELS

ALBA
Santa Vittoria, LL; Santa Vittoria d'Alba; tel. 017 247 8198; credit cards, AE, DC, E, MC, V.
The 15thC bell-tower of this hill-top village is a landmark for miles - and you'll need it, for the miniscule sign off the Alba to Bra road is easily missed. Rooms are spacious with balconies and fine views. Garden with sun loungers; bar/lounge with colonnades and marble floors. No restaurant, but one nearby.

Giardino da Felicin, LL; Monforte d'Alba; tel. 017 378 225; credit cards, V; closed Jan, first week Feb, first half Jul; restaurant closed Sun eve, Mon.
In pretty village 16 km south of Alba amid rolling vine-covered hills. Just 11 rooms. Notable restaurant; try the tagliatelle al pomodoro fresco con tartufi: a wonderful pasta/truffle tomato dish.

ASTI
Locanda del Sant' Uffizio, LLL; Cioccaro, 20 km N of Asti on Route 457 and minor road; tel. 014 191 271; credit cards, DC, E, MC, V; closed Jan, two weeks mid-Aug; restaurant closed Mon.
Old converted farm set in park with swimming-pool and tennis. Bedrooms modern; public rooms traditional and furnished with antiques. Reliable restaurant: the classic Piedmontese fonduta is a highlight of the menu.

Rainero, LL; Via Cavour 85; tel. 014 135 3866; credit cards, DC, E, MC, V; open all year.
Family-run hotel close to the central square, Campo del Palio. Car parking. Restaurants nearby.

CHERASCO
Napoleon, LL; Via A. Moro 1; tel. 017 248 8238; credit cards, AE, E, MC, V; restaurant closed Wed.
New small hotel on edge of sleepy village with views of rolling Langhe countryside. Elegant bedrooms; light and spacious public rooms. Ample car parking. Next door is **L'Escargot** restaurant (**LL**; same phone and credit cards) noted for fine Piedmontese cuisine. Lamb, wild boar, veal in Barolo. The spinach flan was a good starter.

SAUZE D'OULX
Il Capricorno, LL-LLL; Le Clotes; tel. 012 285 0273; credit cards, E, MC, V; closed May, mid-Sep to end Nov.
Small châlet in area dominated by large impersonal ski hotels. In pinewoods above town, reached by chairlift in winter. Just eight rooms and a decent restaurant.

SESTRIERE
Miramonti, LL; Via Cesana 3; tel. 012 277 048; credit cards, DC, E, MC, V; closed Oct, Nov, May.
Châlet-style building with plenty of wood panelling, comfortable rooms, most with terraces. Car parking; restaurant.

STUPINIGI
On Route 23, 11 km SW of Turin. The **Villa Reale**, another Juvarra creation, was built around 1729 as an ostentatious hunting lodge of the Savoy dynasty, baroque-styled and star-shaped. Its sumptuous interior decoration, original furniture and carefully-landscaped gardens make it one of the showplaces of Piedmont.

SUPERGA
See Turin, this page.

SUSA
A great old north-western frontier post between the Romans' Cisalpine and Transalpine Gaul, it is now an attractive bustling town where many tourists stop for a meal and a first or last breath of Italy. Remains of towers and walls survive, also an **arch of the Emperor Augustus** and an 11thC **cathedral**.

SUSA VALLEY
A long narrowing valley of great historical significance. The gap at **Exilles** is overlooked by the fort where Dumas's Man in the Iron Mask was once a reluctant guest. The area is mainly of interest to skiers, hill-climbers and walkers. **Sauze d'Oulx** is the Italian resort most favoured by the British. A longer walk, but a gentle one, leads over Col Basset to **Sestriere** (see Recommended

Hotels, page 141), where elementary winter-sports amenities of the 1930s have now reached epic proportions. There are more than 70 runs and a dozen purpose-built ski hotels at around 2,157 m.

TURIN
Cold, misty, industrial – the popular idea of what they call 'Fiat City'. Yet Turin is a regal place, the first capital of Italy, and it has the capital equipment of squares, colonnades and wide flowing streets where islands of historic buildings alternate with islands of greenery. Magnificent churches and palazzi adjoin elaborate parks and gardens. On **Via Roma**, the city's axis, a line of marble pillars from Piazza Castello to Piazza Carlo Felice is the façade for rows of cosy shops and piole, traditional Piedmontese bar-restaurants. The city itself is like that: warm and cosy behind a superficial hauteur.

The sightseer's route is from the **Egyptian Museum** (the best in the world outside Cairo) to the **Royal Armoury**, the snow-white **Palazzo Madama** (the French polish on Turin's life and character gives its dialect madama instead of signora), the **Royal Palace** with its famous 'scissors' staircase, the eccentric **Mole of Antonelli**, a baroque fantasy originally intended for a synagogue, and the Renaissance **duomo**. On the altar in a black marble chapel of the Duomo lies Christendom's most controversial relic, the **Holy Shroud** in which Christ's body, it is claimed, was wrapped.

The **Sabauda Art Gallery** has a rich selection of Flemish and Tuscan works. The surrealistic **Gallery of Modern Art** is strong on such 20thC masters as Modigliani, Picasso, Klee and Chagall. Arts and sciences are combined in the high-tech crystal, steel-framed **Palace of Labour**, built by Pier Luigi Nervi for the Union-of-Italy centenary in 1961.

Turin was the cradle of automobilism in Italy and its annual motor show is a major event. Another vast modern streamlined building, this time in marble, houses the **motor car museum** which covers the whole history of road transport from a steam-driven landau of 1854 and the first Fiat car of 1899 to the most advanced models.

Do not miss the river promenades and adjoining gardens and fountains (especially the Twelve Months fountain in the **Valentino park**). For a farewell view of Turin, stand on the bridge at **Piazza Vittorio Veneto** and look along the Po, which here is already a broad, placid river. On its banks and beyond the palaces, spires and *campanili* shine like jewels in the sun or pierce the evening mists.

Eight km east of Turin the **Superga Basilica** (early 18thC) was built to the designs of Juvarra, after Prince Victor Amadeus II of Savoy had studied the French battle lines from the hill in 1706 and vowed to erect a church if Turin was liberated. Rich in frescos and mosaics, the basilica is at 670 m. From its balustrade you overlook the whole chain of the Alps.

VALLEANDONA E VAL BOTTO NATURAL RESERVE

See Asti, page 140.

• *The duomo, Asti.*

RECOMMENDED RESTAURANTS

ASTI

Guido, LLL; *Piazza Umberto I, 27, Costigliole d'Asti; tel.* 014 196 6012; *credit cards* E, MC, V; *closed lunch, Sun, most of Aug, Christmas.*

Off main road half-way between Alba and Asti. Booking essential. *Funghi* and truffle dishes are menu's main features.

Gener Neuv, LLL; *Lungo Tanaro* 4; *tel.* 014 157 270; *credit cards*, AE, MC, V; *closed Sun eve*, Mon, Aug, Dec, Jan.

South of town centre, an internationally-famous non-smoking restaurant. Excellent menu; elegant decoration. Great veal (*filetto di vitello all'astigiana*). Wine list includes a fine Grignolino.

AVIGLIANA

La Maiana, LLL; *tel.* 011 938 805; *credit cards* E, MC, V.

Beautiful setting by lakeside with a terrace for outdoor dining. Try the beef braised in Barolo (*bue brasato al Barolo*). Wine list boasts local Dolcetto di Dogliani. Booking recommended. Car parking.

FONTANELLE

Della Pace, LL-LLL; 7 *km* E *of Borgo San Dalmazzo; tel.* 017 138 0398; *credit cards*, DC; *closed Sun eve*, Mon.

With an attractive outdoor terrace where you might choose local specialities such as *fonduta* or *raviolini di erbette*, succulent pasta. Booking essential.

NEIVE

Contea, LLL; *tel.* 017 367 126; *credit cards*, AE, DC, E, MC, V; *closed Sun eve*, Mon.

Historic building in centre of medieval village. Owner Tonino Verro is a larger-than-life character: 'Do you speak French?' — 'No, solo Piemontese.' Don't bother with the menu, just eat what you're served. It will be wonderful. Extensive list of classic wines. Style and great panache – but must book.

Northern Italy

Lakelands of Lombardy

350 km; maps Touring Club Italiano Lombardia

The contrast with adjacent scenery gives the Lombardy lakelands a surprising and inimitable charm. You come down from the Alpine passes among grey rubble, sparse grass and milky, boulder-strewn torrents and suddenly you are in an enchanted land of unnatural and shining beauty: terraced gardens, trees and flowers, magical villas, white church towers, pink roofs and 'emerald isles which calmly sleep On the blue bosom of the deep.' You cannot wait to get on to the lake, where you drift under balconies heavy with roses, boat landings stately with cypress and myrtle, hanging gardens of azaleas, lilies, geraniums and magnolias. Dark green and glossy, the oleanders and citrus bushes are studded with flowers and fruits and the scarlet sheets of bougainvillaea fall to the water's edge.

A similar contrast awaits your approach from the Lombardy plain, which is an uninspiring landscape often veiled in mist. As you drop down to the lakes (they are all deeply embedded in their mountain fastnesses) the splendour of high summer advances and enfolds you. You cannot always pause to savour the moment. These days the Milan conurbation, the cities of Varese and Como and all their malodorous gases come close to the borders of the lakes. Seveso of evil chemicals-industrial memory lies on the main Como-Milan highway. Motorways have accelerated the vehicle flow without easing the congestion. Where lake-side roads are the main routes to Switzerland traffic is a nightmare.

Our tour covers the southern shores of the three major lakes; it could occupy you for three days. It involves minimum hassle, but if you are in a car, some tedious driving between towns is unavoidable. The Maggiore, the longest lake (64 km), partly in Switzerland, resembles an inland sea. Lugano thrusts its inlets into great hills, as though trying to find a way out. This lake is mostly in Switzerland and if you drove all around it you would cross six frontiers, including those of Campione d'Italia, which is a detached fragment of Italy in Swiss Ticino. Como, richest, deepest (410 m) and historically most interesting, is shaped like a slender body with two long legs, striding across the map.

Walking the lake shores is suicidal but mountain paths from most villages deliver you in an hour or so to silence, a viewpoint, a rustic café and a refreshing breeze.

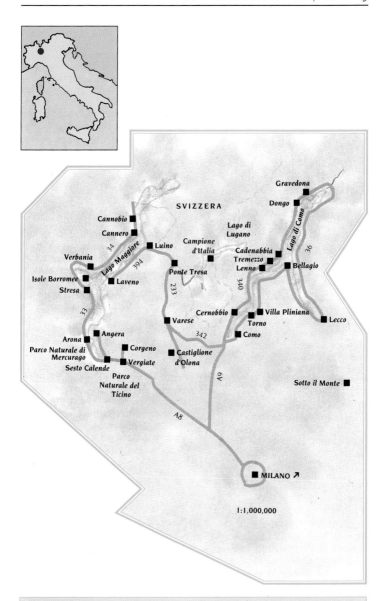

TRANSPORT
Milan is the principal airport.

Main trans-alpine railways go along all three lakes, bound for the Swiss tunnels and northern Europe.

Bus services are comprehensive all over the region. Many excursions to the lakes, including day and night cruises, are available in Milan, Como, Varese, Novara, Lugano (Switzerland) and other major towns.

Among the operators is Autostradale, Piazzale Castello 1, Milan.

Boat services and cruises on Lake Maggiore are run by Navigazione Lago Maggiore, Viale Baracca 1, Arona; on Lake Como by Navigazione Lago Como, Via Rubini 22, Como. Steamers, hydrofoils and car-ferries connect about a dozen places on each of the three lakes.

SIGHTS & PLACES OF INTEREST

ARONA ⊨ ✕

It is the first important lake town you come to when approaching the Maggiore from the south. Two protected areas are close at hand: the **Mercurago Natural Park** 2 km south and the **Ticino Regional Park** near Sesto Calende 9 km south-east. Arona's old crag-top **castle** looks across the narrow arm of the lake at its twin,

---

PLINY, UNCLE AND NEPHEW

Gaius Plinius the Elder and Gaius Plinius the Younger, 1stC Romans of remarkable industry and thirst for knowledge, were born at Como. To the Younger we owe our knowledge of the eruptions which destroyed Pompeii and Herculaneum in AD 79. Their statues flank the main doorway to Como cathedral. In their later years they returned to their native province and set the fashion for acquiring real estate and building lakeside villas. Private ownership since their days has denied long sections of the waterfront to ordinary people – the consolation is that the properties have become overflowing baskets of flowers and shrubs. If you cannot walk among them you can always admire them from a boat.

Uncle and nephew built their villas along the shores of the Como 'leg' of the lake. The Younger's favourites were called Comedy and Tragedy, one on a crag and the other on the shore so that, as he wrote, 'from one you can look upon people fishing, from the other you can fish yourself, even from your bedroom, as though you were in a boat'.

Tragedy may have occupied the spot at Bellagio where Villa Serbelloni now stands. A third villa, called Pliniana, is at **Torno**, 8 km north of Como. Where the others stood is not known, but Milanese rock stars and dress designers will assure you that their villas on Lake Como incorporate steps or pavements hallowed by the footsteps of the two great diarists and historians of the Roman Empire.

Anghera, which once commanded the high road to Milan. Water sports; ferries to all parts of the lake.

Carlo Borromeo of the immensely rich and powerful Lombard family was born here in 1537. At 23 he was Cardinal Archbishop of Milan, an office inferior only to that of the Pope, but he slept on straw, and bread and water was his only nourishment. The bronze and copper statue of San Carlo, as he became after death, is 23 m high. You can climb inside it, crawl into the head and look over Arona and the lake through Carlo's eyes.

BELLAGIO ⊨

Generations of writers have described it as the secret paradise of the lakes: consequently it receives more visitors than a small town far from main roads might expect. Here Como's two 'legs' join the 'trunk' of the lake and some turbulence of wind and current makes for exciting sailing (there is a sailing school here). The lake shore between Bellagio and Como is the most colourful of the whole region. Down the three corridors of water there are wonderful vistas. A network of woodland paths covers the point of land. On rising ground behind the town is **Villa Serbelloni**, sumptuous successor to a residence of the younger Pliny (see Pliny, uncle and nephew, this page). It is now a conference centre run by the Rockefeller Foundation but you can join guided tours of the lavishly-stocked gardens.

CADENABBIA

See *Tremezzo, page 149.*

CASTIGLIONE D'OLONA

See *Varese, page 149.*

CERNOBBIO

See *Como, below.*

COMO ⊨

Duomo and **Broletto Palace** in black-and-white marble make an impressive architectural study but modern Como (an old silk-weaving town) is big, untidy and commercial. The front is pleasant enough, the ferryboats come and go, the Brunate funicular ascends to a splendid viewpoint above the lake. At Cernobbio, 5 km north, the gardens of **Villa d'Este** (now a luxury hotel) retain

some of the glory of a no-expense-spared Renaissance showpiece, complete with follies and fountains, pergolas and pavilions.

DONGO
See Gravedona, below.

GRAVEDONA
On the quieter, less picturesque northern shore of the lake, it was the fort and naval base of the adventurer Il Medeghino (born 1498) who played off the Lombard warlords against each other and made himself master of the region.

Another adventurer, Benito Mussolini, escaping from the ruins of his Salò Republic (see Local Explorations: 5) in April 1945, was caught with his mistress Clara Petacci hiding in a truck at **Dongo**, 4 km south. Further south, at Azzano, while *en route* to partisan headquarters, he and La Petacci were shot. Their corpses were displayed in Milan's Piazza del Duomo and, in an outbreak of vindictive fury more appropriate to the Middle Ages than the 20thC, were mutilated by the mob. Well-dressed women hoisted up their

• *Alessandro Volta Museo, Como.*

skirts and urinated on the remains.

LAVENO
Gateway to some lovely country and panoramic mountain tops. Here you can make the short lake crossing to Luino (see below).

LECCO
At the head of the eastern 'leg' of the lake here called Lago di Lecco, it is an industrial town from which hill roads and cableway facilitate escape to superb viewpoints. Lecco's famous son is Alessandro Manzoni, author of *I Promessi Sposi* (*The Betrothed*), the only 19thC Italian novel anyone outside Italy has heard of.

LUINO
Birthplace of Bernardino Luini, pupil of Leonardo da Vinci and creator of the frescos in the **parish church** – which suggest that the master's mantle did *not* fall on him. The town, on the neck of land dividing Lakes Maggiore and Lugano, is a silk-weaving centre with a ferry-slip and a boatyard.

MERCURAGO NATURAL PARK
See Arona, page 146.

MILAN
See Italy Overall: 2.

PONTE TRESA
Frontier post on the St Gotthard route and a ferry port on a landlocked backwater of the lake. The road to Luino (see page 147) marks the Swiss border.

SESTO CALENDE
See Arona, page 146.

SOTTO IL MONTE
It grows in importance as a place of pilgrimage and general curiosity. **John XXIII**, the people's favourite among 20thC popes, was born here in a farmhouse which, along with his small villa, may be visited. Tasteless trinketry and raucous huckstering pervade the scene.

STRESA 🛏 ✕
'Vast and numerous hotels', says the 19thC guide-book – there are many more now. European royalty, including Queen Victoria, stayed here. Cavour and Napoleon III organized the liberation of Italy, thus inaugurating the international Stresa conferences of the 1900s. Under the headland opposite, in the twin resorts of **Pallanza** and **Verbania**, are a **countryside museum** and the botanical gardens of **Villa Taranto**, 20 hectares of rare plants in

---

RECOMMENDED HOTELS

ARONA
Giardino, LL; Corso Repubblica 1; tel. 032 245 994; credit cards, AE, DC, E, MC, V.
On lake front, close to railway station. Family-run. Shady terrace. Most rooms have views. Restaurant (**LL**) and some car parking.

BELLAGIO
Du Lac, LL; tel. 031 950 320; credit cards, E, MC, V.
Cosmopolitan, friendly, family-run hotel near ferry quay. Terrace bar on ground floor, roof-garden for sunbathing. Outstanding views of lake. Restaurant. This hotel is at the lower end of its price band.

CANNERO
Cannero, LL; on front near ferry slip for Luino; tel. 032 378 8046; credit cards, AE, DC, E, MC, V.
Peaceful location with covered terrace and car parking area. Friendly, helpful staff. Non-smoking restaurant. Heated swimming-pool, tennis; sailing and aquatic sports arranged on request.

CERNOBBIO
Grand Hotel Villa d'Este, LLL; tel. 031 511 471; credit cards, AE, DC, E, MC, V; closed Dec, Jan, Feb.
Italian nobility, British royalty and a Russian tsarina lived here, not all at the same time. Now a horrifically expensive, internationally famous hotel, it seems all chandeliers and dazzling marble. Swimming-pools, tennis-courts, health suite and sauna, 18-hole golf course nearby. See also Como, page 146.

COMO
Tre Re, LL; Via Boldoni 20; tel. 031 265 374; credit cards, E, MC, V; closed mid-Dec to mid-Jan.
Two hundred metres from lake front, near Duomo. Car parking. A comfortably modernized palazzo with terrace and excellent restaurant.

STRESA
Verbano, LL; Isola dei Pescatori; tel. 032 330 408; credit cards, AE, DC, E, MC, V; closed Jan, Feb; restaurant closed Wed out of season.
Only 12 rooms, all with balconies and lake views, in this peaceful, pretty hotel on the least-exploited of the Borromean isles (take ferry from Stresa). Restaurant with floral terrace is noted for home-made pasta.

Villaminta, LLL; Strada del Sempione 123; tel. 032 332 444; credit cards, AE, DC, E, MC, V; closed mid-Nov to early Apr.
A lake-side hotel with private beach, 2 km west of Stresa in attractive location. Flowers, terrace, views, heated swimming-pool, restaurant, car parking. Not wildly expensive.

tumbled profusion, laid out by a Scottish gardener in 1931. After the Renaissance formality of so many parks, this typically English garden, controlled but not strictly disciplined, is a revelation.

Off Stresa's lake front are the **Borromean islands**, two fairylands of old gardens, groves of azaleas and camellias, strutting peacocks, grottoes and villas impressive in their vulgarity; and a third, **Isola dei Pescatori**, relatively unspoiled. Frequent boats and guided tours.

TICINO NATURAL PARK
See Arona, page 146.

TORNO
See Pliny, Uncle and Nephew, page 146.

TREMEZZO
It gazes across the water at Bellagio and sideways at Cadenabbia, a 'capital' of British tourism on the lakes for two centuries. **Villa Carlotta** is the chief attraction of the mountainous shore, ravishing in April and May with masses of rhododendrons and azaleas and terraces of lilies. The house contains Canova's much-reproduced sculpture *Cupid and Psyche*. The lake below is so entrancing that you simply want to sit down and drink it all in.

VARESE ✕
A city that the lakes *aficionados* spend much time trying to avoid. **Sacro Monte**, with church, shrine and stations of the Cross above the chestnut groves, is worth the climb and the surrounding countryside is not entirely ruined by the epidemic of house and factory building. Compared with the real lakes, the **Lake of Varese** is a large stagnant pond. It has a tourist airfield, gliding and some water sports.

En route to or from Milan, make a note of **Castiglione d'Olona**, 15 km south of Varese. The church and baptistery on the hill hold rare paintings by Masolino (1383-1440) the great Tuscan primitive. They were uncovered in 1843 in one of the most satisfying art discoveries of the century. Sixty years later Bernard Berenson found some more frescos, also under whitewash, in a neighbouring villa.

VERBANIA
See Stresa, page 148.

In hotels, faded grandeur competes with sophisticated modernity, but there are many *pensioni* too, including expensive ones. Our restaurants are in the upper price brackets, being exceptional places; but there is no shortage of modest *trattorie* and *pizzerie*.

RECOMMENDED RESTAURANTS

ARONA
Taverna del Pittore, LLL; *Piazza del Popolo 39; tel.* 032 224 3366; *credit cards,* AE, DC, MC, V; *closed Mon, midwinter, last half Jun.*

Lakeside terrace. Fish dominates the menu. Our *filetti di triglia* (mullet) were beautifully presented and the fish terrine made an excellent starter. Wine list includes prestigious local Barbaresco. Essential to book.

STRESA
L'Emiliano, LLL; *Corso Italia 50; tel.* 032 331 396; *credit cards,* AE, DC, E, MC, V; *closed Tues, Wed lunch, Jan, Feb.*

Close to ferry but just off lakeside road. Wide-ranging menu may include delicious *lombatina d'agnello* (lamb chop). A select wine list.

VARESE
Lago Maggiore, LL-LLL; *Via Carrobbio 19; tel.* 033 223 1183; *credit cards,* AE, DC, E, MC, V; *closed Sun, Mon lunch, first three weeks Jul.*

Near Estensi Gardens. Franciacorta wines are a perfect accompaniment to an imaginative cuisine which includes impressive salads and pasta, succulent veal, nuts and fresh herbs. Essential to book.

VERGIATE
La Cinzianella, LLL; *3 km N at Corgeno on one of the Varese lakes; tel.* 033 194 6337; *credit cards,* AE, DC, E, MC, V; *closed Jan, Mon eve in winter, Tues rest of the year.*

Attractive outdoor area for unhurried meals. Excellent *bianco di pollo farcito* (stuffed chicken), tasty desserts and wines from Langhe region.

<u>Northern Italy</u>

Lake Iseo and Franciacorta

150 km, plus lake cruise: map Touring Club Italiano Lombardia

L egend holds that a temple dedicated to the Egyptian goddess Isis gave its name to the town and lake which the Romans called Sebino. The lake comes seventh in the league table of Italian lakes. It is S-shaped and you could drive its perimeter in half a day – though you would see little apart from spectacular scenery; so we suggest you set aside up to two days to do the area justice. A score of picturesque fishing villages lines its shores, with a back-drop of brooding, misty mountains, the final southbound thrust of the Alps.

Most of the towns have medieval origins; some have been carefully developed for up-market tourism. A cosmopolitan air prevails: the Swiss border is just 100 km away, the Austrian border not much farther. Rising to 650 m in the middle of the lake is Monteisola, the largest lake island in Europe. It supports a population of 2,000 and for centuries has supplied half of Italy's fishing nets. Traditional boat-building survives, maintained by a family who opened their doors for business in the 17thC. When you step ashore on Monteisola you feel that era is not so far off.

To the south, between Lake Iseo and the *autostrada*, lies the Franciacorta region. Once an uninhabitable marsh, it is now a verdant plain, noted for the production of quality wine. Two golf courses, a sports centre and a new water-based pleasure park provide outdoor entertainment. There are waymarked trails for walkers and cyclists.

To the north, the road to Bolzano and Austria runs through the Camonica valley where in recent years prehistoric stone carvings have been unearthed. A newly-opened museum celebrates Bienno's former importance for iron and steel production. If you need to shorten your trip turn back at Boario Terme, the third-largest spa town in Italy, to complete your circuit of the lake.

The area is a delightful mixture of old and new. Old towns are mazes of twisting cobbled alleyways; rustic *trattorie* compete with glitzy cafés and discotheques. Shops offer antiques and traditional crafts: beaten copperwork and wrought iron. Across the street, the latest designer fashions from Milan are on show.

You can make numerous excursions and cruises. A most useful organization is Ninfea Cooptur Club, Via Duomo 17, 25049 Iseo (tel. 030 981 154). This co-operative of local tourism-oriented businesses publishes a wide variety of free information.

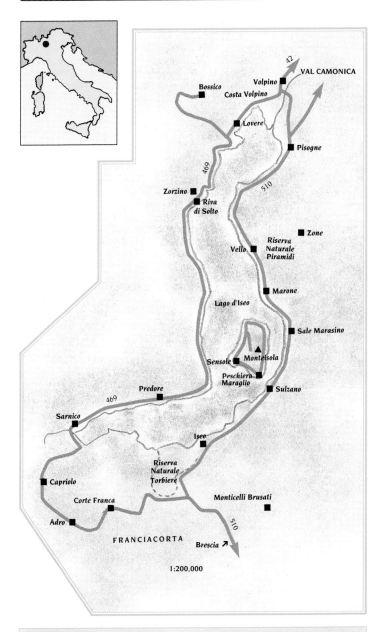

VAL CAMONICA

42

Bossico

Volpino

Costa Volpino

Lovere

Pisogne

469

510

Zorzino

Riva
di Solto

Zone

Riserva
Naturale
Piramidi

Vello

Marone

Lago d'Iseo

Sale Marasino

Sensole   Monteisola

Peschiera
Maraglio

Predore

Sulzano

469

Sarnico

Iseo

Riserva
Naturale
Torbiere

Capriolo

Monticelli Brusati

Corte Franca

510

Adro

FRANCIACORTA   Brescia ↗

1:200,000

TRANSPORT

Nearest airports are Milan
(international) and Bergamo
(domestic). There are regular trains
to Iseo from Milan and Brescia. Buses
connect lake-side towns; minibuses
operate on Monteisola where visitors'
cars are not permitted. The following
towns referred to in the gazetteer of
Sights & Places of Interest are linked
by ferry: (south to north) Sarnico,
Predore, Iseo, Peschiera
(Monteisola), Sulzano, Sale Marasino,
Marone, Riva di Solto, Lovere and
Pisogne. From Sarnico to Pisogne
takes 2¹/₂ hrs.

SIGHTS & PLACES OF INTEREST

BOSSICO
An old village on a 990-m plateau surrounded by pine and chestnut woods, with fine views over Lake Iseo. Narrow streets and houses with tiny doorways and characteristic wooden balconies. 18thC **church of San Rocco**.

BRESCIA
See Italy Overall: 2.

CAPRIOLO
See Wines of Franciacorta, page 153.

CORTE FRANCA
A group of four medieval villages in the Franciacorta region, surrounded by rolling countryside and well-kept villas. Nearby is the **Golf sports centre** with riding school, tennis, swimming-pool and two new golf courses designed by American Peter Dye and Italian Marco Croze.

Also new, the nearby **Acqua Splash** is a huge complex of open-air pools, shutes and slides, bar, pizzeria and ice-cream saloon. Capacity 4,000 with parking for 1,000 vehicles.

COSTA VOLPINO ⇔
At the mouth of the Oglio river. A spectacular hairpin road climbs the hillside, linking seven medieval hamlets which rose from the ashes of fortresses destroyed by warring families 800 years ago. Colourful houses have traditional loggias and mellow terracotta roofs.

FRANCIACORTA
See Wines of Franciacorta, page 153.

ISEO ⇔ ✕
A charming small lake-side resort with excellent sports facilities nearby (see Corte Franca, this page). The centre is medieval, with alleys linking lively shops and restaurants. We recommend a visit to one of several *enoteche*, specialist wine bars. Historic sites include the 13thC **Pieve di Sant' Andrea** with Romanesque bell-tower and the 16thC **Carmagnola Castle**, so carefully preserved you would think they built it yesterday.

West of Iseo lies the **Torbiere Natural Reserve**, habitat of herons,

---

RECOMMENDED HOTELS

COSTA VOLPINO
Franini, L-LL; *tel. 035 971 017; credit cards*, AE, DC, E, MC, V; *restaurant closed* Wed.

Just 14 rooms, so best to book in summer months. Notable restaurant (**LL**). Car parking.

ISEO
Milano, L; Lungolago Marconi 4; *tel.* 030 980 449; *credit cards*, AE, DC, E, MC, V.

Across the road from the lakeside with some reserved car parking. A family-run establishment: the *padrona* is Dutch and speaks most European languages. Bedrooms have large double doors like an old *palazzo*, and are not numbered consecutively, giving new meaning to the phrase 'finding a room for the night'. Bar.

LOVERE
Sant' Antonio, L; Piazza Martiri; *tel.* 035 961 523; *credit cards*, DC, E, MC, V;

restaurant closed Tues *in summer.*

Attractively situated small hotel with outdoor dining area. Restaurant (**LL**). Half-board is very good value.

MONTEISOLA
Sensole, L; Via Beretta 10, Sensole, 2 km from Peschiera; *tel.* 030 988 6203; *credit cards, none.*

18thC building in a beautiful peaceful setting, yet close to the beach and ferry quay. Rooms have large picture windows; roof terrace for sunbathing. Bar and restaurant.

MONTICELLI BRUSATI
Villa Gradoni, LLL; Via Villa; *tel.* 030 652 329; *credit cards, none; open* mid-Apr *to* mid-Oct.

Not a hotel but an up-market *agriturismo*. Monticelli is a wine-producing area in the Franciacorta. This expertly-restored farmhouse preserves many original rustic features. Self-catering apartment for four to six people. Luxury living. Prices are lower at beginning and end of season.

nightingales, wild duck and cuckoos, and numerous fish species.

LOVERE 🚤

At north end of lake, a busy resort with canoeing, sailing and windsurfing. The 19thC **Tadini** *palazzo* houses a rich collection of paintings, sculpture and weaponry. The 3rdC BC **Castle of the Gauls** is a picturesque ruin. Note also the **Torricelli fortress**, the towers of **Soca** and **Alghisi**, the **Basilica of Santa Maria**, and the **church of San Giorgio Martire**, all 13thC-15thC.

MARONE

Pretty town lying in the shadow of Monte Guglielmo (1,948 m). Ruins of a 1stC Roman villa are at **Co de Hela** on the edge of town. A road climbs steeply inland – hairpin bends, memorable views – to Zone and the Pyramids (see page 155). A few kilometres north of Marone is the ancient fishing settlement of **Vello**, with its archaic **church of Cimitero**.

MONTEISOLA 🚤 ✕

The 'Capri of the North' is 10 km around and 600 m high. From the pastel-tinted fishermen's houses to the courtyards and porches of Masse, the landscape is a delight. A thousand years back they made fishing nets here. They still do, along with traditional boat-building – with wood, not plastics.

The shortest crossing is from Sulzano (see page 155) to **Peschiera Maraglio** (10 minutes). Visitors' cars are not allowed: take the minibus service to Siviano and Cure. A walk of 20 minutes through chestnut forests leads to the **Madonna della Ceriola sanc-**

HOTELS AND RESTAURANTS

Except during August, accommodation is easy to find in this area. Around Lake Iseo there are more than a hundred hotels, from the basic but friendly one-star **Piramidi** at Zone (tel. 030 987 0932) to the opulent country club, the **Franciacorta Golf** (tel. 030 913 333). See also Bergamo and Brescia, Italy Overall: 2.

The lake is also studded with camp sites – large ones with swimming-pools and restaurants. There are *Agriturismo* villas and, at Iseo and Sarnico, châlet developments; details from Ninfea Cooptur (see Introduction, page 150). Many of the towns in the gazetteer of Sights & Places of Interest have a large number of comfortable, inexpensive hotels.

The cosmopolitan clientele demands an international cuisine. *Pizzerie* proliferate. So do fish restaurants. Fine wines from Franciacorta (see this page) are available almost everywhere; there are more humble table wines such as Trebbiano (white or amber) and Fortana, a red which goes well with poultry and cheese.

tuary, built on the foundations of a pagan temple.

Siviano was the ancestral home of a Catholic priest called Fenni who taught in England under the protection of Queen Elizabeth I. He eventually died for his religion on Tower Hill, London. At **Sensole** is a stone bench on which, it is said, Chopin composed a sonata.

WINES OF FRANCIACORTA

The Franciacorta label is a rarity outside Italy, but it is applied to some of the most distinguished – and expensive – bottles in the country. Particularly renowned are the spumantes or *méthode-champenoise* varieties. There are some powerful fruity reds too. Of some 60 wine producers, many welcome visitors. The Azienda Agricola of Ricci Curbastro & Son has built up a museum of presses and winery equipment; you can tour the cellars and buy wine inexpensively by the half case. Open all year: Villa Evelina near Capriolo (tel. 030 736 094).

In olden times prospective residents could be tempted to live in Franciacorta's inhospitable country only by the promise of freedom from paying taxes. Today it is a desirable place to live. The *autostrada* provides fast access to the cities of Bergamo and Brescia; the playground of Lake Iseo is nearby and there is great skiing to the north.

San Paolo is a tiny island south of Monteisola, with just room for one villa. It is a holiday home of the Beretta family of gunmakers.

Monteisola is an oasis of serenity. Even the green lake algae, according to Italian writer Petrocchi, 'seems to dance with the sensual and sinuous movements of Scheherazade.'

PESCHIERA MARAGLIO
See Monteisola, above.

PISOGNE
A major resort dominated by the square medieval **Vescovo Tower**. Above the town, paintings by Romanino in the church of **Santa Maria della Neve** have earned it the nickname of the 'poor person's Sistine Chapel'. There is a small harbour.

PREDORE
A resort of the Roman Empire and a fortified town in the Middle Ages. A **tower** and ruined **Guelph castle** above the town, which is a popular fishing centre (eel, trout, perch, pike, tench and carp).

• *Peschiera, from the Iseo motor launch.*

PYRAMID NATURAL RESERVE
See Zone, page 155.

RIVA DI SOLTO
This fishing village is close to the **Zorzino Bögn**, an extraordinary array of vertical limestone slabs forming lakeside cliffs. **Zorzino** village, above Riva, surrounded by vineyards and olive groves, has subterranean passages.

SALE MARASINO
A lakeside town backed by a natural amphitheatre, over-looking Monteisola: 18thC **church of San Zenone**; 17thC **Villa Martinengo**; **Renaissance palace**.

SARNICO
A resort, sailing centre and medieval village, once fortified. Remains of palafitte houses (lake dwellings) suggest a settlement here in prehistoric times. Several buildings are by Sommaruga, a noted Italian art-nouveau architect.

SENSOLE
See Monteisola, page 153.

SULZANO ✕
The main departure point for Monteisola (see page 153). Sailing; fine restaurants; hill walking in the vicinity. A cobbled track leads steeply upwards to the little 15thC **church of Santa Maria del Giogo** at 1,000 m – a superb viewpoint.

TORBIERE NATURAL RESERVE
See Iseo, page 152.

VAL CAMONICA
Follows the Oglio river north from Lake Iseo. **Boario Terme** is an important spa town (liver and gastric complaints) set in attractive parkland with a lake. Nearby, the sports centre offers bowling, minigolf, tennis and an Olympic swimming-pool. Entertainment includes plenty of shops and cafés, a nightclub, fishing.

At **Montecchio** a picturesque single-arched bridge of 1686 spans the Oglio. **Darfo** has old streets and buildings with arches and porches. The 11thC castle of the Federici in **Gorzone** is still inhabited. **Erbanno** boasts a medieval square tower built to defend the town, and the 15thC **Palazzo Federici**.

Bienno in the Valle dei Magli was once a great iron working centre thanks to local mines and powerful mountain torrents supplying energy. A renovated blacksmith's shop houses the **ethnographical iron museum**. An old **water-driven mill** is also a museum, wheels still turning.

Capodiponte has the highest concentration of the rock inscriptions of which more than 150,000 have been found throughout the valley. These incised stones, scattered over the flanks of the mountains, date from the 6,000-year period between the Neolithic and Iron Ages. They are also found at Malengo and other towns.

VELLO
See Marone, page 153.

ZONE ⌂
A hill walking centre in a valley below Monte Guglielmo (1,948 m). The 12thC **church of San Giorgio** has 16thC frescos on the outer walls. On the road

---

ISEO
Al Gallo Rosso, L-LL; *Vicolo Nulli 1; tel. 030 980 505; credit cards, none; closed Thur.*

A typical *osteria* in town centre. Wooden tables, walls lined with copper cooking pots and wine racks; large open grill. Meaty menus.

Il Cenacolo, L; *Via Mirolte 13; tel. 030 980 136; credit cards, none.*

It looks like the rowdiest bar in town – but there's a quieter room at the back, where it's cheap and cheerful. Large pizza menu; house wine by carafe.

MONTEISOLA
Trattoria del Pesce, LL; *Peschiera Maraglio; tel. 030 988 6137; credit cards, none; closed Tues, Nov.*

One hundred metres from the ferry quay (turn right). Ancient building with colonnades and outdoor terrace; fine view of lake. The Archetti family maintains old tradition of serving large stuffed fish on huge platters (locally-caught tench, perch and eel). Wine list includes a fine D.O.C. spumante. Superb value. Last mainland ferry leaves at 1 am in summer.

SULZANO
Trattoria Cacciatore, LL; *Via Mulini 28; tel. 030 985 184; credit cards, E, MC, V; closed Mon eve, Tues.*

Peaceful location at the top of town, with views over lake and Monteisola. Everything cooked to perfection and beautifully presented. You help yourself to starters from a large table of mouth-watering antipasto dishes. Decoration simple but stylish. Ample car parking outside.

---

from Marone you pass the **Pyramids**: curious earth pillars topped by granite slabs, some 30 m high, the result of selective erosion. Similar freaks of geology are found near Bolzano (see Soprabolzano, Local Explorations: 4.)

ZORZINO
See Riva di Solto, page 154.

The Dolomites

360 km; maps Touring Club Italiano Trentino Alto Adige

The facets of dolomite crystals (a magnesium limestone named after the 18thC French geologist Dolomieu) are slightly curved. Hence their diamond sparkle and pinkish pearly glitter. Hence the vivid gleam of those massive outcrops called the Dolomites in the Alpine country of the Veneto, Trentino and Alto Adige regions of north-eastern Italy. From far off the crinkled peaks are a winter fairyland. Closer, amid snows (but the pinnacles are too sheer for much snow to lie), you see a sunny or rosy refulgence. In places there are coloured veins, brown and purple, in the pale stone. These find their way to the souvenir workshops of Dolomite towns and end up in the baggage of tourists in the shape of ashtrays, lamp-bases and paperweights. Sharpness and steepness characterize the mountains. Your road often runs directly beneath crags of amazing perpendicularity and grandeur.

Through the main group of the four Dolomite massifs goes the celebrated Grand Dolomites Highway, opened 1909, broadened several times since. This engineering triumph connects Ponte Gardena on the Bolzano-Bressanone road with Cortina d'Ampezzo, one of the world's most beautiful high-altitude resorts. Our tour (two to three days if you do it all in one go) negotiates the full length of the Highway and brings you back via parallel valleys to the south and high passes from which stupendous panoramas open out. Among them are views from several angles of Monte Marmolada (3,342 m), the highest Dolomite summit and the only glacial one.

Attractive valleys, crossing national parks, link the high points of the circuit. They are burdened with traffic summer and winter, at least half the vehicles wearing the international registration letters 'D' for Germany or 'A' for Austria.

In the Alto Adige two cultures clash. Separatists, calling the region 'Sud Tirol' against geographical logic, demand closer ties with Austria. Between 1961 and 1981 terrorist outrages drove foreign visitors away. Things are quiet now. Tourism is vital to the prosperity of a land starved of natural resources and the activists, stubborn but not stupid, pursue peaceful paths to autonomy. Road signs in Italian and German, a bilingual and trilingual people, a strange mix of Latin and Teutonic cuisines and customs... they enrich the tourist's experience, whatever private animosities they conceal.

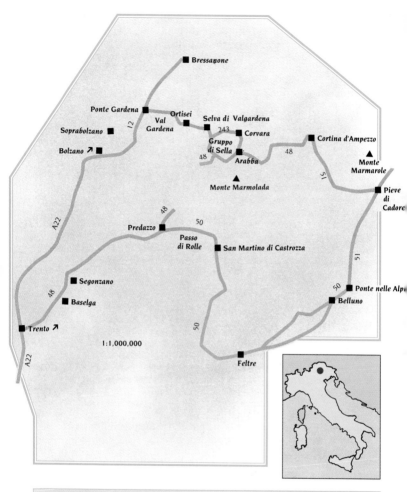

TRANSPORT

The nearest airports are Verona and Milan in Italy, Innsbruck in Austria. An airport for Bolzano is at the discussion stage.

The main Brenner-Bolzano-Trento-Verona railway gives access at three points: from Fortezza (for Brunico and Dobbiaco); from Chiusa (for Ortisei and Plan); and from Trento (for Belluno and Pieve di Cadore by a very roundabout route). At peak times in holiday months the main-line trains, especially the Osterreich-Italien express, are overcrowded and seats must be booked days in advance. In winter, avalanche debris often closes the line at the Brenner Pass and commuter bus services then come into operation.

Dolomiti Bus, Via Sant' Andrea 5, Belluno, is a major bus operator with a comprehensive network of routes. All towns are efficiently linked with the nearest ski slopes. The principal bases for public transport, as for our tour, are Bolzano, Trento and Belluno. National bus and coach operators run Dolomite tours and excursions from many Italian cities.

Through local tourist information offices or hotels in various resorts you can hire bicycles or mountain bikes and tackle some mighty passes and forest trails. In the national parks, and often elsewhere, they are sensibly waymarked for cyclists and walkers.

157

SIGHTS & PLACES OF INTEREST

BELLUNO ⊨ ×
The city stands on a spur above the Piave Valley, its skirts dipped in meadows of corn poppy. Belluno's monuments are concentrated round the **cathedral**: 14th-17thC **Palazzo Rettori** in particular, with typically Venetian arcades and clock-tower. Venice of the Doges has left deep imprints on the house style of the centre – pink and primrose colour wash, balconies, broad low arches, the stern harmonies of façades. From their windows, from descending streets and gaps in hedges, you see cameos of the river valley, reminiscent of the landscapes of local 18thC painters Ricci and Zais. Far to the north, the Dolomite ranges, pictorial emblem of the region, twinkle in the sun.

BOLZANO
See *Italy Overall: 5.*

CORTINA D'AMPEZZO ⊨ ×
Geographical heart of the Dolomites at 1,224 m and the oldest winter-sports resort in the eastern Alps, it is famous for a fashionable appeal and magnificent scenery. Here is a sophisticated, purely Italian day- and night-life (an expensive one too) where designer shops, discos and cabarets replace the thigh-slapping, beer-slurping *stube* culture of 'Sud Tirol'.

The 1956 Winter Olympics gave Cortina exciting installations. The two artificial rinks in the **Olympic Ice Stadium** are unique. The **Olympic ski-jump's referee tower**, the **Monte**

Cristallo cable-cars and the **Olympic bob-sleigh run** exhibit a startling surrealism. There are hundreds of ski-runs at Cortina, bus services to about 30 Italian and Austrian cities and many walks and climbs, clearly defined and punctuated with refuge huts.

(Mountaineering and rock-climbing in the Dolomites are not for beginners. Long-distance footpaths should be treated with respect. The crossing of the Varella, north from Cortina towards Brunico, is a fabulous walk, and a stern test.)

FELTRE
Castle and lofty clock-tower stand behind **San Rocco's church** at the highest point of the old town. Within close radius are the **cathedral**, a **Palladian palace** and a **baroque theatre**: a dignified complex of buildings, tall and straight on sloping steets and piazzas, adorned with statuary. At the **civic museum** you can see Gentile Bellini paintings and learn the contentious history of feudal struggles between church and state which preceded Venetian rule. Alpine scents and colours temper the sunny fertility of the Piave plain. Feltre's graceful architecture and the soothing layouts of neighbouring villages and farms are among the best features of this Dolomites foothill area.

ORTISEI ⊨
Chief town of the Val Gardena (see Ponte Gardena, page 160) and a very popular summer and winter resort. This is a railway station on the 20-km Chiusa-Plan branch line; there are bus services in all directions and ski-lifts and cableways to all neighbouring heights. The cable-car to the Siusi Alps at 2,000 m, an altitude difference from Ortisei of 786 m, surmounts high pastures and meadows which are a naturalist's paradise in summer, an immense blanket of virgin snows in winter. One of the Siusi 'alps' (not mountain but high meadow) is 50 square kilometres, the broadest contained expanse of pastureland in Europe.

The town has mountaineering and climbing schools. A dry bracing climate favours walks and excursions (sleigh-rides included). Grand **parade of horse-drawn sleighs** on New Year's

---

• *Cortina d'Ampezzo.*

Day. In the still air you hear the jingle of harness-bells miles away, also chatter in an unknown tongue: Ortisei is the town of the Ladins, a *montagnard* people who represent 5 per cent of the Dolomites' population and speak a *romansch* language all their own.

PIEVE DI CADORE

Here, in a typically angular farmhouse with a wooden balcony, was born Tiziano Vecellio (Titian), leading exponent of the Venetian school of painting, in 1485. **House** and **museum** are open to the public.

Pieve, meaning 'parish', in this case means chief town of the district. The

159

Cadore, an undulating forest land of the upper Piave Valley at around 2,000 m, sweeps up to the jagged chains of Marmarole and Anteleo, more than half as high again.

Pieve lies in a wide saddle overlooking the riverine lake of Centro Cadore. Skating, ice-hockey and bob-sleighing are offered along with the usual high-altitude amusements and the area is ideal walking territory.

A branch of the Belluno railway has its terminus near the town and in summer there are long-distance road coach services to and from Venice, Milan, Trieste, Bologna, Innsbruck and Vienna.

PONTE GARDENA
The Great Dolomites Highway runs east from here to Cortina d'Ampezzo along the Val Gardena. The valley is typical of the area, woods and meadows and great masses of rock overhanging a wide road which would be a joy to drive on if it were not infested with fast-moving BMWs. Villages along this valley go in for Cembra (name of a dale) pinewood carving, largely of religious statuettes, a traditional cottage industry which has suffered from commercialization.

PREDAZZO 🛌
An historic resting-place where old

RECOMMENDED HOTELS

BELLUNO
Villa Carpenda, LL; *Via Mier 158, off the road to Feltre; tel. 043 728 343; credit cards*, AE, V.

In a silent forest 2 km from central Belluno, this quiet hotel is open all year and has a prestigious restaurant (**LL**).

CORTINA D'AMPEZZO
Cristallo, LLL; *Via Menardi 42; tel. 043 642 81; credit cards*, AE, DC, E, MC, V; *closed Apr-Jun, Sep to mid-Dec*.

Even by Cortina standards it is seriously expensive, but it has everything. Balconies and terraces of generously-sized rooms in this century-old building on the south-eastern edge of town offer grand views. Heated swimming-pool. Car parking. The main restaurant is formal, emphasis on game and meats Italian-style; the other resembles a Tyrolean *stube* (cellar). Piano bar, nightclub.

Fanes, LLL; *Via Roma 136; tel. 043 634 27; credit cards*, AE, DC, E, MC, V; *closed Apr to mid-Jun, Nov to mid-Dec*.

Lower end of the price bracket. South side of town, on exit for Belluno. Châlet-type buildings, cosy rooms with balconies and fine views. Restaurant (**LL**) prides itself on solid home-cooking.

CORVARA
Cappella, LL-LLL; *at Colfosco, 3 km W of Corvara; tel. 047 183 6183; credit*

cards, E, MC, V; *closed Apr to mid-Jun, Oct to mid-Dec; restaurant closed Mon*.

A permanent art collection decorates the interior of this imposing Tyrolean châlet. Gardens and classic views of the Sella group. Sauna, swimming-pool, health club, all at 1,650 m. Restaurant (**LL**).

ORTISEI
La Perla, LL; *Via Digon 8, 1 km from Ortisei; tel. 047 179 6421; credit cards*, AE, DC, E, MC, V; *closed Nov, May*.

Half-board is sound value at this out-of-town hotel in a beautiful garden with tennis court. Heated indoor swimming-pool, sauna. Restaurant is residents only, staid and so-so.

PREDAZZO
Bellaria, LL; *Corso de Gasperi 20; tel. 046 251 369; credit cards*, AE, DC, E, MC, V; *closed May, Oct, Nov; restaurant closed Wed*.

Sauna, swimming-pool and civilized amenities. Value for money. Inexpensive restaurant, varied cuisine.

SAN MARTINO DI CASTROZZA
San Martino, LL; *tel. 043 968 011; credit cards*, V; *closed mid-Apr to end Jun, mid-Sep to mid-Dec*.

Maintains calm, friendly atmosphere amid much to-ing and fro-ing in ski season. Heated swimming-pool, sauna, tennis. Splendid views of Dolomites' most celebrated groups. Reliable restaurant (**L-LL**) is often busy, but you are not hustled.

roads and mountain torrents meet. Christmas and Easter are busy times for the 'white sport'. Thanks to sheltering hills and dry light airs the snows are as crisp and even in April as in December.

SAN MARTINO DI CASTROZZA ⋈

One of the Dolomites' winter-sports success stories. The insignificant village of half a century ago is now a smart town of villas and hotels with the latest in tourist arrangements and ski installations. Its location under the sheer precipice known as the **Pale of San Martino** contributes to its fame. Vast snowfields above are the site of regular national and international skiing contests. A national ski-school is here with every opportunity for novices. San Martino, to which luxury coaches bring people from as far afield as Genoa and Florence, goes like a fair with icy games and sports in winter and early spring.

SEGONZANO

Village of **Val di Cembra**, noted for Earthen Pyramids (see Soprabolzano, below).

SELLA GROUP

See Selva, below.

SELVA DI VAL GARDENA

On Route 243, 20 km E of Ponte Gardena. In a bowl of the mountains at 1,600 m, it is sheltered by pine forests. About 30 ski-lifts transport passengers to slopes 1,000 m higher. Great walking country. A base for mountaineers attempting the conquest of the Sella and Sassolungo peaks. One km from Plan, terminus of branch railway from the main Bolzano-Brenner line.

SOPRABOLZANO

The **Ritten plateau**, calm and leafy in summer, is a delight to the middle-aged and elderly. In winter it has cross-country ski trails. Until 1966 the brown-and-white cars of the Ritten rack (cog and pinion) railway went grinding and clattering all the way from Bolzano. Now it is reduced to a 12-km section between Soprabolzano and Collalbo. To cross the plateau, leave your car in the valley, take the cableway and either follow well-defined hiking paths or ride the rack railway, facing north

for fantastic views of the principal Dolomite ranges.

On your route is the phenomenon of the **Earthen Pyramids** (as at Segonzano, above). They are a group of sandstone towers 20-30 m high, conical with flat stone slabs perched on top. They look artificial but are not. They result from the erosion of a hill, the rocky slabs having prevented the soil under them from being washed away. If, as occasionally happens, a slab slips off, that is the end of the Earthen Pyramid.

TRENTO
See Italy Overall: 5.

VAL GARDENA
See Ponte Gardena, page 160.

Northern Italy

Garda

156 km; map Touring Club Italiano Lombardia

Of all the great lakes of northern Italy, Lake Garda is the greatest. Being of regular shape, a sort of slender triangle, it is one of the shortest to drive around. The touring coaches do it in the day with two or three stops. Twenty times the passengers ask the name of some place briefly glimpsed, with a view to going there for their holidays next year. Comparisons between lakes renowned for their beauty are inappropriate but many people consider Garda the most attractive. Goethe did. He stayed at Torbole and declared the bright blue Garda 'the greatest marvel of creation' – and the German poet was not given to extravagant expression. He was among the first of the German tourists who now arrive by the hundred thousand, by far the most numerous of foreign visitors. From Frankfurt and Munich you can get day trips to this oasis of Mediterranean light and colour.

We suggest a straightforward circuit of the lake: allow two days. Access to the southern shore is from the A4 *autostrada* which passes within metres of Desenzano, Sirmione and Peschiera. Slip roads go to all three. Or you can come in from the Brescia junction, arriving at Salò on what they call the Brescian Riviera (a preponderance of cars with BR number-plates tells you why). From Rovereto or Trento on the A22 Brenner *autostrada* you can reach Lake Garda's narrow northern tip.

Going clockwise from the south, Desenzano to Salò is inland and almost suburban. Salò to Gargnano follows a coastline which grows ever more rugged, precipitous and clothed in greenery. From Gargnano to Riva is an incredible road. We counted 70 tunnels in 40 km. Cliff-framed windows give almost subliminal bursts of sun, lake and fantastic opposite shore until you are dazzled with the stroboscopic flicker. The road is narrow. Clumps of rock thrust themselves in your path. There is rarely a parking bay or passing place and local traffic has developed an unofficial one-way system – southbound mornings, northbound afternoons as we write, but check before leaving Gargnano or Riva.

The eastern or Venetian shore from Torbole to Bardolino is embroidered with forts, villas and resorts. Sixty years ago there was no road, but now you move quite smoothly. The adjacent motorway has creamed off much commercial traffic. The lake's south-east corner is dull – if your eventual destination is Verona, you might as well cut off at Lazise. In that case, see Sirmione before you start the circuit.

TRANSPORT
Airport: Verona (international charters in summer).

The Milan-Venice main railway passes close to the southern shore with stations at Desenzano and Peschiera.

All communities on and near Lake Garda are served by local buses. The principal bus stations are at Desenzano, Salò, Riva and Peschiera. To and from Verona, Brescia and Rovereto there are frequent bus services and excursions to different parts of the lake. A regular service to and from Milan is operated by Autostradale, Piazzale Castello 1, Milan.

Boat services on the lake are comprehensive, some would say too much so. A fleet of 80 vessels operates hourly services between Riva, Torbole, Limone, Sirmione, Desenzano, Peschiera, Malcesine, Brenzone, Gargnano, Salò, Garda and Bardolino. A hydrofoil links Peschiera with Sirmione. The car-ferry between Maderno and Torri del Benaco takes 30 mins. Principal operators are Gestione Navigazione Laghi, Via Lodovico Ariosto 21, Milan; and Navigazione Lago Garda, Piazza Matteoti, Desenzano. The latter company has a programme of summer cruises on the lake.

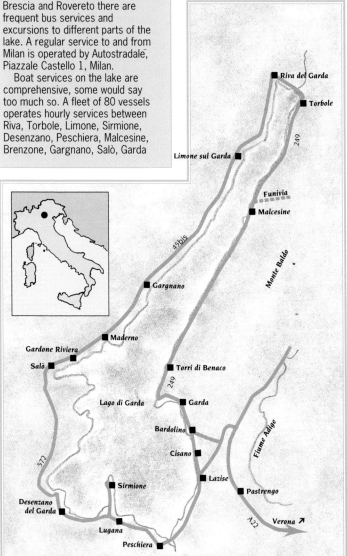

SIGHTS & PLACES OF INTEREST

BARDOLINO
A flourishing resort with a sleepy tourist office. Like Lazise (see page 165) it is partly enclosed in medieval walls. The famous Bardolino wine, grown on slopes behind the town, has suffered, like neighbouring Valpolicella, from over-production. The prestige commodity is D.O.C. olive oil. Its **factory** and **museum**, open daily, are 2 km south at Cisano. Ecclesiastical buffs should seek out the **9thC chapel** dedicated to San Zeno the black saint (see also Verona, Italy Overall: 2).

CISANO
See Bardolino, left.

DESENZANO DEL GARDA ✕
It has watersports, excursion boats and boatyards but has fallen behind in the tourist race. An old castle built on Roman ruins has been turned into an army barracks. A few dilapidated churches are shabby curiosities of the fabled shore. In **Santa Maria Maddalena** is a *Last Supper* ascribed to Tiepolo. Many people pass through Desenzano, few of them stay. The monastery of **Maguzzano**, 3 km west on a barren hill, has dim frescos, vestiges of one-time opulence.

RECOMMENDED HOTELS

GARDONE
Grand Hotel Fasano, LLL; *Corso Zanardelli 160, Fasano; tel. 036 521 051; credit cards, E, MC, V; closed in winter.*
    On a small promontory north of town. Some rooms have balconies. Swimming-pool, tennis, private beach adjacent to water-sports. Terrace garden. Sheer luxury.

Montefiori, LL; *tel. 036 521 118; credit cards, E, MC; closed Nov.*
    Secluded in parkland on hill above the lake. Rooms have balconies and attractive furnishings. Lovely terrace for meals in summer.

GARGNANO
Giulia, LL; *tel. 036 571 022; credit cards, AE, DC, V; closed Nov-Mar.*
    Stunning situation above lake with own beach and heated swimming-pool. Most of the prettily-furnished rooms have balconies. An elegant interior dining-room with chandeliers and antiques is the alternative to a dining terrace among palms.

LAZISE
Case Mia, LL; *on Route 249, 2 km S of Lazise; tel. 045 647 0244; credit cards, AE, E, MC, V; closed mid-Dec to mid-Jan.*
    The modern building in its large garden has 39 roomy apartments, sauna, swimming-pool. Golf course nearby. Half-board is a sound option.

RIVA DEL GARDA
Du Lac et du Parc, LLL; *Viale Rovereto 44; tel. 046 455 1500; credit cards, AE, DC, E, MC, V; closed in winter; restaurant closed Mon.*
    A genuinely 'grand' seaside hotel in large well-kept grounds with statuary. All amenities, everything designed for gracious living. Tennis-courts, sauna, swimming-pool. Prestige restaurant.

TORBOLE
Club Hotel La Vela, LL-LLL; *tel. 046 450 5940; credit cards, AE, DC, E, MC, V.*
    This backstreet villa with its compact little garden was built to meet increasing popularity of a charming resort. Five minutes from beach. Fairly spartan 'utility' furnishings, rooms a tight fit, but we recommend it because the atmosphere is so light and airy and the staff combine military efficiency with just the right degree of friendliness. Restaurant is undistinguished and occasionally crowded with excursion parties.

TORRI DEL BENACO
Gardesana, LL; *Piazza Calderini; tel. 045 722 5411; credit cards, AE, DC, E, MC, V; closed Nov, Dec.*
    On the main piazza near harbour with views across the lake. Furnished with quiet good taste, this long-established hotel has been patronized by British prime ministers and Hollywood stars.

GARDA

The town gives its name to the lake. It did so in Roman times, when both were called Benacus (**Torri di Benaco**, 7 km north, where the car-ferry crosses to Maderno, preserves the old name). A walled stronghold under the striking headland of **San Vigilio**, Garda nestles peaceably among cypress and olive and Venetian villas whose gardens fall to the shore. From the **Camaldoli hermitage** above the town, an easy climb of about 300 m, you have wonderful views to the south and west. Beyond the hill, 3 km from Garda, is a large **German military cemetery**.

GARDONE RIVIERA ⚓ ✕

Here begins the **'Brescian Riviera'** with aquatic fun, noisy speedboats and waterfront fish restaurants in full measure. The **Hruska botanical gardens**, $^1/_2$ km north, remain unaccountably unpopular. It cannot be said of **Villa Vittoriale** next door, one of the lake's most ostentatious villas though hardly the most attractive. Gabriele d'Annunzio (see also Pescara, Italy Overall: 4) was its owner and the gardens are a pompous testimony to his mad career as soldier and poet. The souvenirs are so bizarre that by the time you come to the bow-section of a 4,000-ton Italian cruiser, salvaged from the sea bed off the Dalmatian coast, the incongruity fails to shock. D'Annunzio died in 1938, during the Fascist heyday, when his bellicose deeds and extravagant poetry were taught and recited in schools. Mention him today and the Italians smile and change the subject.

GARGNANO ⚓ ✕

The delicate structure of an antique **Franciscan cloister** is to be admired. Everything else is smart, modern and tourist-orientated. Look at Gargnano from the lake, or look north up the lake from Gargnano and you will see the culmination of that inimitable combination of blue water, glossy foliage and grey cliffs which summarizes the magic of this Italian scene.

LAZISE ⚓

Best seen at a quiet time, which is

RECOMMENDED RESTAURANTS

DESENZANO
Cavallino, LL-LLL; *Via Gherla 22; tel. 030 912 0217; credit cards*, AE, DC, E, MC, V; *closed Mon, Tues lunch.*

Garda cuisine has an international flavour but standards are high. Here the pasta comes with a light fresh parsley sauce and wine list includes the local Lugana.

GARDONE
Villa Fiordaliso, LL; *Via Zanardelli 132; tel. 036 520 158; credit cards*, AE, DC, E, MC, V; *closed Mon; rooms unavailable Jan to mid-Feb.*

Patrician villa once owned by Mussolini's mistress. Attractive lakeside terrace for summer meals. Menu based on local produce is strong on *funghi*. A few rooms are available (**LL**).

GARGNANO
La Tortuga, LLL; *tel. 036 571 251; credit cards*, AE, V; *closed Jan to mid-Mar, Tues.*

Imaginative cuisine includes *soufflé di verdure* (with green vegetables) and *tagliolini ai gamberi* (pasta with shrimps) garnished with courgette flowers. Wine list has vintages from nearby Franciacorta vineyards. Reservation essential.

LUGANA
Vecchia Lugana, LL-LLL; *on 'mainland' near Sirmione promontory; tel. 030 919 012; credit cards*, AE, DC, E, MC, V; *closed early Jan to mid-Feb, Mon eve, Tues.*

Lakeside restaurant with panoramic terrace. Specializes in lake fish and grills. An interesting fish terrine. Wide choice of vegetarian dishes. Lugana, naturally, is the wine.

SIRMIONE
Grifone da Luciano, LL; *Via delle Bisse 5; tel. 030 916 097; credit cards*, AE, DC, E, MC, V; *closed Wed, Nov-Easter.*

Al fresco meals on beautiful lakeside terrace in shade of the famous Scaliger castle. Traditional cuisine, enlivened with local specialities. Near a small hotel of same name (**L-LL**).

• *Regatta, Lake Garda.*

rarely possible, Lazise is like a scale model of itself, a diminutive fortress-by-the-water, locked in a tiny circle of walls, opening through hollowed caverns, each with a fishing-boat parked inside, to a low quayside with a derelict **Customs House** on it and a 14thC **castle** behind. The cottages battle bravely to preserve their character against a rising tide of cafés, bars and motor boats. Six kilometres east on the main road to Verona, at Pastrengo, is the **Parco Natura Viva**, comprising safari trails, a tropical garden, a 'dinosaur' sanctuary and a centre for the preservation of threatened species. Open all day every day with restricted hours in winter. There are picnic areas and a restaurant.

LIMONE SUL GARDA
For centuries the lemon (*limone*) was the life-blood of this town on the Lombard shore of the lake. They claim that lemons were first grown here, which Sicilians hotly deny. Now the groves are full of campsites and Limone,

hemmed in by near-vertical cliffs, trembles with the reverberation of tourist traffic in and out of the tunnels on the Gardesana (lakeside highway). Between here and Riva the scenery is too grand for close-up views. But to compensate you have the aromatic shrubbery and the sight, across 3 km of sparkling lake, of a similar array of cliffs, steep-to to the water and crowned with olives and flowering bushes.

MADERNO
See Garda, page 165.

MALCESINE
One of the largest townships on the Venetian shore and centre of the densest concentration of camping and caravan parks. Its red roofs cluster beneath the clean lines of a 14thC **fort** and **watch-tower** built, as were most of the defences of this eastern shore, by the Scaliger lords of Verona. A

cable car goes 3 km inland to a summit of the **Monte Baldo ridge** at 1,752 m, where a refuge, ski slope and café are established. Tremendous panoramas from this spot, over both lake and Adige valley.

Here you marvel at the daring, or desperation, of the 15thC Venetian military command. Lake Garda had fallen into Lombard hands. A frontal assault from the south was ruled out. Instead the Venetian commander sailed warships up the Adige, drew them with teams of oxen across the mountain and re-launched them on the lake. The effort deserved better success: the Lombards sank all his ships or drove them on to the rocks.

Four centuries later the Austrians maintained a flotilla of warships on Lake Garda and, in the run-up to Italian independence in the 19thC, they were far from idle. Cannon-balls embedded in the walls of lakeside cottages (you can see a few at Gargnano) are souvenirs of attacks on Garibaldi's troops.

PASTRENGO
See Lazise, *page* 165.

RIVA DEL GARDA 🛏

The handsome old town with its sturdy Venetian tower near the shore and its broad front almost level with the tideless lake might be called the capital of the Garda. It is however neither of the Veneto nor Lombardy: it is in Trentino, a region where Austrian government is still remembered by old inhabitants. Riva's lake front is a scene of bustle and change, and so is the town which slopes upwards behind it on narrowing clambering streets full of little everyday shops and perfumed with the displays of florists, fruiterers and greengrocers.

Two major 20thC authors nearly met at Riva. D.H. Lawrence was here with his German bride in 1912. 'Quite beautiful', he wrote, 'and perfectly Italian... roses, oleanders and grapes in the gardens.' A few weeks later that profound and original writer Franz Kafka came on holiday. 'Riva was very important to me', he wrote. He lost his virginity and composed the enigmatic story *The Hunter Gracchus*, inspired by a 'clumsy old craft' which lay moored at Riva's flat quayside.

Every morning the breeze takes hundreds of dinghies out from Riva, every afternoon the never-failing land breeze brings them back (just as well, since many are crewed single-handed by subteenagers). With them go the windsurfers: the Garda's northern shore is the world metropolis of windsurfing, thanks to those predictable winds. All afternoon the multi-coloured sails and the surfers in very wet wet-suits are swept ashore. It makes for some hilarity among the spectators who line the grainy beach between Riva and Torbole.

SALO
It is not among the Garda's most fashionable towns but it is clean and neat and it has had its moment of history. After the collapse of Fascism in 1943 the Germans installed Mussolini here as dictator of the ignominious and short-lived Republic of Salò. It embarrasses the citizens slightly to be reminded of it.

SIRMIONE ✕
The brightest jewel in Garda's crown is a water-borne citadel at the tip of a 3-km sandy promontory. The pedestrian ways, the lush gardens and fruit groves, the grotto, villa, small church with 14thC frescos, hot springs, aqueduct and extreme congestion in the holiday season make it a place to see but not to linger in. Catullus the Roman poet had a villa here; so did Toscanini the conductor, 2,000 years after him.

TORBOLE 🛏
As at Riva, the young and amphibious provide for the shorebound a day-long spectacle of water acrobatics. There are decent fish restaurants along the gritty beach and several old-fashioned sandstone houses in the town centre – one of them identified as the lodging of Johann Wolfgang von Goethe. Torbole is chiefly residential and seems to have more success than most Italian places in coping with noise pollution. Streets at night are deserted and only a keen ear picks up the disco cellar's *leitmotif*.

TORRI DI BENACO
See Garda, *page* 165.

VERONA
See Italy Overall: 2.

Northern Italy
Between Treviso and Trieste

450 km; map Touring Club Italiano Veneto

Bordered on the west by Lake Garda and on the east by Slovenia and stretching from the Alps to the Po Valley and Adriatic Sea, the former domains of Venice La Serenissima – the Veneto and Venezia Giulia – present a diverse range of attractions. In churches and museums the arts are well represented: this is the territory of Palladio and Canova, of Titian, Veronese and Giorgione. The area is better known to Italians than to foreign travellers, who usually stop short at Vicenza, Padua or Venice.

There is also a culture of gastronomy. Local delicacies include *sopressa* (salted pork), *polenta* (savoury porridge), cheeses – and mushrooms. At one restaurant we had seven consecutive courses of *funghi*. Peppers, asparagus, chestnuts and red chicory are important ingredients. The Alps shelter both regions and encourage the growth of cherries, strawberries, peaches and citrus fruits. In Venezia Giulia the local pasta is filled with unusual flavours, even sweet ones, and the overlap of an eastern European cuisine is detectable in the horse-radish, paprika and poppy seed which season meats and game.

Our tour provides something for every taste: lidos of the Adriatic, mountains and lakes of the Valsugana with awe-inspiring prospects of the Dolomites; fortified hill towns such as Asolo and fortress cities of the so-called 'Quadrilateral' of Venice's defensive system against incursions from the north; richly-decorated Palladian villas; two wine routes; and the stately city of Trieste, hardly known to tourists. Students of military history and readers of Ernest Hemingway's *A Farewell to Arms* will recognize place-names on the ground which Italy contested with Austria in 1917-18 – the straggling rivers of Tagliamento, Piave and Isonzo; Caporetto, Italy's disgrace (now Kobarid in Slovenia) and Vittorio Veneto, Italy's redemption.

In the fertile Sile Valley around Treviso piecemeal development and ugly modern factories have done the environment no favours. The urban sprawl is an endless succession of junctions and traffic lights. This is the price you pay to reach some memorable places and it is some consolation that, as you travel farther from Venice, you leave the congestion behind and enter a beautiful natural landscape.

If you have two more days to spare, combine this tour with the Dolomites (Local Explorations: 4) by heading north from Bassano or Vittorio Veneto.

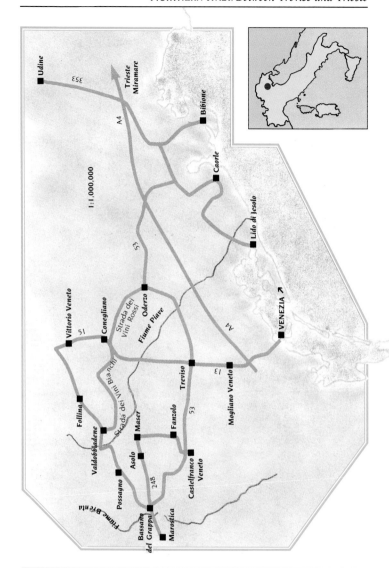

1:1,000,000

TRANSPORT

Airports: international and domestic at Venice (Marco Polo) and Trieste; domestic only at Treviso.

Considering the rail network as erected on the Venice-Trieste axis, the principal lines are Venice-Belluno, Venice-Treviso and Trieste-Udine. Cross-country branch lines link all these places with one another.

Venice is an important destination for long-distance buses Europe-wide. Trieste is a stopover on the routes between northern Europe and Greece and Turkey. The regional networks are comprehensive and it is hardly possible to name a village which is not visited at least once a day by a bus. If progress is slow through urban areas, you fairly skim along the smooth, straight country roads.

The company which operates bus services over most of the Veneto and Dolomiti regions is Dolomiti Bus, Via Sant' Andrea 5, Belluno.

169

• *Bassano del Grappa.*

SIGHTS & PLACES OF INTEREST

ASOLO 🏨
'Town of one hundred horizons,' wrote Carducci the poet. A typical hill-top town of carefully-preserved architecture, it predates the Roman era. Famous residents include Queen Caterina Cornaro who exchanged Cyprus for it; Eleanora Duse the actress; Freya Stark, late veteran travel writer; and Robert Browning, much of whose poetry it inspired. 'Pippa' of Browning's *Pippa Passes* was a weaver here. Browning's son Pen founded the Embroidery School to help employment. **Via R. Browning**, with its shops and ateliers under Gothic arcades, leads to central double piazzas where lively antiques markets are held on the second Saturday and Sunday of each month.

DETOUR – BOSCO DEL CONSIGLIO
On Route 422, about 18 km northeast of Vittorio Veneto, is a regional novelty: a magnificent beech and pine forest, the third largest in Italy, called Bosco del Consiglio or 'Council Wood'.

Note that Vittorio does not mean 'victory' as you might suppose. It honours Vittore Emanuele I, first king of Italy (1866).

Observe the **Zen fountain** and, crowning the hill, the **Rocca** which was first a Roman fort and then Queen Caterina's palace. Inside it is the **Eleanora Duse theatre**. Behind the 15thC **Loggia del Capitano**'s frescoed façade is the civic museum. Important paintings of the Venetian school are also in the **cathedral**, on top of ancient Roman baths. Asolo, the most interesting place for miles around, is said to have inspired the verb *asolare*, to amuse oneself at random in the open air.

BASSANO DEL GRAPPA 🏨
To the north, through the Valsugana gorges (canoes and winter sports) the **River Brenta** is a powerful torrent. It is strong but tame by the time it arrives in Bassano, where it flows under the picturesque **Ponte degli Alpini**, Palladio's 16thC covered wooden bridge. (Many times swept away in floods, it has been many times patiently rebuilt.)

Monte Grappa, 20 km north, 1,775 m, gives its name to the town and its famous fiery spirit *grappa*, drunk all over Italy. Shops also sell ceramics from nearby Nove, noted for Venetian-style pottery.

Marostica, 7 km south-west, a town of the Venetian 'Quadrilateral', offers life-size chess every September, the human 'pieces' wearing 15thC costume – set up originally by a peace-loving local noble as a duel for the hand of his daughter.

BIBIONE
See Lido di Jesolo, this page .

CAORLE
See Lido di Jesolo, this page.

CASTELFRANCO VENETO 🛏 ✕
The *città vecchia* is enclosed within a 13thC citadel. Giorgione the painter was born here and his house is still standing after 500 years. See his *Madonna* in the cathedral: its exuberant colouring scandalized his contemporaries; see also the **Teatro Accademico**, a riot of pink and gold inside, completely over the top. It is visitable when not in use for jazz concerts.

CONEGLIANO ✕
This fortified old town at the junction of Red and White Wine routes (see The Red and White Wine Routes, page 172) has the **birthplace and museum of Giambattista Cima** (1459-1518), innovative Renaissance painter. The date 1492 is scratched under the plaster. A lovely cathedral in the town centre, but car parking is not easy.

FANZOLO
See Detour – Villa Emo, page 172.

LIDO DI JESOLO
Along this once-neglected, marshy littoral a number of mass-tourism resorts flourish. Lido di Jesolo is perhaps the most organized (or regimented) in the

---

RECOMMENDED HOTELS

ASOLO
Villa Cipriani, LLL; *Via Canova* 298; *tel.* 042 355 444; *credit cards*, AE, DC, E, MC, V.

Luxury pad, off-shoot of famous Venice establishment in beautiful surroundings with every facility and all the grovelling flunkeyism that goes with such places. Patronized by royalty. Restaurant noted for rich and creative cuisine based on local produce. Formal dress expected for dinner.

BASSANO DEL GRAPPA
Belvedere, LL; *Piazzale Giardino* 14; *tel.* 042 429 845; *credit cards*, AE, DC, E, MC, V.

The 15thC building is now a hotel in the grand tradition with elegant modern interior, 90 rooms with all amenities, restaurant with shady terrace, piano bar, garage.

CASTELFRANCO VENETO
Ca' delle Rose, L; *Via Circonvallazione Est*; *tel.* 042 349 0232; *credit cards*, AE, E, MC, V.

Three km north-east of town in Salvarosa district, the hotel is conspicuous for flamboyant rose terraces. Bar, secure car parking, access for disabled. **Barbesin** restaurant (see page 173) next door.

MOGLIANO VENETO
Villa Condulmer, LLL; *at Zerman*, 10 *km S of Treviso by Route* 13; *tel.* 041 457 100; *credit cards*, AE, DC, E, MC, V; *closed Jan, first half Feb; restaurant closed Mon.*

Period interior with frescos, chandeliers and antiques restores 18thC Venice to this handsome villa set in parkland with two golf courses at hand. Tennis, swimming. Restaurant (**LL**).

TREVISO
Relais el Toula, LLL; *Via Postumia* 63, *Paderno di Ponzano*, 8 *km N of town; tel.* 042 296 9191; *credit cards*, AE, DC, V.

Delightful small hotel annexed to gourmet restaurant. Exclusive and expensive. Tranquil surroundings, swimming-pool. A really de luxe hideaway. Only ten rooms, so booking is essential.

UDINE
Boschetti, LL; *Piazza Mazzini* 10, *Tricesimo*, 12 *km N of Udine by Route* 13; *tel.* 043 285 1230; *credit cards*, AE, DC, E, MC, V; *closed* 1-23 *Aug; restaurant closed Mon.*

An excellent overnight stop. Half-board a bargain because restaurant (**LLL**) is renowned far and wide. The menu changes with the seasons. Look out for *capesante* (scallops) in summer from Grado. A very good Tokai on the wine list.

matter of hotel-controlled sand strips, umbrellas and chairs; and a vast range of aquatic activities is available. Off National Route 14, between Venice and Trieste, you can head for the beach at many intersections. **Bibione**, **Eraclea** and **Lignano** are sun, sea and sand, like Jesolo. The small seaside town of **Caorle**, 36 km east of Lido di Jesolo, has escaped development and retains its characteristic architecture, including a sturdy **Romanesque cathedral** with a cylindrical campanile. **Grado** on its lagoon, 47 km south of Udine on Route 352, via the classical port of **Aquilea**, now several kilometres inland, has a beautiful beach where, among other attractions, the therapeutic properties of sea water are exploited. Grado also has quaint fishermen's houses and an **early Christian church** (Sant' Eufemia).

MAROSTICA
See Bassano del Grappa, page 170.

MASER
The great attraction is **Villa Barbaro**, joint work of Palladio the architect,

---

DETOUR – VILLA EMO
Eight km north-east of Castelfranco Veneto at Fanzolo is Villa Emo, a Palladian jewel in stone. A long avenue leads up to the porch where Zelotti's mythological frescos begin. They continue through the house. No faded masterpieces here: the colours have retained an almost psychedelic brilliance.

Veronese the painter and Alessandro Vittoria the sculptor. Commissioned about 1560 for a Venetian nobleman, it contains vivid frescos, amazing *trompe-l'oeil* paintings, statuary and fine stucco work. A **collection of carriages** of all eras and nations is housed nearby. Still inhabited, the house has restricted opening times – currently 3-5 or 6 pm, Tues, Sat, Sun.

MIRAMARE
See Trieste, page 173.

ODERZO
Coloured mosaics in the **civic museum** confirm the town's Roman origins. Among palaces and frescoed buildings of great charm is an art gallery dedicated to surrealist engraver **Alberto Martini** with many of his works.

POSSAGNO
Antonio Canova, the neo-classical sculptor (1757-1822), was born here. Inside the museum his studio is intact, with sketches, paintings and outsize models and in the temple close by, which he designed himself, is his tomb.

TREVISO ⊭ ✕
Some guide-books enthuse over Treviso; we find it dull and charmless. The few worthwhile buildings discourage visitors with their short opening hours. A reading of the place-name's derivation – 'three-faced' – is unkindly applied to the citizens. See the **San Nicolo monastery**, the 15thC **Lombard Cathedral** with Titian's *Annunciation* in a side chapel, the 14thC **Loggia dei Cavalieri** with its arcaded cafés and the main street **Via Calmaggiore** with its Palazzo dei Trecento ('trecento' means '300') where the old-time councillors, 150 nobles and 150 commoners, dispensed law and justice.

THE RED AND WHITE WINE ROUTES
The Strada del Vino Bianco pursues a wavering course from the River Piave near Valdobbiadene to Conegliano (see Conegliano, page 171) through 40 km of foothills and vineyards. The Strada del Vino Rosso continues the vineyard route between Conegliano and Oderzo (see Oderzo, this page). Both trails are in-and-out, but signposted; and certain restaurants along them display the wine routes' quality sign.

The white wine is Prosecco, from a grape peculiar to the region. It comes in still (dry) and sparkling (sweet) forms. The reds include Merlot, Pinot, Cabernet and, notably, Raboso, a full-bodied wine from the lower Piave area.

A superior sparkling white, the equivalent of *méthode champenoise* called Opere Trevigiane, is produced at 17thC Villa Sandi near Crocetta del Montello, across the Piave south of Valdobbiadene. Tours of the cellars are sometimes arranged (tel. 042 386 7412).

TRIESTE

The windiest (the cold, fierce *bora* from the Slovenian Alps) and the least Italianate (it was Austria's chief port until 1918) of Italian cities, Trieste ascends San Giusto hill from broad quays, dignified *palazzi*, a 2ndC **Roman theatre**, a baroque **opera theatre** and a huge **museum of history and art** (emblem of the city), meandering into a maze of wine-shops and cheap restaurants and a ramshackle diversity of local colour. Children and adults delight in the venerable **Aquarium** on the front.

Italo Svevo the novelist and his near-contemporary James Joyce lived here – the latter a poverty-stricken exile from Dublin, 1904-06.

Five km west on a promontory is the white dream-castle of **Miramare**, former residence of the Habsburg Archduke Maximilian, later Emperor of Mexico. There is *son et lumière* between June and September. Hereabouts young Henrik Ibsen, emerging from an overnight train journey through the Alps, was overcome by the 'wonderful soft brightness of the South' – start of a lifelong love affair with Italy which, strangely, inspired none of his plays.

UDINE ⛴

Venice has left her mark on this graceful city which traditionally occupies a mound that Attila the Hun built for a viewpoint. The medieval castle, several times rebuilt, now houses the **city museum** and **galleries of ancient and modern art**. **Piazza della Libertà**, one of Italy's most beautiful squares, with arcades and porticoes, has on it a 13thC cathedral with paintings by Tiepolo and the elegant *loggia* of San Giovanni with heroic marble sculptures. Above it rises the short squat Venetian clock-tower with exterior bell and two metal bell-ringers.

VALDOBBIADENE ✕

See The Red and White Wine Routes, page 172.

VITTORIO VENETO

Ever-memorable for the greatest feat of Italian arms, the victory over the Austrians in 1918, this town encompasses two communities, Ceneda and Serravalle. The latter, in a gorge, has a **cathedral** with a Titian alterpiece and fine frescos at the church of **Sant' Andrea**.

RECOMMENDED RESTAURANTS

CASTELFRANCO VENETO

Barbesin, LL; *Via Circonvallazione Est, Salvarosa; tel. 042 349 0446; credit cards, AE, MC; closed Wed eve, Thur, first fortnights in Jan and Aug.*

(See Recommended Hotels, page 171.) The culinary genius of Onorio Barbesin is legendary, his restaurant internationally famed. Varying with season, the menus are strong with artichokes, mushrooms and asparagus; chicory with almost everything, but discreetly applied. Wines including Prosecco and non-Italian vintages are faultlessly presented.

CONEGLIANO

Tre Panoce, LL; *Via Vecchia Trevigiana 50; tel. 043 860 071; credit cards, AE, DC, V; closed Sun eve, Mon, 1-10 Jan, Aug.*

This popular restaurant with garden and easy parking 2 km west of town centre offers some of the best cooking in the region. Traditional and also innovative dishes. Red chicory lurks in former, such combinations as *filetto di gallo al melograno* (chicken with pomegranate) in latter. Tre Panoce is a family concern.

TREVISO

Beccherie, LL; *Piazza Ancillotto 10; tel. 042 254 0871; credit cards, AE, DC, E, MC, V; closed Thur eve, Fri, second half Jul.*

Just north of Palazzo di Trecento, it is busy and lively and serves many regional favourites which other eating places have neither knowledge or patience to bother with. **Campeol Hotel, L**, under same management across the square has acceptable accommodation. Same telephone number, same credit cards.

VALDOBBIADENE

Tre Noghere, L; *at Bigoline, 5 km S of Valdobbiadene; tel. 042 398 0316; credit cards, AE; closed Sun eve, Mon.*

Cheap and cheerful, noted for its careful preparation and presentation of some venerable local specialities.

The Riviera of Flowers

160 km; map Touring Club Italiano Liguria

The Ligurian mountains rush down to the gulf and stop on the brink of the sea. Nevertheless, the Romans managed to squeeze a highway between rock face and water's edge and 19thC Italy went one better with a railway. The highway, the Via Aurelia, is our tour. *Multum in parvo* should be the motto of every town along it: the Italian genius for cramming a great deal into a small space was never more dramatically expressed. With rock-cut steps, lifts and elevators, tunnels and jutting balconies it is astonishing what can be done with a sheer drop.

They call this coastline the Riviera di Ponente ('going down' – west) to distinguish it from the Riviera di Levante ('rising up' – east). Genoa is the midpoint. Our route has no option but to follow the Aurelia – the alternative between Genoa and the French frontier is the *autostrada*, a remarkable road but expensive to travel on and much of it in tunnels. However, it is always alongside you if you feel you can take no more of a road built for two-wheeled chariots rather than 32-wheeled *auto-treni*. The coastal towns run into each other. You will not easily park on any sea front, but turn away at a town-centre crossroads (every town has one) and you will find a flowery piazza, a car-park and an oasis of hotels, restaurants and bars.

This riviera faces south-east. That gives it a climatic advantage over the two rivieras on either side, the French and the Levante. That explains why, before the flower markets of Nice have their spring blooms, you see carnations and gladioli by the truck-load at the railway stations of Savona and Alassio. It also explains why foreign invalids, especially the British, first made Sanremo and Bordighera their Italian winter quarters. A lingering air of elegance and leisure, not yet extinguished by modern tourist impatience, is one of the charms of such places.

Hotels come in two types: *palazzo*-style of fading dignity; and brash new blocks slotted into narrow spaces. Restaurant food is seafood-based but different stretches of the coast have different specialities. In the Ventimiglia area creamed stockfish is a delicacy. Savona is famed for chick-pea pancakes, Noli for fish soup, Alassio for *baci* ('kisses' or sweets), Taggia for *sardenaira* (a salty sardine pizza). Inland villages are blessed with mushrooms, chestnuts, honey and raspberries.

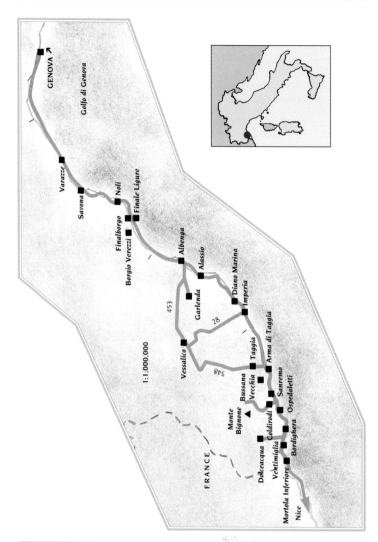

TRANSPORT

The regional airport is at Genoa (Cristoforo Colombo).

The main railway between Genoa and Nice in France runs along the coast. Local trains stop at all stations, fast trains at Savona, Imperia and sometimes Sanremo. All trains stop at the frontier (Ventimiglia). From Ventimiglia a spectacular line goes through the Ligurian hills and across the Colle di Tenda to Cuneo in Piedmont. From Savona there are roundabout rail routes to Turin and Milan.

The principal bus companies, all running frequent services along the coast, less frequently to hinterland towns and villages, are: A.M.T., Via Lagaccio 21, Genoa; Pesci, Corso Perrone 50, Cornigliano (Genoa); and S.A.R., Via Vecchia Morella Albenga, Savona. From Imperia the S.T.P. bus company, of Via Don Abbo il Santo 16, runs buses to Sanremo, Ventimiglia and Nice. An agreeable feature for the not-very-mobile is the frequency of town buses to viewpoints and places of interest within the town or the immediate vicinity.

SIGHTS & PLACES OF INTEREST

ALASSIO
A favourite winter resort of north Europeans for a century. Elgar the British composer celebrated it in music. It has a long stretch of sandy beach, entirely appropriated by hotels. Its most popular building is the **Muretto** or 'little wall' on which every famous visitor inscribes his or her name. Motor-boating, skin-diving, 18-hole golf course. **Jazz festival** in September.

ALBENGA
This town at the Centa River mouth is more spacious than others. It boasts a monumental centre with **early Christian churches** and a **Roman naval museum** (rare finds have been made in the neighbourhood). The **Town Hall** is ancient, a **baptistery** with Byzantine mosaics even older, perhaps 5thC. The **Torsero River** 8 km north has fossil beds. The Centa estuary, though suburbanized, still supports exotic birdlife and **Gallinara Island** offshore is botanically important and a breeding ground for gulls. Visit by arrangement with owner through Albenga tourist office. Networks of **caves** along the shore.

ARMA
A tiny seaport with sunny villas and sub-tropical gardens. The horticultural dazzle of the Riviera of Flowers begins here and runs west, a profusion of bougainvillaea, geraniums, jasmine, magnolia, jacaranda, wistaria and other species.

Arma encourages the arts. The artists are mostly lodged at **Bussana Vecchia**, 1 km inland, their studios, shops and galleries sprouting from the ruins of a place totally abandoned after the earthquake of 1887. Picturesque **Taggia**, 4 km inland, thrives on its antiques markets, every fourth Saturday and Sunday.

BORDIGHERA ⌑ ✕
A haven of the smart set, circa 1900. Lovely gardens on terraces of opulent villas and hotels behind the busy sea front, unseen from road and railway along the sea's edge. Above those wonderful displays of flowers and shrubs, old Bordighera lifts its tiny

squares and alleys. An international **Festival of Humour** – cartoon and poster exhibitions, comedy shows – is held annually, last week in July.

BUSSANA VECCHIA
See Arma, this page.

COLDIRODI
See Sanremo, page 177.

DIANO MARINA
It is distinguished from its neighbours by its package-tour atmosphere. There are two fine old castles: **Diano Castello**, actually a medieval citadel-village, 3 km inland; and **Cervo**, 5 km east along the coast. At Pontedassio, 9 km inland, is the world-famous **Spaghetti Museum**. The 700-year history and mythology of Italy's staple diet is displayed and explained. Open daily, pm only.

DOLCEACQUA
See Ventimiglia, page 179.

FINALBORGO
See Finale Ligure, below.

FINALE LIGURE ⌑
A superior resort patronized by well-heeled Italian families. There are boat trips from the port, skin-diving and water-skiing and a climbing school for the fantastic rocks behind the town. Exceptionally pretty, well-tended gardens. Caves along the shore. An interesting **civic museum** in a nunnery at Finalborgo, the old town 1.5 km away. In the **Valdemino grottoes**, 2 km south-west, classical drama is performed in July. At **Pietra Ligure**, 6 km west, the Nostralino wine *sagra* (feast) is held during the first two weeks in June. Gastronomic *sagra* last week in August.

GENOA ⌑ ✕
See Italy Overall: 1.

IMPERIA
A sizeable town (40,000 inhabitants) where two riviera economies meet. At **Porto Maurizio** on the west side the flower-growing begins, at **Oneglia** to the east the olive-oil, pasta and wine production.

Sailing schools and all aquatic amusements. **Naval museum** is worthwhile, **civic art gallery** so-so.

You could make a foray from Imperia into the sharp-faced hostile-looking hills where cosy little villages are embedded. Cross the *autostrada* and follow the Imperia torrent on Route 28. At Vessalico turn east and return to the coast at Albenga (total distance 47 km) or west to the coast at Arma (71 km).

MORTOLA INFERIORE
See Ventimiglia, page 179.

NOLI
Few travellers stop without particular reason, but in its days as a maritime republic Noli was the biggest port on the coast west of Genoa. Arcaded streets and stairways confirm its antiquity. The old monuments are in decay but **San Paragorio's church** and **Monte Ursino Castle** still put a brave face on the seascape, as they did when giving mariners their bearings past the headland. A fish soup called *ciuppin* is Noli's contribution to culinary variety. The harbour and sea front are popular with small-boat sailors, water-skiers and water-parachutists. Cliff scenery is as impressive as anything in the Gulf of Genoa and the wildlife and botany are rare and rewarding.

As far inland as the *autostrada* (8 km) the whole promontory is a protected area. Panoramic roads give easy access and there are campsites among the forests of maritime pine.

To climb the headland at **Capo Noli** take the steep track from Caverna dei Flasari 100 m west of the cavern mouth and follow the waymark (a red barred circle) to the summit at 280 m.

SANREMO
Best-known to holiday-makers for its **casino**, one of only four in Italy, Sanremo carries into the era of mass

RECOMMENDED HOTELS

BORDIGHERA
Villa Elisa, LL; *Via Romana 70; tel. 018 426 1313; credit cards, AE, E, MC, V; closed Nov, Dec 1-21.*

Situated in residential suburbs near beach but away from noisy town centre. Own swimming-pool, car parking, beautiful sub-tropical garden. Restaurant with terrace. Rooms are large and traditionally furnished.

FINALE LIGURE
Punta Est, LLL; *Via Aurelia 1; tel. 019 600 611; credit cards, AE, MC, V; closed Oct-Apr.*

Luscious terraced garden surrounds this peaceful 18thC villa overlooking sea above the town and main road. Sensitive refurbishment has preserved the character of the house, which is furnished with antiques. Breakfast in conservatory, other meals in rustic-style restaurant noted for seafood. Car parking.

GARLENDA
La Meridiana, LLL; *tel. 018 258 0271; credit cards, AE, DC, E, MC, V; closed Jan, Feb; restaurant closed lunch except Jun-Sep.*

One km from village, 12 km from coast, set in lovely gardens. Rooms have satellite TV. Non-smoking areas. Swimming-pool, sauna. 18-hole golf course at hand.

GENOA
Agnello d'Oro, LL; *Vico delle Monachette 6; tel. 010 262 084; credit cards, DC, E, MC, V.*

Close to old port and main railway station. Thirty-five recently-modernized rooms. Air-conditioning. Very reasonable prices for a city hotel. No restaurant but Genoa has many (see Recommended Restaurants, page 178).

OSPEDALETTI
Delle Rose, L; *Via de Medici 17; tel. 018 468 9016; credit cards, none; open all year; restaurant closed Mon.*

Aptly-named small hotel in garden of exotic plants including thousands of cacti. About 0.5 km from beach. Rooms plain but comfortable. TV lounge, bar, restaurant. Car parking.

VENTIMIGLIA
La Riserva, LL; *at Castel d'Appio, 4 km W of Ventimiglia; tel. 018 422 9533; credit cards, AE, DC, E, MC, V; closed Jan-Easter, mid-Sep to mid-Dec.*

Car parking, swimming-pool, tennis, shady garden; all set in hills at 344 m; distant sea views. Good restaurant, terrace bar.

tourism only a few relics of gracious old watering-place days. Now the action persists day and night to the accompaniment of a ceaseless ground-bass of traffic on the coastal road. Brilliant gardens and scented commerce proclaim the centre of the Riviera of Flowers. The growers supply early blooms, especially carnations, to florists and garden centres all over Italy and neighbouring regions of France.

The medieval nucleus, designated **La Pigna**, is intact. From the central piazza you can ascend **Monte Bignone** (1,300 m) in the cable car and see a long way into France. A few kilometres west of the cableway is the bijou village of **Coldirodi** with its Rambaldi gallery and paintings by Velasquez and Veronese (open daily, pm only).

Sanremo, contemporary with Cannes beyond the frontier, was the Italian Riviera's first resort and is still its largest. Except on artificial beaches which belong to the hotels, bucket-and-spade facilities are poor. It is however heavily into sailing and water-sports.

SAVONA
The chief city of the Riviera di Ponente, the most industrialized, and the main seaport west of Genoa. Tourist boat excursions, sailing and water-sports. Noted for two culinary peculiarities: *farinata*, a flat cake of corn and chick-peas and *fette*, small fried chick-pea cakes.

TAGGIA
See *Arma, page* 176.

VARAZZE
The old maritime stronghold still has its medieval walls and a sandy beach, open to all. Pine-woods to east and west, well-developed water-sports in both neighbouring resorts of **Albisola** and **Arenzano**. Quieter, with more character to its scenery, than most riviera resorts.

RECOMMENDED RESTAURANTS

BORDIGHERA
Le Chaudron, I I -LLL; Piazza Bengasi 2; *tel.* 018 426 3592; *credit cards,* AE, DC, E, MC, V; *closed first fortnights Feb and Jul.*

Trattoria in town centre, popular with locals, best to book. Mainly seafood – lobster sauce was a piquant accompaniment to spaghetti. Proximity to French border accounts for *coquilles St Jacques* and other Provençal treats.

BORGIO VEREZZI
Doc, LLL; 3 km W of Finale Ligure; *tel.* 019 611 477; *credit cards,* V; *closed Feb, Mon and Tues in winter, lunch in Aug.*

Paradise for seafood addicts. Try *trofie con scampi e rosmarino* (a gnocchi-scampi-herbs dish). Seasonal fish are cooked in wine. Black truffles in season (autumn). Excellent wine list.

GENOA
Zeffirino, LLL; Via Settembre 20; *tel.* 010 591 990; *credit cards,* AE, DC, E, MC, V; *closed Wed.*

Popular city-centre restaurant. Bizarre decoration blends ancient and modern. Chef makes inventive use of home-made pasta in all forms. Menu changes often but all is mouth-watering.

7 Nasi, LL; Via Quarto 16, Quarto dei Mille; *tel.* 010 337 357; *credit cards,* AE, DC, E, MC, V; *closed Tues.*

In historic suburb east of city centre. Delightful waterfront location near beach, harbour and swimming-pool. Outdoor meals in summer. Menu is predominantly seafood (a highlight is *zuppa di datteri*, clam chowder, when in season) and strong on desserts.

VENTIMIGLIA
Balzi Rossi, LLL; Ponte San Ludovico, 8 km W of Ventimiglia; *tel.* 018 438 132; *credit cards,* AE, DC, E, MC, V; *closed Mon, Tues lunch, first half Mar, last half Nov.*

Menu varies with season but seafood grill and typical Ligurian cuisine are always reliable and served with panache. Fine wine list includes crisp whites and famous Rossese of Dolceacqua. Eat in summer on panoramic terrace.

• *Albenga, the duomo.*

VENTIMIGLIA 🛏 ✕

It is kept in a state of constant turmoil with the comings and goings of excursionists from the French Riviera. Masses of exuberant flowers cascade down the slopes, the **flower market** is pre-eminent above all others. There are caves on the shore, the wreck of a castle on the hill above the town, an **archaeological museum** in the town itself and a sailing school at the harbour. Do not miss **Villa Hanbury**, the most extensive botanical acclimatization garden in all the Mediterranean lands. The overpowering array of exotic plants and shrubs (even in January, says the curator, there are more than 200 species in bloom) owes its existence to Thomas Hanbury, the English *milord* who laid the place out on the sea-facing terraces of Capo Mortola in 1867. His descendants handed it to the Italian Government in 1960. Villa Hanbury is at Mortola Inferiore, 6 km west of Ventimiglia.

Dolceacqua, 9 km north on an easy road, has on its commanding heights a castle of the Doria princes of Genoa. This dilapidated fortress is haunted by the ghost of the peasant girl Filomena, who appears at dawn and dusk in disarrayed bridal gown and veil. Her story is not documented but she is thought to have been a reluctant participant in the Doria family's *jus primae noctis*, a privilege they conscientiously observed until the 19thC.

VESSALICO

See Imperia, page 176.

Northern Italy

The Po Plain

340 km; map Touring Club Italiano Emilia-Romagna

H ere is an exploration in some depth (two days to cover it all) of the
area crossed by Italy Overall: 2: the *pianura padana*, the 'waveless
plain' of the River Po (Padana in Italian). It is not generally a tourist area,
but it is no less explorable for that.

The Po fulfils all the geographical conditions of a great river but never
looks like one. View it in summer almost anywhere along its 676-km
length and you wonder what black hole has swallowed the myriad torrents of the Alps and northern Apennines almost entirely. On the river's
broad bed quarriers of sand and gravel have set up factories. When you
cross it on a bridge which would not disgrace the Mississippi you see
among marsh flowers a sluggish stream and a trail of stagnant ponds.
On its wide fruitful plain the *condottieri* fought their feudal battles and
paved the way for luxurious ducal courts. The Po presented no obstacle.
Armies could wade across it.

There is not much boat traffic on the Po. Someone some day will re-
establish those massive flat-bottomed barges which, at a snail's pace,
used to transport long-distance travellers (except in summer) stage by
stage. The river is navigable downstream from Ferrara to the sea (about
80 km) for eleven months in the year; from Mantua for about nine; and
from Cremona for about seven. Recently the entrepreneurs of Porto
Garibaldi and other Romagna coastal resorts have been offering boat
trips into the Po delta, where the river's artificial mouths pour out a saturated suspension of mud and you hear the cries of birds trapped in thick-
ets of papyrus.

Our tour follows its windings as closely as roads and lanes permit,
avoiding as far as possible the creeping suburbia of featureless bank-
side towns. You travel through an archetypal 'peasant' Italy (though the
modern mechanized farm-worker will not thank you to call him a peasant). It is a land of shimmering horizons in summer, eerie mists in winter, straggling villages and large farmsteads, rice and corn plantations,
pigs, sheep and oxen. Here, and not in Parma (covered in Italy Overall:
3), you can visit the isolated estates where Parma ham and cheeses are
produced and stored. Lower down the plain, near Ferrara and Rovigo,
you drive through miles of apple and cherry orchards, a lovely sight in
April. Between Rovigo and Padua you can visit the only clump of hills in
400 km of dead-flat landscape.

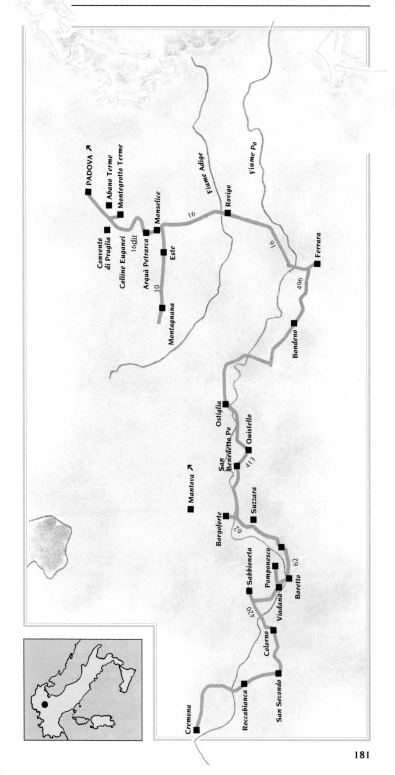

SIGHTS & PLACES OF INTEREST

ARQUA PETRARCA
Another small town to which the name of a famous Italian has been attached. Petrarch the poet (1304-74) spent his last years here and is buried under a green square beside the parish church. Arqua preserves the appearance of old times better than any other place in the Euganean hills, is not so congested on Sundays and is a useful centre for exploring this popular upland area on foot.

See Euganean Hills, page 184.

BORGOFORTE
See San Benedetto Po, page 185.

COLORNO
On a stretch of the Po rich in ancient castles and stately homes, Colorno has one of the best castellated palaces. Corner towers rise above a ground-level arcade. It was a Farnese residence, built in the 16th-17thC. A few kilometres west on the byroad to Cremona are two more antiquated strongholds, **San Secondo** (1448) and **Roccabianca** (1460), with the romains of elaborate interior decorations.

CONVENTO DI PRAGLIA
See Euganean Hills, page 184.

CREMONA ✕
Despite its celebrated tall slender bell-

tower, the **Torrazzo**, Cremona has always seemed to us to hide its light under a bushel. It glories in a provincial market-town simplicity and you see relatively few foreigners on its beautifully-arcaded main piazza. Yet all the symbols of a great city of art and architecture stand around it: a Romanesque cathedral guarded by lions of red Verona marble, a baptistery and public palaces of late-Gothic style.

Cremona's history is rich and com-

TRANSPORT
The nearest airport to the region is Bologna.

Main railways run parallel with the general direction of the Po at some distance from it: Cremona-Mantua-Legnago-Padua to the north; Piacenza-Parma-Bologna to the south. You could travel on branch lines along the valley via (for example) Parma, Guastalla, Suzzara, Quistello, Bondeno and Ferrara to Rovigo, but these are slow, monotonous journeys.

On the Po Plain most people without cars travel by bus. A comprehensive network is based on the major cities and the *autostrada* and '*superstrada*' routes between

them. At the main bus termini of Cremona, Mantua and Rovigo north of the river, Parma, Modena and Ferrara to the south, you can embark for any town or village in the provinces of those towns. Main roads are very busy, the countryside is not exciting. A local bus-ride has little of the magic you experience on the mountain roads and corniche routes farther south.

A tourist boat service, based on Boretto (on the Po north-east of Parma) has been running sporadically: it may prosper and expand, it may disappear. For up-to-date details, contact the Tourist Information Office, Piazza Duomo 5, Parma (tel. 052 123 3959).

plex. It was a cockpit of squabbles, ruled in turn by the Visconti and the Sforza. The harmonious layout, however, reflects its musical reputation. The composers Monteverdi (1567-1643) and Ponchielli (1834-86) were natives; and as everyone knows Cremona was the birthplace and workshop of the Amati, of Stradivarius and of Guarnerius. It is synonymous with violins, especially those of the 17th and 18thC masters, softer and sweeter in tone than anything since produced. You can see violins being made at the **Liuteria School** on Piazza Marconi.

ESTE

See Euganean Hills, page 184.

DETOUR - **THE CITADEL OF MONTAGNANA**

From Este, take Route 10 for 16 km. The 13thC walled town of Montagnana commands the old debatable land between the Vicenza and Verona provinces. The rectangular citadel is in amazingly fine shape. You enter, as did knights of old, through one of three majestic gates (that of 'the Trees' is now a youth hostel). On the large open square which extends in front of you is the 15thC **cathedral** with artistic treasures which would grace a much larger town. The masterpiece, above the altar, is Veronese's *Transfiguration*.

RECOMMENDED HOTELS

FERRARA

Ripagrande, LLL; *Via Ripagrande* 21; *tel.* 053 276 5250; *credit cards*, AE, DC, E, MC, V; *restaurant closed* Mon, *last week* Jul, Aug.

In an 11thC *palazzo* a few blocks south of the Castello Estense, it is in all the guidebooks – so best to book. Sensitively restored. Antique furnishings stretch from the grand entrance hall through to most of the 40 bedrooms, all of which have air-conditioning, television and telephone. Some reserved car parking available. Restaurant (**LL**) serves meals in summer in an internal courtyard of mellow brick.

GUASTALLA

Old River, LL; *Viale Po* 2-4; *tel.* 052 283 8401; *credit cards*, AE, DC, E, MC, V; *closed Christmas, New Year*.

The spacious hotel in its peaceful location on the edge of town near the Po takes its name from the river's nickname, Vecchio Fiume (similar to the American 'Old Man River'). Rooms have air-conditioning and telephones and an air of shabby gentility. Ample car parking. Adjoining restaurant (**L-LL**) claims to specialize in Emilian cuisine but we were served a very British meal with lots of chips. The Lambrusco house wine almost made up for it. Friendly staff.

POMPONESCO

Il Leone, LL; *Piazza* IV Martiri 2; *tel.* 037 586 077; *credit cards*, AE, DC, E, MC, V; *closed first three weeks* Jun, *middle two weeks* Jul; *restaurant closed* Sun eve, Mon.

It could be described as a restaurant with rooms (just nine), so half-board is the best bet. A 16thC town house on the banks of the Po. Courtyard and swimming-pool. Many original furnishings and touches of old world elegance, particularly in the main dining-room. Musty atmosphere which sometimes goes with such decoration is successfully avoided. Bedrooms are comfortable if a trifle stark. Car parking. The restaurant (**LL**) is renowned far afield for typically regional dishes of an impressive genealogy.

SABBIONETA

For an attractive and unique 'museum town' there are surprisingly few places to stay. The two we found were small, basic and very friendly:

Giulia Gonzaga, L; *Via* G. *Gonzaga* 65; *tel.* 037 552 8169; *credit cards, none.*
Ten rooms with bath.

Ca' d'Amici, L; *Via* A. *d'Aragona* 2; *tel.* 037 552 318; *credit cards, none*; *restaurant closed* Tues.
Nine rustic-style rooms with bath and telephone. Restaurant, exceptionally fine wine list. Garden. Car parking.

EUGANEAN HILLS

Volcanic in origin, the Colli Euganei are best known for their spa towns, **Abano**, **Montegrotto** and others which now form one hydropathic unit with more than 130 hotels and scores of swimming-pools, attractively integrated into a landscape of depopulated inner valleys and outer farmland. On Sundays the hills are alive with day tourists and numbers of cheerful *trattorie* cater for them. There are castles, monasteries, Palladian villas and beautifully landscaped 17thC gardens set in old feudal parks. At the **Praglia monastery** you can see the monks busy at their lifelong tasks of restoring old books.

In the southern ramifications of the hills are the historic townships of Arquà Petrarca (see page 182), **Este** and **Monselice**. Long ago they provided guides for crossing the flood plains of Po and Adige, which used to reach to their walls. Este's towers and battlements climb up the hill through garden-like scenery. From this tiny base sprang the all-powerful Este family, lords of Ferrara and Modena.

FERRARA ⌫ ✕

You associate it with swords and swordsmanship and a first sighting of the tremendous **Estense** (Este family) **Castle**, guarded by four gigantic towers and a real moat, transports you into a gory Elizabethan drama. But the beauties of arts and architecture impose a more spiritual dimension.

Ferrara's golden age lasted throughout the Estense dominion when for three centuries (1294-1598) those princes ruled like kings and patronized artists like emperors. The terrible castle contains state apartments softly decorated, arranged around the graceful courtyard. The **duomo** is a perfect fusion of Romanesque and Gothic. All the palaces and churches, distributed over the city, have an individual appeal. Most are built, like the castle, in rose-coloured brick and some have startling façades of geometrically-patterned marble blocks. Most also are jewel caskets of marbles, bronzes, paintings, terracottas and frescoed ceilings. Two of Italy's greatest poets, **Ariosto** and **Tasso**, lived and worked here and you can still visit Ariosto's elegant little 16thC mansion.

Ferrara lies almost at sea-level and is known as the 'horizontal city'. As the Po silted up, the place decayed. Drainage of the lagoons and marshes over a long period brought a ghost town back to life. Now it flourishes as the centre of a prosperous farming region and it has the reputation (disputed with Bologna) of being the North's gastronomic capital. It is an exception-

---

RECOMMENDED RESTAURANTS

CREMONA

Aquila Nera, LL-LLL; *Via Sicardo 3; tel. 037 225 646; credit cards*, AE, DC, E, MC, V; *closed Sun eve, Mon, Aug.*

In the *centro storico*, just south of Duomo and Torrazzo. A pocket of resistance to the eternal *funghi* and *tartufi* of restaurants around it. Specialities include (at a price) frogs' legs omelette and *spuma al torrone* (nougat mousse with chocolate sauce). Wine list has the celebrated Franciacorta (see Local Explorations: 3). Best to book.

FERRARA

La Provvidenza, LL; *Corso Ercole I d'Este 92; tel. 053 220 5187; cards*, AE, DC, V; *closed Mon, one week mid-Aug.*

This trattoria is popular with locals and tourists alike, so it is best to book. In summer meals are served in a delightfully shady garden. They range from obscure specialities of the region to the popular Emilian stand-bys of charcoal-grilled meats and fish. Car parking.

SABBIONETA

Parco Cappuccini, LL; *Via Santuario 30; tel. 037 552 005; credit cards*, AE, E, MC, V; *closed Mon, Jul.*

This 18thC *palazzo* bristles with antiques. It is set in parkland about 1 km from town centre (well signposted) and you can park in the inner courtyard. Mantuan specialities. Try the *riso con salsiccia* (rice with spicy sausage) or the *tortelli di zucca* (pumpkin-stuffed ravioli). A beautiful setting, exquisite food.

ally clean place. The citizens look on their city of warlike towers and dignified mansions with affection and quiet pride.

MANTUA
See *Italy Overall: 5.*

MONSELICE
See *Euganean Hills, page 184.*

OSTIGLIA
The Roman general Hostilius fortified this river crossing, hence its name. Fifteen centuries later the Gonzaga, della Scala and Visconti princes were wrangling over it. Ancient relics are nil, but the **Town Hall façade**, said to be by Piermarini, is worth inspection. A Romanesque sanctuary on the edge of town, the **Madonna della Comune**, has a charming flower-painted ceiling.

PADUA
See *Italy Overall: 2.*

ROCCABIANCA
See *Colorno, page 182*

ROVIGO
The last big town of the Po valley, on the edge of the delta, Rovigo looks out on flat fertile meadows intersected by irrigation canals. Few tourists come here: perhaps the drab landscape puts them off. But it is a new experience to stroll the main streets and squares of a large Italian town among people totally preoccupied with local affairs. Two fine palaces stand close together on Piazza Grande (which is officially Piazza Vittorio Emanuele II): the **Rovigo** and the **Roncale**. The 'rotonda' shape and clean lines of the **Madonna del Soccorso church** with its elaborate Longhena campanile recall a Palladian villa. Its interior is a showcase of Venetian art, nothing very wonderful.

Like Ferrara, this city has had ups and downs, corresponding to the capricious switching of channels of the Po and Adige rivers. Since they have been tamed, Rovigo has prospered and is the 'capital' and commercial centre of the Polesine (or delta) districts.

SABBIONETA 🖃 ✕
Some art-lovers see this as the finest town in Italy, others regard it as an archaeological site, with 16thC build-

ings instead of classical ruins. A Duke of Mantua designed it as a 'model city' around 1580, a principality in miniature. Beside the usual layout of hexagonal walls, palaces and churches, it had its own mint, national library, museum and state theatre. Of that era of lavish patronage much has survived. The **Imperial Gate** and **Garden Palace**, the **Ducal Palace** and **Olympic Theatre** (modelled on that of Palladio at Vicenza) still constitute a formidable architectural complex in a forlorn and useless town. For a pilgrim in the right frame of mind, Sabbioneta is like a corner of Florence without the crowds.

SAN BENEDETTO PO
Benedictine monks established the settlement on an island in the Po in AD 984. The monastery was renowned for its illuminated manuscripts and choral scores and the despot of the Po plain, Countess Matilda of Canossa, chose to be buried there. The town grew up on the south bank of the river. It has a huge austere L-shaped **basilica**, dedicated to San Benedetto (St Benedict). Stucco work and frescos (some by Guido Reni) embellish the chapels. The choir-stall wood-carvings and 12thC floor mosaics in the Immacolata chapel are very precious.

Upriver at **Borgoforte**, 18 km west, motor-boat racing takes place on summer Sundays.

SAN SECONDO
See *Colorno, page 182.*

VIADANA
In an otherwise modern, featureless town, two flamboyant churches will appeal to sacred music and art enthusiasts. **Santa Maria Annunziata** has a great organ and **San Martino** has works by Venetian and Mantuan painters, including Cotignola's well-known *Madonna of the Cherries.*

Central Italy

Northern Apennines

380 km; maps _Touring Club Italiano Emilia-Romagna_ and _Toscana_

On the flight between Milan and Ancona even regular passengers spend time looking out. The route traverses the north wall of the Apennines, abrupt as the north face of the Eiger. Behind it, under the forest fleece, countless ridges slashed with ravines push their different ways. A hopeless land to penetrate. If Italy's northern invaders, from Hannibal onwards, could have seen it as air travellers see it, many a campaign would have been abandoned here.

Part Tuscany and part Emilia (the boundary runs over the watershed), the district divides into ill-defined territories: Garfagnana, Frignano, Lunigiana. They are still unknown to tourism, though very close to La Spezia (see Italy Overall: 6), Pisa and Lucca. On this tour we pay our respects to cities of monumental arts but the chief attractions are the landscape – wild rocks convulsed in primeval cataclysms and the thickly-woven mats of dwarf oak, mountain ash, beech, pine and bracken which cloak them – and the villages. Places of no importance from which the young and fit have departed, they hang on with the tenacity of the tree roots and ferns they grew up with. Their cracked walls are banded with iron straps, their doors tied up with old stockings, their _marsiglia_ pantiles all askew and reinforced with slabs of stone. There are scores of such villages, almost every one with its Malaspina or Visconti or Guidi fortress above it to command the hill passes, now half-buried in a rampant botany. Here and there city-dwellers have disfigured the scene with flashy weekend villas.

Only 50 years ago it was all mule-tracks and gravelled lanes. Now you roll on narrow but well-shod roads – slowly enough, because gradients can be fierce, bends innumerable and the _macchia_ so dense that it interferes with the sight-line. Do not hesitate to explore minor roads: asphalted surfaces lead to the most remote hamlets. Make time if possible to visit a couple of castles in that chain of fortresses along the northern wall, where the history of the dukedoms was written. Allow three days for it all.

Except at garages and some _trattorie_ you will meet few who speak anything but the local dialect. Perhaps that is why nearly all guidebooks ignore what remains to some extent an undiscovered wonderland.

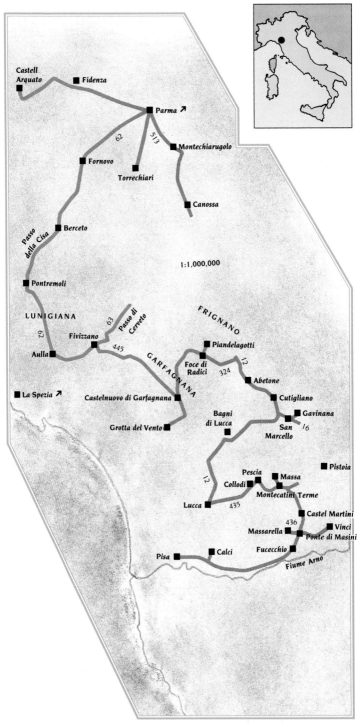

187

SIGHTS & PLACES OF INTEREST

ABETONE
A pioneer ski resort, it became an aristocratic refuge for smart Florentines. The way is steep and the forest promises little in the way of *pistes*, but Abetone commands four beautiful valleys with 30 km of downhill runs. **Cutigliano**, 13 km south (see page 190) and **San Marcello** (18 km south) are more recently developed. With Abetone they form a trio of sophisticated summer and winter holiday locations. Puccini used to come here to walk in the woods. You find skating, bowling, tennis, football and swimming; theatre, discos, cinema, restaurants and snack bars; ski schools and ski hire. Where the Lima river breaks out of the mountain, canoeing (for experts only) is being added to the activities.

Gavinana, next door to San Marcello, has a quieter air and some distinctive arcaded buildings. Gravelled stream beds facilitate walking through fantastic gorges. At San Marcello there is an **observatory** (visitable am weekdays, late evening at weekends); also, $^1/_2$ km south of town, a **park** with lakes and entertainments and an extraordinary foot suspension bridge across the valley bottom.

AULLA
Pausing here to look at some antiques 100 years ago, a British consul was offered the local castle for one *lira*. The problem was access: it stood on a steep crag. He bought it and soon afterwards they brought the railway to Aulla – the sensational Garfagnana line which needed so much ballast. Since a quarry had gone with the castle, Mr Waterfield was able to do a deal: all the ballast the navvies could carry in exchange for a carriage road, a bridge and some landscaping. The castle has been inhabited ever since, one of few Apennine strongholds so to be. Aulla otherwise has no attractions except as the junction of two thrilling rail journeys, east to Lucca or north to Parma.

BAGNI DI LUCCA
'Today', writes Cesare Sardi, 'we shall perhaps have the Queen of Sweden, the King of Denmark, the Spanish Infanta, the Grand Duke of Tuscany, the Princess of Savoy...tomorrow the Duke

---

HOTELS AND RESTAURANTS
Places to eat and sleep are plentiful in the Lucca-Pisa-Montecatini triangle, not always easy to find in the undeveloped Lunigiana and Apennine hamlets. You must have simple tastes for the cheap cottage meal and even cheaper *locanda* (lodging) of the mountains.

Populated centres combine the best of the Tuscan and Emilian cuisine (see also Local Explorations: 10 and 11). Some typical dishes are mentioned below. Local wine is usually a brand of Chianti – *classico*, Pisani, Rufino. The straw-wrapped flask has been replaced by a plastic imitation, but this should not put you off the contents which are sometimes excellent, always drinkable.

TRANSPORT
Air travel: international and domestic flights at Pisa/Florence airport (Galileo Galilei, 2 km south of Pisa).

Two highly picturesque rail routes cross the region. From north to south is the Taro Valley line, Parma and Fidenza to Sarzana and La Spezia. From south-east to north-west is the Garfagnana line, Lucca to Aulla. Many tunnels on both lines, but you have frequent glimpses of splendid untameable scenery. Some tiny stations have been closed, but the train stops at them just the same. You could see the best of both lines by taking a ticket from Parma to Lucca or vice versa, changing at Aulla.

Main bus services through the region have their termini in Florence, Lucca, Pisa, La Spezia, Parma, Reggio Emilia and Modena. The major operator is Lazzi, Via Mercadante 2, Florence. All the minor routes have regular bus services; scarcely a village is neglected. Among the more exciting journeys are Parma-Langhirano-Lagastrello Pass-Aulla; Modena-Sassuolo-Foce di Radici-Massa; and Vignola-Sestola-Abetone.

of Mecklenburg, Count Paar, Prince Ottoboni, Admiral Arrison and the Duke of York.' That was the **Baths of the Val di Lima** 200 years ago, warm springs which caught the fancy of fashionable invalids Europe-wide and became the centre of what Shelley called the 'paradise of English exiles'. Among those resident here were Scott and Trollope, Ruskin and Mark Twain, Heine and Dumas *père*, Liszt and Paganini, Ouida and Mrs Hemans, the Shelleys, the Brownings and Byron. In one of Europe's oldest casinos roulette was invented. The spa is still elegant and picturesque in its deep valley beside the foaming Lima, though a busy main road has ravaged the approaches. **Pieve di Controne**, 3 km north-east, has a curious redstone church with a puzzling façade.

BERCETO
See *Cisa Pass, this page.*

CALCI
See *Pisa, page* 192.

CANOSSA
See *Fornovo, page* 190.

CASTELL' ARQUATO
See *Fornovo, page* 190.

CASTEL MARTINI
See *Fucecchio, page* 190.

CASTELNUOVO DI GARFAGNANA
Recklessly heaped up on two torrent walls, it must have been built for a bet. East and west the Garfagnana valley is impressive, the river tumultuous after rain, but the town has only its 'local colour' to offer. Ten kilometres south by Gallicano is the **Grotta del Vento** ('Wind Cave'), a lesson in geology with its submerged tunnels, snow-white outflows, ancient fossil galleries and great vertical abyss. Tours are of one, two and four hours duration, April to October. Snack bar at entrance. Pebble jewellery and marble artefacts for sale.

CISA PASS
High point of the old military road through the Northern Apennines, 1,039 m, it marks the boundary between Tuscany and Emilia. The ascents north from Pontremoli and south from Berceto are steep with

---

RECOMMENDED HOTELS

GAVINANA
Albergo Franceschi, LL; Piazza Aiale 7; *tel.* 057 366 451; *credit cards,* AE, E, MC, V.

A delightful small hotel in the main square of a medieval hill village. Panoramic terrace adjoining bar/lounge area. Baths, TV and telephone in all rooms. Basement restaurant serves genuine Tuscan cuisine – our starter of cannelloni stuffed with spinach and ricotta was excellent. Informal, self-service breakfast in bar or on terrace.

LUCCA
Villa La Principessa, LLL; Massa Pisana, 4 km S on Route 12radd; *tel.* 058 337 0037; *credit cards,* AE, DC, E, MC, V; *closed Jan-Feb; restaurant closed Wed.*

Luxurious, once a residence of the Dukes of Bourbon and Parma. Formal gardens, swimming-pool, outdoor eating area. The 44 rooms have modern furnishings and air-conditioning. Public rooms more traditional with marble floors, antiques, family portraits. Ample car parking. English-speaking owners.

MONTECATINI TERME
Belvedere, LL; Viale Fedeli 10; *tel.* 057 270 251; *credit cards,* AE, DC, E, MC, V; *closed Nov-Easter.*

This major spa centre boasted 229 hotels at the last count, in all categories – we chose the Belvedere for its location, north end of town, just off ring-road, close to parkland and baths. Private car parking here, neat bar and restaurant, taxi link with station, indoor swimming-pool, tennis-court.

PARMA
Torino, LL; Borgo Massa 7; *tel.* 052 128 1047; *credit cards,* AE, DC, E, MC, V; *closed Aug, last week Dec.*

Small peaceful hotel in pedestrian zone (but with reserved car parking) near duomo. Bar and breakfast room on ground floor. Clean, comfortable bedrooms, some rather old-fashioned in style.

many hairpin bends but the road is magnificently engineered with broad verges where you can picnic and admire the view. The fast alternative, the A15 *autostrada*, goes through tunnels at this point.

COLLODI

Village of Pinocchio, the cautionary-tale character: his inventor Carlo Lorenzini became Carlo Collodi. The 'big house', **Villa Garzoni**, with 16thC gardens, avenues, stairways, statuary, springs and circular ponds in undulating parkland, has long attracted visitors. The **monumental park** established in 1956 in honour of Pinocchio has put it in the shade. Exciting for children, it is also no mean artistic experience. The metal sculptures and mosaics on the Collodi-Pinocchio theme were done by the greatest European artists. Open daily all year round, 8.30 am until sunset.

The old town of **Pescia**, 4 km east, was noted for growing and exporting flowers. Commerce is more mundane today, but lavish flower markets are still held in summer.

CUTIGLIANO

A ski resort of the upper Val di Lima (see Abetone, page 180), it draws you into the Middle Ages with hoary churches and tenements. Coats of arms of the old-time 'Captains of the Mountain' decorate the **Palazzo Pubblico** (Town Hall). In this parish, towards Abetone, is the **ethnological museum of Rivoreta** with ancient weapons and utensils of highland life. Every year the inhabitants declare a 'day of the living museum'. Old people demonstrate obsolescent skills and tell the young how much better things used to be.

FIVIZZANO

It has gastronomic pretensions and holds a 'Golden Fork' food festival annually in April. **Piazza Medicea**, ringed with *palazzi*, is a stern reminder of Florentine suzerainty. At the **Cerreto Pass** (1,261 m), 19 km north-east on trans-Apennine Route 63, is a blossoming winter sports and summer walking and riding centre.

FOCE DI RADICI

By way of the *foce* ('gullet') at 1,529 m the historic **Modena-Lucca road** crosses the Apennine saddle. An invigorating drive in summer. **Piandelagotti**, 5 km north, is a ski resort.

FORNOVO

This market town and rail junction once had strategical importance as the gateway to the mountain passes and pilgrims' roads to Rome. A crucial battle of 1495 between Gonzaga (Italian) armies and Charles VIII's French forces ended in stalemate, thereby (say historians) delaying Italian unification by nearly 400 years.

East and west of Fornovo the Apennine wall rears up above the Po Plain. Numerous castles crown outlying spurs, some with teeth drawn, some in ruins, some belligerent in decay and some restored and provided with museums. Worth visiting are **Castell' Arquato** (south-west of Fidenza); **Torrechiara** and **Montechiarugolo** (south of Parma); and **Canossa** (south-west of Reggio Emilia). Unflinching as the rocky outcrop it sits on, Canossa is the symbol of humbled pride. At its gate in January 1077 the Emperor Henry IV stood bare-footed in the penitent's white sheet, awaiting papal forgiveness. The tale, with other medieval horrors, is explained in the **castle museum**.

FUCECCHIO

A few kilometres north of Fucecchio, on Route 436, turn west for Massarella or Castel Martini into a most un-Tuscan district – not a vine, olive or cypress in sight. Meandering lanes take you into the **Padule** (swamps) **di Fucecchio**. The strange picture of waterways between long curtains of woods is enhanced by poplars and cane-breaks. Punt-like boats of dark wood, occasional disused mills and tiny huts of the L.I.P.U. (a bird-protection society) are the only signs of human life. From Castel Martini you can walk on easy paths (muddy after rain) across the **Paduletta di Ramona**, a more varied marshland with abundant birdlife including bitterns, herons, grebes and snipe.

GAVINANA ✉

See Abetone, page 188.

LA SPEZIA

See Italy Overall: 6.

LUCCA 🛏 ✕

'Towering Lucca, disguised as a wood' – old poem. Some find it claustrophobic however. To a 10thC nucleus were added austere towers and squares, then came late-medieval ochreous brick houses with arcades, open galleries and courtyards, Renaissance palaces and churches with crenellated bell-towers. White marble from Carrara, lavishly used as decoration, made

•*Pisa's Tower, leaning 2 mm more each year.*

Lucca an architectural showpiece unique in Italy. The 16th-17thC city walls and bastions are still in excellent shape; the broad green moat they overlooked now contains sports grounds.

The *lucchesi* say that Gomer, grandson of Noah, founded Lucca when the

191

DETOUR - **VINCI, LEONARDO'S BIRTHPLACE**
Turn east at Ponte di Masino, 7 km north of Fucecchio, for the great Leonardo's birthplace at Vinci, a town of the Albano hill range with a splendid old castle, planted by the Guidi counts. There are several interesting villages and townships along these slopes.

Deluge subsided. Sempronius lay in wait for Hannibal here in 218 BC. The first Roman triumvirate – Caesar, Crassus and Pompey – chose the city for their inaugural conference in 60 BC. Lucca was afterwards chief city of Tuscany for a time and, it is said, Europe's first democracy. The citizens grew rich and proud on goldsmithing, silk-weaving and fighting neighbouring republics and they retained their independence until Napoleonic times.

The new town radiates along leafy boulevards across the Serchio plain. It is commercial and industrial – a place to leave the car if you have time to loiter inside the old walls and view **San Martino's cathedral** with its unsymmetrical façade, sacred treasures, fine paintings by Tintoretto, Ghirlandaio and Filippo Lippi and the marble groups of Jacopo della Quercia. On one of that sculptor's tombs some unknown person has laid flowers every day for the past 30 years.

Other rewarding sights include a well-stocked art gallery in the **Palazzo della Provincia**; the beautifully-decorated church of **San Michele in Foro** on Piazza Michele; the quaintly medieval houses of **Guinigi** and **Monna Vanna**; and the **Travaglio tower**, now restored to its 14thC magnificence.

MASSA
See Montecatini Terme, below.

MASSARELLA
See Fucecchio, page 190.

MONTECATINI TERME ⌂
Hydro cures were offered at Montecatini's six baths 200 years ago, when Grand Duke Leopold of Tuscany made them fashionable. Over the salty, sulphurous waters new baths have been constructed and modern programmes offer such arcane treatments as aerosol therapy, ascendant showers and nebulization.

The town is an integrated architectural whole, its axis the **Grand Avenue of the Baths**. It is visited by more than a million people every year.

Montecatini has hundreds of hotels and restaurants, a wide range of sports and games facilities and, at nearby **Pievaccia**, a newly-opened 18-hole golf course. There are symphony concerts in summer. That essential feature of the up-to-date spa town, a gallery of modern art, attracts visitors on its own account. A cable railway connects the Baths with a mountain suburb, **Montecatini Alto**, where the surviving turrets of a vast fortress recall desperate battles in the old three-cornered Pisa-Lucca-Florence contest. In the hills to the north of town there is pleasant motoring and excellent walking. **Massa**, **Cozzile** and **Buggiano** are historic centres which deserve more foreign visitors. In the Buggiano district, near the Padule (see Fucecchio page 190), stands the abandoned **Bellavissa Villa** with 17thC frescos. Northward again, towards Monte Lignana, you are on the popular **Valloriana trekking route** which ends at Collodi (see page 190). Horses and mountain bikes may be hired at Montecatini Terme.

MONTECHIARUGOLO
See Fornovo, page 190.

PARMA ⌂ ✕
See Italy Overall: 3.

PESCIA
See Collodi, page 190.

PIANDELAGOTTI
See Foce di Radici, page 190.

PISA ✕
The **Leaning Tower**, supreme symbol of tourist Italy, began to tilt while under construction 1173-78. When the campanile was added the Tower was already 1.5 m off-centre. It is now 4.14 m off, the rate of tilt is accelerating (2 mm per annum) and at ground level you descend 2.5 m in walking from one side to the other. In 1992 the Tower was temporarily closed for the second

time in its history. When it is re-opened we shall again stand on the ninth gallery and look down vertically and vertiginously to the ground – as Galileo, a native of Pisa, did when he demonstrated the laws governing falling bodies.

Without this curiosity, the assemblage of Pisan-Romanesque buildings – Tower, **baptistery**, **cathedral** and **camposanto** (cemetery) on the so-called 'Meadow of Miracles' – would still be a marvel. The cemetery especially overpowers the senses with its paintings, monumental sculptures and Roman tombs. Earth around the graves was brought from Golgotha in the Holy Land. Nor should you neglect the 11th and 12thC churches on half a dozen roomy piazzas, all loaded with works of art.

Pisa was a club of small trades and a river port which suddenly grew rich on Crusader loot. Its 15thC **university** and the dim streets and flamboyant palaces of its *borghi* **Sant' Andrea**, **San Martino**, **Borgo Stretto** and **Borgo Largo** – should be sought out. They are witnesses to the Maritime Republic's glorious past.

The city is now a great tourist centre, chiefly the 'Rome-in-a-day-including-the-Pope' brigade, and also a place of ironworks, glass and chemical factories. Industry is mercifully detached from the historic centre. Beyond the suburbs, villas and scattered hamlets put flecks of geranium colour into the greens of vineyard, cornfield and cypress. At Calci on the hillside 12 km east you find an ornate monastery, the **Charterhouse of Pisa**.

Seaward the landscape shelves to the small Pisan riviera of open sands, juniper scrub and pine. At the **Marina** you can hire boats, swim and water-ski and eat in fish restaurants. You can even get a boat-trip upriver into town, an 11-km trip on the cloudy, canal-like Arno, past wrought-iron balconies of orange and lemon *palazzi* which throw out along your course hints of the vivacity, dignity and piety of this once-great Mediterranean power.

PONTREMOLI ✕

See Cisa Pass, page 189.

SAN MARCELLO

See Abetone, page 188.

RECOMMENDED RESTAURANTS

LUCCA

Il Giglio, LL; *Piazza del Giglio 2; tel. 058 344 058; credit cards*, AE, DC, E, MC, V; *closed Tues eve, Wed, first half Feb.*

Just west of duomo, this place of traditional atmosphere specializes in seafood and prides itself on typical Tuscan *crostini* (fried bread with filling) and *stracotto* (braised beef). Faultless cooking and presentation. Outdoor dining in summer. Next door is **Universe Hotel** (**LL**), venerable caravanserai where Ruskin stayed.

PARMA

Parma Rotta, LL; *Via Langhirano 158; tel. 052 158 1323; credit cards*, AE, DC, E, MC, V; *closed Sun in summer, Mon in winter.*

Long-established trattoria with car parking. Typical menu includes famous Emilian *pasta e fagioli* (pasta and bean soup), spit-roasted meats and of course Parma cheese and ham. In summer you eat under the pergola. A non-smoking section provided, a rarity for Italy.

PISA

Sergio, LLL; *Lungarno Pacinotti 1; tel. 050 482 45; credit cards*, AE, DC, E, MC, V; *closed Sun, Mon lunch, most of Jan, last two weeks Jul.*

Pisa's best-known restaurant, located in elegant 11thC *palazzo* overlooking River Arno. Elaborate and expensive menu. We ate a highly imaginative *fantasia* of fishy hors-d'oeuvres and a memorable *portafoglio alla Sergio* (stuffed veal, the house speciality). Formal atmosphere, no riff-raff. Book in advance.

PONTREMOLI

Ca' del Moro, LL; *Via Casa Corvi; tel. 018 783 0588; credit cards*, AE, DC, E, MC, V; *closed Sun eve, Mon.*

Honest-to-goodness country fare. Ever-obliging *padrone* will prepare Tuscan specialities to order (he takes for ever to do so), but the ordinary menu is intriguing enough for most.

<u>Central Italy</u>

Arno and Tiber

390 km; map Touring Club Italiano Umbria Marche

The Arno, river of Florence, rises on Monte Falterona and works its way down into the Casentino (see Italy Overall: 7). The 'Veins' or springs of the Tevere or Tiber, river of Rome, are on Monte Fumaiolo, some 30 km east. At first it looks as though the two rivers will join, but an Apennine spur divides them. One goes west, the other south.

Hereabouts the backbone of Italy is split into short steep ranges along the boundary wall of Tuscany and Romagna. Some are immense bramble patches, some darkly forested with beech and chestnut below, oak and pine above. Others have shouldered themselves into the valleys and staked out further claims for expansion in the shape of tufted cones with square towers and colour-washed villages on top. From a distance the effect is of green hats with badges and rosettes stuck in them. There is hardly as much level ground as would make a billiard table. Before you could spread a picnic cloth you would have to cut down trees.

Our cross-country tour (three days for everything) between Florence and Rimini runs a few kilometres beside the Arno, a shy little brook, and follows the early course of the Tiber, a flashing stream of blue and silver eddies, the river portrayed in Piero della Francesca's *Legend of the Cross* at Arezzo. From San Marino we look over another famous river, the Rubicon. In Caesar's day it was the Roman Empire's northern frontier. When he crossed it without Senate approval he was taking the proverbial irrevocable step.

At weekends on the Apennine *crinali* (crests) you see much traffic. City Italians come to shoot, to gather mushrooms, to fill flasks with spring water, to breathe clean air and let the silence (a rare commodity in modern Italy) soothe their ears. Some famous sites – Camaldoli, La Verna – attract pilgrims. Except where roads cross them, the *crinali* are deserted. The walker needs gloves to part the brambles on overgrown mule-tracks, the only traces of former inhabitants are the fairy rings of the charcoal-burners and the dilapidated cabins where chestnuts were dried. The hill villages remain unsophisticated, each the hub of its own little universe, cherishing a memory of Garibaldi's retreat or an incident in the medieval wars – a miniature San Marino (which the tour also visits) in its passionate parochialism. The valley communities have surrendered to light industry and mechanized farming.

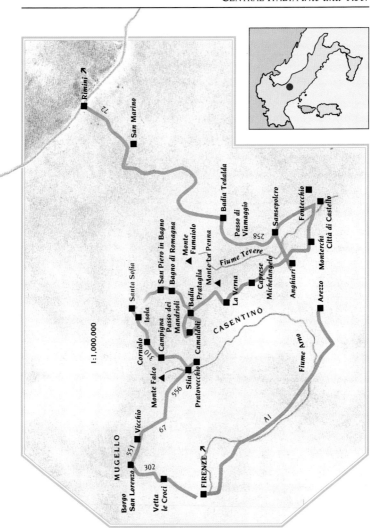

1:1,000,000

TRANSPORT

The airport is Rimini, international and domestic.

The 32-km rail trip from Arezzo to Stia is recommended. Another branch line comes into the region by Città di Castello to terminate at Sansepolcro. Borgo San Lorenzo and Vicchio can be reached by rail from Florence.

The bus companies of Florence and Rimini have frequent fast services between the two cities by way of Forlì and Arezzo. Bagno di Romagna is served by buses from Rimini and Cesena, also from Perugia and Arezzo via Sansepolcro. The chief bus termini for the upper Arno and upper Tiber valleys are Arezzo and Sansepolcro respectively.

From all the major towns within the region buses carry pilgrims to La Verna and the Camaldoli hermitage. At weekends in summer the services are of shuttle frequency. Excursion buses to San Marino, from Rimini and other Adriatic coastal towns, are also frequent. The principal bus companies in Florence are Lazzi, Via Mercadante 2, and SITA, Viale dei Cadorna 105.

SIGHTS & PLACES OF INTEREST

ANGHIARI ⌖
That enthusiastic hill-walker Leonardo da Vinci marked the place in large letters on the map he drew of Tuscany, which is now in Windsor Castle library. Here is a perfect circle of walls with a steep drop to their base, a tight but roomy mass of churches, domestic towers, old four-storey tenements, flagged streets, deep-arched arcades – in other words, an intact Tuscan hill-town. With one difference: the population is indifferent to the occasional visitor. Anghiari is not of this century. We have combed every alleyway and have yet to find the Coca-Cola sign.

AREZZO
See Borgo San Lorenzo, this page. Sansepolcro, page 200, and Stia, page 201.

BADIA PRATAGLIA
A calm little settlement at 843 m, spread along the thickly-wooded ridge above the Casentino. The 10thC **abbey**, often restored but still falling down, is Romanesque and has a crypt. Excellent walking among the hills on tracks where you meet only forestry jeeps. Cheap and agreeable lodging.

BADIA TEDALDA
Site of an ancient religious house at high altitude in the Luna Alps. Here, if heading south, you enter Tuscany from Romagna and begin the final awesome ascent of the Viamaggio Pass (983 m) before dropping down on Sansepolcro.

BAGNO DI ROMAGNA ⌖
The Latin poet Martial praised the warm springs which burst from rocks near the Mandrioli pass (1,173 m). Spa treatment, especially for rheumatic diseases, has been going on since the Middle Ages. The nearby **St Agnes Fountains** are now incorporated into a thriving health and holiday complex. This is a very pretty area. Trekking, fishing, tennis, swimming, riding, canoeing and mountain-biking are offered, along with minibus excursions to the high forests. At summer and winter **music weeks** all tastes are catered for, from chamber concerts to late-night cabaret. There is a permanent **sculpture exhibition**. Art shows

succeed each other with scarcely a break. The go-ahead spa directorate has revived some traditional *feste* and parades at Easter and created others in January and August.

Much sensitive restoration has gone into the old buildings and streets. The modern fountains and ceramic-tiled mansions are impressive and everything is scrupulously clean.

BORGO SAN LORENZO ✕
Under the frowning Mugello hills, on the outer arc of the heights which protect Florence, the Borgo has known violent history; but now it is a civilized market centre. **Vicchio**, 7 km east, is believed to have been the birthplace of Giotto, the supreme Gothic painter.

In this district the grey- and rose-bricked farms and villages evoke memories of Renaissance masters which excite art historians. Usually only the name of a bar or trattoria gives the clue; none could have been more anonymous than those orphan lads and farm boys when they set out for Florence or Urbino and none can now point with certainty to the houses they were born in. But look at the wealth of genius which arose in this one small district: Giotto (at Vicchio); Piero della Francesca (Sansepolcro); Michelangelo (Caprese); Vasari (Arezzo); Masaccio (Loro Ciuffenna); Fra Angelico and Luca Signorelli (Cortona); Paolo Uccello (Pratovecchio); and half-a-dozen more. There probably never was such a seedplot of genius in world art as the area through which this exploration takes you.

CAMALDOLI
Coloured vine adds a welcoming touch to the bleak monastery which stands at 1,111 m among the chestnuts and firs of a rugged tract of hills. The **Hermitage**, a geometrical layout of pantiled cottages at first glance, like a holiday village, consists of the individual cells of the Camaldoli monks. They are used to house visitors – you can stay in these one-roomed, 1,000-year old apartments. Where the San Benedetto Alps end and the Serra Alps begin the mountain crests overlap and break like waves. The approach roads from the Casentino (see Italy Overall: 7) are extremely pretty. Below the Hermitage at Camaldoli and Serravalle bars and cafés are appearing; you can rent cottages here too. From the Hermitage a high-level walk takes you to the head of the Ridracoli Lake (see Santa Sofia, page 200).

CAMPIGNA
A well-maintained road, steep and winding, visits this so-called 'Alpine Village'. Pine, beech, chestnut and sycamore grow in profusion, but on the higher ground there are meadows and pastures where cross-country skiing is popular. Three kilometres south of Campigna, on the Burraia plateau at the summit of the road pass, you can walk or ski to the **Monte Falco peak** at 1,657 m, close to the still pool where the Arno rises. It was a holy site to the Etruscans and we heard of an angler who hooked a 2,500-year old terracotta ear-ring. Campigna and Monte Falco have ski tows. Above the forest sensational views open up. Local propaganda says you can see across Italy from sea to sea.

CAPRESE MICHELANGELO ✕
As Donna Buonarotti's coach made its way down the bed of the infant Tiber (in

---

RECOMMENDED HOTELS

ANGHIARI
La Meridiana, L; Piazza IV Novembre; tel. 057 578 8102; credit cards, none.

A modernized and immaculate albergo in this atmospheric old town above the Tiber valley. A pleasing simplicity, but all rooms have TV, telephone and bath/shower. Quiet little bar. The restaurant prides itself on the old-fashioned Tuscan cuisine. A peaceful spot.

BAGNO DI ROMAGNA
Balneum, LL; Via Lungosavio 17; tel. 054 391 1085; credit cards, AE, DC, E, MC, V; closed Jan, Feb.

Attractive hotel with delightful restaurant in quiet backstreet opposite gardens. Own garden and private car-park. The 40 rooms all have TV, telephone, bath/shower and most have balconies and views across the valley. Free bus service from hotel to thermal baths.

BAGNO DI ROMAGNA
Tosco Romagnolo, LL; Piazza Dante 2; tel. 054 391 1260; credit cards, AE, DC, E, MC, V; closed mid-Nov to Easter.

The same family has been in charge here for 300 years but there is nothing stick-in-the-mud about the hotel or its elegant restaurant. We liked the downstairs lounge of sofas with bold colourful stripes. From the swimming-pool to the grand piano in the restaurant it looks as though a top Milanese designer has been given carta bianca. Rooms are simple but stylish, with TV, telephone and mini-bar. Tennis-court and games room. Shaded terrace, reserved car parking. Being close to thermal baths, it sees some coming and going.

CITTA DI CASTELLO
Le Mura, LL; Via Borgo Farinaro; tel. 075 852 1070; credit cards, AE, E, MC, V.

Spacious up-market establishment in centro storico of medieval town. Airy situation, however, and a great view across mellow pantiled roofs. Modern furnishings, all up-to-date amenities, restaurant which discerning locals are not ashamed to be seen in. Some reserved car parking (this town is difficult to park in).

1476 the only safe route between Florence and Rome), a thunderstorm broke, the horses took fright, the carriage overturned and in the nearest hamlet that night, in a house she happened to own, she gave birth to her child: Michelangelo.

In the courtyard of an old fort which caps the wooded cone above the modern village, a solid square-built house of Tiberine granite, with a characteristic outside stairway, is identified as the *casa natale*. Caprese, disfigured by modern bungalows and *villini*, clings to its medieval atmosphere and parochial pride. Few come here, apart from art pilgrims. As the *carabinieri* sergeant told us: 'This is a place where you say "Good evening" to people, and they reply "Goodnight".'

CASENTINO
See Stia, page 201.

CITTA DI CASTELLO ⌫
Ancient and modern combine harmoniously in this historic town: many hotels, shops and restaurants, a *centro storico* of medieval churches, palaces with ornate façades and a notable civic tower. **Palazzo Vitelli** has the municipal picture gallery with important works by Signorelli and Raphael, coloured terracottas by Andrea and Antonio della Robbia and a quaint *Madonna* by the anonymous early-Renaissance Master of Città di Castello. In the **town museum**, next door to the 11thC cathedral, is another *Madonna* by Pinturicchio.

Two kilometres east is the tiny spa town of Fontecchio.

CORNIOLO
See Santa Sofia, page 200.

FLORENCE
See pages 120-127.

ISOLA
See Santa Sofia, page 200.

LA VERNA
'In Tuscany I possess a mountain which is most favourable to things of the spirit... very secluded and wild, well situated for one who wishes to do penance' – so wrote Count Orlando and so came St Francis of Assisi into possession of La Verna. In his rocky cell amid the oak-woods and brambles above the Casentino he received the stigmata in hands, feet and side. The place has now multiplied into scores of cells, chapels, shrines and a basilica built up against, partly hollowed out of, the limestone crag. It is still a monastery. Countless pilgrims visit this spot, sanctified by the memory of Italy's most venerated friar. On Sundays the monks serve lunch and one hopes their piety exceeds their culinary abilities.

You need an hour to explore the passages, up flights of narrow steps to turret chambers, down into dank cellars: more when impeded by pilgrims, some in states of uncontrollable ecstasy. The saint's rope, girdle, *flagella*, sandals and bed are on display. The chapels are loaded with sacred art which impresses believers and non-believers alike. The scenes of St Francis's life were unfortunately entrusted to Collina-Graziani, a mediocre 19thC painter – you can ignore them, and concentrate on the beautiful blue-and-yellow bas-reliefs of Andrea della Robbia (1435-1528) and his sons: their *Annunciation*, *Nativity* and *Ascension* are worth going a long way to see. Their *Crucifixion* is probably unparalleled in monumental sculpture of the enamelled kind.

In 1926, the 700th anniversary of the saint's death, an organ of more than 5,000 pipes was installed at La Verna. Recitals are given as part of a regular programme of sacred music.

Count Orlando's 'very secluded and wild' mountain is nowadays trodden by hill-walkers as they climb above La Verna and cross the summit of **Monte La Penna** (1,283 m), a moderately testing expedition with magnificent views towards the Adriatic and SE along the Val Tiberina.

MONTERCHI
In the cemetery chapel of this insignificant village, protected only by a frayed rope, hangs one of the most famous and enigmatic paintings of the Renaissance master Piero della Francesca. It is the *Madonna del Parto* (*parto* is 'childbirth') and when de Gaulle persuaded the mayor to let him borrow it for a Paris exhibition the women of

• *Monastery of San Leo, near San Marino.*

Monterchi lay down in the road and refused to allow it to go. Like Anghiari a short distance away, this village had more than a footnote in the history of Italian independence: here, during his retreat from Rome in 1849, Garibaldi and his men achieved a midnight escape through the Austrian lines.

MUGELLO
See Borgo San Lorenzo, page 196.

PRATOVECCHIO
See Stia, page 201.

RIMINI
See Italy Overall: 4.

SAN MARINO
'Not a pebble on this mountain', says the patriot, 'but can tell some tale of heroism and the defence of liberty.' Europe's tiniest republic, a citadel and a few villages floating on a crag, was established about AD 500 by Dalmatian refugees. Inaccessibility kept it aloof from the wars that destroyed the proud dukedoms at its feet. For 14 centuries its inhabitants lived by taking in each others' washing but now they have created an 'industrial triangle' with cement, leather and soap factories and paper mills.

Old grey watch-towers and machicolated ramparts bristle on the heights. Cottage windows resemble arrow-slits. Guards and sentries strut in plumed hats, epaulettes and gauntlets. Flags and lanterns decorate façades of charm and distinction in a dramatic setting. There is a **historical museum**, a **museum of arms and armour** and a picture gallery in the **Valloni palace** with works by Guercino, Strozzi and Domenichino. But the great sight is the Romagna coastal plain, on which you look down vertically from 500 m. The nearest river, the Marecchia, may be the Rubicon of Roman history. A short distance north the river now called Rubicone is almost certainly not.

San Marino's pageantry is make-believe, like its coinage, postage-stamps and reproduction 'national' costumes. Where other invaders failed, tourism has conquered. Cramped though the Republic is, it has made space for a dozen hotels and restaurants, an aerial railway, camp- and caravan sites, clay pigeons, tennis and skating and night-clubs – and the steady procession of cars and buses from the coast.

SANSEPOLCRO ✕
The small city of ancient renown has always held its own in martial spirit and historical tradition with larger centres such as Arezzo, Gubbio and Siena. Its Company of Crossbowmen, now 700 years old, preserves the fame of a picturesque and lethal weapon. Citizens of all degrees, indifferent to modern sports, practise its difficult art in the town's arenas. Every May the crossbowmen of Sansepolcro travel across the regional boundary to Gubbio for a contest; every September the men of Gubbio come into town for a return match. The excitement aroused by this **Palio dei Balestrieri** and the brilliance of the costumed parades, banner-waving and cavalcades which attend it have to be seen to be appreciated.

Sansepolcro means 'Holy Sepulchre'. The paved streets, sturdy walls and gatehouses, pyramidal bell-towers and pedestrianized piazzas give this ancient place of pilgrimage a natural frame for serious and enthusiastic spectacles. Two major works by the native master Piero della Francesca in the modest **civic gallery** add the cultural dimension. Aldous Huxley described one of them – the *Resurrection*, a jacket illustration for many an art book – as the most beautiful picture ever painted.

Spectacle, culture – and industry. This small town is one of Italy's spaghetti capitals. The venerable house of Buitoni, long-established makers of pasta and pasta sauces, has had its headquarters here for 180 years.

SANTA SOFIA
Its **Oratory** has a fine wooden crucifix of the 12thC. Going south-west on Route 310, keep left at Isola for a short and attractive detour. (If coming north from Campigna, turn sharp right). In about 9 km you will reach **Ridracoli** and a hydro barrage, behind which a wonderfully sinuous, crooked lake extends south for another 6 km – almost to the watershed where the footpath comes over from Camaldoli (see page 197).

At Ridracoli the **Museum of Mammals** in Palazzo Giovannetti contains tableaux and stuffed items of local fauna past and present. It is open only at weekends and holiday times.

The company which runs the museum and, to some extent, tourism, is conscious of the environment. It has replanted trees and wild flowers along the lake shore and it offers guided walks and short courses in the wildlife and ecological field. The same company has renovated some empty houses at Ridracoli and also **Corniolo** (on Route 310 near Campigna) and offers them for holiday renting.

STIA

Here the Arno is a dribbling stream, narrow enough to be jumped over. Its course down the valley is marked with tottering single-arched bridges and here and there a box-like tower of a Guidi stronghold. Two of these towers, dating from the 11thC when the Guidi counts ruled the Casentino, are close to Stia. **Porciano**, the largest tower in the valley, is 5 km north on the Arno bank. **Romena**, a better-preserved tower with prison, postern, draw-bridge, bailey and keep almost intact, is also beside the stripling Arno, 5 km south. Here spurts the Fonte Branda, a spring mentioned in Dante's *Inferno*.

Stia is the terminus of the railcar line from Arezzo; and is the near neighbour of Pratovecchio where the painter Paolo Uccello came from. Stia is also the foothill village of Monte Falterona, where the Arno rises, and is an obvious starting-point for excursions by car or on foot into the bowl of mountains which closes the northern end of the Casentino (see Italy Overall: 7).

VICCHIO
See Borgo San Lorenzo, page 196.

RECOMMENDED RESTAURANTS

BORGO SAN LORENZO
Feriolo, LL; *On Route 302, Vetta le Croci; tel. 055 840 9928; credit cards, applied for.*

This strange little hostelry, medieval from top to bottom, has stood near the celebrated viewpoint of Vetta le Croci, 15 km south of Borgo San Lorenzo on the road to Florence, for at least seven centuries. It is now a superior haven for travellers. From *bistecca alla fiorentina* (the classic unadorned steak) to *zuccotto* (an elaborate pastry shell with a heart of ice-cream), the true Florentine cuisine is managed with pride and care. This place is *just* too far from the city to be invaded by Florentines in large numbers.

CAPRESE MICHELANGELO
Buca di Michelangelo, LL; *tel. 057 579 3921; credit cards, none; closed Wed; rooms available all year.*

Menu is limited and heavily *cacciatore* (game, funghi, fruits of the forest) but excellent value considering the location. *Scaloppine ai funghi porcini* were a dream. Rooms are available here (**L**) – smallish but nice with beautiful views.

SAN PIERO IN BAGNO
Bar Ristorante Italia, L-LL; *Via Battistini 76; tel. 054 391 7216; credit cards, none.*

Renowned for home-made pasta. The *cappelletti* and *maccheroncini piccanti* are supreme. Menu is also strong on *funghi*, truffles, wild boar and game. Outdoor terrace for al fresco meals in summer.

SANSEPOLCRO
Al Coccio, LL; *Via Aggiunti 83; tel. 057 574 1468; credit cards, AE, DC, MC, V; closed Wed.*

A busy establishment popular with locals. It specializes in charcoal-roasted and grilled meats and some imaginative variations on run-of-the-mill dishes – *gnocchi* in walnut sauce, for example. In Sansepolcro's close huddle of streets, car parking is strictly limited; this restaurant provides permits for customers.

Central Italy

Southern Tuscany

405 km; map Touring Club Italiano Toscana

From northern Italian cities the popular 'roads to Rome' by car or train are the coastal route through Livorno and the valley route through Florence. It was not always so. One of the most important staging-posts for travellers, a place that stuck in the memories more than most, was Siena. They had to navigate the Sienese domains, a territory of villages, forests and stark hills, some of them desolate with tufa crags and drifts of white shale, indicating an unusual geology. A feature of the route today is the number of convents and monasteries, formerly hermitages and rustic abbeys, which grew rich on the passing trade of pilgrims.

The small pugnacious town of Siena was in its day a capital city strong enough to challenge Florence, Pisa and Arezzo, to develop a culture of its own and to become a metropolis of architecture, music and painting. Crowning a hill, compressed within high walls, it packed all its splendour into a small compass, which is convenient for sightseers.

Many foreigners visit Siena, generally on day trips from Florence or from the Tuscan coast. This tour covers the middle ground between the motorways A1 and (incomplete) A12 on minor lines of communication, byroads which can never see a hill in the distance without turning aside and making for the top of it. You can take in one notorious tourist trap, San Gimignano, and another town nearby – Volterra – which deserves to be one but is not. You skirt the Chianti country, where the first Italian wines to make a reputation outside Italy were produced; and you cross the district of the *vino nobile* which, you may observe, Italians on the move by train or ship most frequently ask for with their meals.

There are pockets of warm springs, one of which is responsible for a savage attack on the landscape with shiny metal pipes and chimneys – the waters are harnessed for industry. This is in the metal-bearing mountains north of Massa Marittima where misshapen wastelands briefly interrupt the flow of hill and vale – just long enough to give you a heightened appreciation of the natural visual wonders that Siena's domains have spread out so lavishly behind you and a keener anticipation of the wonders still to come.

Our circuit based on Siena is no great distance, but much of it is on slow and wayward roads. Particularly around Monte Amiata, the highest mountain in Tuscany, prepare to travel at a crawl. If you want to cover it all, allow three days.

TRANSPORT

There are no airports.

Two railways run south-east from Siena, one to Chianciano Terme and the other to Monte Amiata and points west. Siena station is far below the city, a 10-minute bus-ride from the centre; Monte Amiata, nowhere near the mountain of that name, is about 15 km south of Montalcino. From the main Pisa-Rome railway a branch line links Cecina on the coast with Saline, 8 km short of Volterra, with a connecting bus to Volterra.

Country buses, frequent and prompt, link all the marked towns and villages. There are excursions to spa towns such as Chianciano Terme from all parts of central Italy. Long-distance express buses pass through the district on main roads: Florence-Siena-Grosseto is a major route. They are operated by numerous companies, prominent among which are Lazzi, Via Mercadante 2, Florence and SITA, Viale dei Cadorna 105, Florence.

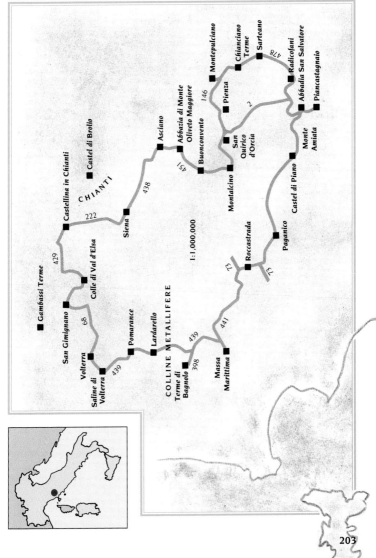

SIGHTS & PLACES OF INTEREST

ABBADIA SAN SALVATORE
Set at nearly 1,000 m on the rippling slopes of **Monte Amiata** (1,734 m), this small town made its reputation long ago as a summer holiday and winter sports resort, a fount of medicinal springs and a base for the ascent of Tuscany's highest mountain. The climb to the top is not hard: you have a choice of sleigh-lift, ski-lift or well-trodden path. The **Mountain Ring** is a circuit (30 km) of byroads at the altitude of Abbadia. You can drive nearly to the summit, to a car-park and some cheap souvenir stalls. *En route* you pass the Madonna del Scout viewpoint, where the Virgin's statue is plastered with Boy Scout emblems and patches.

At Abbadia you have all-round views of wide tracts of Lazio, Umbria and Tuscany. On the outskirts there are mercury mines: you are not far from the rough treeless uplands they call the Colline Metallifere ('metal-bearing hills').The rectangular **Abbadia** (abbey) originated in Lombard times and was once a nest of religious painters. The Medicis removed the pictures to Florence, but some noble architecture remains.

Five kilometres south is the rustic retreat of **Piancastagnaio**. Buried among groves of sweet chestnuts, the survivors of the ancient Tuscan wildwood, are cool scented footpaths and a few springs.

ASCANIO
The partly-walled town has two museums, chiefly for the specialist: a **picture gallery** with 14th-15thC Sienese school paintings and an **Etruscan museum** where finds from the Poggio Pinci necropolis 5 km distant are exhibited. In a house on Via Vento a Roman mosaic floor is preserved under a layer of sand.

BUONCONVENTO
The stout 14thC walls encircle a modest little town which boasts a museum with Renaissance paintings of the Sienese school, a fairly modern hotel and a couple of family-type *trattorie*.

CASTELLINA IN CHIANTI ⌁
Heading north from Siena you climb

into veritable 'Chiantishire' – the Chianti hills, delight of old-time British globe trotters and the source, at one period, of the only Italian wine foreigners had heard of. A medieval fortress with swallowtail crenellations – hallmark of the Ghibelline warlords in the Middle Ages – towers over Castellina, which is not otherwise remarkable except for its views and, of course, its Chianti. Several cellars are visitable in this district, but the process is heavily automated and totally lacking in peasant *joie de vivre*.

Some 25 km east of the Castellina-Siena road, deep in Chianti country on 'communal' roads, stands **Brolio Castle**, a large pentagonal structure with big bastions and long ramparts. Its excellent condition is a testimony to the prosperity down the ages of the baronial Ricasoli family (they came here in 1141) as producers and marketers of the most prestigious Chianti wines. The family seat is a palace inside the castle and close at hand are the Brolio cellars, much modernized and expanded, which may be visited.

'Chiantishire' suggests the good life in a Tuscany of beech and chestnut, vine and pasture, romantic crags and deep dark valleys thick with the autumnal leaves that Milton wrote of in *Paradise Lost* 'that strow the brooks In Vallombrosa'. Parts, however, are arid and suburban and certain little towns with evocative names are frankly ugly. West of Siena, where a thin topsoil exposes the geology, you could imagine yourself in the badlands of Dakota. But it is still an up-market holiday district, as numbers of cafés with striped blinds, discreet country-house hotels and a great range of vacation cottages testify. To northern Europeans 'Tuscany' still has a magic sound – especially the Chianti section.

CHIANCIANO TERME 🛏

Hypochondriacs know this for one of Europe's most pleasing spa towns. Its **Acqua Santa spring**, unique in Italy, is said to hold a miracle cure for liver complaints. The spa complex also embraces the **springs of Sant' Elena**, prescribed for kidney and bladder problems. Italians take their healing waters seriously – the analogy with miracle-working statues and the like is inescapable – and a well-run little town of stylish modern architecture in very pretty surroundings, such as Chian-

ciano is, attracts many visitors but not many foreigners among them. Some come simply to enjoy concerts and summer theatre, a bracing atmosphere (altitude 549 m), brilliant gardens and fountains and enchanting walks in mature broad-leaved forests – to take a mug of spa water for form's sake and to have a good time far from the hurly-burly of organized tourism.

COLLE DI VAL D'ELSA

An untidy lower town and a beautiful upper town with walls extending along a ridge. Of three museums the one devoted to sacred art is worth looking at. Glassware is Colle's speciality: the workshops in the **Vicolo della Fontanella** are open to visitors.

LARDARELLO

This industrialized town, reeking of sulphur, is the nexus of geo-thermal pipelines of the metal-bearing hills, which you cross between Volterra and Massa Marittima. A 19thC Frenchman devised the system for harnessing hot springs and the town is named after him.

MASSA MARITTIMA

You have to climb a flight of steps to

RECOMMENDED HOTELS

CASTELLINA IN CHIANTI
Villa Caselecchi, LLL; *Castellina; tel.* 057 774 0240; *credit cards,* AE, DC, E, MC, V.

Luxury living in this elegant old villa with swimming-pool and tennis-courts, all surrounded by a mature oak forest. Rooms furnished with antiques, Tuscan specialities in restaurant. Off the beaten track – all roads to Castellina involve miles of hairpin bends. Very expensive by rural standards.

CHIANCIANO TERME
Raffaello, LL; *Via dei Monti 3; tel.* 057 864 633; *credit cards,* AE, DC, E, MC, V; *closed in winter.*

Has all the amenities of more expensive places – beautiful garden, sports activities, heated swimming-pool – and is more welcoming than most. Excellent restaurant, restrained

decoration. If you lack something, merely ask.

SAN GIMIGNANO
La Cisterna, LL; *Piazza della Cisterna;* tel. 057 794 0328; *credit cards,* E, MC, V; *closed* 10 Nov-10 Mar.

A 14thC building on main square of *centro storico.* Furnished with impeccable Florentine taste. All amenities. Rooms with a view cost a little more.

VOLTERRA
Albergo Nazionale, LL; *Via dei Marchesi* 11; tel. 058 886 284; *credit cards,* DC, E, MC, V.

Completely renovated, the venerable hotel, where D.H. Lawrence stayed in 1925, still has stunning views over terracotta pantiles to open country. Not large, but all 36 rooms are properly furnished and equipped. Spacious restaurant – minimalist even – a rendezvous for the country-folk. (No shortage of folksy *trattorie* in the town.)

the 13thC **cathedral**, a harmonious pile. Faded frescos inside are all the more impressive for never having been retouched. One group is probably by the Sienese master Duccio (1418-1481). The main piazza slopes away and its exits trickle down among medieval tower houses.

MONTALCINO ✕

After the fall of the Sienese Republic refugees took to this mountain and built a replica Siena, a classic Tuscan hill town. Just like Siena, it even has twice-yearly contests between rival *contrade* (town districts or 'wards') – but here it is archery, not horse racing. At the Palio of Siena (see page 209) the bowmen of Montalcino sit in seats of honour.

A short walk from the Palazzo Civico, whose tower resembles the Mangia of Siena, brings you to the **Rocca**, a ruined stronghold in a park. From its walls you can sometimes see Siena itself. Montalcino is an enterprising festival centre: theatre last half of July, music in mid-August, the archery *palio*

• *San Gimignano.*

on May 8 and again the second Sunday in August.

MONTE OLIVETO MAGGIORE

The **Benedictine abbey** is planted on a ridge of grey shale like a square turret on a battleship. It is the seat of the Olivetans, a sect founded by a Sienese bishop in 1313. In its austere halls paintings, ceramics and marquetry show up to advantage. The abbey's priceless treasure is the cycle of 36 frescos in the great cloister. They portray the life of St Benedict, who was born just across the regional border in Umbria and is now patron saint of Europe, and are the joint work of Luca Signorelli and Giovanni Sodoma. Some of the monks here are scientists, engaged in metallurgy.

MONTEPULCIANO

Up to 50 years ago scarcely a foreigner had set foot in this aloof little town on its tufa escarpment, where tiny rivulets spring from mossy clefts and flow east to the Tiber or west to the sea. The few who did found themselves in a place of tiny squares and alleyways, nooks and crannies which led them to splendid viewpoints and expired above a precipitous drop. The town is now popular as an archetype of the old undisturbed Tuscany. Its Medici heritage (it was under Florence's rule) attracts architectural students. See the **Palazzo Comunale** on Piazza Grande with its 13thC Gothic towers; the **lion-and-griffin fountain** beside Palazzo Tarugi; and **Palazzo Contucci**, a *cantina* for the wine trade where you can taste and buy bottles of Montepulciano's dark *vino nobile*. Tarugi was designed by the celebrated Vignola, Contucci by the more celebrated Sangallo the elder. Above the foundations of **Palazzo Rucellai**, where cinerary urns are built into the walls, are Latin and Etruscan inscriptions. On the hour, above the angles and machicolations of the **Palazzo Comunale**, the incongruous figure of Pulcinello, the Commedia dell'Arte clown, strikes the town bell.

• *Siena, the duomo.*

Palazzo Nero-Orselli houses a **civic museum**. At the end of a cypress avenue 2 km north-west from town stands the huge Greek-cross church of **San Biagio**, with a well in the grassy clearing. Its chanonry has a double loggia by Sangallo the elder. Church and chanonry have been described as 'the most harmonious creation of Renaissance Italy' – a bold claim.

PIENZA
Built as a 'summer city' to replace the miserable village where Pope Pius II was born in 1405 (hence its name), Pienza is a post-medieval 'new town' – a careful grouping of late Renaissance buildings in sterile perfection. Comparisons with a Hollywood set for *The Agony and the Ecstasy* come to mind. The two best things about Pienza are the Flemish tapestries in the **museum** and the view from the hanging garden of the **Piccolomini Palace**. The adjacent village of Monticchiello boasts a popular Little Theatre (Teatro Povero or 'theatre of the poor').

RADICOFANI
Climb a pyramidal mound to the medieval village, then climb higher to a

tower once inhabited by monks who may have chosen it for its panoramic outlook. Another inhabitant was the legendary brigand Tacco, before whom Rome and Florence trembled.

SAN GIMIGNANO   ⊯ ✕
The fame of this 'town of 100 towers' has spread worldwide and the result is crowds, vulgarity and overpriced souvenirs. The town is ringed with car parks and no vehicles are allowed in the historic centre. The **Collegiata** and **Sant' Agostino** churches have frescos by Ghirlandaio and Benozzo Gozzoli respectively. A macabre attraction is the **Inquisition or Medieval Criminology Museum**, a small chamber of horrors on Via del Castello.

SAN QUIRICO D'ORCIA
Noteworthy for the **Horti Leononi**, an indoor and outdoor exhibition area for science, botany and horticulture. International sculptors have adorned the woods and gardens.

SARTEANO
Another high town (384 m) but its massive fortress with a drawbridge, like a nightmare vision of a toy fort, is higher. This is one of the best examples of an old Sienese castle.

SIENA
Strongly medieval, handsomely Gothic and Renaissance, suffused with all the dignity and self-respect of an old city-state, Siena should be high on every traveller's list of places to visit and revisit. The place is just right for size: its fabulous monuments and works of art are all within easy walking distance of each other. Town mansions, slotted into narrow streets, are marvels of domestic architecture. The **Piazza del Campo**, best seen from the top of the 13thC **Mangia Tower** above the municipal palace, is an irregular triangle and is considered the finest city centre in Italy. In front of the great black-and-white **cathedral** in which the city culminates you stand open-mouthed with wonder.

Duccio, the early Renaissance painter, led the Sienese school of art. Sassetta, Beccafumi, Pinturicchio and the Lorenzetti were among those who followed him. Jacopo della Quercia, Ghiberti and Donatello were responsible for the city's most beautiful sculptures and statuary.

At **San Domenico's church** the head of Catherine of Siena, saint and martyr, is venerated. (She is not the martyr the manner of whose death gave rise to the Catherine Wheel of fire-

---

RECOMMENDED RESTAURANTS

GAMBASSI TERME
Il Castagno, L; *Castagno Val d'Elsa*; *tel.* 057 167 8074; *credit cards*, DC.

Typical Tuscan *osteria* by the roadside with large car-park opposite. Chequered tablecloths, unpretentious home cooking with many desserts. Highly drinkable house wine. Vegetarians may be put off by the stuffed boar and mounted fox heads; others by slightly out-of-the-way location (detour 22 km north from San Gimignano).

MONTALCINO
Taverna dei Barbi, LL; *Fattoria dei Barbi*; *tel.* 057 784 8277; *credit cards*, *none*.

Kill two birds with one stone by touring the *fattoria* (wine-producing establishment) and eating in its rather self-consciously Tuscan-rustic tavern

in the vineyards. English chef handles traditional dishes with aplomb. The wine is *brunello*, the quality product of the district.

SAN GIMIGNANO
Le Terrazze, LL; *in same building as hotel (see page 205); tel.* 057 794 0328; *credit cards*, E, MC, V; *closed* Tues, Wed *lunch*.

Panoramic views over Val d'Elsa. Smart place with pasta made on premises. Try the fettuccine *all'uovo ai funghi*.

VOLTERRA
Osteria dei Poeti, L; *Via Matteoni 55*; *tel.* 057 186 029; *credit cards*, AE, E, MC, V.

The restaurant occupies the ground floor of a medieval tower house and you eat between stone walls under a vaulted ceiling. Fixed-price tourist menu, sound value, swift service if you need it.

• *Volterra.*

works displays.) At **San Francesco's church** 223 sacred wafers are kept, as fresh and white as when they were baked in 1730 – they are considered the greatest eucharistic miracle in religious history. The **heart of St Bernard of Siena** is kept in the oratory named for him. These and other churches contain paintings and frescos which, for the art student, repay hours of study.

Always a vibrant town, a market and banking centre for a wide region, Siena really explodes in **Palio week**. Bands of costumed performers, like rival gangs of football supporters but more civilized, parade the streets with the insignia of their *contrade* (city wards) – Goose, Caterpillar, Giraffe, Unicorn, 17 in all – until the Palio itself on July 2 and August 16. On those days a pagan frenzy seizes the city. In the Piazza 100,000 spectators are jammed, all standing for hours in a torrid heat, to see a bare-back horse race which lasts about two minutes. (We watched a woman who nervously gnawed her handkerchief – in that two minutes she had swallowed it.)

The Palio, brutal, no-holds-barred, not for the squeamish, is possibly the greatest of Italy's 'traditional manifestations'. It is best seen from a balcony if you can afford the extortionate prices. If you intend to stand in the Piazza, arrive early. The horses do a double circuit around you, but you see almost nothing unless you are against the barrier. The atmosphere, of course, is a grand spectacle in itself.

Siena is a city of gastronomy. Confectioners sell *panforte* (spiced bread – you can tour the factory) and marzipan. A labyrinth of air-conditioned cellars in the Medici fortress is the **Italian Wine Centre**, the only one in Italy, where you can inspect, taste and buy every wine of the nation: best sellers are the regional Chianti, Montepulciano and Montalcino. Smart expensive shops handle typical *alta moda* sweaters and leather goods and their quality souvenirs include chic little dolls clad in the colourful heraldic uniforms of the Palio contenders.

VOLTERRA ⋈ ✕

It hangs between heaven and earth at the top of what was once a mountain railway, a focal point in the landscape for miles around. Town houses adorned with armorial bearings, a Saturday market with striped umbrellas spread on the piazza, the **Guarnacci Etruscan Museum** with wonderful Giacometti-like figurines and ornaments of 2,500 years ago...and the cutting of alabaster, the pure white or black-streaked rock on which Volterra is built. See it done and buy finished products at **Bessi Ghebo Vero** in Via Turazza. Many flock to San Gimignano, few to Volterra, but the latter town has more personality and more stable and homely traditions. It is however open to all the winds, icy in winter.

Central Italy

Green Hills of Umbria

290 km; map Touring Club Italiano Umbria Marche

The happy hunting grounds of Tuscany stand between the foreign tourist and a region which, just as much as 'Chiantishire' (see Local Explorations: 11), is the essence of the Italy we most admire. The region is Umbria. Our tour (two to three days to cover it all) takes in its central districts, geographically the heart of the nation. No great cities are here apart from the regional capital Perugia; no lavish displays of art, though many a humble church and civic gallery can boast works of the greatest masters; no really stunning scenery, no high mountains, but yellow earth, fruit blossom, vineyards and olives. Through it all flows the Tiber, not yet 'Tiber, Father Tiber, to whom the Romans pray' but a docile shallow stream, canalized between files of poplar and riverside walks. Old towns and fortresses mark out its windings and its prolific tributaries. 'Without Nera, the Tiber would not be the Tiber' says the proverb. This route follows the Nera into Valnerina, one of Italy's most pleasant and least-exploited lowland dales.

Out of the valleys, the hill towns are all of a pattern. You see from afar a crumbling citadel or nodding belfry and decide to visit it if only for the view. You pass through tentacles of suburbs and try not to look at the cheap, flimsy constructions which desecrate the approaches. You climb into streets which become narrower and steeper as you progress. The old town is closing in on you. Better park while you can – if you can. The summit complex – medieval churches, towers, arcaded *palazzi* – is bound to be all-pedestrian. From the upper piazza or the frail-looking campanile, the view is eminently viewable. The towns are of a pattern, but each has its own prized panorama.

We choose some short stretches of main roads, no motorways. Much of the route is on secondary roads which in Umbria are peaceful enough even in high summer. You could do this tour in one day if you missed out the byroads of Assisi's hill and the Tiber Regional Park and if you gave Perugia and Spoleto only a passing glance. But that would be a pity. There are sights on this tour which everyone should make a point of seeing at least once in a lifetime.

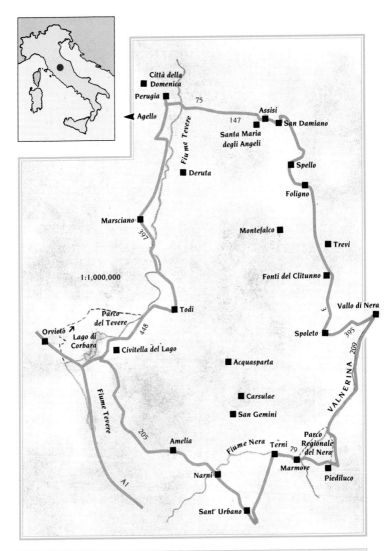

TRANSPORT

There are small domestic airports at Perugia and Foligno; no scheduled national or international services.

A branch of the main State Railway (Florence-Rome) goes via Perugia and Foligno to Terni and Narni. The Umbro-Aretine private line with railcars connects Perugia with Todi and Terni.

Every town on the tour is linked more or less directly with every other town by a regular and efficient bus service. From larger towns such as Perugia express buses travel to cities outside the region, including Ascoli Piceno, Arezzo, Florence, Macerata and Rome; and in summer there are daily services to Cattolica, Cesenatico, Fano, La Verna, Pesaro, Riccione and Rimini. Mainline bus stations: Perugia (Piazza dei Partigiani); Assisi (Piazze Santa Chiara and San Francesco); Deruta (Piazza dei Consoli); Foligno (Porta Romana); Narni (Piazza Garibaldi); Spoleto (Piazza Vittoria and railway station); and Terni (Piazza Dante).

SIGHTS & PLACES OF INTEREST

ACQUASPARTA
See Terni, page 215.

AMELIA
One of the oldest towns in Italy, founded by obscure Pelasgian tribes whom some consider the aboriginals of the peninsula, precursors of the Etruscans. A Roman cistern survives in mint condition. Parts of sturdy polygonal walls are still visible; these are much older than the Roman and medieval defences alongside.

ASSISI 🛏 ✕
Having toiled up the slope from which this town surveys the wide Tiber valley, you hardly know where to start, so crowded and compelling are the sights of Italy's spiritual metropolis. If you come from the south our route takes you across Monte Subasio at about 1,000 m, via San Damiano. On the way down, pause for view of the **basilica of San Francesco**, apparently isolated in the greenwood, as it was in the time of St Francis himself. When you arrive at it you will be hustled and elbowed among crowds of pilgrims and hucksters of garish pictures and plastic statuettes.

St Francis of Assisi (1182-1226) is buried in the crypt of this basilica of two halves, upper church and lower church. The cycle of frescos on the walls is attributed to Giotto.

High-rise **Piazza del Comune** still exhibits the pavement of a Roman forum. The corroded pillars of a temple to Minerva, now a church, remind you of Assisi's flourishing life centuries before St Francis. The architectural plan of the main square is admirably harmonious, as is most of the town. Note the elegant fountain in front of the Town Hall and the trailing potted plants at cottage windows.

Take the cobbled path to **San Rufino's church** (12thC); he was Assisi's first bishop, predating St Francis. Going downhill, look in at **Santa Chiara** in the piazza of the same name which usually escapes mass tourist attention. Its design reflects that of San Francesco, which is appropriate because St Clare, founder of the 'poor Clares' was the feminine equivalent of St Francis.

The austere and ascetic Clare died of under-nourishment at San Damiano's convent. Earlier, when the place was a country chapel, St Francis had heard a voice saying: 'Go, repair my house which is crumbling' – the inspiration of his religious mission. At Santa Chiara you have some sense of the simplicity and self-denial of the Franciscan message.

CARSULAE
See Terni, page 215.

HOTELS AND RESTAURANTS

As Umbria becomes more of a holiday destination, so the range of facilities increases. Assisi, Perugia, Spoleto and Terni all offer places of varying price and quality to stay or to eat at. Parking can be a problem, as in all historic cities never designed for cars. The places we recommend are mostly a little way out of town.

Agriturismo (farmhouse accommodation) is developing fast and is worth investigating if you have your own transport. Contact Agriturist, Corso Vittore Emanuele 101, Rome. It is not always cheap.

The cuisine resembles that of Tuscany. Spit-roasted and charcoal-grilled meats are the region's signature. The former include porchetta, sucking pig with fennel and garlic; the latter agnello a scotta dito, lamb flavoured with rosemary. Terni is renowned for its bread, used in minestrone, in bruschette (garlic toast) and crostini di fegatini (chicken liver croutons). Ravioli, called cappelletti, in broth are a Perugian speciality. The cakes and candies of Perugina are, as the name implies, made in Perugia.

Fine local cheeses include sheep's milk caciotto and raviggiolo. Olive oil is produced around Spoleto and Spello, truffles abound in Valnerina and the lakes supply eels, river trout and coarse fish. Wines come from the Trasimene and Montefalco districts but the most famous is Orvieto, available as dry or sweet white.

DERUTA
One of the classier souvenir outlets, specializing in high quality ceramics which sustain a long tradition.

FOLIGNO
The town has a shy exterior and inner fascinations. The **duomo**'s carved angels and red marble lions look across the piazza at the 500-year-old business of Orfini, the printing house which first brought out Dante's *Divine Comedy* in 1470. Nearby Palazzo Trinci has paintings by Alunno and Gozzoli.

FONTI DEL CLITUNNO
East of the main road a thick clump of poplar, willow and cypress has failed to protect the **spring of Clitunno** (hymned by Carducci and Byron and

---

DETOUR - **MONTEFALCO**
About 11 km south-west of Foligno, high above the valley, it is the 'Balcony of Umbria', rich in age-old buildings. San Francesco's church, now the civic gallery, has paintings by Perugino and Gozzoli.

---

memorably painted by the great 19thC landscape artist Corot) from shacks catering to visitors. The **early Christian temple** of Clitunno, of pagan origin, not quite so accessible to passing traffic, is 1 km north, across the river.

NARNI
Hedged in with disastrous suburbs, Narni's monumental artistic patrimony

---

RECOMMENDED HOTELS

AGELLO
Rossano, L-LL; *Off Route 220, 17 km SW of Perugia; tel. 075 695 370; credit cards*, AE, E, MC, V; *restaurant closed Aug.*

Agello is a tiny township of very narrow streets. From the hillside hotel you look south over rolling country, with a glimpse of Lake Trasimene to the south-west. If the views are expansive, the rooms are rather small and of monastic simplicity. The prestigious restaurant (**LL-LLL**) offers a variety of fish dishes and you may also be offered beefsteak *al curato*, local ham and salami and tagliatelle with *ragoût* or mushrooms; homemade pasta is a *sine qua non*.

ASSISI
Villa Elda, LL; *San Pietro Campagna 137-9; tel. 075 804 1756; credit cards,* AE, DC, E, MC, V.

A large hotel complex set in parkland surrounding an old country house on Via Patrono d'Italia, 1 km or so south of Assisi. The place has been in the family for 100 years. Rooms have been modernized but are still traditionally furnished. Solarium, American bar, ample shaded car parking. Attractive restaurant (**LL**) has fanlight windows and an open fireplace for spit-roasting. It specializes in the Umbrian cuisine, especially

roasted and grilled meats. Tables under the trees in summer.

SANTA MARIA DEGLI ANGELI
Porziuncola, LL; *tel.* 075 804 0833; *credit cards*, AE, DC, E, MC, V.

The small town is close to the main Perugia-Foligno road, about 6 km from Assisi. The hotel, up-market for its location, run since 1860 by the Biagetti family, stands opposite the basilica of St Mary's church. Comfortable, spacious; simply but elegantly furnished; all rooms with bath/ shower and telephone, some with balconies. The public rooms have traditional Umbrian arches and are furnished with antiques. Private car-park and garden. The restaurant (**LL**) is walled with cosy mellow brick and it maintains the gastronomic standards of the Umbrian cuisine.

TODI
Bramante, LLL; *Via Orvietana 48; tel.* 075 894 8382; *credit cards*, AE, DC, E, V.

Names of local poets or architects often lead one to reputable hotels, if decrepit ones. Bramante's medieval convent exterior will not prepare you for a scene of deep armchairs and banquettes and fussy modern decoration, nor for the faint echo of the disco. The rooms are comfortable, however, the food beyond criticism and there is a swimming-pool and a tennis-court.

• Assisi.

includes a broken **Roman bridge** (subject of one of Corot's greatest paintings), a 10thC **duomo**, and a thoroughly medieval centre. The **hermit's cave** of Sant' Urbano, in a picturesque spot, is 13 km south-east.

ORVIETO
See *Italy Overall: 7*.

PARCO DEL TEVERE
The Tiber Park is an area of roughish undulating country with some quiet roads and picnic places. The route looks over Lake Corbara, through which the Tiber flows. Carp and pike fishing, boating, riding on lakeside tracks. Camping at southern end.

PIEDILUCO
See *Terni, page 215*.

PERUGIA
The biggest hill-top city of them all, pedestrianized on top, difficult to park in down below. Animated air is enlivened with fresh-faced students from languages university. Old Perugia, a sort of medieval Pompeii, is enclosed in a 16thC papal citadel with a garden-belvedere on top. Carvings on elaborate 13thC fountain in Piazza Grande

are attributed to the Pisani brothers. Perugino is the top artist. Duccio did the bas-reliefs on the San Bernardino oratory. This is a fine place to linger in but uphill streets and stairways are a test of stamina.

Città della Domenica ('Sunday City'), 8 km west on Route 75*bis* is a large funpark for young children with fairytale tableaux, a zoo, a sports arena and restaurants, open daily 9 am to dusk. Parents be warned: one adult and two children pay about L40,000 admission.

Perugina candy factory, the best-known in Italy, is open to visitors. Contact Tourist Office, Largo della Libertà 13.

Jazz festival in July.

SAN GEMINI
See *Terni, page 215*.

SPOLETO ✕
It used to be a quiet town above a gorge, rarely visited by tourists despite the rare attraction of Ponte delle Torri ('Tower Bridge'), 80 m high. Exquisite little **Via di Fonte Secca** with flight of steps to Piazza Pinciani; a **Roman**

wall which delayed Hannibal after the Battle of Trasimene; astonishing carvings on **San Pietro's façade**, of which parts date back 1,500 years – these features of a typical Umbrian 'city of art' are now revealed to thousands who flock to well-publicized cultural demonstrations every summer. The Festival of Two Worlds, a June-July operatic fortnight, which genuine opera-lovers tend to avoid, sees Spoleto at its most chaotic.

TERNI
A city of the plain which suffered destruction several times. Its one distinguished citizen's grave, that of Tacitus the Roman historian, is lost. Surviving relics of a murky past include the Dark Age church of **San Salvatore**, formerly a pagan temple; **San Lorenzo** and **San Francesco**, both 12thC; **Palazzo Spada**, the last great edifice of the military architect Sangallo; and pieces of an **amphitheatre** of 32 BC.

West on Route 79 you enter the delicious Valnerina, the wooded vale of the Nera river. The **Marmore Falls** 7 km from Terni (170 m high) are one of Italy's chief aquatic spectacles when water is coming over them. Old-time engineers created them when controlling the river but the Falls are in full spate only on holidays and (best of all if you can manage it) on summer Saturday evenings under floodlights.

On the same road, 13 km from Terni, is the secret lake of **Piediluco**, a spot of natural beauty in the green forest and the haunt of canoeists and trout fishermen who have not yet wrecked its rustic tranquillity.

North-west of Terni on Route 79 and off Route 3*bis* are the Roman remains of **Carsulae** (10 km from Terni) with discernible stretches of the Via Flaminia, also an arch and two theatres of classical times. Off the same road are **San Gemini** (10 km) and **Acquasparta** (16 km), two bright little spa towns. There are campsites and discos.

TODI ⌂
High on its hill above the placid Tiber, this was a sacred citadel dedicated to Mars. The best views are probably from Piazza Garibaldi. A compact cluster of domes, like Florence's Duomo in miniature, catches the eye on the outskirts of town. They are the church of **Santa Maria della Conciliazione** and are said to be the work of Bramante.

TREVI
All this place has in common with Rome's most celebrated street spectacle, the Fontana di Trevi, is the derivation of the word. Trevi probably means 'three ways' – *tre vie* or a T-junction. The small pretty town perches precariously on a hill blanketed with olive woods to which the romantic poet Leopardi wrote an ode.

VALLO DI NERA
Heart of the Valnerina. The town's coat of arms, three castles, recalls the days when Vallo's Swabian overlords ruled the roost in Umbria. Even Vallo's castle is now a hoary ruin. From the river bridge there are quiet walks along the reaches of the Nera. A more strenuous expedition on foot is east over the Coscerno range of hills to Roccaporena (birthplace of Saint Rita) and Cascia (see Local Explorations: 13).

RECOMMENDED RESTAURANTS

ASSISI
Giardino Paradiso, L; V*ia* M*adonna dell' Olivo 8; tel. 075 812 843; credit cards, applied for; closed Mon.*

A paradise garden indeed, with a shaded terrace looking south. Public car park across the road. Check your bill – the cooking is better than the arithmetic.

SPOLETO
Il Tartufo, LLL; P*iazza Garibaldi 24; tel. 074 340 236; credit cards,* AE, DC, MC, V; *closed Wed.*

During the Two Worlds Festival this is a honeypot for highbrows, which is perhaps why it closes for three weeks immediately afterwards (mid-July). At other times it is one of central Italy's great restaurants, famous for grills, game and sausage, for Christmas *gnocchi*, Easter cheese cake and sweet pizza. Wines of the Umbrian hills.

Central Italy

Eastern Apennines

500 km; maps Touring Club Italiano map Umbria Marche

Here is an exploration of the area known as the Marche. This is usually translated 'marches' – a borderland – but historically they were a
group of German counties or *marken*, each ruled by its margrave, in the
time of the Hohenstaufen (Swabian) emperors. In a sense it *was* border
country, an outlying, ultramontane region of the Papal States, constantly
in conflict with the Holy Roman Empire, constantly juggling with the bal-
ance of power. That made for confusion of cultures, a defensive style of
architecture and an independence of local character, features that still
give the Marche a colour and life all their own.

Our roads are not easy to travel: some are reminiscent of the forest
sections of an international automobile rally, and they go across the
grain of the country, up hill and down dale. If marks were awarded for
hairpin bends, the Marche provinces and not those of the Alps would
earn the highest grades. To cover it all, allow about three days. You will
not want to hurry from A to B. Though slow, your journey will be wonderfully quiet, for the Marche do not yet rank among the major tourist destinations. Almost uniquely in Italy, you can walk main roads without having
continually to leap aside or flatten yourself against a wall. On secondary
roads, on foot, you may be passed by about ten cars in an hour – and
three will stop to offer you a lift, which is also uncharacteristic of modern Italy.

The route we suggest, roughly parallel with the coast and 30-60 km
from it, connects towns, villages, lakes, gorges and mountain passes of
particular interest. They are fairly typical, however, of the general scene.
East-west roads, from the coast to the watershed and down into Tuscany and Umbria, cross the route. New highways and improvements to
the old ones are beginning to lessen the ordeal of those journeys. Within
a few years the Marche will be a different world. For the present, a casual detour can bring you to other places of memorable scenery, wrapped
in solitude, undiscovered by travellers, bathed in age-old simplicity. Join
our route at any point by following upstream roads from the pleasure
beaches of the Adriatic – and note how, as you climb, you are ascend-
ing the stream of time.

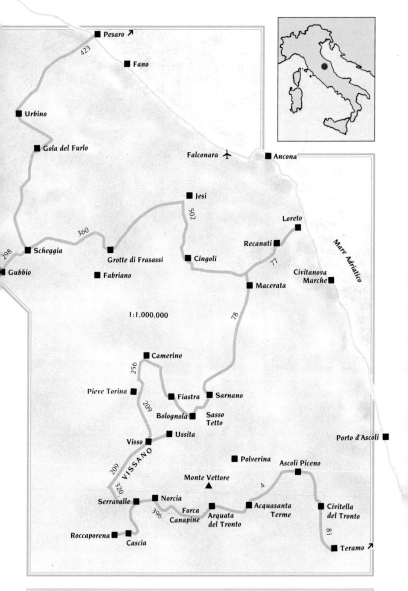

TRANSPORT

The regional airport is at Falconara, 10 km north-west of Ancona.

There are fascinating rail journeys on branch lines into the mountains from stations on the Adriatic coastal line (Milan-Bologna-Ancona-Pescara-Bari). You can get trains from Fano to Urbino; Falconara to Gubbio (and on to Rome); Civitanova Marche to Macerata and Fabriano; and Porto d'Ascoli to Ascoli Piceno.

From the coastal resorts and larger towns of the region – Ascoli Piceno, Macerata, Jesi and Urbino – there are scheduled bus services and summer excursions to all the places of interest on our tour. In the hills some villages see only one bus per day. The whole area away from the coast is lightly trafficked.

SIGHTS & PLACES OF INTEREST

ACQUASANTA TERME
A bustling little township in a gorge of the Tronto river where, heading west, you begin the stiff climb to the Forca Canapine (below). The waters have a centuries-old reputation for easing bone and muscle diseases. Mud packs and baths in the thermal grotto; beauty therapy.

ANCONA
Airport (Falconara) for the region. **Trajan's Arch** overlooks the harbour, which is sheltered in an angle of the coast (Ancona means 'elbow'). Handsome churches gaze out to sea. The **Cavalli Fountain** and the **Ferretti Palace** (National Museum inside it) are worth seeking out. From the port you can sail to Corfu, Greece, other Balkan states, Turkey, Cyprus and Israel.

ARQUATA DEL TRONTO
A noted upland resort (777 m), it slopes from a cone of rock above the Tronto ravine with a medieval fortress above and delightful flower beds and shrubberies below. A centre for excursions and walks into the **Sibillini Mountains** (vast panoramas from Monte Vettore, 2,378 m).

ASCOLI PICENO
Provincial capital and a well-built city strategically poised above the Tronto where that stream escapes from the hills and descends on the Adriatic (a railcar takes you to the coast in 25 minutes). Boulevards carry the impression of a place which has moved with the times: crowded streets unexpectedly open out on **Piazza del Popolo**, a great rendezvous ringed with shops and bars. Under the arcades you might be in an old Lombardy city, especially with **San Francesco's church** and the **town hall**, both elaborately Gothic, surveying the scene. The **Torneo della Quintana** with a 1,000-strong cast in fancy dress, first Sunday in August, is a historical joust similar to that of Arezzo.

BOLOGNOLA
For ski slopes all to yourself, look no farther than the looping road which encircles the Sassotetto massif at 1,100 m. Regional ski contests are held on extensive snowfields but the amenities so far are limited.

CAMERINO ⚰
A neat little hill-top town of narrow streets and steps to which few foreigners find their way. It is impossible to park a car here.

HOTELS AND RESTAURANTS
Away from the coastal resorts, places to eat and sleep at resemble those of Calabria and the Abruzzi. In parts, a foreign car is a rare sight and hotels cater mainly to the Italian business traveller.

Exceptions are Norcia and Cascia, each with a clutch of attractive hotels and *trattorie*. Large cities such as Macerata and Ascoli Piceno have relatively few places to stay at but *Agriturismo* (farmhouse accommodation) is beginning to catch on. One such place, recommended, is on the mountainside south of Acquasanta Terme, with impressive views over the Tronto valley.

Menus are dominated by *funghi*, as elsewhere (perhaps there will soon be a campaign against them, as against macaroni consumption in the 18thC). Other specialities are: *brodetto*, fish soup from the Ancona coast, either tomato-based or the saffron-yellow *brodetto recanatese*; pasta *alla marcheggiana*, made with risen bread dough; *vincisgrassi*, filled oven-baked pasta; *salame* Fabriano, made from a mixture of pork and beef; *caciotto*, a cheese made from both cows' and sheep's milk. Around Ascoli Piceno you may be offered olives stuffed with meat and herbs. Truffles are abundant in the Norcia area.

From vineyards around Jesi comes the white Verdicchio – according to Elizabeth David 'pleasant and refreshing to drink on the spot, but grotesque when put on the market in fancy bottles and sold abroad at the price of vintage claret'.

CINGOLI

A formidable climb from either direction to this charming old-fashioned little town which, for its views over the coastal towns, is known as the 'Balcony of the Marches'.

CIVITELLA DEL TRONTO ✕

Typically picturesque hill town with an old fortress and a couple of hotels. The terrace-like sloping piazza is another 'balcony of the hills' opening on the theatrical set of the coastal plain and the backdrop of the sea.

FIASTRA

The town is set in a small lakeland, in excellent hill-walking country, along the fast-moving Fiastrone river, which becomes the Fiastra lower down. Leisure activities centre on boating and fishing. Some relatively unobtrusive campsites.

FORCA CANAPINE

One reason for including Norcia (page

• Ur*bino*.

221) in this tour is to take you across the wild **Canapine Fork**. From either side your ascent is like that of a jumbo jet gaining altitude after take-off, but by no means in the same straight line. Miles of hairpin bends deliver you at last to pass level (1,543 m), to a large holiday hotel and winter sports installations. The broad **Castelluccio snowfields** 10 km north have sophisticated facilities. From Forca Canapine you can join walking excursions through the lonely, mystical Sibillini mountains, visiting **Lake Pilato** at 2,200 m and the **Sibyl's grotto**, about which guides tell tall tales. A road tunnel 20 km long will soon abandon these picturesque heights to the skiers.

GOLA DEL FURLO

Here a venerable consular road, Via Flaminia (State Highway 3), Rome to Fano on the Adriatic, dives into a narrow twisting gorge (*gola* is 'throat'). The main road goes through a 2-km tunnel but a short detour takes you down the gorge on the old road.

GROTTE DI FRASASSI
Among the limestone ravines of the Sentino torrent, these 'caves of between-the-rocks' are part of a maze of underground warrens and chambers, with some strange rock formations. Guided tours.

GUBBIO
See *Scheggia*, page 221.

JESI
Also spelt 'Iesi', it was a famous Swabian stronghold of the Middle Ages, commanding the Ancona coast. Frederick II, called 'Stupor Mundi' for his accomplishments, was born here in 1194.

Jesi still preserves its medieval fortifications. There are typical Venetian-school paintings in the **Palazzo della Signoria**. The town was also the birthplace of the composer Pergolesi (1710-1736).

LORETO
See *Macerata, this page.*

MACERATA
A much underrated, little-visited town. It breathes the authentic air of the old rustic red-brick Marche. A big walled centre holds itself aloof from 20thC developments and the broad piazza, town walls and wandering alley-ways make for leisurely exploration. Old-world courtesy prevails – ask for an address and you will be taken there, not merely directed.

Macerata's glory is its amazing **Sferisterio** above the main piazza, a Roman-style amphitheatre actually built in the 1820s. In July and August al fresco opera is staged.

On Route 77, 17 km and 25 km respectively downhill towards the coast are the interesting towns of **Recanati** and **Loreto**. The former has the much-publicized birthplace of the poet Leopardi (1798-1837), who for Italians is Keats and Byron rolled into one, and the more obscure birthplace of Beniamino

---

RECOMMENDED HOTELS

CAMERINO
I Duchi, L-LL; *Via Favorino 72; tel. 073 763 0440; credit cards*, AE, E, MC, V.

In the historic centre of an attractive walled town. Some reserved car parking in the piazza below. Hotel is large for the locality (49 rooms with TV and bath), rather anonymous but a safe bet for short-notice booking. Restaurant.

CASCIA
Cursula, LL; *Viale Cavour 3; tel. 074 376 206; credit cards*, AE, DC, E, MC, V; *closed Jan, Feb.*

In the new, lower part of town as you enter from the north. Old-fashioned air, but 34 rooms with bath/shower and telephone are clean if homely. Shaded car parking area. Restaurant renowned for typical local cuisine.

NORCIA
Dei Cacciatori, L (winter), LL (summer); *Via Case Sparse 14, Biselli; tel. 074 381 8147; credit cards*, AE, V.

Log-cabin style with covered terraces, signposted off Route 396 west of Norcia. Public areas glitzy but rooms bright and modern. Garden has a children's playground. Ample car parking. Fishing, shooting, canoeing and pony-trekking are available at this peaceful spot. Wood-panelled restaurant serves traditional food.

NORCIA DISTRICT
Canapine, LL; *Forca Canapine, on S396, 18 km E of Norcia; tel. 074 381 7568; credit cards, none (applied for).*

Dramatic situation at summit of 1,500-m pass: amazing views. Mainly a ski hotel, this place is agreeably quiet and friendly outside the winter season, but can be very busy in August.

POLVERINA
Albergo del Sole, L; *Strada Statale 77, No. 59; tel. 073 746 115; credit cards, none.*

Peaceful establishment above the main road, overlooking Polverina lake. Only ten rooms – even the passing traveller is made to feel at home. Restaurant specializes in truffle-based dishes at modest prices.

Gigli (1890-1955), last of the *bel canto* tenors. (The woman who took us looking for it in the suburbs, certain it was 'here somewhere', found the plaque she had never noticed on a small post office next door to her own house.)

Avoid Loreto if the religious trinket industry irritates you. You can see the gross basilica and apostolic palace from far away. Loreto leaped from humble village to rich town when the faithful accepted that a musty little sanctuary, now embedded in the basilica, was the Virgin Mary's house, miraculously translated in two bounds from Nazareth in Palestine.

NORCIA 🛏

An important art centre, walled, aggressively medieval in idyllic surroundings. Gastronomes equate Norcia with truffles. At **Serravalle**, 6 km west, you find tranquillity and an Arcadian valley accompanying Route 320 to Cascia and beyond. Both towns are holiday resorts and hang-gliding centres. Strong walkers should try Norcia-Ospedaletto and Cascia-Roccaporena, both six hours return. Free pocket-sized itineraries and maps from Cascia tourist office.

PESARO
See *Italy Overall: 4*.

RECANATI
See *Macerata, page 220*.

SARNANO
Showplace of the region, with a helter-skelter approach road surging through three tiers of ancient dwellings and flagged lanes. Rustic *trattorie*, camping and winter sports.

SCHEGGIA
A junction of roads through fine scenery. **Gubbio**, on Route 298, 13 km west of Scheggia, is one of Europe's best-preserved medieval towns. Traditional 'Race of Giant Candles' annually on May 15.

SERRAVALLE
See *Norcia, this page*.

TERAMO
See *Local Explorations: 15*.

URBINO
A major centre of Renaissance art.

Birthplace of Bramante and Raphael. **Marche National Gallery**, where a dozen old masters are represented, is housed in the rambling ducal palace, an architectural marvel. A very pretty pink-brick town.

USSITA
See *Vissano, below*.

VISSANO
It comprises the holiday district of **Visso** and **Ussita**. Beautiful walking country, rock-climbing and mountaineering. The ski scene is notable for downhill runs of varying distances. At Fontignano near Ussita they are up to 4 km long.

VISSO
See *Vissano, above*.

RECOMMENDED RESTAURANTS

CASCIA
Il Grottino, L; *Via Roma; tel. 074 376 420; credit cards, none; closed 9.30 pm and Tues in winter.*
Humble village *trattoria* in historic centre, but tender care goes into cooking and presentation. Veal in red wine, *rigatoni rustici*, spaghetti with truffles.

CIVITELLA DEL TRONTO
Fortezza, L; *off main piazza; tel. 086 191 321; credit cards, none.*
Grilled meats, pizza from wood-fired furnace – but the location and view are everything. A few rooms (**L**), clean and neat.

PIEVETORINA
La Camilluccia, L; *Strada Valnerina 6; tel. 073 751 8021; credit cards, V; closed Mon.*
Not much to look at, but cooking has won awards. Pizza, crayfish, wild boar and truffle dishes often on menu. Bar decoration includes fish tanks and a stuffed porcupine. Beside main road, car parking opposite.

Central Italy

North-West of Rome:
Etruscan Homeland

400 km; maps Touring Club Italiano Lazio

The Romans thought them vicious. In their painted wooden villas they perpetrated the worst excesses of a permissive society, such as taking their meals *en famille*, husband and wife reclining on the same couch. Yet Rome adopted their religious cults (vestal virgins and household gods), their arts of divination (thunder, sheeps' livers and the flight of birds) and their entertainments. From flute-and-dance routines with which, after capture, they amused their masters on Capitol Hill, Roman comedy was born. Before that, long before Rome's monuments were built, they ruled as kings. Their emblem of authority, twelve rods bound to an axe, became the badge of Empire and later of Fascism.

They were the Etruscans, the 'long-nosed, sensitive-footed, subtly-smiling Etruscans' as the novelist D.H. Lawrence called them. (His book *Etruscan Places* thoughtfully describes parts of the tour.) They founded cities from Lombardy to Campania but this region north-west of Rome was their homeland. Here is the great concentration of subterranean tombs with paintings and sculptures of surrealist artistry and high quality. They tell us as much as we know of a race which came from nowhere and vanished as mysteriously and spoke a language not yet properly deciphered. Of an Etruscan ruin Propertius wrote, 2,000 years ago:

> You, old Veii, were once the dwelling of princes,
> Where on the open mart glittered the lawgiver's throne;
> Now your streets are filled with the fluting of wandering
> shepherds,
> Over the graves of kings the goodman drives his plough.

In fact, you can see ancient Etruria without leaving Rome, in the glittering collections of the Villa Giulia (at Villa Borghese, closed Mon) and the Vatican (Gregorian Museum, closed Sun except last Sun in month; closed public holidays). Then, taking to the road and looking out for the 'TOMBA ETRUSCA' signs, without attempting too much, you can survey splendours *in situ*. They lie under archetypal pastures along earth-faults and round the black perimeters of volcanic lakes. Our route is adorned with clusters of surface ruins and tumuli (grave-mounds); for the tombs it is best (sometimes compulsory) to take a guide.

Travelling anti-clockwise, leave Rome on Via Trionfale or Via Cassia (north of St Peter's Square), not failing to look back from Monte Mario at a wonderful cityscape. Clockwise, leave on Via Aurelia (just south of St Peter's Square). Allow four days.

222

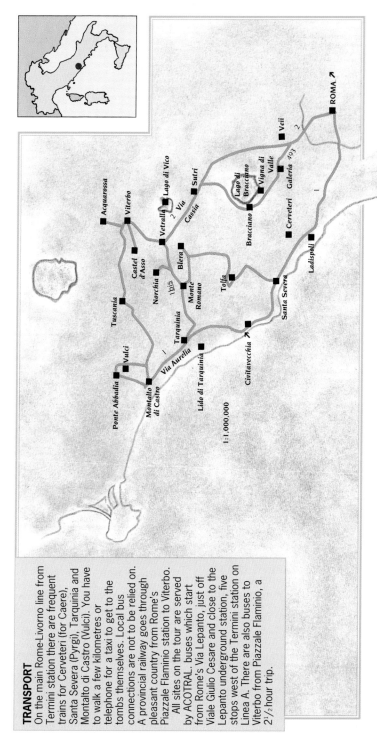

TRANSPORT

On the main Rome-Livorno line from Termini station there are frequent trains for Cerveteri (for Caere), Santa Severa (Pyrgi), Tarquinia and Montalto di Castro (Vulci). You have to walk a few kilometres or telephone for a taxi to get to the tombs themselves. Local bus connections are not to be relied on. A provincial railway goes through pleasant country from Rome's Piazzale Flaminio station to Viterbo. All sites on the tour are served by ACOTRAL buses which start from Rome's Via Lepanto, just off Viale Giulio Cesare and close to the Lepanto underground station, five stops west of the Termini station on Linea A. There are also buses to Viterbo from Piazzale Flaminio, a 2½-hour trip.

SIGHTS & PLACES OF INTEREST

ACQUAROSSA
To reach from Viterbo, leave the main route by Viale Francesco Baracca. An Etruscan town older than Viterbo, destroyed and abandoned about 500 BC. Unusually, traces of private dwellings have been found. The late King Gustavus of Sweden, a passionate Etruscologist, was reported to have uncovered a house near the warm springs. While insisting on gorgeous stone chambers for their dead, the Etruscans when alive inhabited timber houses, hence their rarity today. Clay and tile decorations from Acquarossa are in the Villa Giulia Museum in Rome.

BLERA
From Route 1bis, E at Monte Romano crossroads, signposted Barbarano Romano. Like many other Etruscan centres, Blera sits over a deep ravine. It is still outlined by sections of original walls. In the neighbourhood are about 1,000 tombs and dozens of tumuli. Excavations continue. But the tombs, having done duty for 1,000 years as stables and wine cellars, are a disappointment to the ordinary visitor. Soak up the atmosphere, savour the patriarchal landscape – more thinly populated now than in ancient times, but just as mild and fertile in climate and character.

BRACCIANO ✍
Famous for Roman baths, for the tremendous fortifications of the Orsi-

ni/Odescalchi castle and for giving its name to Italy's eighth largest lake. There are guided tours of the still-inhabited castle on Thursday, Saturday and public holidays. Massive construction, cylindrical towers, rich 15thC frescos, period furniture and a breathtaking view of the lake. Swimming and camping on lake front. At Vigna di Valle, 6 km east, is the **Aeronautical History Museum**, one of Europe's largest collections of vintage aircraft.

CASTEL d'ASSO
See Viterbo, page 229.

CERVETERI ✕
The 'modern' town is medieval and picturesque, draped over a spur of the soft, easily carved volcanic rock called tufa, within earshot of the motorway. Here are few traces of what was a great Etruscan centre of commerce except in the **Cerite Museum** (inside Ruspoli Palace near Piazza Santa Maria; open daily except Monday and public holidays).

The Etruscan urban plan was a city for the living and a city, equally important, for the dead, usually on adjacent hills. The Caere necropolis is 2 km north of Cerveteri on a minor road.

HOTELS AND RESTAURANTS
If really grand hotels and gourmet restaurants do not exist, establishments of superior quality are found everywhere in the region. The smallest towns have three or four reputable hotels and, though some close in winter, most remain open. Hotels in the new developments along the coast may lack character but they are invariably clean, neat and very moderate in their prices compared with not-so-distant Rome.

On the coast the diet is seafood, seafood and seafood. Inland a varied cuisine, based on traditional rural recipes, comes into its own with appetizing arrangements of game, lake fish, woodland herbs and fruits. If ingredients are hard to identify, you can be sure they are part of a pure and authentic tradition. The famous crop of the coastal plain is artichokes, which come in all shapes and sizes.

ETRURIA IN BRIEF
The best single destination is Tarquinia, 92 km from Rome on Route 1 or the A16 motorway.

A crisp introduction to Etruria would be a day trip Rome-Veii-Bracciano-Cerveteri-Rome, 98 km.

Before or after your Etruscan tour, try to see the Etruscan rooms in the Villa Giulia Museum (north-west corner of Villa Borghese, Rome) and the Gregorian rooms in the Vatican museums. When the wealth of Etruscan art first came to light, this area of Lazio was part of the Papal States and the Vatican took charge of it.

Ticket office and a snack bar are in the entrance square. You walk among long rows of tombs which have been denuded of most of their furnishings and paintings but cleaned up and made presentable. Not all the tumuli (earth-covered rock mounds above tombs) survive but those which do are wonderfully evocative of a distant past. Greek vases are placed here and there but the real treasures of old Caere have been distributed among the local Cerite Museum, the Gregorian at the Vatican, the Villa Giulia in Rome and, sad to say, many world museums and private collectors. The pillaging of this city as soon as it was unearthed was a bonanza for the illicit art markets.

A peasant farmer, ploughing the hillside in 1834, saw his oxen suddenly disappear down a hole. Thus the most famous of Etruscan tombs came to light. It is called **the Regolini-Galassi** and is visitable at **Sorbo**, south of Cerveteri village, about 4 km from the main Caere complex. The tomb is architecturally interesting but the sumptuous treasure which surrounded the princely corpse in its central chamber – gold, ivory, bronzes, ceramic jars – is now in the Gregorian Museum.

Walk among Caere's tombs on sandy tracks between low cliffs and tumuli, as the ancient Etruscans did in this city of their dead. You can even drive down Main Street, which is Via Sepolcrale Principale. To enter the central or **Banditaccia** system of tombs,

RECOMMENDED HOTELS

BRACCIANO
Casina del Lago, L; *tel.* 069 024 025; *credit cards, none; closed* Tues.

If you can secure a room in this small *albergo* you will enjoy ease, friendly informal care and tremendous views along the lake shore. A most attractive garden. Restaurant brings people out from Rome (**LL**).

LADISPOLI
La Posta Vecchia, LLL; *Palo,* 3 *km* S *along shore; tel.* 069 949 501; *credit cards,* AE, DC, E, MC, V.

Probably the most exclusive hotel on this stretch of coast. The small 17thC mansion has everything: lovely setting in own mini-park, great views, indoor swimming-pool, faded gilt and plush modernized with taste. Only 12 rooms, so you live like one of the family. Elegant restaurant (**LL-LLL**, must book if non-resident).

LIDO DI TARQUINIA
Velcamare, LL; *tel.* 076 688 380; *credit cards,* AE, E, MC, V; *closed* Oct-Feb, Tues until May.

Part of the modern sea-front complex of an extensive resort development. Flower-beds and shrubbery have not yet achieved the mature look. Hotel has privacy, own garden, easy accessibility to beach of volcanic sand and is small enough for staff to know you by name. To Tar-

quinia 6 km, to famous Etruscan tombs 9 km. Restaurant has unstereotyped seafood cuisine.

SANTA SEVERA
Pino al Mare, L; *tel.* 076 674 0027; *credit cards,* DC, E, MC, V; *closed Christmas and New Year.*

A quiet retreat in one of the quieter resorts. Delightful outlook from most of the 50 bedrooms, which are neatly and economically arranged. Restaurant (**LL**), offers variety of regional dishes, fish predominating.

TARQUINIA
Tarconte, LL; *Via Tuscia* 19; *tel.* 076 685 6141; *credit cards,* AE, DC.

Leading hotel of Etruscan district, discreetly sited at top of town. The bright clean stripped-pine look acts like a tonic. Lounge, bar, halls have appropriate Etruscan decoration, not over the top, and some modern paintings. One of the new-look hotels of the 1970s, this is still a favourite and its restaurant (**LL**) is much in demand for weddings and official banquets. Garage for car parking.

VITERBO
Leon d'Oro, L; *Via della Cava* 36; *tel.* 076 134 4444; *credit cards,* AE, DC, E, MC, V; *closed Christmas and New Year.*

An old provincial 'commercial' hotel which has come up in the world without sacrificing its atmosphere of solid comfort. In heart of old town, but Viterbo is not a noisy place.

• Tuscania.

which is like a collection of gigantic turf-topped beehives, you need a guide. Tomb of the Marine Waves, the Five Chairs, the Tarquins – tumuli of the Shields, the Painted Animals, the Boat – stripped of their glory, they hardly live up to their picturesque names.

CIVITAVECCHIA
See Italy Overall: 6.

GALERIA
At the Osteria Nuova crossroads turn S and then W to Santa Maria di Galeria, 4 km from crossroads. Continue along a stony lane for 2 km to River Arrone and ruins of Galeria. It was Etruscan Careiae. (Not now a major site; the striking view of the ruins from the main road against the background of Lake Bracciano and the sea may be enough.)

LADISPOLI ⋈
It has one of the longest sandy beaches on the Roman shore with ample

room to park a caravan, as thousands do. Highway One, the old Via Aurelia, is a busy road at the best of times and the Rome-Ladispoli section is exceptionally congested and unavoidable unless you take to the motorway. Bumper-to-bumper on summer Sundays. On the shore, another formidable Odescalchi fortress. Town is noted for its artichoke festa in April and its proximity to Cerveteri.

NORCHIA
See Vetralla, page 229.

ROME
See pages 106-119.

SANTA SEVERA ⋈
Palm-trees on the shore and a burly Odescalchi castle half seaborne distinguish this small resort from a score of others on the flat Tyrrhenian strand. From the castle you can walk to the excavations at Pyrgi, a one-time Etruscan seaport. It flourished from the 7thC to 3rdC BC, when the Romans

took over. Two temples have been identified and their clay decorations and friezes are in the Villa Giulia in Rome, along with the most sensational discovery: three golden sheets with bilingual (Phoenician and Etruscan) inscriptions which have enabled scholars to move deeper into the mysteries of the Etruscan language.

SUTRI

On lakeside road and unclassified lane, 25 km N of Bracciano. Quaint little town of tufa-built medieval and Renaissance buildings. The Roman amphitheatre, also dug out of tufa, must originally have been Etruscan. The small chapel of the Madonna del Parto (childbirth madonna to whom many pregnant women pay their devotions) was for-

merly a Mithraic temple, before that an Etruscan tomb.

TARQUINIA 🚢

If you have time for only one Etruscan site, this is it. From the low citadel of the lovely old town you look over parapets at a countryside which, from a distance at least, has changed hardly in 2,500 years. The **national museum**, spread over three floors of Palazzo Vitelleschi on Piazza Cavour, has the region's most comprehensive Etruscan collections. Here you see the famous stone sarcophagi with life-sized statues reclining on the lids; Greek-style red and black cups and pots, intricately

• *Viterbo.*

decorated; painted slabs from the tombs; and the most exciting of old Etrurian sculptures, the *Winged Horses*, two animals harnessed together and stepping out proudly and gracefully towards you. At the Museum, which is open daily except Monday, you can apply for a tour of the tombs, which lie underground beside a country road on Monterozzi Hill 4 km east.

Of about 20 large tombs, each frescoed with amazing action paintings which reveal so graphically the daily lives of the Etruscans at work and play, the guided tour allows time for about five. (You cannot enter without a guide.) Descriptions of the frescos' vivid colouring and varied subject-matter convey very little: you must see them for yourself. The names of a few tombs suggest the noble occupants' interests, hobbies or claims to fame: tomb of the Warrior, of Hunting and Fishing, of the Lioness, of Jesters, of Chariots, of the Bull, of the Typhoon (a mythical monster) and of the Dying Man.

TOLFA

Coming this way from Blera (see page 224) on minor roads you pass a **nature reserve** on the left and the **San Giovenale archaeological zone** on the right, with tumuli and ruins of mainly specialist interest, and 6 km west the **Pian di Luni plateau**. Here stands a huge Bronze Age construction with a cave in which Etruscan relics have been found. There is now a church on top of it.

Tolfa at 470 m is a small old-fashioned health resort half-way up a conical mount which has a medieval fortress of the Frangipani on top. The area is wooded, pleasing to the eye and rich in wildlife. They produce hams at Tolfa and sell them locally. The first Sunday in August is the *festa* of the hams. That is also the month of the *butteri* (cowboys), marked with tournaments and horse-races. In Tolfa's gift shops you can buy *cattane*, soft leather purses and wallets, and *incerrate*, rough rainproof coats as worn by the cattle-men.

TUSCANIA

Take Via Cassia Nord and turn left after 2 km. It is huddled on a hilltop in lonely country between two river gorges. Though damaged by earthquake, there are substantial Roman and medieval remains. The Etruscan finds are in the **civic museum** next to St Peter's church and the numerous 'rocky necropoli' from which they have come are scattered within a 2- to 3-km radius of the town, picturesquely wedged against cliffs beneath tangles of undergrowth. The big cube-shaped Peschiera tomb dates back to the 6thC BC.

VEII

Near the Madonna di Bracciano fork turn east to Isola Farnese on its cliff between gorges with the Ferraioli castle above. A narrow cutting leads past a broad Etruscan road and, crossing the Mola riverbed (pretty mill and waterfall), arrives at Portonaccio arch-

---

RECOMMENDED RESTAURANTS

BAGNAIA
Biscetti, L; *Via Gandin* 11; *tel.* 076 128 8252; *credit cards, AE; closed Jul.*

Sophisticated catering for discerning visitors (they flock to see the celebrated formal gardens of Villa Lante). Ingenious vegetable *antipasti*, stuffed aubergines and pumpkins, *frittate* (omelettes with ham, cheese, pork, many vegetables), red wine and rosé of Viterbo. There are a few rooms to rent (**L**).

CERVETERI
Oasi da Pino, L; *tel.* 069 953 482;

credit cards, none; closed Mon, most of Nov.

Attractive garden restaurant, country fare presented with style, a most reasonable à la carte menu.

VETRALLA
Primavera, L; *at Cura di Vetralla, 3 km S*; *tel.* 076 147 1029; *credit cards, AE, E, MC, V.*

A small *albergo* (**L**) whose restaurant has built up a reputation disproportionate to size or price. Fish casserole with numerous side-dishes of uncommon vegetables; oxtail *vaccinara*; *pagliata* of veal. Fine wine list includes the renowed Est Est Est of Montefiascone.

way and the excavations of Etruscan Veio, *Roman Veii.* You make out the lines of an ancient swimming-pool and the stalls of a sanctuary. Continue along the narrow road to Ponte di Formello. Here is a 75-m Etruscan rock tunnel on the bed of a rivulet. The Bell tomb, a frescoed chamber, is in the hillside above. Closer to Portonaccio, at **Riserva di Bagno**, are a few tombs lined up on terraces. They include the Tomb of the Geese, believed to be the oldest painted tomb in the region.

Ancient Veio was a buffer city against Rome and the first to fall in the Roman conquest (369 BC).

VETRALLA ✕

One of the oldest towns in classical Rome's domains and a significant staging-post on the Via Claudia (sometimes written 'Clodia'), a military highway in the 3rdC BC and now a state highway. For all that, its history is sketchy. It seems to have kept out of trouble and settled for a humble agricultural existence. The Romanesque **church of St Francis** is worth a visit. The **duomo** has a fresco by Antonio da Viterbo, an early Renaissance painter of provincial importance. The nearby **Rocca dei Vico**, an aggressive crag-top fortress, was garrisoned in the Second World War and almost entirely destroyed.

At Vetralla you are in the heart of metropolitan Etruria, surrounded by buried treasures. We deal separately with Blera (see page 224) but here you can run west on Route 1*bis* and after 9 km turn north for **Norchia**. Its 'rocky necropoli' – tombs hollowed in tufa rock – have unusually refined effigies and friezes on their sarcophagi. A deep split in the rocks, about 0.5 km long, is for walking through or viewing from the main road which crosses it.

VITERBO 🚲

A notable city of art, an undiscovered central Italian gem. The whole city, gathered on undulating hills, is a storehouse of domestic architecture of seven centuries. Overlooking the principal piazza are the 15thC **town hall**, the towered 12thC **Palazzo del Podestà** and the medieval and 18thC **prefecture**. **Palazzo Chigi**, one block south, **Palazzo Farnese**, south again, and the **Papal Palace** (13thC Gothic, brilliantly restored) must not be missed; nor the graceful churches of **Sant' Angelo**, **Santa Maria della Salute**, all part of the central complex. The medieval quarter has houses and shops of curious trades still intact. Near Santa Maria della Verità, 0.5 km east beside a railway, is a handsome **civic museum**. Follow the railway 0.5 km north and you come to the **Santa Rosa Sanctuary** where Rosa's body and her 'Machine' are kept. The 'Machine' is a top-heavy pillar 30 m high, newly-decorated every year and festooned in coloured lights. On 3rd September a force of strong men carry it through the streets and, for a climax, run full tilt with it up the steep street back to the sanctuary.

Though an Etruscan city, crucial to the old civilization's economy and defence, Viterbo preserves only fragments of the original walls in Piazza Duomo. Off Route 2, 9 km south-west, at **Castel d'Asso**, are 70 tombs with monumental façades, dating back to the 4thC BC. Nothing inside – art thieves got here before the authorities did. But stroll the narrow tufa-cut lane between them and, where it opens on olive-groves, you will feel you are really in tune with those shadowy folk of long ago.

VULCI

On a defenceless plain beside the River Fiora, Vulci led the pre-Roman world in bronze manufacture. By the 7thC BC it was Etruria's fancy goods emporium, turning out fascinating ornaments – tiny statuettes, decorated ostrich eggs, Egyptian scarabs and painted vases and jewellery. Much of what survived is now in the British Museum, London. Architecturally, the François tomb is the most remarkable. Its contents have been detached and reassembled in Rome's Villa Albani. Other material is at Villa Giulia.

Guided tours of the tombs leave Casale dell'Osteria most days in summer. The tour includes the excellent **State Museum** in Abbadia Castle, which is approached by a 1stC BC bridge of stone, delicate and fragile. (If you are unguided, take the rough lane upstream and come back to the river after 4 km. You can return to Vulci across the ravine by a startlingly modern bridge.)

Central Italy

Abruzzo: the Roof of Italy

233 km; round trip 452 km; maps Touring Club Italiano Lazio and Umbria Marche

Abruzzo or Abruzzi? Both are correct. Abruzzo is the region, Abruzzi describes the four provinces which make it: Aquila, Teramo, Pescara and Chieti. Close to Rome but separated by a mountain barrier, Abruzzo used to be notoriously a no-go area. Here the Apennines culminate in towering massifs. They have snow all year round and their slopes are split by dark forested gorges sometimes wide enough only for the torrents which rush through them. Traditionally, Abruzzi people led tough secretive lives and had little knowledge of the world outside. Emigration was a fact of life; emigrants in the New World supported those who stayed at home and that is why you may meet an old *abruzzese* who has no idea where London and Paris are but is familiar with Brooklyn and the Bronx.

Since the middle of this century hydro schemes, winter sports developments and now the motorways have been bringing a patriarchal lifestyle into contact with what we call civilization. To plan a local tour along motorways may seem strange but our two routes, the A24 and the A25, are no ordinary motorways. They forge through some of Europe's most dramatic scenery. It is as well that your view is obliterated now and again by tunnels several kilometres long – it gives you time to recover from the stupefying grandeur of forest and ravine, of towers and small belfries at impossible heights and powerful destructive torrents at impossible depths.

If you start this tour from Rome your motorway splits just beyond Tagliacozzo, the A24 going north by Aquila and the Gran Sasso tunnel (17 km long) to Teramo, the A25 by Avezzano to Pescara. The Adriatic *autostrada*, the A14, almost closes the gap between the two ends, so you could make a round trip of it. As an alternative to the long tunnel we suggest an exhilarating climb over the Gran Sasso itself.

Beware the rush hour morning and evening on the approaches to Rome. Every commuter seems to favour this stretch of motorway. We recommend Tivoli and the Sabine villages as escape routes of some fame and great charm. In 1993 the motorway toll Rome-Pescara was L1,300-L1,500 depending on size of vehicle; Rome-Teramo, including Gran Sasso tunnel, L1,100-L1,300. See also Local Explorations: 16. Allow one to two days for it all.

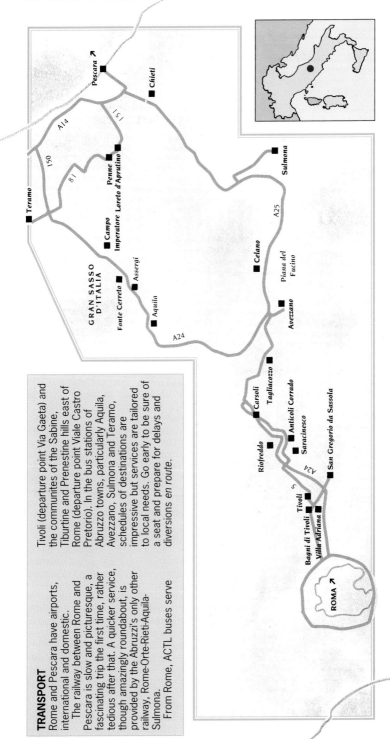

TRANSPORT

Rome and Pescara have airports, international and domestic.

The railway between Rome and Pescara is slow and picturesque, a fascinating trip the first time, rather tedious after that. A quicker service, though amazingly roundabout, is provided by the Abruzzi's only other railway, Rome-Orte-Rieti-Aquila-Sulmona.

From Rome, ACTL buses serve Tivoli (departure point Via Gaeta) and the communites of the Sabine, Tiburtine and Prenestine hills east of Rome (departure point Viale Castro Pretorio). In the bus stations of Abruzzo towns, particularly Aquila, Avezzano, Sulmona and Teramo, schedules of destinations are impressive but services are tailored to local needs. Go early to be sure of a seat and prepare for delays and diversions en route.

SIGHTS & PLACES OF INTEREST

ANTICOLI CORRADO
See The Sabine Villages, page 235; other Sabine villages covered in that entry, and marked on the map, include Saracinesco and San Gregorio in Sassola.

AQUILA ⌖
Regional capital, once the second city of the Kingdom of Naples, Aquila is an introverted hill-top place cherishing a few remarkable monuments. The **Collemaggio basilica**, dazzlingly faced with pink and white marble, has the tomb of Abruzzo's favourite Pope, Celestine V – he who *fece il gran rifiuto*, 'made the great renunciation' by resigning the papacy. See Dante's *Inferno*. The moated 16thC castle is now the **National Museum of Abruzzi History and Folklore**. A strange **fountain** with 99 spouts and a nightly carillon of 99 bells represent the 99 churches which once graced this pious town.

Aquila's little country-style shops have craftwork to offer in wood, copper, iron and lace. Buses go to Assergi for the Gran Sasso.

AVEZZANO
Tree-lined boulevards near the railway station suggest an elegance which the town does not sustain. An earthquake destroyed Avezzano in 1915 and the place was hastily rebuilt. The great lake of Fucino on its doorstep was dried out last century for cultivation and is now the **Plain** (Piano) **of Fucino**, 60 km round, like a fancy chessboard with parallelograms of crops edged with spiky poplars. There are said to be 782 km of small canals. The original lake outlet can be seen at the Incile buildings, 5 km south on Highway 82.

CELANO
A stupendous 15thC citadel sits four-square on a hill overlooking the drained Fucino lake, with grey and russet houses plastered to its skirts. Celano was a Roman station, then a Lombard town. People look subdued, and no wonder: the town was sacked many times and wrecked in three earthquakes, the most recent in 1915. Celano's **cathedral** has 15thC frescos and there is a macabre little chapel decked with human skulls.

CHIETI
Legend says that Achilles founded Chieti but its ancient monuments are all Roman: capitol, baths, water tanks, theatre, a clutch of restored temples. Chief medieval relics are a 14thC **tower** and the **cathedral**. The **archaeological museum** has one unique exhibit, the 6thC BC *Warrior of Capestrano* in limestone, a majestic souvenir of a culture about which little is known.

The **provincial library** has some of d'Annunzio's manuscript poems (he was born at Pescara). From the upper town there are fine views of the sea and the Maiella and Gran Sasso ranges.

GRAN SASSO D'ITALIA
The roof of the Apennines. Monte Corno, highest of a group of summits, is 2,914 m. On an easy gradient you climb from Aquila to Assergi and Fonte Cerreto, the cable-car station. A 12-minute ride deposits you at an Arctic settlement: hotel, restaurant, snack-bar, observatory, tiny black-and-white chapel, husky dogs and sleigh-rides. You can reach the same spot on a well-shod road (17bis/6) from Assergi. Walk for ten minutes along the uphill trail to Monte Corno and before you have reached the first refuge hut you are surrounded by edelweiss. (It is illegal to dig them up by the roots. Pick-

---

HOTELS AND RESTAURANTS
In the old provincial towns you will find old provincial hotels. They rarely rise above the mediocre in comfort or service (none of Rome's grovelling flunkeyism here), they economize on electric light but sometimes you are surprised by elements of refinement. An *Albergo Moderno* is usually the oldest for miles around.

Near and on the Gran Sasso and the Adriatic coast hotels and restaurants are more up-to-date and sophisticated, matching the vacation clientele they serve. See also Local Explorations: 16.

ing them could be unlawful, too: this depends upon local by-laws – enquire first rather than suffer embarrassment; a precaution which holds good for wild flowers all over Italy.)

Stroll the other way, down a slope, and you are on the Campo Imperatore, in winter a snowy table cloth and in summer a quaking bog of Alpine flora.

In Mussolini's time this was Rome's winter playground. Mussolini himself was here, a prisoner after the 1943 coup. The Germans rescued him in a daring airborne snatch. (Some visitors ask to be given his room at the Campo Imperatore hotel, but the proprietor has forgotten which it was.)

The ascent of Monte Corno from this side is not for amateurs. Slightly easier is the chairlift-assisted climb from Pietracamela on the other side of the massif. In winter the Gran Sasso is busy, though winter sports facilities are still rudimentary by Alpine standards. In summer everything is strangely neglected and peaceful.

LORETO D'APRUTINO
Aprutino means 'of Abruzzo'. The church of **Santa Maria in Piano** is a rare example of Lombard architecture. The pleasant little Acerbo art gallery exhibits a collection of antique Abruzzi ceramics.

PENNE
A typical old-fashioned highland town, reached without difficulty. Roman origins, a medieval flavour. One of the most wide-open views of Abruzzi landscapes from its mini-ring-road: fertile valleys close at hand, the windswept wastes of the mountains farther off.

PESCARA
See Italy Overall: 4.

ROME
See pages 106-119.

SULMONA
It was the birthplace of Ovid and despite its location it has been for cen-

---

RECOMMENDED HOTELS

AQUILA
Grand Hotel e del Parco, LLL; *Corso Federico* II 74; *tel.* 086 241 3248; *credit cards*, AE, DC, E, MC, V.

Dazzlingly bright modern hotel in city centre, just downhill from Duomo and overlooking a park. If you do not take advantage of the impressive health centre with sauna, solarium and Turkish bath you may feel you have been overcharged. Car parking.

FONTE CERRETO
Cristallo, LL; *tel.* 086 260 6688; *credit cards*, AE, E, MC, V.

An Alpine-style building which incorporates the old cable car station for the plateau of Campo Imperatore (where you find another hotel, very quiet outside the skiing season). The Cristallo has ample car parking and a high standard of comfort. All rooms have colour TV and telephones (a novelty in darkest Abruzzo) and the place is thronged and cheerful in the ski season. It is very close to the south entrance of the Gran Sasso tunnel (leave motorway at Assergi juction).

RIOFREDDO
Villa Celeste, L; *tel.* 077 492 9145; *credit cards, none.*

Villa Celeste is more like the *Marie Celeste* when you call on an autumn evening – deserted, a football match flickering on TV to an empty lounge. It turned out to be a useful overnight stop with easy car parking and a tennis-court and we ate well enough, and cheaply, at the unpretentious restaurant/pizzeria. Riofreddo is 55 km east of Rome, just off the motorway (leave at Mandela-Vicovaro or Carsoli junctions).

TAGLIACOZZO
Bocconcino, L-LL; *Via Vittorio Veneto* 25; *tel.* 086 366 866; *credit cards, none.*

A 3-star modern hotel tucked away in back streets of lower town, only five minutes' walk from historic centre. Peaceful. All rooms have bath, TV, telephone. Bright and roomy restaurant. Private car parking. Management organizes guided tours of local attractions, such as Abruzzo National Park. Discounts on town entertainments (tenpin bowling, swimming-pool, disco). In high season only half-pension or full board is available.

•*Fountains at the Villa d'Este, Tivoli.*

turies a commercial centre and market-place, much livelier than Aquila. An excellent base for the Abruzzo National Park (see Local Explorations: 16). Centre of *confetti* production – the coloured sugared almonds which go with baptismal and bridal ceremonies. **Palazzo Tabassi** is charming. An **aqueduct**, built in 1256, gives the town centre a look of its own.

TAGLIACOZZO 🛏 ✕
Pine forests drape the slopes and shelter the town, which is a grey stone ladder of cottages propped against the mountain. Allow an hour for walking to the topmost house from the piazza where you arrive. Being within an hour or so of Rome and having smooth snowfields above the tree line, this place has acquired a fashionable gloss. Round **Piazza del Obelisco** (the obelisk is the centrepiece of a fountain) signs such as 'BABY SHOP' and 'SNOOPY CLUB' look incongruous.

Rome clashed with the hill tribes here in 321 BC at the Battle of the Caudine Forks and was beaten. The Battle of Tagliacozzo took place in 1268 between Spaniards and Swabians. The **ducal palace** and **San Francesco's church** date from 1300. Swimming, discos, civilized bars and hill walking.

TERAMO ✕
Strange that such a solid, respectable town should have a history of brigandage, but it has. Flights of steps guide you to **Castello della Monica**, a 19thC medieval pastiche; to a small **Cappuccino church** with a wooden altar; and to the **Collurania observatory**. The Roman **amphitheatre** turns out to be a vague mass of rock, the Roman **theatre** consists of two mean alcoves. Curious coats of arms on old buildings, a pretty **Villa Comunale** (public park) with lake and civic museum. Everything low-key and parochial.

TIVOLI

A town older than Rome, well equipped with antiques, crafts and gift shops. Thronged with touring buses, all converging on **Villa d'Este** for the renowned fountain displays. By contrast, the cascades of **Villa Gregoriana** down the road are not much visited. See Tivoli's fountains also by night (summer-time only) if possible, when fireflies compete with the discreet floodlighting.

VILLA ADRIANA

Hadrian's Villa at Bagni di Tivoli, 2ndC BC, is a collection of replicas of the wonders which the imperial master-builder had admired on his Mediterranean travels. Scaled-down temples, forts, libraries, pavilions, the Athens Academy and Egypt's Canopus Canal are set along avenues peopled with marble heroes and haunted by lizards and butterflies. On a quiet day it is a magical spot. You can stay the night – the Adriano restaurant at the main entrance normally has a few rooms to rent.

THE SABINE VILLAGES

Savage gradients on gravelled roads, fortress walls and crowded houses, a rectangular piazza with fountain and plane trees, donkeys stumbling down cobbled lanes – such are the Sabine villages, close to Rome but a world away. You don't find them in the holiday brochures. Licenza is in classical literature as the Sabine farm to which Horace retired and gave a mention in his *Odes*. Anticoli Corrado has its niche in art history – its inhabitants were sought by artists and photographers of Rome. One greybeard, known as Padre Eterno for his patriarchal looks, appears in numerous 19thC Biblical pictures. Anticoli peasant girls modelled for several Roman fountains. Their grand-children had walk-on parts in the movie *The Secret of Santa Vittoria*, shot at Anticoli in 1969. Other Sabine villages, cut by the motorway but aloof from it, relatively easy to get at from Routes 5, 636 or the A24 (Tivoli and Vicovaro junctions) are Marcellina, Saracinesco, Ciciliano and San Gregorio in Sassola.

RECOMMENDED RESTAURANTS

CARSOLI

L'Angelo d'Abruzzo, LL; Piazza Aldo Moro; *tel.* 086 399 7429; *credit cards*, AE, DC, E, MC, V; *closed* Wed.

Leave motorway at Carsoli junction and in town follow ' STAZIONE FS' (railway station) signs. The place is popular with locals, unknown to tourists. Menu is dominated by *funghi* – and truffle-based dishes. The *filetto al tartufo* (fillet steak with truffles) was mouth-watering.

RIOFREDDO

La Tana dei Lupi, L-LL; *tel.* 077 492 9094; *credit cards*, AE, E, MC, V (*applied for*); *closed* Mon.

It occupies the uninviting ground floor of an apartment block, but the new (1992) owner has trained in Hiltons and Sheratons worldwide. Mushrooms and truffles enhance the standard regional cuisine. Try the *fettuccini ai porcini*, an out-of-this-world pasta dish. A tourist menu (**L**) is planned. See Recommended Hotels (page 233) for location of Riofreddo.

TAGLIACOZZO

Al Corradino di Svevia, L; Piazza Obelisco 48; *tel.* 086 368 246; *credit cards*, AE, E, MC, V (*applied for*); *closed* Tues eve.

They do not come more determinedly rustic than this: low wood-beamed ceilings, walls lined with wine bottles. Central situation opposite fountain on main piazza. Vegetarians delight in broad choice of salads, wide range of wood-fired pizzas, but the charcoal-grilled meats are done to a turn. Impressive wine list opens with an excellent cheap house wine.

TERAMO

Duomo, LL; Via Stazio 9; *tel.* 086 124 1774; *credit cards*, AE, DC, E, MC, V; *closed* Mon, most of Aug.

A noted rendezvous for locals in the tranquil heart of the town. Charges may seem a little steep for the sort of place it is, but the regional cuisine is presented with care and expertise.

<u>Central Italy</u>

Gorges of the Abruzzi

220 *km*; *map Touring Club Italiano Abruzzo Molise*

An Italian sky, an Italian climate, snow and sunshine on the heights – and no art. Can the foreign traveller imagine anything more delightful? It is not strictly true. There are relics of great art in the wilds of Abruzzo, but they have to be sought out. There are no concentrated collections. You come across the treasures in dead townships and unfrequented valleys, chipped and cracked and reset in a lamentable fashion.

Local Explorations: 15 went through this wild land on the motorways, looking at peaks, gullies and untameable massifs from a distance. Here you diverge from the motorways, from the Chieti-Pescara junction at one end and the Cocullo junction at the other (the A25). On the west you pass through the Abruzzo National Park, on the east you surmount the shoulders of the Maiella, a great knot in the Apennine chain which touches 2,795 m. The route goes through a web of obstacles thrown up by Nature and it follows ancient lines of communication between the high pastures, where you may meet a shepherd as primitive as a shepherd of Tibet, and hill villages to which people have clung obstinately for centuries. Although the roads proceed in endless flourishes of hairpin bends, they are beautifully engineered and for the most part highly panoramic. Stick to the route, otherwise you could find yourself in a dead-end valley or on a mountain-top with nowhere to go; all in all, two days.

Italians rarely came into this region, convenient as it was to Rome, Naples and the Adriatic coast. Abruzzo was to them only part of that poverty-stricken, troublesome South which gave politicians and economists headaches. Within the past 30 years the cable-cars have begun skimming up the mountain slopes and there are points on our route – Rivisondoli, Roccaraso, Pescasseroli – which, with their pink-and-green roofs, timber chalets and weekend crowds, resemble an Alpine resort. Motorways and ski areas have introduced colour into the old rusty villages and their towering rocks. New hotels and *trattorie* and souvenir shops are slowly (because the *abruzzesi* are a conservative folk) persuading the lifeless taverns and *locande* to smarten themselves up.

Not content with ringing the region with motorways and improving existing roads, the authorities are now pushing *superstrade* up the torrent valleys. Abruzzo may not much longer be a country reserved for the eagle, the mountain hare and the hardy walker. At present however you can still park the car on a mountain pass, wander off along a line of snow posts and soak up a divine air and a sublime solitude.

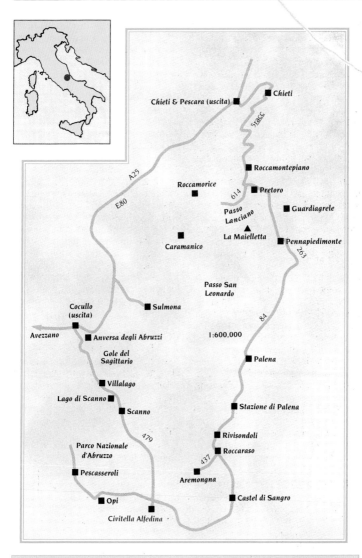

TRANSPORT

If possible, take a ride on an Abruzzo railway. The network is not complicated but the principal line (Ortona-Guardiagrele-Castel di Sangro-Sulmona-Pescara) and its offshoots have scores of little stations for scores of villages and hamlets. As usual in mountainous Italy, village and station may be far apart. Scanno, for instance, is 23 km from its station. These trains hang on by their eyebrows. They scale crags and burrow through spurs and take

for ever. Country folk walk briskly through tunnels, confident the train will not overtake them. Even a short trip between two wayside halts, from which you can walk back over the hill in little more time than it took the train, shows railway engineering at its most audacious. An especially dramatic section is between Sulmona and Castel di Sangro (90 minutes). Its summit at around 900 m is among the highest of ordinary railroads in Europe.

See also Local Explorations: 15.

SIGHTS & PLACES OF INTEREST

ABRUZZO NATIONAL PARK
About 45 km S of Sulmona on unclassified roads. The park is part of the landscape and you do not know, without a map, when you are in or out of it. Over the years it has shrunk from a protected area covering all the central Apennines to its present 40,000 hectares and the shrinkage has made a dragnet of this craggy mountainland, altitude 700-2,000 m. Flora and fauna banished from other parts find a refuge here. Rare, but still around, are the Marsican brown bears, exclusive to the district. Wolves are rarer still. Chamois show themselves, particularly in the mating season. Other species include roe deer, wild cats, badgers and otters. Birdwatchers report eagles, eagle owls and some rare small bird species.

Our route runs for 20 km just inside the park. If you see no wildlife you cannot miss the splendour of beech forests and, above them, the *karst* (limestone) plateaux with crags and caverns and the pines which grow out of the sheer sides of profound gullies. Spring is the flowery season with masses of crocuses and gentians, daisies and irises among noble broad-leaved trees in the river meadows of the Sangro, which runs through the park. From Civitella Alfedena you could detour inside the park to **Pescasseroli** (birthplace of philosopher Benedetto Croce, 1866-1952; botanical garden, museum of natural history) and the source of the Sangro. This detour adds 24 km to the trip.

CASTEL DI SANGRO
You see its twin-towered **baroque cathedral** and **mini-acropolis** from far away. The **Corso**, across the rushing Sangro river, is a winding street of many colours with a patterned piazza. Townsfolk chatter, children shout, small trades are plied at cottage doors; life seems more spirited and easy-going than in other stern, dark Abruzzi communities. Craft shops deal in the typical *montagnard* products: wood carvings, wrought iron, woollen rugs, garments and tapestries. Veterans of the Second World War will recall that Allied and German troops were locked in combat along the Sangro, between here and the sea, for many months.

CIVITELLA ALFEDENA
A medieval hamlet above a serpentine reservoir at the east entrance to the National Park. It has a museum of wildlife and folk history, a visitor centre, mountain refuges for climbers and a company of wolves in an enclosure.

COCULLO
Early in May you meet the *serpari* or snake-charmers carrying sacks of

---

HOTELS AND RESTAURANTS
The sombre *alberghi* of Abruzzo towns, old-fashioned travellers' inns with wooden chairs around the reception counter, doing duty as a sitting room – a minimum of decoration – a cathedral-like gloom along the corridors – a bathroom to every floor, furnished with hand-towels like napkins and bath-towels like sheets – sparse bedrooms with unmanageable *persiani* (heavy wooden shutters)... these are to be found but are being replaced by 'business' hotels in major centres and chalet-type seasonal hotels in the mountain resorts.

You may eat well and interestingly but not as cheaply as you might suppose. On the large breadchest in every *trattoria* kitchen, among the hammered copper pots, lies the *chitarra* ('guitar') with steel cords, used for slicing narrow strips for *maccheroni* and egg pasta. *Maccheroni alla chitarra* is the Abruzzo's contribution to the national cuisine. It may come with a minced lamb sauce. Expect a variety of nourishing soups – chicken broth with chicory, lentil soup or minestrone *della virtù*, with meats and vegetables in profusion. Lamb or kid may be cooked in a huge cauldron out of doors, or in a pan with sweet peppers and herbs. On the coast you find sole, cuttlefish, sardines and most seafoods. *Pecorino* and the soft round *caciocavallo* are the most 'regional' of Abruzzo cheeses. Sweets are plentiful – sugary cakes and bonbons. Even the *confetti* of Sulmona (sugared almonds) may be offered for dessert.

vipers into town. By the power of their arts they draw snakes from dark crevices and nests in the bracken. Waiting for the saint to be brought out of church they offer to inoculate you against snake-bite with the scratch of a fang. It is unnecessary: on San Domenico's Day (first Thursday in May) the reptiles declare a truce. (More likely the vipers are drowsy after hibernation.) The saint's statue, crowned with roses and clothed in snakes, tours the village whose cottages fit into the slits of the mountainside like pieces of an

•*Near Scanno, edge of the Abruzzi National Park.*

interlocking puzzle. Then, on a tiny piazza adorned with gladioli in olive-oil drums and ankle-deep in snakes, Cocullo prepares for its annual al fresco supper dance.

Cocullo is quaint at any time, but San Domenico's day is a day to remember. He lived in the Sagittario gorges (see page 241) and like St Francis had a way with birds and beasts. Like many saints he also had a

RECOMMENDED HOTELS

AREMOGNA
Boschetto, L-LL; *at the foot of the Monte Greco ski-tow, 9 km W of Roccaraso; tel. 086 462 297; credit cards, none; open mid-Jul to end Aug, early Dec-Apr.*

The steep road to this thriving ski resort should not deter you. The hotel has superb views, is warm and comfortable on an icy day and, though well equipped for an energetic clientele, also provides a rest-cure. Humdrum cuisine (**L** available to non-residents).

PESCASSEROLI
Grand Hotel del Parco, LLL; *tel. 086 391 2745; credit cards, AE, DC, E, MC, V; open mid-Jun to end Sep, early Dec-Apr.*

Embedded in the depths of the National Park, this is probably the nearest thing the Abruzzo knows to a luxury hotel. Cool in summer, warm in winter. Splendid views, swimming-pool, agreeable garden. Restaurant (**LL**).

ROCCARASO
Motel Agip, LL; *1 km from town on road to Sulmona; tel. 086 462 443; credit cards, AE, DC, E, MC, V.*

Welcoming, efficient, no problem getting in, a picturesque situation.

SCANNO
Miramonte, L; *edge of town on the Anversa road; tel. 086 474 369; credit cards, none; open Easter-Sep.*

Commanding the entrance to this most charming of Abruzzi towns, it was Scanno's first modern hotel and has moved with the times while keeping charges very moderate. Easy car parking, a starting-point for pleasant walks, very quiet after dark.

MAIELLA MOUNTAINS
Though not quite the height of the Gran Sasso they are rougher, lonelier and streaked with crevices, each with its toy chapel, statue or crucifix. They flaunt their snows blatantly in the face of a summer sun. Paths cross their rounded summits and edelweiss decorates the snowy fringes. 'Never pick edelweiss,' they say, 'it grows in dangerous places.' On the Maiella you can hardly avoid trampling it. In intervening hollows the clearings are edged with pines and deep in fir-cones and on the high pastures poppies, delphiniums and all the flora of a cultivated garden grow in profusion.

Follow a stream from Caramanico, Roccamorice or Pennapiedimonte to its Maiella source and you will pick up another, trickling down the far side. If you have no time for a trans-Maiella hike, drive the looping highway from Pretoro to the Lanciano pass (10 km) or from Palena station to the San Leonard pass (25 km). At the former there is a chalet-style hotel, a restaurant and ski tows. When we were there some plainsmen were building summer cottages of limestone rock (it does not hold water, therefore will not freeze and split), so one day this will be a smart little high-altitude village. A road from the Lanciano Pass climbs a few kilometres south to about 2,000 m. There, we are assured, with a telescope you can see both Naples and Ancona, cities 400 km apart. More staggering is the view of Pennapiedimonte's roof-tops, defying gravity on a Maielletta outcrop, like a village temporarily halted in the course of a miraculous translation. Our route passes under this village (Route 263); you could photograph it through the sunroof of a car.

If you cross the Maiella on foot, take local advice about the weather. Mist on a summer day not only disorientates, it rapidly reduces the temperature by 30 degrees.

PRETORO
A village of artisans in wood, buried among pines on a zigzag ascent to the Maiella. For centuries it supplied the implements Italian housewives needed for the main task of the day, namely making the pasta. The *chitarra* or harplike frame, the serrated mallet, the ravi-

short fuse. He stopped at Cocullo to have his mule shod. When the farrier asked for payment he struck him dumb for his impudence and the mule kicked off its shoes in disgust. Anyone who doubts this story can see one of the horseshoes in the parish church.

oli mould, the metre-long paddle for stirring – they all originated at Pretoro and people still come from far afield to buy them.

ROCCAMORICE
Also Caramanico and Pennapiedimonte: see Maiella Mountains, page 240.

ROCCARASO ⇥ ✕
An expanding township of Alpine chalets, already (with nearby Pesco-costanza and Rivisondoli) among the top ten mountain holiday and winter sports resorts of central Italy.

SAGITTARIO GORGES
The river starts as the Tasso in the National Park (Torquato Tasso the 16thC poet was often a visitor to the feudal castles of the district). Below Scanno (this page) it breaks out into Lake Scanno, emerald-green and silent with feathery trees and towering cliffs around it, a famous place for trout and nightingales and the biggest natural lake in the province. Under Villalago the river hurls itself at a series of cascades and becomes the Sagittario. Compressed into 10 km of fantastic *gole* ('throats') of limestone, foaming with a wild turbulence, it opens out beyond Anversa and goes sedately to a squalid destiny in the industrialized Pescara river. Our road goes through the gorges, entwined with the torrent, tunnelling through the rock, demanding caution and alertness in motorists.

Spanning the road, overhanging the Scanno lake, is the **sanctuary of Santa Maria del Lago**, 'Our Lady of the Lake', a chapel to which local women have brought many votive offerings. All the district comes to her *festa* in July.

Villalago, poised on a rock which shoots up from the Sagittario abyss to nearly 1,000 m, is a holy place. It shares San Domenico with Cocullo (when you see a saint in a niche with the wolf-and-serpent emblem, that is San Domenico) and the pathway to his rustic chapel, bare and frugal, is lined with Stations of the Cross. Like many others in these mountains, the chapel is hollowed out of living rock. Comically naïve pictures of the miracles San Domenico performed are painted on the loggia.

RECOMMENDED RESTAURANTS

RIVISONDOLI
Da Giocondo, L-LL; *tel.* 086 469 123; *credit cards*, AE, DC, E, MC, V.
Very small and you should give prior notice. A genuine traditional *trattoria*.

ROCCARASO
La Preta, LL; 4 *km* E *on mountain road to Ateleta; tel.* 086 462 716; *credit cards*, AE, V; *closed* Tues.
Another gem of a restaurant where intriguing country specialities can be relied on.

SCANNO
Grotta dei Colombi, L; *Viale dei Caduti; tel.* 086 474 393; *credit cards*, E, MC, V; *closed* Wed.
Of two dozen hotels and restaurants now flourishing in Scanno, this is the best value. Very much a family affair: son shaping well as a waiter, grandma's muffled oaths from the kitchen indicating who is really in charge. Only a step from farce in certain respects – they give you the menu and tell you most dishes are 'off'. *Il padrone* carries everything with unshakeable aplomb. Food uncomplicated but stylish. A dozen rooms (**L**) to let, clean and comfortable. And all incredibly cheap.

SCANNO ⇥ ✕
A surprising town, a town of women. The streets have a passion for gradients. Tall houses with decorated lintels bend over them, archways and balconies span mysterious alleyways. The women too are tall and dignified. On Sundays they wear a sombre costume of blue and green and, under turbans, their hair is braided and woven with tresses of coloured wool. Long ago Scanno grew rich on wool. The men tended distant flocks, the women stayed at home knitting. They developed a matriarchy and took Saracen slaves for their servants, who taught them Oriental embroidery. South-west, under the Terratta ridge, are ski slopes and a chair-lift.

VILLALAGO
See Sagittario Gorges, this page.

Central Italy

South-East of Rome: the Pontine Way

180 km, plus Ponza detour 70 km; map Touring Club Italiano Lazio

In the last reel of *La Dolce Vita* the sweet lifers end a night of *dégringo-lade* by going down to Rome's lido to watch the sun rise over the sea (apparently unaware they are facing west). A strange dead creature has been washed ashore, a behemoth of the deep. It symbolizes decadence and corruption. It could also symbolize the desperate ugliness which has come upon parts of the Roman shore. We no longer have to contend with the evil-smelling Pontine marshes which once barred the traveller's way between Rome and Naples: that land is now under cultivation. But you must traverse miles of bungalows, cheap shacks, tents, caravans, grey sea, grey sand and groynes and concrete walls many times patched.

Nonetheless, our tour (one to three days in all) has its moments, and this guide would be incomplete without it. Nowhere in Italy, not even in Rome, has history sunk its roots so deep as on this littoral of tombs, temples and place names (Lavinio, Enea, Latina, Cincinnati) carried forward from nearly 3,000 years ago when the first arrivals on the Tiber struggled to gain a foothold. Forget the vacationlands, concentrate on a timeless landscape, the renowned and unmistakable Roman countryside of open valleys and hunting woodland, crumbling towers and aqueducts, green hills and quiet lakes. If the beaches are skimpy and artificial, the towns have a stubborn unchanging character. For all the influence Rome has had, they might be in another region altogether. Do not miss Ostia Antica, one-time port of Rome, a superb example of a prosperous city of the imperial era, today a little-publicized peaceful place where you can wander for hours, or just sit dreaming, and feel all the better for it.

If you come down from Rome at dawn, like the *Dolce Vita* crowd, you find Via Ostiense and Via del Mare only moderately busy. Later you encounter congestion, delays and always an accident up ahead. From central Rome head south and keep to the east (left) bank of the Tiber; cross it and you end up at the airport (Ostia Antica and Fiumicino village are however equally accessible from that road). Avoid these busy roads altogether by finding Via Cristoforo Colombo, near Caracalla baths, and following it through the EUR zone (the big sports complex) to the sea 4 km east of Lido di Ostia.

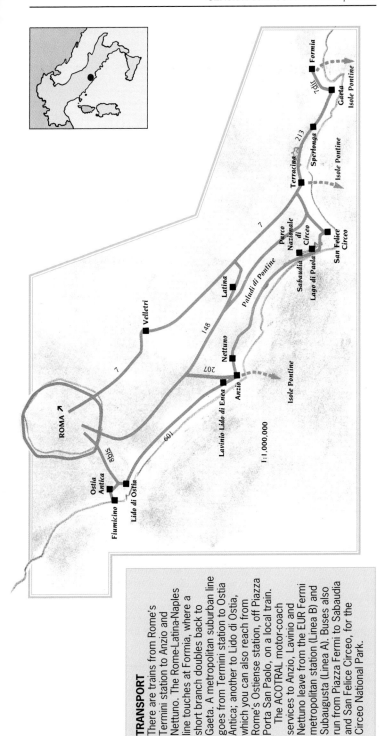

TRANSPORT

There are trains from Rome's Termini station to Anzio and Nettuno. The Rome-Latina-Naples line touches at Formia, where a short branch doubles back to Gaeta. A metropolitan suburban line goes from Termini station to Ostia Antica; another to Lido di Ostia, which you can also reach from Rome's Ostiense station, off Piazza Porta San Paolo, on a local train.

The ACOTRAL motor-coach services to Anzio, Lavinio and Nettuno leave from the EUR Fermi metropolitan station (Linea B) and Subaugusta (Linea A). Buses also run from Piazza Fermi to Sabaudia and San Felice Circeo, for the Circeo National Park.

SIGHTS & PLACES OF INTEREST

ANZIO ⌗

Ancient Antium, the 'goodly city' of Coriolanus, has a compact harbour and traces of imperial villas, notably that of Nero from which some of the world's greatest sculptural treasures were taken. The *Apollo Belvedere* and *Dying Gaul* are now in the National Museum on the Campidoglio in Rome.

Anzio thrives on fishing, on the tourist industry (major regattas bring crowds and create excitement), on the coming and going of yachts and ferries and on visits from war veterans. The **U.S. military cemetery** is 3 km east at Nettuno, the **British** 4 km north on Route 207. The casualties came from Allied landings in 1944, when Britain's Grenadier Guards spearheaded the assault. A little girl named Angelita, found wandering in the battle and adopted by an army unit, has become the emblem of war-orphaned children. Her monument is west on the sea-front road.

Anzio is the ferry port for Ponza (see page 245).

HOTELS AND RESTAURANTS
Seaside hotels are sprinkled along the coast. Being seasonal, they do not all inspire confidence. Experience shows that out-of-town hotels tend to be more self-contained and to have a more settled clientele than those in the resorts. They also offer better value for money.

Restaurants spring up and die down. This year's favourite may be next year's flop. Proprietors, chefs and waiters display enthusiasm and anxiety to please: they aim for a quick reputation and a move to Rome. A typical meal of the Lazio coast might include chicken broth with *quadrucci* (small pasta squares); *gnocchi*, *bucatini* or spaghetti *carbonara* (with streaky bacon); lamb with peppers, spitted or roast; and fishy, salty salads. The strong, dry red wines of Velletri are very drinkable. The classic dry whites of Frascati, Albano and Genzano di Roma are normally available.

CIRCEO NATIONAL PARK

As Mussolini's drainage campaign steam-rollered its way across the Pontine marshes in 1934, conservationists took steps to save a corner of a unique environment. They created the Parco Nazionale di Circeo, so-called because ruins on a headland along the Park's seaward border were associated with Circe, the charmer who turned men into swine, in the *Odyssey*. The conservationists failed to halt the post-1945 spread of roads and villas along the coast, but since 1974 building development has been brought under control. Some more land, and the Pontine island of Zannone, 32 km offshore, have more recently been included in the Park.

This antediluvian botanical survival takes in lakes, mountain and forest. To reach the higher ground you must tread difficult paths through cork and holm oak woods. It is easier to get along on the seaward side, which is mostly heathland with juniper, palmettos and wild flowers, especially wallflowers. Many uncommon birds, including sheldrakes, ospreys and grebes, frequent the lakes on the sea's edge, while secluded ponds in the woods are the watering holes of roe deer, badgers, wild cats and pine martens. Keen walkers, botanists and ornithologists could spend a few days here, staying at one of the two townships on the edge of the Park, Sabaudia and San Felice Circeo (see page 246).

FIUMICINO

See Ostia Antica, page 245.

FORMIA

A fine sandy beach shelves gently and the Gaeta promontory protects it against south-westerly gales. In the calm waters of the Vindicio beach water-sports flourish; they hold water-skiing championships. There are ferries to Ischia and the Pontine islands.

Classical **Formia** stood on the old Via Appia and was a Roman bathing station. You can see the outlines of hanging gardens and swimming-pools on the sea-front. Among the ruins of large, luxurious Roman villas is that of Cicero, now Villa Rubino. Cicero's tomb, a conical tower set on bricks and bordered with evergreens, is 2 km west on the Gaeta road.

GAETA ⊯

It keeps intact the character of the historic seaport towns of the Rome-Naples shore. Some old streets are mere flights of steps between gaunt white-painted houses. The important ecclesiastical sight is the lavishly-decorated **Column of the Easter Candle** in the 13thC cathedral. The **Diocesan Museum** (it keeps short and unpredictable hours – try 9 am or 5 pm) portrays a turbulent religious past.

Gaeta's **Serapo beach**, 1.5 km long, has reasonable bathing and, at either end, excellent sub-aqua possibilities. From above the **Crucifix sanctuary**, wedged in a chasm, you have good seascapes. On the coast road 15 km west are natural marine caves, including a large one associated with Emperor Tiberius; objects found in them are now in the museum at **Sperlonga**, 2 km west.

LIDO DI OSTIA ✕

See Ostia Antica, below.

OSTIA ANTICA ✕

The settlements at the Tiber mouth are, from west to east, Fiumicino, next door to Rome's international airport, a fishing village on the canal by which the Tiber reaches the sea; Ostia Antica the ancient port of Rome; and Lido di Ostia, a seaside resort with a long sandy beach backed by pine-woods and an area reserved for hunting.

Fiumicino has excellent fish restaurants, a safari park and a ship museum with reconstructions of Roman galleys from Ostia Antica.

Ostia Antica is among Italy's most evocative classical sites. A complete 4thC BC city has been exposed without too much archaeological tampering: forum, temple, a long main street, a street of balconies, an amphitheatre, shops, public baths with hot and cold showers (advertised with a wonderful mosaic of Neptune driving seahorses through shoals of fish), a market-place with oil jars still casually scattered, warehouses with mosaic pictures on the dockside in front of them, telling you where to unload your fruits, wines and timber. The wall decorations in the merchants' houses, inspired by the exotic wares which passed through the port, are very pretty. There is much to see at Ostia Antica and the site is never

THE PONTINE OR PONZIAN ISLANDS

They lie about 36 km SW of Anzio: Ponza (@) with its two islets of Palmarola and Zannone; and Ventotene further east. The chief attraction is **Ponza**. Its port takes car ferries but otherwise landing-places are few and there are only 12 km of rough roads. Tunnels in the volcanic tufa rocks communicate with outlying communities and provide access to postage-stamp-sized coves, grottoes and rough bastions of cliffs. A great deal of wild mountain scenery is crammed into Ponza's few square kilometres. The town resembles a Greek island town: square, flat-roofed white houses, precipitous alleyways between high white walls. Ponza was a Roman playground, later a place of political exile. The Abyssinian princes lived here after 1936 and in 1943, after Mussolini's overthrow, the *carabinieri* brought him here for some days before taking him to the Gran Sasso.

The spectacular beach is **Chiaia di Luna**, which you reach through a 0.5-km subway – a cool walk with a current of air even on the hottest day.

'From what kingdom are you?' Maria Aprea, aged 86, asked us, brandishing her Bible. The island is a small hotbed of Jehovah's Witnesses, mostly returned emigrants from the U.S.

Sea services to Ponza and Ventotene from Anzio, San Felice Circeo, Terracina and Formia (summer only) take an hour (hydrofoil) or three (car ferry). From Fiumicino there is a fast catamaran to Ponza. From Anzio you could do Ponza in the day, spending about six hours there; long enough for a boat trip round the grottoes of Palmarola (you need a calm day for this). Ponza's hotels and restaurants increase apace, but they are still inadequate for summer traffic.

Ventotene has basic accommodation. Palmarola and Zannone are uninhabited.

crowded (closed Monday); but it is the atmosphere of the old cosmopolitan uninhibited life of a seaport in its far-off heyday which comes across most vividly.

ROME
See pages 106-119.

SABAUDIA
The small town was built on reclaimed land in 1934 when the Circeo National Park came into being. Its lido extends about 8 km along the coast and to get to it you have to cross Lake Paola, which winds round the town. Most summer Sundays they have motorboat races on this lake. On its eastern shore is the **Fount of Lucullus**, a mineral water spring from ancient times. Sabaudia is slowly becoming a tourist destination, but has yet to acquire a personality. There is still something desolate about this shoreline where snake-infested, fever-ridden swampland once oozed into the sea.

SAN FELICE CIRCEO
Gateway to the National Park; on the headland, an **acropolis** with polygonal

• *Sperlonga*.

walls of great antiquity; in town, crouched under the mountain, towers and houses of the **Knights Templar**; in neighbouring sea-cliffs many **grottoes** (a Neanderthal skull was found).

SPERLONGA
See *Gaeta, page 245*.

TERRACINA ×
Another old, good-looking town, clambering shorewards from the hills. The paving of a Roman forum survives. **San Cesario's cathedral** (11thC) has bright mosaic-tiled floors. There are ruins of a 1stC BC temple to Jupiter Anxur (Anxur was the town's original name). An immense rock, **Pisco Montano**, 100 m high, disfigures the shore. The sandy beach west, well furnished with campsites and caravan parks, extends almost to San Felice Circeo 17 km away.

If you are returning to Rome from Terracina, take the fast inland highways 7 via Velletri or 148 via Latina (108 km); or the more interesting 156 through Priverno and Sezze.

RECOMMENDED HOTELS

ANZIO
Dei Cesari, LLL; Via Mantova 3; tel. 069 874 751; *credit cards*, AE, DC, E, MC, E, V.

Commanding the beachhead a short stroll from the harbour, it is superior to anything else you may find along this coast. Swimming-pools indoors and out, attractive garden to rear; sauna and gymnasium; garage. Unremarkable restaurant.

GAETA
Summit, LL; 7 km W on Route 213; tel. 077 174 1741; *credit cards*, AE, E, MC, V; *closed in winter*.

A really attractive, well-organized hotel with uninterrupted sea and coastal views. Garden terrace for drinks and meals. An unadventurous but first-class seafood cuisine. Plenty of space, own beach, sauna in hotel.

LAVINIO LIDO DI ENEA
Succi, L; Tor Materno, 8 km NW of Anzio on coast road; tel. 069 873 923; *credit cards*, AE, DC, E, MC, V.

One of the best of the quiet hotels which are spaced out along the coast some distance from major holiday attractions. Patronized by a faithful clientele which values tranquillity and a soothing atmosphere. Enchanting views along the coast. An excellent restaurant (**L-LL**).

LIDO DI OSTIA
Sirenetta, LL; Lungomare Toscanelli 46; tel. 065 626 700; *credit cards*, AE, DC, E, MC, V.

Looks a little bleak, or bleached, but is neat and cosy inside with a roomy lounge, bar and elegant restaurant. Ring-side views of the seafront fashion parade. The beach is just across the road. Short on amenities – you could be bored in winter, but the train to Rome (25 minutes) is just round the corner.

RECOMMENDED RESTAURANTS

OSTIA ANTICA
Sbarco di Enea, LL; Via Romagnoli 675; tel. 065 650 034; *credit cards*, AE, MC; *closed Mon, Feb.*

Here you come for a Lucullan feast, or what the management imagines it to be. No peacocks' tongues, in fact a standard Roman cuisine, a grand array of pastas with intriguing seafood sauces. Your evening stands or falls by your reactions to the ancient-Roman hype: waiters in tunics and togas bearing torches, archaeological vehicles and weapons scattered about the arbours where you dine. It is done with flair and is not as ludicrous as it sounds. The decorations of mosaics, bogus frescos, terracotta columns, old stone pots and trailing plants is most attractive in daylight. You can come here for a light lunch (**L**) after viewing the real ruins next door.

PONZA
Acqua Pazza, LL; tel. 077 180 643; *credit cards*, AE, E, MC, V;
La Kambusa, L; tel. 077 180 280; *credit cards*, AE, DC, E, MC, V;
Bellavista (hotel), L; tel. 077 180 9827; *credit cards*, MC.

All have attractive situations with views of the rockbound coast, all are within minutes of the port, specialize in seafood and are *closed between Sep and Apr*. You should book at least 24 hours ahead. *Pizzerie* and snack bars are the alternative on this island.

TERRACINA
Meson Feliz, LL; Via Pontina, W of town; tel. 077 371 026; *credit cards*, AE, DC, E, MC, V.

Delightful setting and outlook, flowery and secluded. Exotic seafoods, Neapolitan dishes, chicken and lamb done to old-time country recipes.

<u>Southern Italy</u>

Molise: Between Two Seas

287 km, plus detour 82 km, plus island excursions; maps Touring Club Italiano Campania e Basilicata and Abruzzo Molise

Some feel a thrill in following paths hallowed by the footsteps of 30 centuries. Others get satisfaction from boldly going where scarcely a traveller has gone before. This part of Italy, more or less corresponding to the region called Molise, offers both options on our route across the peninsula from sea to sea. West of Naples are the shores and isles to which the Greeks retired when masters of the Mediterranean – vacationlands soaked in classical mythology; while north of Capua and Caserta, which today are almost part of the Naples conurbation, you exchange the most over-populated territory for the most under-populated.

Molise, newest, smallest and least-inhabited of Italian regions, was always a lonely land. Backward in communications, in social services and job opportunities, it continues to drive its people abroad. The world acknowledges Molise's existence only when floods or earthquakes devastate towns and villages and the international relief agencies move in. As to tourism, this is one part of Italy where you will see no campsites or caravans until you get to the beaches.

Molise however is waking up. If you travel our route you see the new Guardialfiera reservoir, use a new arterial road to the Adriatic coast and cross the River Biferno on the longest viaduct in Italy.

The region is a cure for cultural indigestion: art, architecture and antiquities are thin on the ground. It was not always so. Molise has suffered from systematic vandalism down the ages. It paid dearly for its resistance to Rome in the Samnite wars (ended 288 BC). The Saracens behaved brutally to the heirs of the Samnites: at the 'mystic city' of San Vincenzo, an immense abbey covering 11 churches and crammed with sculptures, paintings and mosaics, the invaders smashed everything and slaughtered a thousand monks. Today only one crypt survives.

Travel slowly through Molise and you will admire desolate mountain scenery and improbable mountain-top villages and will come across a wealth of little trades. Bell founding, lace making, copper embossing, leatherwork, rope making, blanket weaving and bagpipe making... Molise's casket of hidden treasures contrasts with the hard-sell souvenir glitter of the Neapolitan shore at the western end of the trip. That shore is for most of us a journey of recognition. The byways of Molise are voyages of discovery.

For a return journey across the peninsula, combine this expedition (three days if you take it all in) with Local Explorations: 15.

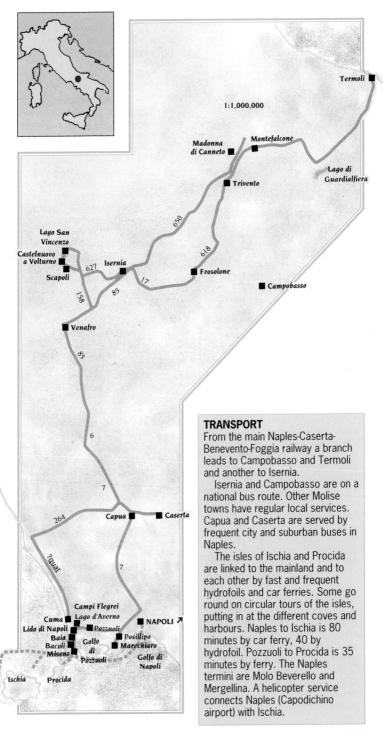

TRANSPORT
From the main Naples-Caserta-
Benevento-Foggia railway a branch
leads to Campobasso and Termoli
and another to Isernia.

Isernia and Campobasso are on a
national bus route. Other Molise
towns have regular local services.
Capua and Caserta are served by
frequent city and suburban buses in
Naples.

The isles of Ischia and Procida
are linked to the mainland and to
each other by fast and frequent
hydrofoils and car ferries. Some go
round on circular tours of the isles,
putting in at the different coves and
harbours. Naples to Ischia is 80
minutes by car ferry, 40 by
hydrofoil. Pozzuoli to Procida is 35
minutes by ferry. The Naples
termini are Molo Beverello and
Mergellina. A helicopter service
connects Naples (Capodichino
airport) with Ischia.

SIGHTS & PLACES OF INTEREST

BACOLI
And other places marked on the Gulf of Pozzuoli (such as Pozzuoli and Posillipo) – see Pozzuoli Gulf, page 252.

CAMPI FLEGREI
Myth, legend, natural phenomena and uncontrolled building development join hands on this area whose name translates as the 'Burning Fields'. Low hills surround hot bubbling springs called *solfatare*. At Pozzuoli's *solfatara* is the cave where the custodian used to walk his dog for the amusement of visitors. Thanks to heavier-than-air fumes the animal would collapse, the custodian emerge unscathed.

CAPUA
Home of the **Campania Museum**, where you trace the confused history of the Naples region, Old Capua in particular: from Etruscan to Samnite, from Roman to Lombard, from Norman to Swabian conquests. Columns and carvings from those eras make incongruous buttressings for modern buildings. They have all been pillaged from **Santa Maria Capua Vetere** ('Old Capua') 4 km east, but that classical city still has archaeological riches. See the Campanian **amphitheatre**, built when gladiators from the famous Capua training school made their debuts; also a 3rdC **temple crypt of Mithras**. Its explicit frescos first revealed the nature of the initiation rites of a Persian cult which for a time looked like annihilating Christianity.

CASERTA ✕
A palace as grand as Versailles, built by neo-classicist Vanvitelli for the megalomaniac Neapolitan Bourbons. It has 1,200 rooms, 34 staircases, 1,800 windows and four courtyards with statuary and furnishings of suitable richness. The beauty of the park, pools, cascades and fountains relieves the oppressive grandeur of the building. It is a sort of dream landscape with great trees, waterways and rustic buildings. An English garden of flowery glades, intimate paths and arbours is said to be the finest in Italy. A minibus is available to take you round the park.

CUMA
It is Greek Cumae, the first Hellenic settlement in Italy. A rock tunnel leads into the sanctum of ancient Rome's most distinguished prophetess, the Cumaean Sibyl. She offered nine books of wisdom to Tarquin, last king of Rome. He thought the price too high. She burned three and came back with six for the same price. Again he declined. She burned three more and he gave in, paying the full price for the remaining three. (The Sibylline Books were said to contain instructions for placating the gods after natural disas-

---

> **HOTELS AND RESTAURANTS**
> Visitors to the Naples coast (see also Local Explorations: 21) can run the whole gamut of hotels, both commercial and resort-type. Ischia bristles with them, ingeniously fitted into limited spaces as only the Italians and the Japanese know how. On the Adriatic shore, around Termoli, things are moving the same way but at present the seasonal demand exceeds the supply. In peak months remember that there are also useful stopovers along the state highway.
>
> Food on the Naples shore is cosmopolitan, from the traditional to the ethnic to the tomatoes-with-everything. Undiscovered Molise has a surprising gastronomy. From that part of the world came those chefs who followed Catherine de' Medici to Paris and laid the foundations of the sophisticated French cuisine. On the Adriatic coast most is made of the harvest of the sea – look out for octopus *in purgatorio* and marinated fried fish with spicy sauces. Inland, in unpretentious *trattorie*, you may find pasta *alla chitarra* (cut into strips with our old friend the 'guitar'), excellent lean meats from the herds and flocks of the plateaux, river fish and mountain spinach. Pastries, grape jam tarts, crunchy wafers and chocolate fruit cake lead a catalogue of desserts – a sweet tooth is a characteristic of the Molise people. On the coasts, the service industries are polyglot; inland, even Italians have difficulty in making themselves understood.

• *Molise hill village of Pianisi.*

ters. They were destroyed when the Capitol of Rome was burned down in 83 BC.) **Lago d'Averno**, classical Avernus, the descent to Hell, is 0.5 km south of Cuma.

A longer but easier route between Cuma and Capua is by Castel Volturno, the grey sands, lidos and chalets of the Domiziana coast road (Route 7*qua*) and the open valley of the Volturno road (Route 264).

FROSOLONE
Scissors and knives are its claim to fame – if you meet an itinerant knife-grinder on your travels he is likely to hail from this town. Its healthy upland setting (900 m) is beginning to attract summer visitors.

LAKE GUARDIALFIERA
On the new trunk road, 35 km SW of Termoli; via Acquaviva on an indecisive highland route with a steep descent to the lake, 31 km E of Montefalcone. The 13-km long expanse with one of Europe's largest barrages where civil engineering surmounted serious challenges has turned the awesome Biferno river into a dejected ribbon of mud and marshplants. The reservoir makes amends by bringing 30,000 hectares of barren land under cultivation.

The lake shores attract cave-explorers, anglers, picnickers and lovers of the captivating Molise scenery: wide, meandering valleys shaded by rolling hills where the villages have perversely chosen heights instead of lowlands, and the courses of rivers are deserted and bleak with gravel banks and stagnant pools.

Between Guardialfiera and Termoli the new Fondovalle ('valley bed') highway is another triumph of engineering skills. The longest viaduct in Italy is at the north end of the lake.

ISCHIA 🛏
Larger than Capri and becoming almost as crowded, Ischia is a cluster of dormant volcanoes, one of which occasionally emits smoke. Hot springs are everywhere and hotels may soon outnumber them. The isle is fertile and pine-scented away from the claustrophobic white town of Oriental character. The port is a volcanic crater with taverns, seafood restaurants and folkloristic night-clubs all around it; also thermal baths.

Hire a donkey for mountain ascents and visions of splendour over Naples Bay. You come across pretty white churches and troglodyte dwellings. There are water-sports and a pleasant beach at Casamicciola, 1.5 km west of the port.

Procida, a flatter islet, is a stepping-stone from Ischia to the mainland. A three-hour boat-trip discloses many grottoes but ashore the isle is run down. You might bathe here without hearing the accents of Leeds and Frankfurt all round you – the best sandy beach is on the extreme western tip of the isle.

ISERNIA ⌨ ✕
The provincial capital is an overgrown village, long and narrow, straggling to the confluence of two highland torrents. A new town centre, Largo Ponzio, proclaims faith in a commercial and light-industrial future. A gipsy rodeo is held in July, a music festival in September and an Onion Festa in June.

MADONNA DI CANNETO
On minor road 18 km N of Trivento and 11 km W of Montefalcone, crossing Termoli-Isernia highway. A lonely sanctuary on the Trigno river bank, much revered throughout Molise. It contains medieval bas-reliefs and a wonder-working 15thC wooden Madonna.

MONTEFALCONE
A falcon on the wrist of the mountain ridge, its gaze fastened on the Trigno gorges. The austere **ducal palace** is in poor shape. A **Capuchin monastery** is now a parish church.

POZZUOLI GULF ✕
Bathing beaches line this gulf: Baia, once the private bathing station of Roman emperors, Marechiaro, Lido di Napoli, Bacoli and Miseno. Being only a few minutes from central Naples they rate highly for overcrowding and pollution. Posillipo on the headland, accessible by zigzag road or cable car, is more up-market with villas, flower-gardens and a busy night-life.

PROCIDA
See Ischia, page 251.

TERMOLI ⌨
A sea-port from the dawn of Mediterranean trade. Old Town is confined to its jutting promontory, New is a flourishing resort and ferry port, sprawling along a rather featureless coast. Government aid to Molise, notably the roads programme, has enabled Termoli to expand. The industrial estate has a Fiat factory and a sugar refinery and the fish market is becoming one of busiest on the Adriatic. The **cathedral** is aggressively Romanesque, the **Swabian castle** (1247) a daunting piece of architecture with sheer sides, corner towers and high square keep.

Campomarina Lido, 5 km southeast, has camping and caravan parks and offers seaside fun and games. **Campomarina town**, embosomed in olive groves on a hill, originated with 15thC Albanian refugees and you still hear something like medieval Albanian spoken.

TRIVENTO ✕
Perched on a ladder of steps, overlooking the gorges of the River Trigno, the village recalls times long passed away. In the 3rdC BC it was Terventum, the Samnite stronghold, the sharpest thorn in Rome's flesh.

VENAFRO
Historic village above the Volturno valley with fragments of **Roman theatre**, **amphitheatre** and **aqueduct**. The **Pandone castle** is Angevin, the **Caracciolo Palace** 15thC. The **Annunziata church** has frescos and alabaster panels.

DETOUR – **SCAPOLI AND THE SOURCE OF THE VOLTURNO**
Take the attractive road, *Route 627, 32 km N of Venafro,* to Scapoli, the bagpipe metropolis. Bagpipe fair in July entices foreign enthusiasts and buyers for these instruments made from traditional materials – cherry and olive wood, and goatskins. The Scapoli bagpipe school takes pupils (boys only) from seven to 11.

Continue 8 km north to Lake San Vincenzo and the source and gorge of the mighty Volturno river. Near the river bank are the remains of an 8thC Benedictine abbey. The crypt of San Lorenzo on the river has 11thC frescos.

RECOMMENDED HOTELS

ISCHIA
Villarosa, LL; *Via Giancinto Gigante 5;
tel. 081 991 316; credit cards*, AE, DC,
E, MC, V; *closed in winter.*

A first-class family hotel, not large,
only five minutes from harbour, ten
from beach. All rooms have bath or
shower. Leafy garden, heated swimming-pool. Restaurant is for residents
only. Those who stay here keep coming back for more, and the clientele
now built up obliges the proprietor in
summer to restrict the terms to half-
pension only; but he resists the temptation to increase rates.

Il Monastero, L; *Castel Aragone, Ischia
Ponte; tel. 081 992 435; credit cards, none.*

Cross the bridge to Ischia's castle
rock and you cross into the Middle
Ages. This *pensione* occupies the
small monastery in the shelter of the
fortress. Monks' cells have become
cosy cabins with showers and incomparable sea views. Refectory cuisine
verges on the *nouvelle*, assists meditation.

ISERNIA
Santa Maria del Bagno, LL; *on valley road 3 km E of town; tel. 086 545
1397; credit cards*, DC, E, V.

Quiet country-style hotel with unexpected degree of sophistication and
attentive service. Unostentatious
restaurant (**L**) offers a small choice of
regional favourites, perfectly cooked.
Above-average wine list.

TERMOLI
Mistral, LL; *Lungomare Cristoforo
Colombo; tel. 087 570 5246; credit cards*,
AE, DC, E, MC, V.

You could mistake it for a chain
hotel, but the stamp of individuality
and careful decoration set you right
when you step inside. Bright outlook
on sea, own beach. Front rooms are
exposed to traffic noises, rear rooms
have no view. Excellent restaurant,
cool and airy.

Jet, LL; *on Route 16, 4 km W of town;
tel. 087 552 354; credit cards*, AE, DC,
E, MC, V.

Superior, roomy, secluded motel-
style establishment. Private beach,
swimming-pool, no restaurant. Ideal
for short-term stay.

RECOMMENDED RESTAURANTS

CASERTA
Antica Locanda Massa, L; *Via
Mazzini 55; tel. 082 332 1268; credit
cards*, AE, DC, V; *closed Mon, mid-Aug.*

Go-as-you-please *trattoria* near
Palace, tables under trees, air of
studied rusticity. Pink truffles generously sprinkled on your pasta.

ISERNIA
Emma, L; *Valgianese, 5 km SE of town;
tel. 086 541 4886; credit cards*, AE, DC,
E, MC, V.

Typical of better class of rural *trattoria*. Abruzzi red wines and all the
liqueurs: *nocino, amaretto, strega* of
Benevento. Some rooms generally
available (**L**), basic but in peaceful and
romantic surroundings in countryside
which should really be explored on
foot.

MARECHIARO
La Fazenda, LLL; *Calata Marechiaro
58; tel. 081 769 7420; credit card*, V;
closed Sun.

Large restaurant on point of gulf,
foreign visitors' favourite. Chicken
and rabbit *cacciatore* and desserts
always outstanding.

POZZUOLI
La Ninfea, LL; *on bank of Lake Lucrino,
5 km W, close to Averno and Cuma; tel. 081
866 1326; credit cards*, AE, DC, MC, V.

Lush garden deadens sounds of
motorway traffic. Conventional cuisine is enlivened with some inventions
– try pasta *cresciuta* or *sfogliate rus-
tiche* made with buffalo milk; soused
squid; oven-baked bass.

TRIVENTO
Meo, L; *on valley road, 6 km NE of vil-
lage; tel. 087 487 1750; credit cards*, AE,
DC, E, MC, V.

Attracts discerning diners from a
distance. We lunched on chick-pea
soup, *ricotta*-filled ravioli and barbe-
cued trout with garlic.

Southern Italy

Puglia: Gargano

270 km; map *Touring Club Italiano Puglia*

The Gargano is the spur above Italy's heel: a huge limestone mass thrusting out into the Adriatic, pitted with grottoes, crevices and the sink holes typical of limestone country. Its coastline is an almost uninter-rupted succession of headlands and narrow coves, with triangles of firm clean sand in tiny inlets. Along its coast natural rock-arches and detached pinnacles stand out. Particular features are the top-heavy off-shore monoliths, undercut by the sea, which look in danger of crashing 50 metres into the water at the next low tide. This truly beautiful promon-tory, often compared to the Sorrentine, is most impressive in the evening and in winter, when a softer light brings out rosy tinges in the cliffs and blue-green streaks in the sea.

The Gargano was always accessible as a spectacular introduction to the versatile region of Puglia for those travelling south down the Adriatic shore; yet its coastline remained unvisited by tourists until recent times. Now it is even easier to get to. The A14 motorway borders its landward side. Touristic development proceeds unchecked and our route is a busy one at weekends.

Two religious celebrities preside over the Gargano: the Archangel Michael, who appeared in person at Monte Sant' Angelo (see Monte Sant' Angelo, page 256); and Padre Pio, the stigmatized friar of San Giovanni Rotondo (see San Giovanni Rotondo, page 258). Both places belong to the Gargano hinterland, where the limestone crown and its coiffeur of twisted wild olives reach 1,055 m.

A sinuous highway, magnificently engineered, replaces the precipice paths by which, not long ago, the Gargano coastal villages communicat-ed with each other. The villages themselves, rising in tiers on stony bluffs, each more picturesque than the last, are besieged with camping parks and tourist complexes but have not yet been stripped of their char-acter or their preoccupation with the lifestyle they pursued in bygone ages. The highroad, by the way, has a bad accident record: the scenery is a distraction. Most of our tour, equally sensational in either direction, goes along this road. It also detours to the two sacred spots and to Foresta Umbra (see page 256), still remote from the world, a delight to picnickers and a revelation to dendrophiles. Allow two or three days if you wish to cover it all.

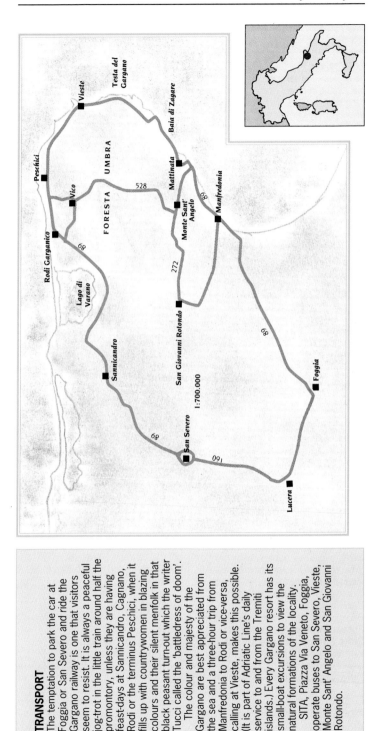

TRANSPORT

The temptation to park the car at Foggia or San Severo and ride the Gargano railway is one that visitors seem to resist. It is always a peaceful jog-trot in the little train around half the promontory, unless they are having feast-days at Sannicandro, Cagnano, Rodi or the terminus Peschici, when it fills up with countrywomen in blazing colours and their silent menfolk in that black peasant turn-out which the writer Tucci called the 'battledress of doom'.

The colour and majesty of the Gargano are best appreciated from the sea and a three-hour trip from Manfredonia to Rodi or vice-versa, calling at Vieste, makes this possible. (It is part of Adriatic Line's daily service to and from the Tremiti islands.) Every Gargano resort has its small-boat excursions to view the natural formations of the locality.

SITA, Piazza Via Veneto, Foggia, operate buses to San Severo, Vieste, Monte Sant' Angelo and San Giovanni Rotondo.

SIGHTS & PLACES OF INTEREST

FOGGIA ⇌ ✕
As an essential rail junction this provincial capital suffered intense aerial bombardment in 1943. Two centuries earlier an earthquake wiped it out and two centuries before that the French devastated it during their anti-Spanish campaigns. Little therefore remains of Foggia's days of glory when the Holy Roman Emperor (Frederick II) chose it for his southern capital and built its **imperial citadel** (13thC). Only a fragment survives, re-erected near Porta Arpana and the **civic museum**.

Umberto Giordano (1867-1948), pioneer of *verismo* opera (he introduced tennis rackets into *Fedora*), was born here. His monument is supported by sculptures of his heroes and heroines.

Foggia straddles routes across the Tavoliere ('tableland'), an open plain of pastureland and cereal crops. Few Italian cities have so little to show architecturally, outside the heavily-rebuilt baroque churches, but Foggia is an active modern city, not over-burdened with tourists, an excellent centre for the Gargano and the northern Puglia seaside.

FORESTA UMBRA
This densely-wooded corner of the promontory at 800 m is reached by forbiddingly steep minor roads from the coast. Tall and slender, tightly packed, the trees form wavering green curtains which draw apart as you enter. The variegated foliage, unique and classed as 'Garganic' by botanists, includes holm oak, white poplar, cornelian cherry, Aleppo pine, maple and birch. You may approach by way of **Vico**, a small hillside town of red-pantiled white houses with the remains of Emperor Frederick's 13thC fortress, a single tower built into a modern house. Still climbing, this road arrives at the **Foresta Umbra visitor centre**, the **State Forestry Bureau**, a **roe deer sanctuary** and a few small natural and artificial ponds with rudimentary watersports facilities.

LUCERA
Another massive imperial fortress once glowered across the Tavoliere (excavations in progress inside still-formidable

HOTELS AND RESTAURANTS
Hotels and vacation centres have sprung up to meet a rapidly-increasing tourist demand. They monopolize the best beaches, access to which is confined to residents. Restaurants of character are submerged among fast-food outlets and ubiquitous snack bars and *tavole calde*. The standard diet – pasta, seafood, salads, excellent bread – may be enlivened with local specialities based on traditional Greek, Arab and Neapolitan recipes.

ramparts), but the historic quarter is gathered round the **cathedral**. See **Palazzo Lombardi** (18thC) and **Palazzo de' Nicastri**, which houses the local museum. Outside the town tombs and traces of antique dwellings surround a 1stC BC amphitheatre.

MANFREDONIA ✕
The Gargano's chief port takes its name from the Swabian king Manfred Hohenstaufen who established its chessboard layout in 1256. The Swabian-Angevin fortress matches that of Lucera in decrepit grandeur. It contains the **National Gargano Museum**, mostly geology and archaeology. **Santa Maria di Siponto**, a strange pale-stone Romanesque church of many arches and a fortified appearance, is on the way to Siponto lido, 2 km south of town. **Mattinata**, 16 km north, has the Gargano's longest beach, a sight to behold as you wind towards it down the zigzags of the coast road. In Zagare Bay, on the edge of that strand, are some of the promontory's most contorted caverns and islets.

MATTINATA ⇌
See Manfredonia, *above.*

MONTE SANT' ANGELO ⇌
In a grotto on the mountain at 800 m in AD 490 the Archangel Michael appeared to shepherds. Luckily he chose a very large grotto, for over succeeding centuries it was to accommodate a basilica and hundreds of pilgrims at a time from the length and breadth of Christendom. Crusaders,

emperors and kings worshipped here and left precious gifts. You may have to queue to get in but it is worth waiting for. The sanctuary (built 5th and 6th centuries) contains works of art including a very ancient bishop's throne and an alabaster statue of the archangel carved, it is said, by Sansovino.

Crude votive offerings, painted or pinned to walls, touch or amuse according to taste. Touts and hawkers abound, every type of religious trinket is on sale, every useless object from coloured pebbles to painted feathers is pressed on the visitor. Quietest places in town are two museums: the **Tancredi** of popular traditions and the **St Michael** of religious history.

Recover from the heat and stuffy atmosphere by walking uphill through woods on the mountain; or wander round the Junno, a medieval quarter; or drive 6 km south to **Pulsano abbey**, founded 6thC, and its gorge

whose steep rock faces, pockmarked with hermits' caves and echoing to the screams of seabirds and ravens, plunge 250 m.

PESCHICHI ✕
Founded 1,000 years ago by Dalmatians, it looks vertically down on what was once a semi-landlocked secret cove and is now a bottleneck of marinas, campsites and holiday villages. Fantastic caves in the cliffs. Sea anglers catered for.

RODI GARGANICO ✕
A seaport township of great antiquity, dropping down from orchards and flowery slopes (Rodi means roses). Tourism has snapped up its creeks and coves and their names – Ischitella, San Menaio, Baia Santa Barbara – appear in travel brochures. Rodi is the nearest port to the Tremiti islands (see Italy Overall: 9).

RECOMMENDED HOTELS

Pugnochiuso, LLL; *off Route* 89dir, 24 *km* NE *of Mattinata*; *tel.* 088 470 9011; *credit cards*, AE, DC, E, MC, V.

The **Faro** ('lighthouse'), first luxury hotel on the Gargano coast, commanded the hidden cove of Pugnochiuso ('closed fist') with a lift/elevator to the untrodden beach and unrivalled sea views from bedroom balconies and restaurant. Now the nucleus of a vacation centre it embraces all types of holiday activity but remains exclusive.

FOGGIA
President, LL; *Via degli Aviatori* 130; *tel.* 088 161 8010; *credit cards*, AE, DC, E, MC, V.

Suburban setting, no car parking problems. Modern, superficially spartan. Swimming-pool. Largely business clientele.

MATTINATA
Alba del Gargano, L; *Corso Martino* 102; *tel.* 088 447 71; *credit cards*, MC, V.

Standards of comfort and service above its price range are consistently maintained. Town-centre site but

free bus takes you in 10 minutes to not-overcrowded beach. Courtyard for summer dining, a pavement café enthusiastically patronized.

MONTE SANT' ANGELO
Rotary, L-LL; 1 *km* W *of Monte Sant' Angelo*; *tel.* 088 462 146; *credit cards*, *none*; *closed* Nov.

Named for a legendary king of the Lombards buried in the cave of the archangel, not for the businessmen's club. Small refuge from noise and dust of town, sited pleasantly amid olives and almonds with balcony views of Gulf of Manfredonia. Restaurant's imaginative cuisine makes it a noted rendezvous.

VIESTE
Pizzomunno Vieste Palace, LLL; *Via Litoranea*; *tel.* 088 470 8741; *credit cards*, AE, DC, E, MC, V; *closed in winter.*

A surrealist seaside complex whose amenities include watersports, tennis, handball, archery and in-house movies. Restaurant (**LLL**) is noted for clams, calamari, assorted *frutta di mare*.

SAN GIOVANNI ROTONDO

We assembled in the chapel passage at dawn to see Padre Pio. Piggy-eyed with a spade beard and a vindictive expression, he pushed through, hitting with his rope girdle those who knelt to kiss his gown.

The 'priest in prayer on the Cross', as promotional literature calls him, came here as a young man to meditate. One day he awoke to find nail wounds in his hands and feet and a scar in his side. That event, authenticated by the Vatican (he became father

• Almond cracker, Monte Sant'Angelo.

confessor to Popes), transformed a poverty-stricken village into a flourishing mountain resort with 30 hotels, futuristic villas and blocks of flats, a huge ornate cathedral, a new sanctuary, a multi-storey hospital, several charitable institutions and a supermarket. When Padre Pio died aged 90 in 1969 San Giovanni suffered no setback. It has its own momentum. Souvenir shops still offer blurred photographs of his hands. In backstreet boutiques (a few backstreets with ankle-wrenching flagstones survive) his old bloodstained bandages are sold. Cynics say that the blood comes from chickens.

SAN SEVERO ✕

A baroque town and agricultural centre, home of the south-east's finest

---

DETOUR – SANNICANDRO

It is worth the short detour for its silent cobbled piazza, its San Giorgio courtyard in the medieval Terravecchia quarter and the *karst* grottoes of the neighbourhood.

---

white wines. Terminus of the Gargano railway.

TESTA DEL GARGANO
See Vieste, this page.

VARANO, LAGO DI
Barred from the sea by a 15-km strip of dunes, this large lake and its elongated shallow neighbour **Lago di Lesina** are part of a primeval landscape noted for eels, wading birds, heather, rosemary and misty twilights which have given rise to macabre superstitions. Hardly touched by tourism, Varano is a silent reproach to the adjacent, more populated lagoon, where inns and fish restaurants proliferate.

VICO
See Foresta Umbra, page 256.

VIESTE 🏖
From blunt headlands and sea arches the Gargano's most important holiday centre pushes out, like a crocodile's snout, a little promontory of its own, covered with houses, edged with the narrowest of promenades.

Already a port when the ancient Greeks came to Italy, Vieste has the usual **Swabian castle** and **Romanesque cathedral** and, in the **Saracen Cave** on the shore, some catacombs. On its doorstep, east and west, are golden kilometres of yacht moorings, beach clubs, discos, hotels of neo-Moorish type, 58 campsites and 16 holiday villages. The hotel consortia have pounced on the best coves and opened them up (for residents only) with steps, lifts/elevators in the cliffs and motor boats. Old Vieste remains an enclave of tiny alley-ways and white-washed cottages. Do not miss the **Castello beach**, a 4-km arc of sand with safe bathing south of the town; or the sharp-edged, dazzlingly-white 26-m **monolith of Pizzomunno**, in dialect 'edge of the world'. In summer, local boatmen offer trips which thread caves and arches inaccessible from land.

The inland attraction is a well-wooded hillscape – here you are on the edge of Foresta Umbra. Climb for ten minutes for a broadening view of exceptional coastal scenery, stack rocks offshore and **Testa del Gargano**, the culmination of the capes, 10 km south.

RECOMMENDED RESTAURANTS

FOGGIA
Sarti, LL; *Via Gorizia 20; tel. 088 171 686; credit cards*, AE, MC, V.

Hallmark of excellence: an aged waiter in a soup-stained dinner-jacket with a napkin on his arm. His first customer, 40-odd years ago, was the great tenor Beniamino Gigli. 'He just walked in.' What did he order? 'Mountains of spaghetti and six or seven oranges.' Gigli was so fond of San Severo's white wines that he nearly bought a house there. (We ate first-class roast lamb with baby artichokes.)

La Mangiatoia, LL; *Viale Virgilio 2; tel. 088 134 457; credit cards*, AE, DC, E, MC, V.

Old farmhouse much tarted up. Standard menu includes outlandish pasta dishes with assortment of seafood sauces.

PESCHICI
La Grotta delle Rondine, L; *Peschici*, 1 km W *of town; tel. 088 496 4007; credit cards*, AE, DC, E, MC, V; *closed Oct-Easter.*

Intriguing situation in cranny (the name means 'swallows' cave'). Usual selection of seafoods is augmented by mixed grills, vegetable sauces and forest herbs which attract gourmets. Eat al fresco or indoors, but avoid weekends.

RODI
Ciccio a Mare, L; *Via Scalo Marittimo 22; tel* 088 496 5409; *credit cards*, E, MC, V.

Fish and seafood, pasta dishes peculiar to the region. Generous portions. Nothing very refined, but excellent value.

SAN SEVERO
Le Arcate, L-LL; *Piazza Cavallotti 29; tel. 088 226 025; credit cards*, AE, DC, E, MC, V.

Typical old-town atmosphere, traditional country cuisine, unhurried service. This is where to relax over superior wines and watch provincial life slide quietly by.

Southern Italy

Puglia and Basilicata:
Trulli and *Sassi*

310 *km; map Touring Club Italiano Puglia*

This expedition is both picturesque and unusual, mostly on quiet open roads which wind through silent valleys and mountains. Villages are lost in a tranquillity which may be broken only by the sound of your car. You penetrate a region unknown to most Italians except from the biblical movies which have been shot in the *calanchi* (badlands) of Basilicata: Pasolini's *St Mark's Gospel* and Paramount's *King David* among others.

The route we recommend jogs along minor roads and country lanes, always with a fast main road at hand if you are running late. Travelling east to west you climb a steady gradient from sea level to about 400 m at Matera, midpoint of the journey. Thereafter, in the Basilicata highlands, you climb more steeply to about 1,200 m before descending on Potenza at 819 m. Be careful to stick to the route, however wildly it meanders and doubles back. The road network is thin and a wrong turning could lead you miles astray. Doing it all could take two days.

At the eastern end of the route, in the Valle d'Itria, the supreme curiosity of the *trulli* is laid before you. *Trulli* are conical stone huts, white and grey, topped and painted with strange symbols – ball, cross, egg, diamond, pointed cap. Years ago they sheltered whole populations. Few are inhabited now, although most are still in use as stables or tool-sheds. A modern fashion for designer *trulli* in garish shades – like the mock-Elizabethan of the English stockbroker belt – desecrates the countryside here and there. (The British firm, Vacanze in Italia, of Bignor, West Sussex RH20 1QD, offers a genuine *trullo* as a holiday villa. It is at San Vito dei Normanni, 20 km west of Brindisi.)

Over the *sassi* or rock dwellings of Basilicata hangs another primitive aura. The *sassi* were the homes of neolithic peoples, then Byzantine monks and shepherds, then poor peasants of recent times. They spiral down from rocky heights into *gravine* (ravines) tangles of walls, steps, roofs, caves and rock-cut chapels. A few are now crafts workshops. You can wander through on a 'tourist trail' or accept the guidance of small boys who know everything and can take you everywhere.

Beginning or ending this tour at Potenza you have a motorway spur (40 km) to the Naples-Cosenza *autostrada* A3 (see Italy Overall: 8).

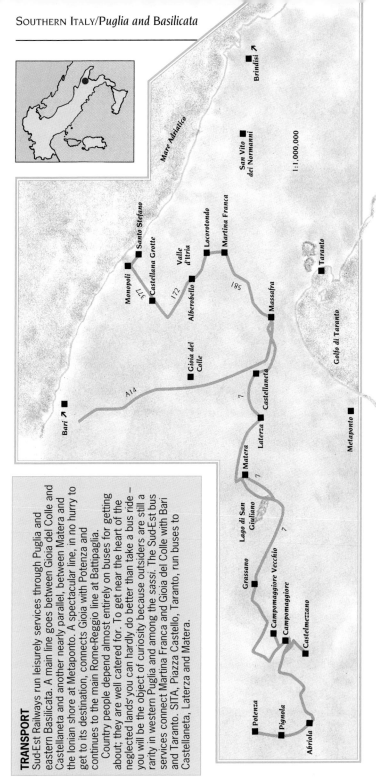

TRANSPORT

Sud-Est Railways run leisurely services through Puglia and eastern Basilicata. A main line goes between Gioia del Colle and Castellaneta and another nearly parallel, between Matera and the Ionian shore at Metaponto. A spectacular line, in no hurry to get to its destination, connects Gioia with Potenza and continues to the main Rome-Reggio line at Battipaglia.

Country people depend almost entirely on buses for getting about; they are well catered for. To get near the heart of the neglected lands you can hardly do better than take a bus ride – you will be the object of curiosity because outsiders are still a rarity in western Puglia and among the *sassi*. The Sud-Est bus services connect Martina Franca and Gioia del Colle with Bari and Taranto. SITA, Piazza Castello, Taranto, run buses to Castellaneta, Laterza and Matera.

261

SIGHTS & PLACES OF INTEREST

ABRIOLA
Ancient Arab settlement, now a large village and base for the ascent of Monte Pierfaone. Ski slopes here and at **Pignola** 16 km north.

ALBEROBELLO ⇔ ✕
Trulli capital and a national monument. The old town of uphill lanes is full of *trulli*, like a prehistoric Disneyland.

BARI
See *Italy Overall*: 9.

BRINDISI
See *Italy Overall*: 10.

CAMPOMAGGIORE
A phoenix of a town, abandoned after a rebellion against Angevin lords but rebuilt in the 17thC. Base of the Carbonari, 19thC secret society which undermined papal power in the Risorgimento. Overwhelmed by a landslide in 1885, the place was again abandoned and is now 5 km north-east of the present-day village, marked Campomaggiore Vecchio on the map.

CASTELLANA GROTTE ✕
The underground *karst* (limestone) caves, formed by dripping surface water, were not properly explored until 1938. They became at once the most celebrated in Italy. Tunnels, passageways, crystalline columns, stalactites, stalagmites, natural bridges and echoing vaults go on for 2 km, glowing and sparkling in artificial light and bursts of sunlight from apertures high above where the roof has fallen in. Coloured rocks evoke a response from the most blasé cave-explorer. Open daily, all year round. The full tour takes about three hours.

CASTELLANETA
A car stopped. The driver helped out an old woman all in black. Walking with difficulty, she took a wreath of red roses to the memorial. It commemorated local boy Rodolfo Alfonzo Raffaello Pierre Filibert Guglielmo di Valentina d'Antonguolla, died 1926. He started his career in the Italian Navy but was thrown out as a weakling and a thief. Relatives clubbed together to send him to America. In the First World War, when men were scarce, he throve as a taxi-dancer (a professional dancing-partner) in nightclubs, then the theatre, then Hollywood. He was Rudolf Valentino.

The pink-and-grey marble slab still attracts floral tributes. The labels read 'To the Great Lover' – 'Incomparable Rudi' – ' Rudi, *Mon Amour*'.

Castellaneta, important in Roman and Norman times, has a lovely 13thC **cathedral**, restructured in the baroque style. All the houses, frail-looking as paper houses, are crumpled on the brink of a tremendous ravine. Streets wind at alarming heights and stop short on the edge of the abyss. Hawks nest among the crags below, which are also honeycombed with rock-chapels. Difficult to get down to them.

CASTELMEZZANO
Turn south at Campomaggiore station and keep right at Pietrapertoso turning. You climb to a fine viewpoint over the pinnacled hills and ravines of the Lucanian Dolomites (Lucania is the old name for Basilicata). Caves and natural curiosities decorate the surrounding wilderness.

GRASSANO
San Giovanni's baroque church, reared up over two valleys with wide prospects north and south, pinpoints the place from afar. At nearby Caracoia you have a dramatic view of the clay gullies of the *calanchi* or badlands.

LATERZA
Many rock churches and cave settlements of incalculable age perforate the crags and ravines above which Laterza is balanced on a dry gulley 200 m deep. Patches of forest soften the arid landscape. The **Laterza gully**, 10 km long, is popular with rock-climbers and egg-collectors (vultures, kites, buzzards, even sea-eagles have been seen). On its bed is a **nature reserve** where, by arrangement with the Laterza tourist office, visitors may spend a few days roughing it.

The town itself is untidy, the 14thC castle, abbey and many old churches are unremarkable. Tombs of the 2ndC BC have been unearthed here.

The whole scene is typical of west Puglia's landscape of crypts and clefts.

LOCOROTONDO

An attractive old town on a hill, overlooking the cultivated Valle d'Itria. You survey many *trulli*, a rash of pale molehills, standing in clusters or alone. The town's name – 'Round Place' – is appropriate: a circular plan, narrow radial and concentric streets of white terraced houses.

MARTINA FRANCA

The demure little town seems to have been drenched in thick cream. You need sunglasses. Only the black wrought-iron balconies with their overhead tracery, billowing candelabra and climbing pink roses have escaped. If Puglia hosted a best-kept town competition, Martina would surely go forward to the national finals and perhaps win. Among numerous masterworks of baroque art and architecture the façade of the **Martino collegiate church** is exceptional. Various *palazzi*, town houses of old-time gentry, vie with each other in the restrained splendour of their ornate loggias. The handsomest is the **ducal palace** on Piazza

• *Massafra.*

Roma, built for the despotic Caracciolo nobles of Naples. The piazza itself is triangular with flower-beds and a dolphin fountain.

Martina was settled by refugees from the coast in the 10thC. The medieval Angevin lords had to bribe people to come and live there – hence 'Franca' or freedom from taxes. The place is all the more attractive for being set above the Valle d'Itria's red earth, white *trulli* and vast green market-gardens striped with black polythene.

MASSAFRA

The town's sorrowful drama of oppression and hopeless rebellion was played out on a stage of crag and ravine, chopped, scarred and wind-sculpted. A ravine actually splits the town in two, with a bridge connecting old part with new. In a few visitable grottoes there are traces of frescos. The best rock-chapel is **San Leonardo** but the most interesting site is the **sanctuary of**

263

HOTELS AND RESTAURANTS
Eastern Puglia caters for tourists but few visit the west or the Basilicata highlands for grand hotels or gourmet restaurants. In summer you will find places to stay and to eat; after September facilities are much reduced. For the touring motorist a main-road motel is often the best option – there you will find someone who speaks your language.

Puglia produces much of Italy's olive oil, a fact reflected in the cuisine, which is built around the standard Mediterranean diet of pasta, fish or lamb, cooked and raw vegetables in profusion, cheese, fruit and wine.

Basilicata augments the basic pasta with regional herbs (celery, fennel, radishes). One popular recipe uses turnip tops fried in oil. Goat, mutton and pork sausage appear as main courses. *Dolci* (sweets) have no place in Basilicata's culinary traditions. Flavours are authentic because the basic ingredients are pure. The resemblance to imitation-rustic city *trattorie* is slight.

Amaro Lucano is a respected *aperitivo*, known all over Italy. In Puglia you find sparkling white wines of controlled origin at Locorotondo, Martina Franca and Gravina; Basilicata's red wines, fair to middling, are labelled Aglianico when they come from the best stock.

the Madonna della Scala – the *scala* being an ornamented stairway of 125 steps down into the ravine. From the sanctuary you tunnel into the **Magician's Pharmacy**, a complex of linked cells lined with pigeon-holes where, it is thought, Graeco-Syrian monks experimented with medicinal herbs.

MATERA ⌫

A provincial capital, hemmed in with badlands, lumpy outcrops of rock and precipitous *sassi* (see page 260). The **Ridola Museum** on Via Ridola tells the whole story of the one-time cave dwellings, and 100 m south you can embark on the **Strada Panoramica dei Sassi**, which takes you along the rim of the gorge to the north end of town, about 1.5 km.

Artists, archaeologists and crafts workers have made their homes at Matera, which has historical links with, and a museum devoted to, **Carlo Levi** (*Christ Stopped at Eboli*).

You might believe that you were coming into a lively modern city, unless it is noon, when the men gather in Piazza Vittorio Veneto for patriarchal discussions. No woman dare show her face.

An austere **Romanesque cathe-**

RECOMMENDED RESTAURANTS

ALBEROBELLO
Il Poeta Contadino, LL; *Via Independenza 21; tel. 080 721 917; credit cards, AE, DC, E, MC, V; closed mid-Jan, mid-Jun, Sun eve, Mon except Jul and Sep.*

A country trattoria with a refined cuisine based on Valle d'Itria's rich farm produce. Intriguing nomenclature: *sckattata* is pasta with hot peppers and strong herbs; *quaggfijaried-de* is mutton haggis with egg and cheese, baked in clay; *zavizicchje* are sausages.

CASTELLANA GROTTE
Da Ernesto e Rosa, L-LL; *Via Matarrese 27; tel. 080 896 8234; credit cards, none; closed Dec, Thur in winter.*

Also called 'Artists' Tavern'. Near cave's entrance, 2 km from town, large clientele at weekends overflows to large garden. High-quality home cooking. Dishes masquerade under fanciful names on the speleological theme. Very tasty *risotti*.

POTENZA
Taverna Oraziana, L-LL; *Via Orazio Flacco 2; tel. 097 121 851; credit cards, none; closed Sun.*

Renovated but keeps a traditional character. Eat cheaply from the standard menu; regional specialities take time and cost more. Try *strascinate* pasta with veal, basil and chilli sauce; *minestra spersa* (meat and vegetable soup, with garlic and chilli); or *ciamarucchede* (tiny snails fried with garlic and tomato in oil).

dral has some sculpture worth looking at. Annexed to **Palazzo Lanfranchi** is a picture gallery with works of the Neapolitan schools, from Mattia Preti to Salvatore Rosa. One large church called **Purgatorio** is dedicated to the dead – a common custom in Basilicata. On the north-east shore of Lake San Giuliano, 12 km south of town, is a **wildlife reserve**.

MONOPOLI ⌂

It presents a tattered appearance from seaward, consistent with its history of pirate incursion and sturdy defiance. Under the Byzantines, 1,000 years ago, it was a flourishing seaport. The Aragonese castle looms over the harbour and bastions protect the medieval quarter. Some churches are built above rock-chapels in the cliffs – the **crypt of San Procopio** is the best-preserved. Bathing from rocks at **Santo Stefano**, 3 km south on Route 379.

PIGNOLA

See *Abriola, page 262.*

POTENZA ⌂ ✕

The regional capital, the highest in Italy. Foundations of the 11thC BC underpin a straggling collection of red-roofed tower blocks, and the most ancient sites, in the Via Pretoria area, disappeared in the dreadful earthquake of 1980, the latest of many.

Some historic churches are being restored. The **provincial archaeological museum** houses nothing especially exciting, but it is prettily laid out. For strangers the charm of Potenza, not immediately apparent, is its inhabitants' conservatism, the result of centuries of isolation. There was no road to Naples until 1872 and no railway until 1880.

The May festival, called **Maggio Potentino**, with its cavalcades and gangs of little knights with wooden swords and little Turks in table-cloths, is a characteristic throwback across centuries of some splendour and much misery.

SANTO STEFANO

See *Monopoli, this page.*

RECOMMENDED HOTELS

ALBEROBELLO

Dei Trulli, LLL; *Via Cadore 32; tel. 080 932 3560; credit cards, AE, E, MC, V.*

A group of *trulli*, custom-built, pink and totally bogus but set among rose gardens and flowering shrubs. Determined simplicity is the furnishing keynote. Large bedrooms have exquisite tiled floors and rustic outlooks. Garden restaurant, swimming-pool, agricultural bric-à-brac around main buildings.

MATERA

Il Piccolo Albergo, LL; *Via de Sariis 11; tel. 083 533 6491; credit cards, E, MC, V.*

Small, neat and tidy, the desire to please was agreeable. No restaurant but **Da Mario** on *Via XX Settembre; credit cards, AE, DC, E, MC, V,* is recommended.

If you arrive during a *festa* without prior reservations, **Motel Park, L-LL**; *on Route 99, 5 km N of Matera; tel. 083 526 3625; credit cards, none,* may fix you up.

Nearby restaurant, famous for regional delicacies, is **Nonna Sara, L**; *1 km along Route 99; tel. 083 525 9121; credit cards, E, MC, V.*

MONOPOLI

Il Melograno, LLL; *Contrada Torricella 345; tel. 080 690 9030; credit cards, AE, DC, V; closed Nov.*

'The Pomegranate' – those fruits and others thrive in lovely gardens at this oasis of luxury and elegance, new and very smart, 4 km from the dilapidated old town. Swimming-pool. Restaurant (residents only) offers a short but select menu.

POTENZA

Motel Agip, LL; *on Bari-Naples superstrada 407, 5 km SE of Potenza; tel. 097 147 2204; credit cards, AE, DC, E, MC, V.*

Modern, efficient, convenient, no space wasted: regular travellers in southern Italy know the form. Restaurant above average and reasonable.

A similar **Motel Agip** is at **Pisticci** on *Route 407, 42 km S of Matera; tel. 083 546 2007; credit cards, AE, DC, E, MC, V.*

Southern Italy

The Bay of Naples

214 km without detour to Capri; map Touring Club Italiano Campania e Basilicata

Like all the other tours and routes in this guide, you can tackle it in any way that suits you. However, it makes a particularly good three-day break if you approach it like this:

Arrive Capodichino (Naples) airport am, hire a car (BA/Hertz deal) and head for Pompei. At T-junction out of airport all traffic turns right and so do you; but left at first opportunity to Rome *autostrada* A2, then Salerno *autostrada* A3 as far as Pompei junction.

Park right of Porta Marina entrance to Pompeii excavations ('Scavi') and allow at least two hours. Then make for the Sorrentine peninsula along Salerno motorway A3 and turn right at Vietri junction. You now exchange the chaos around Naples for the twists and turns of a narrow corniche, where parking is impossible but everyone parks just the same. Beware rear-ends of cars sticking out on dangerous bends. Turn right at Atrani, uphill to Ravello, if only for a little relief from petrol fumes. Descending again from Ravello, see Amalfi. Enough for one day.

Day two: continue around the peninsula. Visit Capri, but to do that continue around the headland to Sorrento. Give up your hire car at the Hertz office, which is on the right entering the town; they will take you to the hydrofoil terminal for Capri, two-hourly service, 15-minute voyage. Staying the night on the island could be a rip-off but it would allow you to see Capri after the day trippers have gone home.

Day three: hydrofoil to Naples, taxi to the airport; or go back to Sorrento, pick up another hire car and continue north and west around the Bay to Torre del Greco *or* Ercolano motorway junctions, then right on mountain road or toll road to summit of Vesuvius. You have to walk the last bit, about 25 minutes. Return to Capodichino by A3/A2, airport sign-posted at Napoli Nord junction.

Scenery is superb, that goes without saying; this is the world's most celebrated bay. The rich volcanic soil of its shores has encouraged a dense population and an anarchic concentration of industry and agriculture. The recklessness of Neapolitan motorists is proverbial even in Italy. Auto theft, even from moving vehicles, is common and foreign tourists are fair game. Longer-term visitors to the fabled shore put their cars away and use public transport, which is cheap, efficient and easy to understand.

For the not-so-intensively-hyped but equally splendid sights on the western side of the Bay of Naples, see Local Explorations: 18.

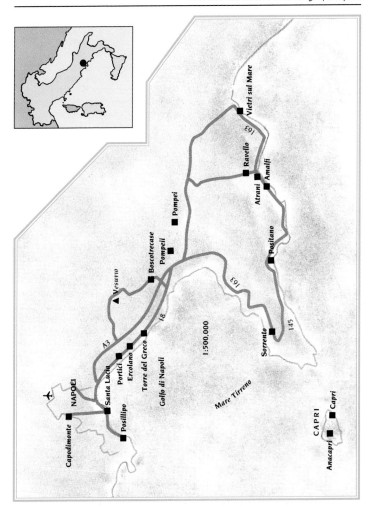

TRANSPORT

The main Rome-Naples-Salerno railway follows the shores of the Bay. From the Circumvesuviana Station in Corso Garibaldi, Naples, frequent little trains rattle round the foothill villages of Vesuvius, a 65-km round trip (see Vesuvius, page 271). You view the great sleeping monster from every angle.

No area is better furnished with transport - rail, bus, suburban train, funicular railway, ferryboat, hovercraft, hydrofoil and helicopter. Services neatly dovetail. You could move through all those options in the course of a day's adventuring in Naples and environs. CIT and SITA are long-established companies who offer half-day tours round the peninsulas and across the Bay. Appian Line, Via Barberini 109, Rome, have express buses through Naples and the Sorrentine towns for Capri. Shipping services are multifarious and various – just go down to the Santa Lucia waterfront in Naples and pick a boat. The principal ferryboat operators, all at Molo Beverello, Naples, are Lauro, Caremar and Navigazione Libera. Hydrofoil and catamaran operators, all at Via Caracciola 10-13, are Alilauro, Aliscafi SNAV and Med Mar. There is a helicopter service between Capodichino (Naples) and Damecuta (Capri).

SIGHTS & PLACES OF INTEREST

AMALFI
Walled in by cliffs, the town climbs on zigzag streets. It seems incredible that little Amalfi was once a Republic of the Sea. Above the shingly beach (windsurfing, water-skiing) the sea-front shops and stalls are bright with relatively inexpensive gold-and-pink-coral trinkets. Visit the **cathedral** (supposed bones of St Andrew in its crypt) and look down on its green-and-yellow cupola from the back streets. Try the woodland walk up Amalfi's old millstream, where they hand-make paper, to the cliff-top village of **Pogerola**.

BOSCOTRECASE
See Vesuvius, page 271.

CAPODIMONTE
See Naples, this page.

CAPRI 🛏 ✕
Worldwide symbol of blue skies and romance, it has a large daytime popu-

---

lation. At night the *piazzetta* of **Capri town**, five minutes by funicular railway from Marina Grande where you land, is less congested and the vaulted streets with their little shops and luxury boutiques, striped umbrellas and masses of flowers and cacti, look more civilized. Private cars are banned.

The isle was a state penitentiary, before that a corsair's hideout, before that an Emperor's holiday home. Three of Tiberius's 12 villas have been located, the most-visited being **Villa Jovis**, 4 km from town, fragmentary but you can identify the balcony from which he allegedly threw those who displeased him.

Discovery of the **Blue Grotto** (1826) brought the first tourists.

See the isle on foot if possible: **Villa San Michele**, where Axel Munthe wrote his best-seller *The Story of San Michele*; the **gardens of Augustus** and **grotto of Matermania**; the **Belvedere of Tragara**; **Marina Piccola**, a must for Noel Coward fans; and **Siren Rock**.

Buses go to **Anacapri** (ten minutes), a more restful little town among the vines and olives of **Monte Solaro** (589 m). From Anacapri you can walk to the **Blue, Green and White Grottoes**. In summer the queues of boats lined up to enter are a sight more curious than the caves themselves. Best of the poor bathing is west of the wharf at Marina Grande.

ERCOLANO ✕
Hercules founded Herculaneum, they say. The rectilinear town was badly damaged in the AD 62 earthquake. The Vesuvius eruption 17 years later completed its destruction but that bolt from the blue, constituted of ash and boiling lava, time-capsulated it. Surprising cameos of everyday life in a Roman 'new town' or 'garden suburb', more sophisticated than Pompeii (see page 270), include board games and toys, carpentry and kitchen work.

NAPLES 🛏 ✕
Amphitheatrically set around a curving waterfront, Naples extends from the Campi Flegrei to the slopes of Vesuvius. The *autostrada* tunnels in from Posillipo on the west, and comes in from Pompei on the east, right up to the main railway station.

HOTELS AND RESTAURANTS

In this area you run the gamut of hotel categories from the old urban alberghi and pensioni of Naples, dark and decrepit with suspect plumbing but cheap, to the bright caravanserais of the Sorrentine peninsula, fresh and colourful, overlapping the cliff faces and making the most of the incomparable outlook on the Bay. At the latter, do not expect individual attention from the hotelier; tourist groups are his wine and pasta.

From this fertile volcanic soil sprang the ingredients which went to make Roman banquets: olive oil, tomatoes, eggplant and cheeses (mozzarella and *provolone*), all shapes and sizes of pasta and pizza, generous doses of basil, garlic and hot pepper, varieties of shellfish, some rather dubious. Butter is unknown, rice rarely used, meats – apart from highly-spiced salamis – do not figure prominently. Among scores of excellent local wines are the red or white Falerno, celebrated in classical literature.

Via Roma, running north from Piazza Plebiscito near the front, splits Naples in two. Its extension, Corso Amadeo di Savoia, takes you to the royal palace of **Capodimonte** in the northern suburbs. In its fine park are a porcelain factory and a museum noted for silverwork and weaponry. Capodimonte and another royal palace on the front recall the Bourbon heyday, the 18thC, when the Spanish king's eldest son took the title King of Naples.

Important sights convenient to the Maritime Station on the harbour include the 13thC **Angevin castle** and the **San Carlo**, an opera theatre second only to La Scala in Milan (Naples is the city not only of Punchinello and pizza but also of Caruso).

Museums abound. An amusing one is the **Diego Cortes** on Riviera di Chiaia, two blocks from the front, where all the panoply of the elaborate Neapolitan festivals is on display. Chiaia ends at Castel dell' Ovo, supposedly built on an egg, which guards the breakwater of Santa Lucia. Yacht moorings, restaurants and a busy ferryboat traffic have brought the old slummy Santa Lucia quarter up in the world.

For the Naples stereotype, the sordid malodorous steps, alleyways, lofty nodding tenements and a teeming population, go behind Santa Lucia into the Spaccanapoli district. Scores of blackened churches with nothing remarkable inside stand on a network of underground lanes and passages which give old Naples a sinister dimension. (They say Naples has more catacombs than Rome.)

The Italian Government, 100 years

RECOMMENDED HOTELS

CAPRI
Villa Sarah, LL; *Via Tiberio* 3; *tel.* 081 837 7817; *credit cards*, AE; *closed Nov-Mar.*

Quiet situation on road to Villa Jovis, but a ten-minute walk from Capri town. Attractive shady garden, no restaurant. Simple rooms, family atmosphere. Small, so book ahead.

NAPLES
Cavour, L; *Piazza Garibaldi* 32; *tel.* 081 283 122; *credit cards*, AE, DC, MC, V.

Former station hotel and badly run down until recent face-lift made it the showplace of the city centre. Old doss-house street-level lounge is now a stylish, popular restaurant (**L**). With bus station and main railway to hand it could hardly be bettered as a base for the Bay.

Excelsior, LLL; *Via Partenope* 48; *tel.* 081 417 111; *credit cards*, AE, DC, MC, V.

Trailing creeper from the terrace almost touches the private mooring on Santa Lucia's harbour where you have parked your yacht. The eight-storey hotel with its panoramic balconies to almost every suite and room is a visual delight amid the shabby old tenements of the fishermen's enclave. Sizeable garage.

Restaurant offers buffet, diet, vegetarian and kosher options. Satellite TV in bedrooms. A restrained modern style with flashes of opulence, such as crystal chandeliers.

POSITANO
Le Sireneuse, LLL; *Via Colombo* 30; *tel.* 089 875 066; *credit cards*, AE, DC, E, V.

The very chairs and tables on the *terrazzo* are marvels of wrought-iron filigree and the colour harmonies and Moorish touches of the general decoration go well with Positano's ceramic-domed church, on to which you could toss a cocktail stick. The 18thC house has an enviable site, looking across the theatrical tiers of houses, splattered across a conical hill. Cool, spotless grape arbours over a terrace restaurant, a bar with walnut panelling and a balcony to every room.

RAVELLO
Caruso Belvedere, LL; *Via Toro* 52; *tel.* 089 857 111; *credit cards*, AE, DC, E, V.

Dignified ex-*palazzo* on ridge, entered from piazza side-street. Large cool rooms, garden belvedere. A guide-book once rhapsodized over the restaurant's soufflés and now you can drown in chocolate or lemon soufflé at any meal. But cuisine is beyond criticism.

• *Sorrento coastline.*

ago, seriously proposed to demolish Naples: there seemed no other answer to its squalor and disease. But that would have deprived us of many monuments of grandeur, of brilliant street markets and a lovable citizenry.

There is a brighter, airier Naples. Sail over the Comero's boulevards and smart shops in the cable-car from Cumana station, alight on Montesanto and a 'high town' of viewpoints, notably **Villa Floridiana** (the national Ceramics Museum), **Castel Sant' Elmo** and the Charterhouse gardens of **San Martino**.

The **National Archaeological Museum** on the road to Capodimonte embraces Greek and Roman history and the Borgia collections of Egyptian treasures. Do not miss the Farnese Bull, a massive work carved from a single block of red marble; or the *Aphrodite* ascribed to the ancient Greek sculptor Praxiteles (350 BC).

POMPEI

Like Herculaneum, classical **Pompeii** (note spelling) was destroyed in the volcanic eruption of AD 79. Ignore the scent of *caruncula hamburgensis* from a Macdonald's tastefully sited near the main entrance and immerse yourself in a vanished past, marvellously recreated after another, quite recent earthquake. Temples, patrician villas, mosaics and painted walls, with all the hotels, baths and storehouses of a Roman town are spread over 66 hectares. The wealth of relics and the atmosphere distract and pacify the loudest talkers among visitors. On a first visit, try at least to see the **Forum,** the **two theatres, Via dell' Abbondanza,** the **Amphitheatre,** the **Stabian baths,** the **houses of Menandro** and the **Vettii brothers** (the last formerly the *casa pornografica* whose frescos were not shown to women until recently, but they are thin stuff compared with Italy's late-night TV fare) and the **Fauno,** the **Villa of Diomedes** and the **Misteri** ('Mysteries'), famed for its exceptionally beautiful and well-preserved frescos.

Pompei the modern town, 2 km away, has a florid 19thC sanctuary, several charitable schools and orphanages (whether lonely bachelors still come to select brides we do not know, but they used to); and a **museum** devoted to the history of Mount Vesuvius – *Funiculi funicula* and all that.

POSITANO 🛏 ✕

Brightly-painted houses, climbing on each other's shoulders for a better view of the Gulf of Salerno, make Positano one of the most romantic-looking places. Santa Maria, the principal church, has the typical majolica dome. For its oleanders, bougainvillaea, magnolias, gladioli and sub-tropical greenery and for its impecunious painters and poets, this resort was the 'poor man's Capri' - but it has raced ahead, establishing aquatic activities and letting in the snack bars and discos and is now one of the peninsula's most popular holiday destinations.

RAVELLO 🛏

Victorian philanthropists Francis and Sophia Reid 'discovered' it, provided a water supply and a school and died in the knowledge that the *ravellesi* would love and honour the British for ever. The arrival of a different kind of foreigner, led by Jacqueline Kennedy and the Radziwills, shook but did not destroy that sentimental loyalty.

The small township trembles on the bluff above Atrani. From Amalfi, energetic walkers do the climb on woodland paths in two hours. The Reids gave Ravello fertile gardens, prolific shrubbery and seats on the sloping piazza. They restored villas, terraces and statuary. Romanesque **duomo and cloisters** date from the 11thC. **Villa Cimbrone** has a cool garden and a famous belvedere. Arabo-Norman **Villa Rufolo** was the inspiration for the magic garden in Wagner's *Parsifal*.

SANTA LUCIA

See Naples, page 268.

TORRE DEL GRECO

See Vesuvius, this page.

SORRENTO

Not tucked in a crevice or riding high above cliffs, it occupies a relatively flat site bright with flowering trees and citrus groves (which are a hallmark of the whole peninsula) and has all the amenities which the international package tours demand.

VESUVIUS

It rises to two cones, the higher at 1,277 m. Foothill towns are interesting in themselves: **Portici**'s Bourbon palace, now part of Naples University; **Boscotrecase**'s Lacrima Cristi, the wine of Vesuvius; **Torre del Greco**, manufacturing centre for pasta, straw hats and pink coral souvenirs.

Roads end at 400 m from the summit, then you walk, unless they have repaired the old chair lift. Whether you take a guide or not you will probably pay for one. Get him to do his party trick, bringing the volcano to life with a lighted cigarette.

RECOMMENDED RESTAURANTS

CAPRI

Al Grottino, LL; *Via Longano* 27; *tel.* 081 837 0584; *credit cards*, AE, DC, MC, V; *closed Tues and in winter.*

Typical island setting, arches, alcoves and roses, provides *milieu* for genuine home cooking. Shrimp pasta, lobster *caprese.*

ERCOLANO

La Piadina, L; *Via Cozzolino* 10; *tel.* 081 771 7141; *credit cards* AE, DC, E, MC, V; *closed Tues.*

Unusual medley of seafoods, also sautéd lamb, gnocchi, thick bean soup, macaroni and tomato, presented with a convincing flourish at no great cost to the consumer.

NAPLES

La Sacrestia, LLL; *Via Orazio* 116; *tel.* 081 664 186; *credit cards*, AE, V; *closed Mon, Aug.*

On Vomero slope, with a sea breeze and a distinguished menu. Seafoods are complicated and costly; we economized by choosing chicken and rabbit *cacciatore.*

POSITANO

Bucca di Bacco, LL; *Via Rampa Teglia* 8; *tel.* 089 875 699; *credit cards*, AE, DC, E, MC, V; *closed in winter.*

Eat al fresco above Positano's smartest café. The chef is a seafood specialist – clam pasta, shellfish mixed grill; but also very tasty veal with ham and mozzarella.

271

Southern Italy

Puglia: Salentina

260 km; map Touring Club Italiano Puglia

Salentina in the region of Puglia is the flat, tapering extremity of Italy's heel. It expires at Cape Santa Maria di Leuca, which to the ancients was Finibus Terrae. Our journey is a pilgrimage to this 'Land's End' and to the shrine where those who built the Apulian Aqueduct (see Capo Santa Maria, page 274) are remembered. That extraordinary piece of civil engineering (1919-1939) brought tap water to dwellings across all of Puglia Sitibonda ('Thirsty Puglia'). Do not look for a procession of arches over the countryside: everything is underground until you come to the final outfall on the very tip of 'Land's End'.

Salentina's roads are fast, straight and quiet, growing quieter as you descend ever gently on the Cape. No through traffic. Except for Lecce the provincial capital, towns are village-sized. This may change. The coast of Salentina is a beautiful riviera, just as you would expect of a limestone littoral with glossy foliage and white grottoes – just the sort of 'costa' that Mediterranean tourism, fighting a losing battle with pollution, must some day seize on.

Inland Salentina is agricultural, sunny and waterless. If village fountains run they run only on festive occasions – with wine, not water. You may meet a housewife in her Fiat, the weekly wash piled on the roof, heading for laundering facilities in some neighbouring village.

You could do this tour comfortably in one day but we suggest you allow two if you wish to take it all in. You have to idle along to appreciate limestone-and-citrus Salentina and her rainbow-streaked waters where the sea caves are hung with chains of coloured lichen. Stop here and there to gaze down on the gullies of astonishing depth but hardly any width which you have just crossed. Make the most of the pinewood fringes and the hopeful little resorts – you are a long way from the foreign tourist's Italy and you may not come this way again.

The low backbone subsides, the low cliffs draw together and you know you are coming to the end of something. The Apulian Aqueduct monument is the end: a stony paean to neo-Roman grandeur, a fitting climax for a peninsula whose limestone ribs give it the character of one large classical site, remote in time, haunted by the glories of a distant past, untouched by archaeological interference.

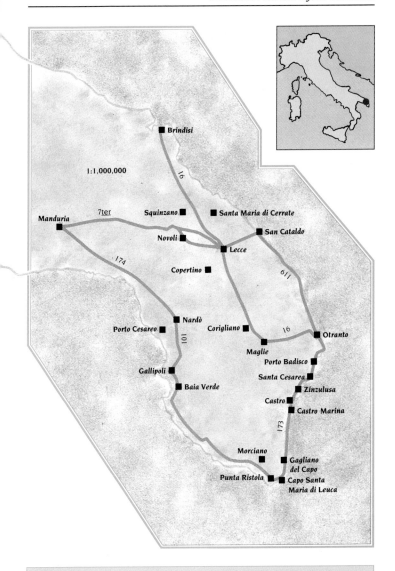

1:1,000,000

TRANSPORT

There are no commercial airports on the peninsula and the only sea services are between Otranto and Corfu/Igoumenitsa.

Main railways connect Brindisi, Lecce and Manduria. The subsidiary Sud-Est line runs from Lecce almost to Cape Santa Maria di Leuca, makes a U-turn and comes back via Gallipoli, Nardò and Copertino to a mainline junction at Novoli, near Lecce. There is a branch line from Maglie to Otranto. This is the slow way to travel. The small pink-and-cream diesel cars stop everywhere.

There are two bus companies. The auto services of Sud-Est Railways, Viale Quarta 38, Lecce, cover coastal resorts and main road towns. The Società Trasporti Pubblici di Terra d'Otranto, Via Imbriani, Lecce, looks after coastal places and most inland towns and villages.

Self-drive hire is available in Lecce; elsewhere it will be difficult.

SIGHTS & PLACES OF INTEREST

CAPO SANTA MARIA DI LEUCA

You stand below the **hill-top sanctuary** and **lighthouse** as in the bows of a ship, where two seas meet. Up the cliff the **monumental staircases** ascend, one labelled REX, the other DUX. A Byzantine copy of the original **Roman column** stands at their top, like an exclamation mark, at the terminus of the Apulian Aqueduct.

'A suggestive cataract', says the promotional literature of 1939, 'is conducted to the terminal fountain, which forces stentorian torrents of water from its base'. No longer. The staircase is arid and forlorn, the famous aqueduct which runs underground from Caposele in Campania, 200 km away, with its 2,500 km of piping to water 360 towns and villages, is dried up by the time it reaches here. Puglia's thirst

---

HOTELS AND RESTAURANTS

Accommodation expands to meet tourist demand and in our view standards do not improve. Apart from a few places well established in Lecce, newly built along the coasts, Salentine hotels must always be a gamble — the risk being minimized, perhaps, if you sample the *pensioni*, of which there is a selection at reasonable rates.

The land is no gourmet's paradise. Salentine restaurants fall short of standards achieved elsewhere. Wines with their long history of promiscuous cultivation are noted more for strength than quality, although the dessert Salento is highly thought of. In the traditional dishes of the peninsula local herbs and vegetables add character to fried and grilled meats and fish. You may eat *tielle*, fish pie with layers of vegetables; mustard, garlic and anchovy or bean, chicory and wild onion salads, offered as a first course; and pastas in curious shapes with unpronounceable names, doused in lamb sauces or fishy ragouts. A picnic can be made on Salentina's excellent bread and *ricotta* cheese. Mussels, oysters and lobster may usually be had for the asking.

---

has increased faster than the system can slake it.

Legend says the hill-top sanctuary is the spot to which St Peter will come to open the gates of Paradise. Down on the shore, all round the promontory, the sea has eaten into grottoes of fantastic shape which look as though they might lead to somewhere quite different. You can enter them by small boat from the holiday hamlets at the water's edge, anywhere between Punta Ristola and the Marina di Novaglie.

CASTRO

Conflicting traditions claim both Cretan and Hellenic origins for Castro, which looks out on a dramatic seascape with the small resorts of Castro Marina and Marina di Marittima at its feet. One km of cliff road and several flights of rock-cut steps bring you into the most remarkable of Salentina's sea caves: the **grotto of Zinzulusa**. In dialect this means 'rags' – a reference to the stalactites and clusters of algae which hang like streamers from the roof. A walkway, submerged at high tide, takes you right into this grotto. The overhangs and pinnacles of limestone above a clear sea of ever-changing blues and greens are a fascination, whether you clamber over the precipice walk or go round them in a small boat from Castro Marina or Santa Cesarea (see page 277).

CORIGLIANO

Make a detour here for a glimpse of the other Salentina, the wine-and-olive-oil country, away from the coast, where corrupt Greek, not Italian, is spoken. Several small towns dotted along the Lecce-Otranto inland route (State Highway: 16) have populations who descend from refugees of the medieval Byzantine wars. One village is **Calimera** – Greek for 'good morning', possibly getting its name from the newcomers' courteous reply when asked where they came from. In a sense the aliens were coming home, for local museums display marbles from a 4thC BC Attic colony.

Culture shock is a constant hazard in these superficially unremarkable townships. You do a double-take at the sight of Corigliano's 16thC castle, the **De' Monti**, so handsomely fronted with heraldic carvings and elaborate stat-

• *Baroque archway to old part of Lecce.*

ues in niches that you suspect it to be a Venetian villa mysteriously translated 1,000 km south. Much of Salentina has its outcrops of pseudo-Palladian and Baroque flamboyance. The princely palaces, relics of feudal grandeur, are never as grand as they first appear to be. Behind magnificent façades these great houses are insignificant enough.

GALLIPOLI 🏨

The connection with that other Gallipoli of First World War memory is only etymological: the word means 'beautiful city'. More Aragonese than Greek or Italian, with its hexagonal fortress thrusting into the harbour, the town covers a low tongue of land within a circle of walls. Inside them, among winding streets and white houses built round little courtyards, you could be in old Tunis. The **cathedral** has a baroque façade of dizzying complexity and the **Hellenic fountain** (1560) is worth looking at but Gallipoli as a town fails to live up to its situation. Immediately south are tourist villages and

camping parks: **Lido Piccolo** on Via Galilei and **San Giovanni** (with a riding centre) 4 km south on the road to Leuca.

LECCE 🏨 ✕

A strange town, promiscuously and haphazardly built up, enclosing a centre almost unparalleled for the beauty and exuberance of its Baroque, the finest flowering of the soft, pink-tinged Salentine stone which was clearly such a joy to work with. Among churches **Santa Croce** next door to the **Palazzo del Governo**, famous for its huge rose window, is the most ornate – some would say most frivolous. The **duomo** with a five-storey bell-tower and the bishop's palace beside it lead the rest of the city's churches and palaces in elegance and *floridezza*. If a little of this 'Salentine Baroque' goes a long way, confine yourself to the churches of **Saints Niccolo & Cataldo** and of **Del Rosario**.

Lecce's main square, Piazza Sant' Oronzo, is partly occupied by a Roman amphitheatre brought to light in the 1930s. Roman and pre-Roman finds from the excavations at Rudiae, 3 km south-west, are in the city's **Castro-mediano Museum**, Viale Gallipoli.

The place is considered a cultural capital. You find many bookshops, a theatre, a (modern) Greek 'little theatre'. The **Chinese Missionary Museum** on Via Monte San Michele must be unique in Italy. The **permanent exhibition** of provincial craftwork at Via Rubichi 21 has wrought-iron and wood sculptures but chiefly papier-mâché items, a line in which the *leccesi* have always excelled. You can buy display items at this exhibition. Antiques shops abound – we liked the look of **Antichità Ann** on Via San Trinchese and **Epoque** on Via Braccio Martello.

Among vineyards east of Squinzano, 16 km north-west off Route 16, the large abbey of **Santa Maria di Cerrate** contains the Salentine Crafts and Folk Traditions Museum, an expanding venture. Lecce's night scene is livelier than average, with the floodlighting of buildings rating high among spectacles.

MANDURIA ✕
Oil and wine, grain and tobacco enter this market town, negotiating a shabby industrial estate *en route*. Near the Capuchin church a section of **cyclopean walls** (5thC BC) is identifiable. The grotto called **Fonte di Plinio** is actually mentioned in Pliny as sacred to some water-god. A few large town houses give the place dignity. **Palazzo Imperiali** is not as extravagantly named as it sounds: the owner's surname was Imperiali.

NARDO ✕
Stop only if Lecce has whetted the appetite for ornamented churches and Baroque configurations. The best-looking church is **San Domenico** (16th-18thC). Round about Nardò are some *masserie* or fortified farmhouses (com-

---

RECOMMENDED HOTELS

GALLIPOLI
La Sirenuse, LL; *Baia Verde; tel. 083 322 536; credit cards*, AE, DC, E, MC, V.

One of several new open-plan tourist hotels which gleam white along the coast south, 6 km from town. Lovely sea views from terraces, snack bar on private beach, swimming-pool, tennis, sailing, restaurant (**L**).

For something cheaper and more traditional, try *pensione* **Cala Scirocco, L**; *Via Urso 49; tel. 083 347 3927*.

LECCE
Grand Hotel Tiziano e dei Congressi, LLL; *on Lecce-Brindisi superstrada; tel. 083 247 18; credit cards*, AE, DC, E, MC, V.

The biggest and most sophisticated new hotel in the province, strategically sited on the main road south into Salentina. Expert service, non-committal decoration, bedrooms could be roomier but public rooms are spacious and rarely crowded except for weddings and suchlike. Not *very* expensive. The restaurant table d'hôte is cheap and sound value.

Risorgimento, LL; *Via Augusto Imper-atore 15; tel. 083 242 125; credit cards*, AE, DC, E, MC, V.

A modern *palazzo* enclosing an interior redolent of more gracious days. Quiet, though close to the central piazza. From the roof-garden terrace you see all Lecce's roofs.

For budget accommodation in Lecce try the following *pensioni*, all **L**, credit cards not welcome, parking no problem:

Faggiano, *Via Cavour 4; tel. 083 242 854;*

Milanese, *Via Re Sole 46; tel. 083 231 1969;* and

Oasi, *Via Mangionello 3; tel. 083 235 1359.*

OTRANTO
Previtero, LL; *Via Poppi 17; tel. 083 681 008; credit cards, none.*

A pretty little house, only eight rooms, with excellent amenities.

SANTA CESAREA
Grand Hotel della Salute, LL; *Via Roma 173; tel. 083 694 4008; credit cards*, AE, DC, E, MC, V.

Queen of the spa, having long aspired to old-time Carlsbad opulence without quite making it. The restaurant (**LL**) is probably the best in this popular resort.

---

pare these with the *mas* of the Cevennes). This countryside was not always as peaceful and sleepy as it seems today.

OTRANTO 🚌 ✕
Horace Walpole's Gothic tale *The Castle of Otranto* is no guide to this white, sun-baked seaport: he picked the name at random and never saw the place. It has had its horrific moments, however, as you realize when the sacristan shows you the **cathedral crypt** and opens a cupboard and 400 human skulls fall out. They are of townsfolk who kept a Turkish fleet at bay and, after capture, were beheaded for refusing to abjure their faith. Four centuries later a chapter of First World War history was written when the British Royal Navy sealed the Adriatic with a mine barrage from Otranto.

The only serious seafaring activity today is the ferry service for Corfu. Tourism is quietly taking hold of the sandy beaches, rocks and pine groves – in the latter are two holiday villages, **Valtur** and **Club Méditerranée**. The two **Alimini lakes**, 8 km north, are stagnant pools but fragrant with cypress, pine and aromatic shrubs – excellent places for picnics, and the fishing (mullet, dory, eels) is first-class.

PORTO BADISCO
See Santa Cesarea, this page.

PORTO CESAREO ✕
The promontory and columnar islets are photogenic. A reclaimed sandy beach has encouraged the spread of campsites. The marine museum need not detain you long.

SAN CATALDO
A crescent beach backed by pine woods, gratefully enjoyed by Lecce's population in the heat of summer.

SANTA CESAREA 🚌
A well-wooded, cliff-top resort with hydropathic pretensions. The cliffs, perforated with grottoes, stretch north and south in jagged disarray. People take winter holidays here. **Porto Badisco**, 8 km north, is identified with the first landing of Aeneas, fleeing from Troy (in Virgil's *Aeneid*, Book III).

SANTA MARIA DI CERRATE
See Lecce, page 275.

ZINZULUSA
See Castro, page 274.

Some reputable *trattorie* and cafés at different points on our tour, all **L**, probably no credit cards, are:

I Tre Moschettieri; *Via Paisiello* 9, *Lecce (near exit to Otranto); tel.* 083 228 484);

Re Sole; *Via Leuca, Gagliano del Capo; tel.* 083 354 8057;

Rizzo; *Via Tasso* 11, *Nardò; tel.* 083 356 1625;

Da Cosimino; *Via Monti* 98, *Porto Cesareo; tel.* 083 356 9076;

La Roccia; *Via del Mare* 128, *Morciano; tel.* 083 374 3545; and

Al Castello; *Piazza Vittore Emanuele, Manduria; tel.* 099 879 5153.

Southern Italy

Calabrian Highlands

490 km; map Touring Club Italiano Calabria

When tourists penetrate Italy's 'boot' they normally follow two coast roads, the Ionian (see Italy Overall: 10) or the Tyrrhenian (Italy Overall: 8); or they speed through on the *autostrada*. This local tour examines the bony interior structure of Italy's foot, between the two seas. Here the Apennines have their last fling, throwing up summits and ridges of 2,000 m or so, walling off – until modern times – one of the least-known mountainlands in Europe. Along the central spine you can see two coastlines at once, east and west. From hill-top cottages at Tiriolo the snow melts off one roof into the Ionian Sea, from another into the Tyrrhenian.

Much of our route (three days to cover it all) is daunting (one sign says 'DANGEROUS CURVES FOR THE NEXT 65 KM') but rarely difficult. Yesteryear's problems for motorists – petrol and repairs – have largely disappeared with the recent encouragement of skiers and tourists. Some roads are blocked with snow, or passable only with chains, between November and mid-April: signboards in foothill villages advise on conditions. In that period accommodation is hard to find outside the largest towns.

Spring is flowery with almond, Judas, peach and pear; upland meadows are dense with clover. In the blazing summer months the cool lakes and tall trees of the Calabrian Sila come into their own and a thousand species of wild flowers are in bloom. Of those three mountainous forest lands, the Greek, Grand and Little Silas, now the Calabrian National Park, Norman Douglas wrote (*Old Calabria*, 1927): 'Travellers could think they were in Scotland.' Our tour goes through all three Silas and also across Aspromonte, the bunion on Italy's toe, where the journey through orange groves from the foot of the ski-tow to the hot sands of the Costa Viola takes 25 minutes.

Townships and hamlets of the old Calabria where brigands with blunderbusses and pointed hats once held sway still exist: dusty, dispirited, depopulated, devoid of culture, cracked with earth tremors. Oases of tourist development increase, however, and you should not despise the simple châlets of so-called 'holiday villages' – they are a foretaste of better things to come. And what another writer, Paul Louis Courier, said last century ('Calabrians are nasty people, they dislike everybody, especially the French') is certainly not true today.

TRANSPORT

The railway map of Calabria looks like the physical map: the main lines trace the outline of the coast. You may cross the peninsula between Paola and Sibari and between Sant' Eufemia Lamezia and Catanzaro Marina but you cannot follow our tour by rail. See also Little Trains of Calabria, page 280.

Check Calabrian station names against the places on the map, to avoid being stranded. Acri is 23 km from the station which bears its name and we disembarked on a rainy evening at Roccabernarda Station to learn that Roccabernarda village was 31 km distant. Bus services designed to bridge the gap do not always coincide with train times.

Castrovillari

Spezzano Albanese

Fiume Crati

Santa Sofia d'Epiro

SILA GRECA

Acri

Luzzi

Parco Nazionale della Calabria

Camigliatello Silano

SILA GRANDE

San Giovanni in Fiore

107

Lorica

Lago Arvo

Lago Ampollino

Parco Nazionale della Calabria

SILA PICCOLA

179

109

Taverna

109bis

Nicastro

280

Catanzaro

Maida

1:1,000,000

Chiaravalle Centrale

Serra San Bruno

Polistena

536

111

Oppido

183

Gambarie

Parco Nazionale della Calabria

Reggio Calabria ↗

All towns of this local tour are accessible by bus. Fares are cheaper here than elsewhere on the Italian mainland. Reggio and Catanzaro have flat-fare city buses. We know of no excursion buses. Bus information for Cosenza region, including Sila Grande: Autolinee Scura, Via Vittorio Emanuele, 87064 Congliaro, Cosenza.

SIGHTS & PLACES OF INTEREST

ACRI ✕

From afar a white crown on lumpy foothills, close up a survival of feudal Calabria with a few 17thC mansions in poor repair. Here old travellers met the 'biggest brigand in the South' – the local innkeeper.

Acri was Acherontia, its torrent the Acheron. Here died Alexander of Epirus, as foretold by soothsayers. Having crossed the more famous Greek river of that name, he thought he had successfully called destiny's bluff.

CAMIGLIATELLO SILANO ✕

It was once a wayside halt on the mountain railway. Then came the artificial lakes and it started to flourish as

---

LITTLE TRAINS OF CALABRIA
It is recorded that on founding the FCL (Ferrovia Calabro-Lucane) last century the directors invested in enough gorgeous uniforms, swords and trappings to last 200 years. The gauge is Italian colonial – 96 cm, about three feet – and the system is informal and a byword for unpunctuality. ('He met a terrible death in Calabria, brigands tied him to the rails.' – 'Was he run over?' – 'No, he died of starvation waiting for the train to arrive.')

FCL lines once connected a dozen hill towns with the coast, besides operating the wonderfully picturesque route between Cosenza and Catanzaro. Surviving routes, always under threat of closure, are:

Cosenza-Catanzaro Marina (114 km); Cosenza-San Giovanni in Fiore (69 km); Soverato-Chiaravalle Centrale (23 km); Gioia Tauro-Cinquefrondi (32 km); Gioia Tauro-Sinopoli (28 km).

The most remarkable rail journey in Calabria, however, is between Paola and Cosenza. The 28-km trip, two thirds of it in tunnels, takes two hours. Little Train timetables: Ferrovia Calabro-Lucane, Via Papilio 45, Cosenza.

DETOUR – LAKES ARVO AND AMPOLLINO
The burgeoning resort is Lorica on the E846. Midway between Camigliatello and San Giovanni in Fiore turn south, at Lake Arvo, then turn right.

---

an angling, watersports and ski centre. It is the gateway to the **Sila forests**, now a National Park, where beech, chestnut and Corsican pine (descendants of trees spared by the Romans when they came for ship-building timber) reach grand heights. One 'botanical colonnade' has pines 500 years old; on a tree of enormous girth we saw a plaque: 'I am the Queen of the Sila.'

Rich wildlife browses on brilliant flora, including orchids. Townsfolk come to gather mushrooms and soft fruits. Calabria's last wolves, about 100 of them, roam east of Camigliatello, heard but rarely seen.

CASTROVILLARI ⌂ ✕

Calabria's northern outpost, anciently a staging-post on the Sybarites' route to Etruria (see Italy Overall: 10) **Aragonese castle** (1490), **Santa Maria's church** (1090) – eight marble panels on **main piazza fountain** tell its story. Great views from this church, but a stiff climb.

CATANZARO ⌂ ✕

A golden cliff-top silhouette from far off, it is 'Queen of Panoramas' and city of three Vs: *veluti* (velvets), *venti* (winds) and Vitaliano (local saint). A resident likens it to a man in a handsome cloak with a dirty shirt underneath. Shoddy high-rise tenements overlook a Shanghai of packing-case and corned-beef-tin dwellings. Litter swirls in the updraught from the valley.

The sights of this city of age-old cor-

DETOUR – LUZZI
37 km north of Camigliatello Silano is Luzzi, a tightly-knit village with seven churches in and on its gorges. Its splendid Easter processions attract national news coverage.

HOTELS AND RESTAURANTS

Rag-trade tycoon Count Marzotto wanted to expand into Calabria and Sicily but his salesmen could find nowhere to stay. So he set up his own chain of staging-posts and called them all *Jolly* (Italian name for the joker in a pack of cards). The first was at Nicastro on the road between Cosenza and Reggio Calabria. Now there are more than 100 *Jollys* in Italy, mostly in the south. See one and you have seen them all: design, decoration, furnishings and even cuisine are standardized, though some places are more luxurious than others. They never make the gourmet guide-books but they are a reliable bet. Unlike many Calabrian provincial hotels they are open all year and you can usually get into them at short notice.

The accommodation situation in Calabria, especially on the west coast and the ski slopes, continues to improve but still lags behind the rest of Italy. Of the places on this local tour, the following deserve marks for effort, if not much else.

ruption are the **Cavatore** or Miner's Monument in front of the main-street Castello (dedicated, they say, to the man who actually discovered a trickle of clear water); **Villa Trieste gardens**, magnificent in spring with flowering trees; **the train from Cosenza**, engaging cogs for a precipitous descent to Catanzaro Marina; and a mish-mash of a **cathedral**, built in haste to replace a casualty of the Second World War.

CHIARAVALLE CENTRALE

End of the line for an FCL train (see Transport, page 279) from the coast, the point at which it runs out of breath. Nothing else disturbs the populace's *triste far niente*. An amphitheatrical Capuchin convent surveys the foothills.

GAMBARIE

A tidy, brightly-coloured hill town like an Alpine resort. Main winter playground is Monte Scirocco (1,676 m) 0.5 km south-east. North is the high

RECOMMENDED HOTELS

CASTROVILLARI

President Joli, LL; *Corso Luigi Saraceni 22; tel. 098 121 122; credit cards, AE, DC, E, MC, V.*

A well-furnished small central hotel with modern amenities. Has ambitions to be a conference centre, something hitherto unheard-of in this mountain town. Car parking.

CATANZARO

Motel Agip, LL; *Viadotto sulla Fiumarella; tel. 096 177 1791; credit cards, AE, DC, E, MC, V.*

One km east of town on the exit road which leaps across Catanzaro's gorge on a fine single-span bridge. Bright, modern and efficiently-run, it likewise bridges the gap between the stuffy vintage caravanserais of the towns or the depressed inns of the mountain villages and the kind of tourist hotels which the new generation requires. Locals come to eat in its restaurant, which offers nothing adventurous but is cheap (**L**).

LORICA

Grand Hotel Lorica, L; *tel. 098 453 7039; credit cards, DC, V; closed mid-Oct to mid-May.*

Up-to-date chalet-style hotel on the shores of Lake Arvo in the Sila highlands. Cableway/chairlift to winter sports ground. Great walking and botanizing country. Rooms and service, though fairly basic, stand comparison with many at twice the price. One might do worse than stay a couple of days in this up-and-coming mountain resort – by which time you will have run through the Lorica's limited menu.

POLISTENA

Mommo, L; *tel. 096 693 2734; credit cards, E, MC, V.*

If you have come over the choppy sea of mountains from north or south you will welcome the sight of this oasis with its tidy little à la carte dining-room.

wasteland of **Aspromonte**, where a red-white-and-green fence 6 km from town protects the **Garibaldi monument**. He was wounded and captured here in 1862, after King Victor Emmanuel disowned him. More to local taste was Benedetto Musolino, the last Calabrian brigand and a Robin Hood figure. Captured at Gambarie in 1928, he died in prison 30 years later.

LORICA 🚤
See Detour – Lakes Arvo and Ampollino, page 280.

MAIDA
Hens clucking along narrow windswept streets outnumber the population of this grubby hill town cowering under a gap-toothed castle ruin. Lombards built Maida, 15thC Albanians moved in and set up the local carpet-weaving industry. Maida Vale in London takes its name from this place: a victory for British land forces against the French in 1806.

OPPIDO
Latin *oppidum*, 'the city', and since 1987 American archaeologists have

• *Graceful Serra San Bruno.*

been unearthing a 1stC BC settlement.

POLISTENA 🚤
One of a trio of hill towns (with **Cittanova** and **Taurianova**) built in baroque and Renaissance styles after the 1783 earthquake. Citizens still cross themselves when walking their streets. Elaborate parades of 'mysteries' (Biblical effigies) here at Easter with *penitenti* enthusiastically brandishing whips, broken bottles and thorns.

REGGIO CALABRIA
See Italy Overall: 8.

SAN GIOVANNI IN FIORE
Picturesque on granite outcrops near the Sila forests, the town keeps up old weaving traditions and is said to maintain the last silk worms in Italy (you may have better luck in finding them than we had). Graffiti on empty houses lament a declining population. **Museum of the Sila** – ecology, botany, social history – was opened in 1984 but has so far achieved only two of the projected seven halls.

SANTA SOFIA D'EPIRO

One of a string of 'minority' townships on the northern slopes of the Sila Greca. The others are **San Demetrio Corone, San Cosmo, Vaccarizzo** and **San Giorgio**. Common to all are black umbrellas and long black cloaks (men), threadbare finery (women, Sunday only), lacklustre appearance and no respectable inns or cafés.

They were 15thC Albanians, driven out by the Turks after the death of their champion Skanderbeg, who put down roots in Calabria and Sicily. They have about 25 villages, a college at San Demetrio, their own Orthodox bishop at Lungri, a newspaper in Albanian and cultural links with Albania itself.

SERRA SAN BRUNO

Forest setting under highland passes of the **Stone Sword** (1,335 m) and **Panaro Cross** (1,210 m) with 11thC ecclesiastical ruins under a 16thC **Carthusian monastery** (rebuilt: only the façade is authentic; admits men only). Decent houses with wrought-iron balconies give the town an aloof, graceful air. **Statue of Saint Bruno** kneels on its islet in the lake. Traditional craftwork in stone, iron and wood is offered to tourists.

SPEZZANO ALBANESE

Most accessible, least Albanian, of the 'minority' towns. Five km north is Spezzano's spa on five springs. Great hopes were pinned on this curative centre for all kinds of respiratory, arthritic and gynaecological ills in the 1930s, when the hotels and baths were built. The place, a relic of Fascist architecture, is not much used now.

South and west the **Crati**, Calabria's main river, trickles to the sea. Irrigation schemes have dried it up but there are plans, with EC funding, to canalize it and encourage watersports.

TAVERNA ✕

Snug village of **Sila Piccola**, birthplace of Mattia Preti, Calabria's only major painter (the 'Southern Raphael'), born 1613. A few of his paintings here, not much to modern tastes. Catanzaro people drive up to Taverna at weekends to buy local wine and collect local spring water, then move on 13 km north to the holiday villages of Mancuso and Racise.

ACRI

Panoramik, L; *tel.* 098 495 4885; *credit cards*, AE, MC, V.

Another hotel restaurant where you may eat the veal-and-pork haggis called *morseddu* and drink the locally famous *lacrima* wine of Castrovillari.

CAMIGLIATELLO SILVANO

La Tavernetta, L; *on Route 177, near Cecita lake*; *tel.* 098 457 9026; *credit cards*, MC, V; *closed Wed, last half Nov.*

Agreeable setting, country cuisine.

CASTROVILLARI

Alia, LL; *Via Jetticelle 69*; *tel.* 098 146 370; *credit cards*, AE, DC, E, MC, V; *closed Sun.*

A genuine find. Much thought and ingenuity go into food preparation with particularly interesting salads based on highland fruits and vegetables. Vegetarians could do well here. Alia sometimes has a few rooms to rent (**LL**).

CATANZARO MARINA

La Brace, L; *Via Melito di Porto Salvo*; *tel.* 096 131 340; *credit cards*, DC, E, MC, V; *closed Mon, first half Jul.*

A very superior little restaurant attached (as the best Calabrian restaurants often are) to the hotel on Catanzaro's beach, 14 km south of city. *Frutta di mare* and Ionian fish, spiky but always fresh and palatable.

TAVERNA

Il Roseto, L; *Villaggio Mancuso by Taverna; closed in winter.*

Do not despise the bars and restaurants attached to the holiday villages of the Sila Piccola, of which the *Roseto* is among the best. If you are travelling north on Route 179*dir* this is the last civilized stop for many miles. Shuts down for winter around the end of September.

Western Sicily

370 *km; map Touring Club Italiano Sicilia*

You could be familiar with this landscape of ragged hills, dusty plains, Agave and cactus: covered wagon country, the locations that Italian movie-makers use for their 'spaghetti westerns'. It was bandit territory not long ago. The last bandit, Giuliano, died in 1950. His base was Montelepre near Partinico, his corpse ended up at Castelvetrano. All the long hot day he lay hidden in scrub, surrounded by *carabinieri* sharpshooters. Towards evening, to allay his raging thirst, he eased open his little box of fruit pastilles. The setting sun struck a gleam from the tin lid, a marksman fired one shot and that was the end of banditry in Sicily.

Your route is rough and wild through the interior, smooth and swift around the coast – even swifter when you take the toll-free motorways, the least-trafficked in Europe; if covering it all, allow three to four days. Remember that the country roads are the highways of pedestrians, animals and – emblem of Sicily – donkey-carts decorated with scenes of chivalry from the troubadours' songs which came in with the 11thC Norman invasion.

Signposting is adequate and you will never be more than 30 kilometres from a garage or a petrol station.

This journey induces both uplift and sadness. Incomparable in beauty and harmony under the hot, harsh mountainland stand the honey-coloured Doric temples, the works of Greek architects, engineers and thousands of slaves nearly 3,000 years ago. Do not miss Cusa, where the columns for Selinunte were quarried. For some reason everyone downed tools. The result is a step-by-step guide to temple construction: some granite 'drums' half-excavated, some half-fluted, some with joining sections half-chiselled, some rejected or abandoned on the road to Selinunte. Eight drums, weighing hundreds of tons apiece, made a column; there were 64 columns to a temple. Each drum took two years to quarry and cut to shape and several months to roll along the track to Selinunte, 16 km away.

Contrast that industry and vision with the sleeping-sickness of western Sicily today: insanitary beaches, sand-blocked drains, flyblown cafés, the dearth of art in ugly, pompous churches, the chronic apathy of the people. Marvel at the scenery and move on.

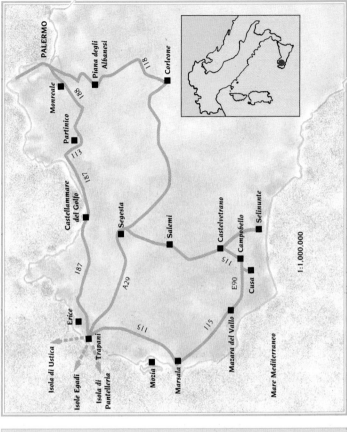

1:1,000,000

TRANSPORT, INCLUDING MAINLAND CONNNECTIONS

Western Sicily's airports are Palermo and Trapani. Limited services from both to mainland airports and offshore islands.

From Palermo the main railway goes east and west along the spectacular coastline. A branch line continues round west and south coasts from Trapani to Marsala. Castelvetrano and points east. Another branch heads north from Castelvetrano to join the main line at Castellamare del Golfo and Alcamo. Trains in Sicily move at a jerky 40 km per hour.

Of bus companies offering year-round daily services the most useful to the visitor is Saistours, Via Libertà 169, Palermo (tel. 091 343 698). This company operates the round-Sicily 'Golden Tour' of 8 days with conducted excursions *en route* and special hotel terms for passengers. (It starts and ends at Catania; see Local Explorations: 25).

Shipping services link Palermo with Cagliari (11 hours), Genoa (22 hours), Livorno (18 hours), Naples (10 hours) and the island of Ustica (2½ hours). From Trapani you can sail to the Egadi islands by hydrofoil; to Ustica (5 hours), Cagliari (11 hours) and Pantelleria (6 hours, or by hydrofoil 2 hours). To Pantelleria from Marsala is 4 hours, from Mazara del Vallo 6 hours. Aliscafi SNAV, Molo Norimberga 23, Messina (tel. 090 774 862) operate a Naples-Palermo-Naples hydrofoil (5½ hours each way) on Mondays, Thursdays and Saturdays.

• *Figures on gateway, near duomo, Palermo.*

CASTELLAMMARE DEL GOLFO
Pause to walk on the breakwater for a view of the sparkling coast, but do not probe beach or town too closely. West of Palermo places that look like Paradise from afar turn out to be neglected close up. Someone writes that four males out of five in Castellamare have served prison sentences.

CASTELVETRANO
A large market town and wine centre. Has a Jolly hotel. A dozen churches, none remarkable.

CUSA
See Selinunte, page 289.

CORLEONE
A former Saracenic stronghold and robbers' lair; no obvious connection with Hollywood's Godfather. Very wild country hereabouts.

ERICE ⇥
This you must see. A dreamy little citadel of thick walls and wynds on the summit of a conical hill (762 m), surveying miles of ocean and the 'sickle' of Trapani (see page 289). Clean, silent, well-kept but no trace of the mammoth Venus temple which made it renowned throughout the ancient world. You could take a short cut through woodland on steep paths to Trapani, about 5 km; the ascent on foot *from* Trapani is exhausting.

MARSALA
Coming from Trapani you pass **Mozia** close offshore, a 7thC BC Phoenician island seaport which yields exciting discoveries. Boat excursions from Marsala. With its limestone shelves, tiny lagoons and evergreenery, Mozia is delightful but you may not land without permission from the Whitaker Foundation, Villa Malfitano, Via Dante, Palermo. At Marsala, an exposed town, the sea-front can be windswept and waterlogged. Here nevertheless Garibaldi landed with his Thousand and a **monu-**

ment records the event. In a feature-less tangle of streets the chief sight is **Stabilimento Florio**, the wine and brandy house set up in 1773 by John Woodhouse and Count Florio. (They sent a speculative consignment of Marsala wine to London, lacing it with alcohol as a preservative. It immediately caught on.) Few drink Marsala these days, though you see tanker-loads leaving town for Naples. Tour the cellars, see the memorabilia and statues to Garibaldi, Florio (his nephew is better-known: he launched the Targa Florio road race round Sicily, said to be the oldest motoring event) and, surprisingly, Mussolini in bronze, black shirt, tunic, bearskin *biretta* and all.

MAZARA DEL VALLO
The second fishing port of Italy. Picturesque stern-lanterned boats, a venerable canal harbour.

MONDELLO
See Palermo, this page.

MONREALE
It is uphill all the way here from Palerma. Show-place of the **Conca d'Oro** ('Golden Shell') of orange groves girdling the Palermo basin. The **cathedral** is the finest Norman church in existence, with an amazingly florid cloister and a series of mosaics comparable only to those of Ravenna.

MOZIA
See Marsala, page 286.

PALERMO
It is called Città Felice and it looks a 'Happy City' indeed, at least in situation and climate, when you approach from seaward (the dramatic way): the twin headlands draw apart to reveal the sweep of domes and towers embraced by protecting hills. West of the bay is **Mondello**: soft sands, night spots, water-sports, a yacht harbour, Palermo's playground.

From the Maritime Terminal a broad avenue lined with *palazzi* runs straight uptown and peters out in chaotic sets of crossroads, among market stalls and fruit shops. Streets are wide enough for a small car if you keep the doors shut. A few cracked thoroughfares come together to form a piazza: **Piazza Rivoluzione** as old people still call it, the piazza of noble causes.

Here in 1282 the spark of revolt against Sicily's French overlords was struck. An officer insisted on searching

• *Selinunte.*

a Palermitan bride for concealed weapons, the wedding party lynched him, bells tolled for evensong and riots broke out. The affair went down in history as the Sicilian Vespers.

Here in 1848, year of revolutions, they launched the rebellion against the Spanish Bourbons. Here, 12 years later, came Garibaldi and his Thousand, crying 'Rome or Death'. And here in 1944 began the uprising against the Italian government which led briefly to civil war. No wonder they say that when Palermo plucks her mandolin Rome begins to dance.

A personal message to each hotel guest says steer clear of these quarters of the city. A shame, because the spirit and character of Palermo reside in the hucksters, bag ladies, truck drivers and vegetable sellers of the overgrown urban villages.

Churches, *palazzi* and sub-tropical gardens are the official sights. Among villa gardens the so-called **'English'** on Via Libertà is a shady refuge on a torrid day. On Corso Calatafimi, southwest towards Monreale, the **Palazzo dei Normanni** has the island's best Norman-Saracenic carvings and mosaics in its gorgeous Palatine Chapel. The cathedral is not attractive. Our favourite church is the bullet-domed pink **San Giovanni degli Eremiti** (1148) with a pretty flowered cloister and the remnants of a mosque. This church is empty and deconsecrated and usually locked up.

You could describe the **regional museum**, in a former monastery near Piazza Teatro Massimo (the opera theatre) as Sicily's prime archaeological site. The collections' quality and the way they are displayed make this a vehicle for a memorable voyage back in time. On Via Vittore Emanuele near the harbour is the amusing **marionette museum**. This entertainment, as the costumes and actions confirm, has been popular in Sicily for eight centuries. Most towns have marionette theatres and audiences get very involved. A puppet-master tells us: 'A young man stormed into my lodgings at 3 am demanding the release of the marionette Rinaldo, left in chains after the previous evening's instalment of my *Death of Roland*. I had to get up, take him to the theatre, unbind Rinaldo and hang him up with the others. The youth dried his tears, gave me his benediction and went home happy.'

PANTELLERIA
See Islands of the West, this page.

PARTINICO
An undistinguished town where Danilo Dolci, priest and social reformer, established in 1955 his first rehabilitation centre for vagrant children.

PIANA DEGLI ALBANESI
A high township with splendid views and a population of Albanian origins much addicted to fancy dress. Their

---

ISLANDS OF THE WEST
The three Egadi islands are the rocks which in Homer's *Odyssey* the Cyclops hurled after Ulysses.
Favignana, 8 km west of the Trapani shore, has a neat island town, hotels and a holiday village. There is even agitation for a bridge to the mainland. Squeamish people avoid the island in May when the annual massacre of tunny takes place and the harbour becomes their 'chamber of death'.

Levanzo next door is all rocks, rough tracks and crystal sea – 'so clear you want to drink it' says the only hotel-owner. Interesting botany among the crags.

Round **Marettimo**, 40 km west of Trapani, the tunny leap and the flying fishes play. On this mass of coloured rocks and a few derelict cottages tourists are rare – fisherfolk rent rooms and the Tourist Board turns a blind eye.

Ustica belongs to the Lipari or Aeolian island group but is nearest to Palermo (61 km). Population divides into fishermen, underwater explorers and drop-out artists. Four small hotels.

Pantelleria is a rough carpet of lava half-way to Africa with some vines (the super-heated shrivelled grape which produces *passito*) and a smart front with bars, restaurants and yachts. Strong Moorish flavour: one-room Arab *domus* (cottages) on the hill, fish-based couscous in restaurants. Air service to/from Palermo.

costumed **parades** at Easter draw big crowds.

SALEMI
In the wine country of Val di Mazara. Badly knocked about in the 1968 earthquake, the town centre was abandoned. Ecclesiastical buildings are repaired and a new monastery has been built; work on the humble dwellings of victims proceeds more slowly. It is dangerous to enter houses marked 'O'.

SEGESTA
One of the oldest archaeological sites, traditionally associated with immigrants from Troy (Virgil located the *Aeneid* in Sicily). A **Greek theatre** of rough-cut stones (3rdC BC), turned towards the distant coast, overlooks hills where the earliest known settlers lived about 1,000 BC. On a plateau, blending wonderfully with surrounding land forms and colours, stands the stateliest of **Doric temples** (5thC BC), complete though roofless, perfect in beauty and silence – until the State built a railway junction. The Transport Ministry has gone one better by merging two motorways at the same spot. Many touring buses visit Segesta but with the continual clanking of rail trucks and the roar of traffic it hardly matters now whether you are alone or in a crowd.

SELINUNTE
First visit the **Cusa quarries**, 3 km west of Campobello, where the classical temples' raw material came from (see also the introduction to this tour, page 284). Selinunte, 16 km southeast, is a never-completed Greek city of docks and villas, of eight great temples and six smaller ones. You see about six, which have been renovated amid much controversy.

Technical and historical arguments aside, it is a magical spot. Divine is not too strong a word for this miracle of architecture and city planning: the Greeks knew how to do it and Selinunte's silence carries more weight than words or lizards, than acanthus or wild celery... until a noisy bridal party arrives and breaks the spell. This is a perpetual hazard at Selinunte. The elegant, two-toned pillars and pediments, amber and dark grey, make excellent backdrops for wedding photographs.

TRAPANI
Beyond the oleanders and colour-washed villas of the approach road it is the very fag-end of Sicily, shaped like the handle and blade of a sickle (Greek *drepanon*, hence Trapani) – the implement the harvest goddess Demeter threw down in despair when she saw Pluto carrying off her daughter Persephone to the underworld, according to myth. This sickle of a seaport is a graveyard of old boats, a jigsaw puzzle of steps, alleyways, dirty washing, horsemeat butchers and rats: a promontory of mudflats washed by two Mediterranean seas yet never clean. You would despair of Sicily among the tenements of old Trapani, so airless and unhygienic, were it not for the warmth and cheerfulness of the people, their ignorance of gloom and misery, their capacity for extracting enjoyment out of simple pleasures. In the street under our hotel we had one night a sword-swallower, the next a Jehovah's Witness rally (the maritime communities favour the evangelical faiths), the next a blind accordionist playing Bellini and Verdi like an angel – and the next a small earthquake.

In the many churches and few *palazzi* we found only one notable work, Andrea della Robbia's enamelled *Madonna* in **Santa Maria del Gesù.** Trapani has its smart façade, of course. It is south of the all-pedestrian hub along the quays for the island ferries – only ten minutes from the mudflats, but the sleek white palaces of the shipping offices and the sleek white ferry boats and hydrofoils seem a world away in space and time.

USTICA
See Islands of the West, page 288.

RECOMMENDED HOTELS

See Local Explorations: 25.

RECOMMENDED RESTAURANTS

See Local Explorations: 25.

Eastern Sicily

730 km; map Touring Club Italiano Sicilia

First sight of Sicily, for most, is across the Messina Strait: the isle of dreams, Italy with an extra dimension. Was not this where the ancient Greeks came for their holidays and liked it so much that many never went home? You stop and stare. There before your eyes are the glossy evergreens and golden fruits of the Lemon Riviera, the strips of tawny rock, prickly pear and palm trees which run down to Siracusa; farther back an arid hinterland where Doric temples stand, so noble and so little understood, baked in the heat of 2,500 Sicilian summers. Near the peaks of mountains which have been trimmed by some mythological axe are tiny white smudges. Patches of snow? Aureoles of mist not quite evaporated? Incredibly, they are villages, but how you shall get to them without crampons and ropes is a mystery.

The white coastal towns will be real enough and you can almost believe in the subtle harmonies of cliff and surf, foliage and volcanic sand – but there must have been a spillage of aniline dye in the sea. 'Mediterranean blue' was never as blue as this.

Fisherman's taverns will line the fabled shore. Little carts whose every square inch is covered in paintings of the paladins, drawn by donkeys festooned in paper rosettes, spin down chalky lanes. Yes, you may well hesitate. The reality of Sicily may not match the dream. Finally you cross, after dark, and find your hotel. Next morning the porter draws your curtains, eyeing you for your reaction to the view framed in the double window: Etna in a calm sunrise, breathing smoke, a point of fire at its tip. Now you know it will be all right. Sicily will be everything you imagine it to be. And more.

Our route – four to six days for it all – is the well-trodden coastal highway round the eastern, more civilized half of Sicily; and from coast to coast through a once-impenetrable interior. Between Messina and Catania the riviera route is in and out of villages, frustratingly slow. The toll-free motorway is an alternative, as it is across the interior between Enna and Cefalù where we prefer difficult but outstandingly attractive roads (Routes 290 and 286). You may find other options: all over eastern Sicily ambitious '*superstrada*' projects are under way.

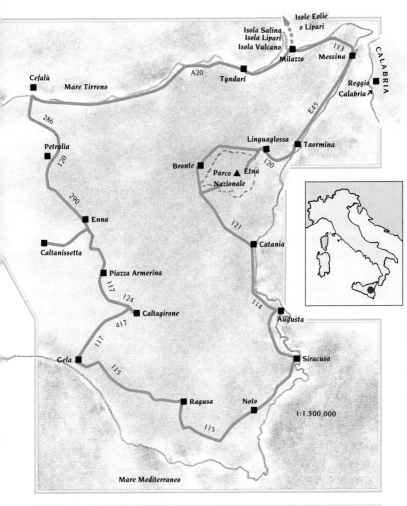

TRANSPORT, INCLUDING MAINLAND CONNECTIONS

Catania is eastern Sicily's airport, with connections to all parts of Italy and some other European cities.

Rail services are frequent on the coastal lines Messina-Cefalù and Messina-Siracusa-Gela and across the interior Catania-Enna-Caltanissetta. Trains stop everywhere. The little Circumetnea train, round the skirts of Mount Etna from and to Catania (136 km) navigates a troubled landscape among villages as sombre and jumbled as the basalt and lava-blocks around them.

Express buses skim between coastal cities and along the west-bound motorways. Companies which specialize in tourist services are Etna Trasporti, Via San Giuseppe La Rena 25, Catania (tel. 095 340 076) and Saistours, Via Libertà 169, Palermo (tel. 091 343 698). The latter runs the eight-day 'Golden Tour' of Sicily, starting and finishing in Catania.

Train ferries, car ferries and hydrofoils shuttle ceaselessly between Messina and Reggio Calabria/Villa San Giovanni on the mainland. There are also Reggio-Catania (3 hours) and Catania-Siracusa (2¹/₂ hours) ferries. From Messina to Lipari and Vulcano takes 3¹/₂ hours, from Milazzo 1¹/₂ hours. Inter-island ferries in the Lipari group do not carry vehicles.

SIGHTS & PLACES OF INTEREST

AEOLIAN ISLANDS. ⇌
See Milazzo, page 294.

AUGUSTA
A modern city by Sicilian standards – only 750 years old. Give it a passing glance. The most interesting feature of this industrial town and naval base is its situation on a clump of rock with a 2 km **bridge** to the shore.

BRONTE
The tattered village with Etna's congealed overflow all around gave **Admiral Nelson** his Neapolitan title (Duke of Bronte) and the ducal seat is 15 minutes down the road. The short straight cypress-and-azalea avenue leads to an exquisite monastic-style house. Chapel, cloisters and courtyard are hung with coloured vine. The ship's bell, dated 1765, may have come from HMS *Victory*. The liveried major-domo rings it on Trafalgar Day (October 21). Nelson never saw his Sicilian estates. His successors the Lords Bridport (Nelson-Hood family) kept them afloat on walnut, pistachio and orange production and tolerated visitors but the place has been up for sale and all may be changed when you get there.

CALTAGIRONE
Its key position at a junction of valleys gave it importance from 1,000 BC at least – the date of its **necropolis** of 2,000 rock-cut graves, many of the Mycenean 'beehive' type, 1 km north. This town of narrow medieval streets was once 'Queen of the Mountains' and amid modern developments some handsome architecture survives. From main square to Santa Maria del Monte's church a long flight of steps is paved with coloured majolica tiles. The **ceramics museum** has collections of Sicilian potters' work from prehistory to the present day.

CATANIA ⇌ ✕
A city of geometrical streets and substantial buildings, very little pre-1693, the date of the most disastrous earthquake. Some churches are ostentatiously impressive (**San Nicolò** is Sicily's largest) but short on art. The opera theatre, **Teatro Bellini**, is named for

Catania's famous citizen and any evening in the **Bellini gardens**, on the hour, you will see the rock groups, children and political orators stop and listen to a few bars of a Bellini aria – *Casta diva*, perhaps – played over loudspeakers. The **Bellini Museum** has manuscript scores of the operas and some fascinating biographical material on this supreme *bel canto* composer who lived hard and died young.

The main street, Via Etnea, runs dead-straight to the foot of the volcano. The best excursions start from Catania – one in the small hours, seeing the glow of fires on the slopes and reaching the summit at sunrise. Catania is also the terminus for the Circumetnea narrow-gauge railway, which encompasses Etna at a respectful distance.

The city has quality shops, well-kept gardens and a go-ahead atmosphere. The centre, **Piazza del Duomo**, is adorned with an absurd fountain, an Egyptian obelisk on top of an elephant carved out of lava, surmounting classical sculptures. Its designer was the monk Vaccarini, an amateur architect who reconstructed most of Catania after the 1693 earthquake and otherwise made a decent job of it.

CEFALU ✕
The old fishing town, trembling on sea cliffs, looks as though it fell off the back of a lorry. Bars and craft shops are taking over, the new Cefalù with hotels for the glitterati a few km along the coast being a major resort. The 12thC **cathedral** with its two solid towers and pillared arches along its façade is formidable inside and out. See also the **Mandralisca Museum** with a fine portrait by Antonello da Messina and

rare antiquities. A pre-Hellenic **Temple of Diana**, possibly 9thC BC, has a commanding position on a rocky summit. South of the coast, where the Madonie mountains rise sharply to 1,980 m, skiing is a growth industry.

ENNA
Central citadel of the island and a very old town, much fought over by Greeks, Carthaginians and Romans. It was called 'Holy City' for its temples and religious cults. Livy pronounced it 'absolutely impregnable'. Maybe for that reason the relics from different eras are prolific and largely intact. They are collected in the **Archaeological Museum** and the **Alessi Museum** – the latter has beautiful gold coins and other precious items on display.

Lake Pergusa, 7 km south with a holiday village on its banks, is unusual in having no inflow of water. It depends entirely on rain, a phenomenon hardly known in the interior of Sicily. It also turns red periodically at the 'flowering' of its invisible plankton.

LINGUAGLOSSA
'We have a patrimony in the house,' says the mayor, referring to winter sports potential just above the town on the northern slopes of Etna. You drive in a jeep through groves of tightly-packed evergreens to the foot of the downhill run, which starts at 2,440 m. On this track, before refrigeration, mule-trains descended with cargoes of snow, insulated in volcanic ash, to be shipped to Naples to cool the palaces and make ice-cream. In this small town, not yet another Courmayeur, you can sit on a sunny piazza, eat the juicy *fichi d'India* (prickly pear) which grow rife along tufa walls and drink *amaro d'Etna*, the local *digestivo*.

MESSINA ⌫ ✕
Here, as the Italian writer d'Arrigo pointed out, 'the sea is more sealike.'

RECOMMENDED HOTELS

CATANIA
Excelsior, LLL; *Piazza Trento 13; tel. 095 316 933; credit cards*, AE, DC, V.
Modern, high standards of comfort and cleanliness, if slightly conveyor-belt. American bar attracts Americans. Roof-top garden is city's smart-set rendezvous. Better-than-average restaurant.

ERICE
Moderno, L; *Via Vittore Emanuele 63; tel. 092 386 9300; credit cards*, A, AE, DC, E, V.
These 'Modernos' are often a locality's oldest hotel. This one, on Erice's cool mountain top, from which you can toss a stone on the port of Trapani, has moved with the times and is an excellent base for touring western Sicily. Bar, mini terrace, romantic surroundings, intriguing seafood choices in restaurant.

PALERMO
Villa Igiea, LLL; *Acquasanta; tel. 091 543 744; credit cards*, AE, DC, MC, V.
Sicily's premier hotel in exclusive seashore park 3 km north of city. All rooms spacious and masterpieces of interior design. Two restaurants (terrace and candle-lit). Own beach, tennis, all possible amenities.

PANAREA
Raya, LL; *no telephone; no credit cards*.
Architectural fantasy on outlying isle of Lipari group. Spartan furnishings, a simple island cuisine. Sea bathing, yoga and massage, a lifestyle stripped of essentials – in short, a health cure. Boats for hire but no cars.

SIRACUSA
Motel Agip, LL; *Viale Teracati 30; tel. 093 166 944; credit cards*, AE, DC, V.
Essentially a superior motel, but has airy rooms and a surprisingly satisfying restaurant. Minutes away from the Greek temple complex.

TAORMINA
Jolly Diodoro, LLL; *Via Bagnoli Croci 75; tel. 094 223 312; credit cards*, AE, DC, E, MC, V.
Jolly flagship, holding its own with more expensive palaces on same cliff-top avenue. Big garden, swimming-pool, sauna. Adjacent to main classical sites.

• *Bronze statue, Castello di Lombardia, Enna.*

The strong current of the famous Strait sweeps past an invigorating, monumental and cosmopolitan city which could have shed reflections of a most distant past on our present, had not a series of earthquakes and the heavy bombardments of the Second World War brought the place many times to its knees. Even so, more than a sketch of the city's rich heritage is displayed in the **regional museum**, a large and expertly arranged building which used to be a spinning mill.

The modern city is low-built with broad thoroughfares to minimize future earthquake damage. Festivals, trade fairs and art exhibitions keep it on the map. The prettiest church, **San Giovanni di Malta**, is in ruins. The majestic **duomo** on the tree-lined central piazza has been carefully restored

although its ancient art works were beyond repair.

Antonello da Messina (1430-1479) was the most distinguished native artist. Both he and Caravaggio are represented in the museum, north end of town on the sea front.

From the terraced **cemetery** south of centre you have marvellous views over Calabria and the procession of shipping through the Strait. Strange creatures from those waters lurk in Messina's **Aquarium**, Villa Mazzini, opposite the Neptune fountain on the sea front at the junction of Via Garibaldi and Via della Libertà. A **beach** of sorts lies south of the harbour. Leisure options include tennis, mini golf, go-karting, pigeon shooting, sea angling, sailing, water-skiing, windsurfing, discos galore and delightful walks in the **Peloritan hills** south of the industrial zone.

MILAZZO

One of several Sicilian ports where the petroleum boom has improved the economy and spoiled the scenery. Relics of antiquity include, on the isthmus of Milazzo, **tombs** of about 1,250 BC. A crucial sea fight of the Punic wars (260 BC) took place here. In one of these battles the soothsayers advised the Roman admiral not to close with the Carthaginian fleet because the sacred chickens would not eat. 'Then let them drink,' he said, and threw them all overboard.

From Milazzo a ferry sails to the Lipari or **Aeolian Islands** (1½ hours). **Lipari** itself gets quite crowded with visitors in summer and its small town is rich in archaeology dredged up from the sea. **Vulcano**, next door, is less interesting. **Stromboli**, 'Lighthouse of the Mediterranean' to old-time mariners, manages to support a population of 400 and receive visitors, despite having one explosively active volcano at 918 m. Its offshore pinnacle, **Strombolicchio**, offers a stiff climb up rock-cut steps to 43 m for an uninterrupted view of distant horizons. The attractions of the other islands of the group Alicudi, Filicudi, Panarea, Basiluzzo and Salina – do not compensate for the hassle of travel.

NOTO

Old Noto, first a Greek city and then a

• The old Roman theatre, Taormina.

Saracen and Norman stronghold, was nearly demolished in the 1693 earthquake. The modern town, aggressively Baroque, is capital of the Siracusa province with a dignity to match its statues. While no buildings are grand, none is mean. Observe a fondness for animal flourishes – the carved figures on **Palazzo Villadorata** in Via Nicolaci, the lions in **Piazza Mazzini** (they came from Old Noto) and the large polychrome mosaics of beasts and legendary creatures at the **Imperial villa** 3 kilometres from town at the mouth of the Tellaro river.

PETRALIA
Route 290, or Route 286, on which you approach Petralia, are wild but not really troublesome, and convey some-

thing of the torments and delights of cross-country travel in olden times. Take them steadily and do not be tempted on to more strenuous byways. The Imera-Enna motorway is a boring alternative. (If you are exploring by train, note that Imera station is 65 km from Imera.)

Petralia has lower and upper towns proudly set at over 1,000 m. The latter, draped over a spur of the Madonie mountains, is an old climatic station and is now forging ahead as a base for the winter sports grounds.

PIAZZA ARMERINA ⌂ ✕
Have a look at the **cathedral** (17thC) and its precious relic, a Byzantine

295

ETNA

Southern Italians call it Mongibello, 'lovely hill'. To Sicilians it is simply 'La Montagna'. Geographically it is Etna which rises from the coastal plain to, according to the latest calculations, 3,323 m. Ascend from Catania by car, bus or excursion coach; then cable car; then jeep; then the final short section on foot.

Etna is not the smooth symmetrical dome you admired from afar. It is a bumpy ride, a no-man's-land of coagulated lava and drifts of grit, without bird or animal or blade of grass. Cones can launch tracer barrages of red-hot cinders, crevices can spout boiling lava and pour out blasts of sulphurous smoke. They have to keep re-routing the cinder-track: it costs money, says Etna's director, to maintain La Montagna.

Though closed to visitors as we write, Etna is normally accessible. You can walk to the very lip of the main crater with its brimming, strangely silent lake of fire. Your guide breaks off pastry-like pieces of lava and tosses them in, trying to stir up some action. Etna does not respond. You remember the tale of Empedocles, the 5thC BC philosopher, who committed suicide by jumping in. Some time later Etna threw out one of his sandals.

Serious eruptions occur every three or four years and with local knowledge can be predicted. The worst in history was in 1669, when Catania, 35 kilometres away, was overwhelmed with ash and lava. Within living memory lava has reached the sea. Six times villagers on the slopes have fled; but they always return.

Half-way up there is an excellent hotel, the **Grande Albergo Etna**. Its restaurant serves the dark, glowing Etna wine. At the end of the road from Catania and the beginning of the cableway stands Rifugio Sapienza, where you can also eat and sleep.

In clear weather this mountain commands a view of all Sicily and half of Calabria.

painting called the *Madonna of the Victories* in a silver casket. Typical medieval architecture in orchards and woodlands give the town an air of quiet prosperity. The luxurious villa of **Casale**, a Roman survival with a magnificent spread of multi-coloured mosaics of perhaps AD 350, stands 4 km south of town. The themes are lively – bathing scenes, hunting scenes – and suggest a naïve African influence. There are traces of wall paintings too. Debate continues about Casale's origins and the identity of its owner. It may have been the retreat of an Emperor who exchanged power politics for a meditative retirement. Six km south of this secluded site are the remains of a village significantly called **Philosophiana**.

RAGUSA

Not the Ragusa whose commercial fame produced the word 'argosy' – that was the Dalmatian port of Ragusa, now Dubrovnik. This Ragusa lies across three heights divided by two gorges. Old narrow streets and houses with curved balconies are now cheek-by-jowl with oil-related industry. The oldest quarter is **Ibla**, a name known to Virgil, who praised Iblaean honey.

REGGIO CALABRIA

See Italy Overall: 8.

SIRACUSA 🛏

Epicentre of 'Magna Graecian' culture, most splendid of Hellenic cities in Sicily, where the ancient world still speaks to us across the centuries. The stylish, functional complex of the **Paolo Orsi Museum** (he was a well-known archaeologist) is an education in itself. Among the marbles is de Maupassant's 'ideal woman' – a 2ndC BC *Venus*. All around are grouped the evocative **temples** of Diana, Demeter, Jupiter and Apollo; the sensational and unique **Greek theatre** (classical drama in May and June); and a rock-hewn **Roman amphitheatre**, second only to that of Verona in size. Explore grottoes and catacombs in the historic centre and wander among the papyrus beds of the **Ciane river**, one of Sicily's best natural habitats, despite environmental pollution.

TAORMINA 🛏

The English 20thC novelist D.H.

Lawrence, who perpetually moaned about Italy but spent most of his time there, found it a 'parterre of English weeds, all cultivating their egos hard against one another.' There is still an air of genteel one-upmanship about some of the discreet and contented-looking residences, but you come here to feast your eyes on the panorama of the sea, on Etna looming overhead, on two rivieras and a far-off ring of mountains. See all this from the little **acropolis** (214 m) where a gaunt old Roman theatre, brick and marble, carries you straight back to the old world. In summer this small town surrenders completely to tourism.

• *Naxos, Etna in the background.*

RECOMMENDED RESTAURANTS

The best Sicilian cuisines are conditioned by climate and soil; also by sun, volcanoes, salt water and semi-tropical vegetation. Seafood *risotti* and pasta – lobster, anchovy, sardines – are specialities. Pine nuts, eggplant and capers give flavour to meat dishes. Sweets are many and various. Cassata (ice-cream with candied peel) is Sicilian. Wines are strong and tangible. Marsala and the *passito* of Pantelleria have nationwide *réclame*.

CATANIA
Costa Azzurro, LLL; Via de Cristoforo 4; *tel.* 095 494 920; *credit cards*, AE, DC, MC, V.

Has sea-front terrace and is perhaps the best place in town. Famous for swordfish steak.

CEFALU
Bracce, LL; Via Venticinque Novembre 10; *tel.* 092 121 495; *credit cards*, AE, DC, MC, V; *closed Mon, mid-winter.*

It is where off-duty waiters and hoteliers come to eat. Has seen more pretentious places come and go in Cefalù. Stuffed vegetables, rice croquettes, honest grills and superb home-made cassata.

MESSINA
Pippo Nunnari, LL; Via Ugo Bassi 157; *tel.* 090 293 8584; *cards*, AE, V.

Elegant decoration and expert service go with typical Sicilian *antipasti*, grilled steaks and desserts based on *pasta reale* (almond and lemon-peel filling). Meals to discuss with ever-obliging staff; and to linger over.

PALERMO
Toto, L; Via dei Coltellieri 5; *no telephone; no credit cards.*

Not in the most salubrious district, but a no-nonsense trattoria of authentic character with fish soups and many fish dishes. Fine white wine. Evening customers are one big happy family; late at night waiters may give a floor show.

West and south of Palermo the emphasis is on the slipshod and lacklustre. The following are notable exceptions:
    Re Aceste, LL, Erice, the classical citadel above Trapani; and
    La Taverna, Piazza Armerina.
    Restaurants at the various **Jolly** hotels and **Motels Agip** are unexciting but at least clean and professionally run.

Sardinia

Southern Sardinia

370 *km; map Touring Club Italiano Sardegna*

'**N**othing to see. Sights are an irritating bore' – do not be misled by D.H. Lawrence's petulant reaction (*Sea and Sardinia*) to this magical island. You are guaranteed isolated havens, a treasure island uncorrupted by mass-market tourism.

Sardinia is densely populated – with sheep. Humans are thin on the ground even in the high season, which means an agreeable absence of litter, pollution and the rip-offs common in resort areas. The Mediterranean is shimmeringly inviting and algae-free. Inland, tortuous roads link remote villages where a pale skin may invite curious stares. In mainstream Italian cities to call someone a Sard is the equivalent of calling him a bog-trotter – backward and unworldly. Brigands do exist but, though hyped by the media, they are few and mostly preoccupied with private vendettas.

Its position made Sardinia strategically important in Mediterranean power politics. Before Admiral Nelson failed to buy it for £$^1/_2$ million the Spanish established vines and before them the Phoenicians, Carthaginians, Romans, Pisans and Saracens planted landmarks of their different civilizations. Before that, perhaps around 2,000 BC, a mysterious people of unknown origin built conical stone citadels called *nuraghi (singular: nuraghe)*, peculiar to Sardinia but having affinities with those equally enigmatic dwellings the *trulli* of Puglia and the Pictish brochs of Scotland. There are some 7,000 *nuraghi* in Sardinia and our tour includes the most spectacular of them.

The briefest historical survey must not omit Sardinia's role in the making of modern Italy: it fell to Victor Emmanuel, King of Sardinia and Piedmont, to ascend the throne of the new kingdom of Italy in 1861.

Those Spanish vines have flourished and there are many regional wines in Sardinia, mostly of high strength. They should be approached with respect, as should the local brandy, nicknamed *su fil e ferru* – 'barbed wire'. Restaurant cuisine majors in fish and seafood – everything but sardines; and there are delicious hams, cheeses, spit-roasted pig and lamb to be savoured.

Sardinia is worth a week, so we have devised two tours, north and south, to explore the fertile plains, wild highlands, firm white sands and rocky coves. To cover everything on this exploration of the south of the island, allow three nights.

TRANSPORT, INCLUDING MAINLAND CONNECTIONS

Shuttle flights connect Elmas airport, Cagliari, with Rome. There are less frequent links with Palermo and half a dozen Italian mainland cities, plus Paris, Frankfurt, Munich and Zurich.

Sea ferries connect Cagliari with Genoa, Civitavecchia and Naples, also with Palermo and Trapani. It is not easy to get a ferry booking at short notice in holiday months. Trips take from 12 to 22½ hours. Better to fly and hire a car. Outside Cagliari roads are uncluttered. There are no motorways.

Regular bus services link the main towns of southern Sardinia, following such routes as Cagliari-Oristano-Bosa, Cagliari-Villasimius-Muravera, Cagliari-Oristano-Nuoro, Cagliari-Sant' Antioco. Current details are issued by the Sardinia Region Tourist Department, Viale Trieste 105, 09100 Cagliari. Local hotels provide information on bus excursions.

From Cagliari a railway goes west to Iglesias, Carbonia and Sant' Antioco; another north to Oristano and the northern ferry ports. The exciting Green Train (see Trenino Verde, page 300) links Cagliari with Mandas and Arbatax.

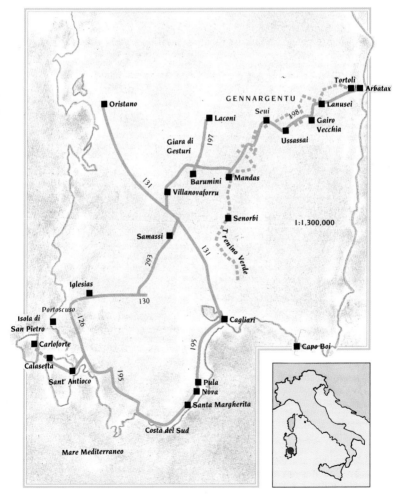

SIGHTS & PLACES OF INTEREST

ARBATAX ⇌

A quiet ferry port and popular seaside resort with seafood restaurants. Sandy bays alternate with rocky coves. Plenty of underwater fishing, canoeing and wind-surfing. Boat trips to **Seal Grottoes**.

BARUMINI ✕

The neglected village became famous in the 1950s when Sardinia's largest *nuraghe* site was excavated and restored. A prehistoric hamlet had been enlarged some time between 2,000 and 500 BC into a fortress now called **Su Nuraxi**. Now you see the central cone, four towers north, east, west and south and a girdle of walls with combat towers. Outside the military complex are huts, bakeries and dwellings. You must be active to climb all over Su Nuraxi but it justifies a few aching limbs.

The ancient stronghold commands views of rolling hills, the aboriginals' homeland. **Giara di Gesturi** northwest, a basalt plateau, is the habitat of semi-wild ponies called *cavallini della Giara*. With its rainwater pools and thick belts of oak the whole park is so natural that it has not yet been designated one. Allow half a day unless you have a 4-wheel-drive vehicle. Near **Laconi**, north again, is another park with a beautiful waterfall and a 'growing museum' of long-established trees from all over the temperate world.

Barumini village, close to the *nuraghe*, is charming, peaceful and scrupulously clean.

CAGLIARI ⇌ ✕

The capital of Sardinia and busiest town is surrounded by marshes and lagoons where remains of prehistoric lake-dwellings have been found. Flamingos stalk the flats and herons and cormorants are common sights.

Cagliari is a commercial centre and seaport by no means devoid of historic gems. The **University** preserves an enlightened code of laws drawn up in the 14thC – by a woman. Fragments of town walls, ramparts and wrought-iron balconies proclaim the Aragonese influence. The **Roman amphitheatre's auditorium** is carved out of a hillside.

Pisans of the 13thC left a **Romanesque cathedral**, the 14thC **Elephant Tower** and the **Tower of San Pancrazio**. Church visitors make for **San Michele** and **San Domenico**, the latter with impressive cloisters. A splendid **archaeological museum** contains *nuraghi* relics and items from Carthaginian and Roman times. Great views from **Terrazzo Umberto**, southeastern corner of city walls. This somewhat subdued city explodes on May Day at one of Sardinia's celebrated festivals, that of **Sant' Elisio**, intense and unself-conscious, lasting four days. In August, citizens escape to Poetto, a huge beach 4 km east.

CALASSETTA
See Sant' Antioco, page 302.

CARLOFORTE
See Sant' Antioco, page 302.

COSTA DEL SUD ⌂
A magnificent stretch of coastline boasting 305 sunny days in the year. The little town of **Nora**, overshadowed by its 16thC watch-tower, is an archaeologist's delight. Here the Phoenicians built a double harbour, one sheltered from western winds, the other from the mistral. An earthquake in the 3rdC AD threw most of Nora into the sea. You can see the rubble when the water is calm. Salvage operations have brought to light a Roman temple and baths and mosaics of refined geometrical design. Around **Pula** endless tracts of fine white sand have encouraged up-market resort developments. By-laws keep buildings well back from the sea front. At **Is Molas** is southern Sardinia's only international golf course, a very superior playground amid woodland and lakes. Sailing, fishing, windsurfing, scuba-diving along the shore. Shoppers head for hand-crafted ceramics,

---

RECOMMENDED HOTELS

ARBATAX
Villaggio Saraceno, LL; *San Gemeliano; tel. 078 266 7318; credit cards*, AE, DC, E, V.
  Superior bungalows set on beach slope with central restaurant, bar and boutique. Huge swimming-pool, tennis, canoeing, windsurfing, archery. Children's organized activities. Polite, careful instructors. Magnificent rock formations, exciting sub-aqua exploration.

CAGLIARI
Panorama, LLL; *Viale Armando Diaz 231; tel. 070 307 691; credit cards*, AE, DC, E, V.
  Roomy, modern, eight-storey hotel on broad avenue, ten-minute walk from centre. Clean and bright, insulated from traffic noise. Spacious bar on top floor with views. Garage, swimming-pool. Above-average restaurant.

LANUSEI
Villa Selene, L; *Coroddis; tel. 078 242 471; credit cards, none.*
  A quiet leafy situation on outskirts of a mountain resort. Garden, swimming-pool, tennis-court. Local people patronize the restaurant.

ORISTANO
Mistral, LL; *Via Martiri di Belfiori; tel. 078 321 2505;* and
  Mistral 2, LL, larger and more expensive; *Via Venti Settembre; tel. 078 330 2445; credit cards* AE, DC, E, MC, V *at both.*

Without pretence of *gran lusso* these twin hotels are better equipped with amenities and a quality regional cuisine than you expect to find in a Sardinian provincial centre. **Mistral 2** has a swimming-pool.

SANTA MARGHERITA DI PULA
Is Morus, LLL; *tel. 070 921 171; credit cards*, AE, DC, MC, E, V.
  Gracious living on southern Sardinian shore. Ultra-modern Saracenic style, cool arcaded terrace, rooms opening to lush garden and courtyard. Tennis, pine-woods and all water-sports. For international beautifully-landscaped golf course, shuttle bus connects **Is Molas, LLL**, similar establishment, slightly cheaper.

SANT' ANTIOCO
Moderno, L; *tel. 078 183 105; credit cards*, AE, V.
  Very small, so book before crossing to isle of Sant' Antioco on causeway (south-west coast). Restaurant, bar, shrubbery, a pleasant air of contented simplicity.

VILLASIMIUS
Capo Boi, LLL; *Capo Boi; tel. 070 798 018; credit cards, none.*
  Set in orchards on island's southeastern tip with rough sand and sea in front and mountains behind, the stark trefoil-shaped hotel opens on to a secluded private cove. Rustic beach restaurant, buffet and drinks amid prolific foliage. Two large swimming-pools at hotel, innumerable water-sports on private beach. Shoreline ripe for development.

jewellery and tapestries in the village of Pula.

GAIRO VECCHIA
See Seui, page 303.

GIARA DI GESTURI
See Barumini, page 300.

IGLESIAS
Romans exploited the rich minerals of the area, Pisans built the town. Old town walls, castle, cathedral and some churches were rebuilt in the Aragonese Gothic style. Tourist highlight is the **mineralogical museum**. Tourism on the adjacent **Costa Verde** replaced the traditional mining economy and left Iglesias a typical market town. Buy picnic cheese and ham here.

LACONI
See Barumini, page 300.

LANUSEI 🛏
The tidy little town is chief centre of the Ogliastra region. Inhabitants' casual car parking habits turn the steep main street into an obstacle course. Some fine parks here and the newish hotels

• *Cagliari, Sardinia.*

and gift shops tell you that Arbatax and the seaside are not far off. If you have arrived via the Gennargentu highlands they will be a welcome sight. If you are heading west, say goodbye to civilization.

MANDAS
See Seui, page 303.

NORA and PULA
See Costa del Sud, page 301.

SAMASSI
Well-preserved archetypal village of the Campidano wine-producing district. Houses are of Roman *domus* type, built of sun-dried mud and straw, with arched doorways, inner courts and south-facing porticoes on wooden columns called *lolle*. Wine is stored in large casks in ground-level cellars.

SANT' ANTIOCO 🛏
Island with a fine shoreline of beaches and caves, reached by a causeway which has superseded a Roman bridge (traces still visible). There are prodi-

gious remains of the Phoenicians and Carthaginians. Funerary urns at **Tophet** contained sacrificed corpses of first-born children. The African martyr Sant' Antioco is thought to be buried among tombs and catacombs of a large **necropolis** on the western side. There are also atmospheric ruins of a temple and a fort.

Local restaurants specialize in seafood – mullet, white bream and eels are among the more exotic ingredients and the fish soups *ziminu* and *sa cassola* are renowned. The best local wine is Gregorius. From Calasetta the ferry takes you to Carloforte, a pretty little town, formerly a Phoenician settlement.

SEUI

Typical mountain village in the depths of historic brigand country, the Barbagio Seulo. Major event of the day is the arrival of the train (see Trenino Verde, page 300). A mild climate favours this wine-producing area. Seui at 800 m is dominated by **Gennargentu**, as high again. Eating places make the most of the agri-pastoral economy: a country cuisine.

This is the midpoint of a spectacularly hairpinned mountain road between Mandas and Lanusei, along which villages cling precariously to cliff walls. Now and again they fall: **Gairo Vecchia**, 36 km east, is deserted by inhabitants who, tired of seeing their cottages slide down the mountain, built new homes on flatter ground.

VILLANOVAFORRU ✕

The **Genna Maria**, a major *nuraghe* complex recently excavated, consists of prehistoric houses and workshops surrounding the central cone. Shards and pots of futuristic design suggest this was an important ceramics centre. There are hopes that this site will yield information about the *nuraghi* builders, of whom so little is known. Local archaeology is well displayed and cleverly expounded in a newish architect-designed **museum** which is putting the town on the map. **Ales**, 19 km north, a centre of farming, has a piazza designed by the modern sculptor Pomodoro and dedicated to Antonio Gramsci, whose writings inspired Mussolini in much the same way that those of Nietzsche inspired Hitler.

RECOMMENDED RESTAURANTS

Regional food based on lamb and kid with artichokes, fennel and herbs and cooked in patriarchal fashion (such as in a pit in the ground) is best sought in homely taverns and *trattorie*. On the coast, expect a choice of about 20 fish dishes. Smart restaurants are few.

BARUMINI
Zia Annetta, L; *no telephone; credit cards, none.*

Cottage courtyard chophouse presided over by 'Auntie' Annetta herself with anxious frowns and mutterings about poor quality of present-day fruits of the earth. Brilliant table d'hôte for all that. *Gnocchetti sardi* (stuffed pasta, ewe-milk cheese), *porceddu* (roast pork) and *sebadas* (honey soufflé) with golden Vernaccia wine constituted the best meal, and one of the cheapest, we ate in Sardinia. This farm kitchen was as memorable as the famous Su Nuraxi down the road (see Barumini, page 300).

CAGLIARI
Dal Corsaro, LL; *Viale Regina Margherita 28; tel. 070 664 318; credit cards, AE, DC, E, MC, V; closed Sun, Christmas, Aug.*

Foreigners make for this best-known of waterfront restaurants where spit-roasted pork and seafood are of consistent standard and excellent value.

PORTOSCUSO
La Ghinghetta, LL; *Via Cavour 28; tel. 078 150 8143; credit cards, AE, DC, E, MC, V; closed Sun and in winter.*

An oasis in the culinary wilderness, worth a detour if you are among the south-western islands. Rooms to rent.

VILLANOVAFORRU
Le Colline, LL; *tel. 070 930 0134; credit card, AE.*

Peaceful location, painstaking country cuisine. This place also offers limited accommodation at fair rates.

Northern Sardinia

470 km; map Touring Club Italiano Sardegna

Fantastic rock formations, sculpted by the winds – deserted beaches of flat white sands – limestone grottoes bristling with stalactites – smoky taverns, scented pine-woods, bowers of sea-angling bliss, sub-aqua wonderlands – multifarious cottage crafts and customs from a melting-pot of ancient cultures... and the jet set. The Costa Smeralda, the coastal indentations which admit a limpid sea near Sardinia's north-eastern tip, is the patrician playground. Expensive yachts have supplanted patched-up fishing boats. Night-clubs, bistros and hideaways in flamboyant gardens parody with antiseptic cleanliness the simple lime-washed dwellings they have swept away. All this is superb, but it is not exactly Sardinia.

The Costa was invented by the late Aga Khan who happened to be stormbound in a yacht. He could have been stormbound almost anywhere else on the north Sardinian coast and been similarly inspired. Some visitors will prefer the lovely lonely stretches, the unsophisticated townships where there turns out to be plenty to see and do; and everywhere, in town and country, the vivid reminders of far-off peoples who came and settled, planted their cultures, died or were driven out.

Northern Sardinia is the antiquarian's hunting-ground. The most ancient _nuraghe_ complex is at Santu Antine. Elsewhere, man-made grottoes 4,000 years old are threaded into cliffs as termites might thread the uprights of antique furniture. The Romans and Carthaginians are well represented in forts and settlements. Among some intriguing churches the Saccargia basilica near Sassari takes the palm with its bold chess-board stonework.

This being Sardinia, pagan rituals are scrupulously observed and pageantry takes priority. See if possible, on the third Sunday in May, the Cavalcata Sarda at Sassari, where a furious horse-race (the jockeys _stand_ on their mounts) precedes a three-hour costumed procession.

Old habits and occupations dictate rural life-styles. Encircled by our tour (three days to see it all), on minor roads, are Pattada, home of the notorious _pattadese_ or shepherd's knife; and Nule, where dazzling geometrically-patterned carpets are woven. Historic centres of coastal towns teem with little shops offering souvenirs of more recent pedigree. If you are into pink coral, you have the choice of a myriad trinkets.

TRANSPORT, INCLUDING MAINLAND CONNECTIONS

Alghero and Olbia have flights to and from several mainland airports, with summer charters to and from various Continental cities.

The rudimentary rail system of southern Sardinia is continued here, the line which comes north from Cagliari splitting, west to Sassari, Alghero and Porto Torres, east to Olbia and Golfo Aranci. There is also a route designed for slow-train enthusiasts between Sassari and Palau on the Bonifacio Strait.

Car ferries link Corsica and La Maddalena with the Sardinian mainland. Porto Torres is the ferry port for Toulon in France (summer only, 12 hours), Genoa (12 hours) and Livorno (12 hours). The short sea route is between Olbia and Civitavecchia (7 hours). Book well in advance – the rule book says two months minimum.

Buses serve the principal towns and tourist areas, except that nothing so plebeian as a bus is normally seen on the Costa Smeralda. The long-distance bus routes are Olbia-Nuoro, Porto Torres-Sassari-Oristano and Olbia-Sassari. Bus excursions are detailed in seasonal information from local hotels.

General information on ferries and excursions: Provincial Tourist Agency, Viale Caprera 36, 07100 Sassari; tel. 079 299 544.

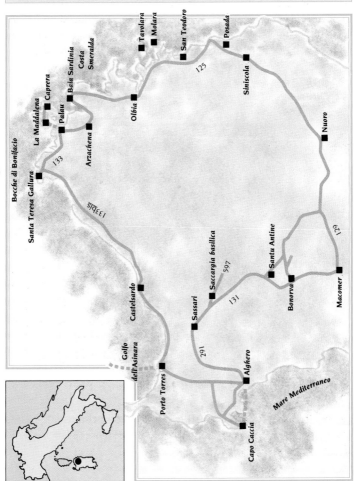

SIGHTS & PLACES OF INTEREST

ALGHERO ⊨ ×
A walled town on the so-called Coral Riviera, originally an Aragonese colony (the cathedral is Aragonese Gothic) and now developed for tourism. Ramparts overlook the harbour, there are good beaches along the corniche roads north and south and the town has cafés, seafood restaurants and a couple of expensive hotels.

The obligatory excursion is to **Neptune's Cave**, an echoing vault in the headland of Capo Caccia with interior pools and limestone curiosities near sea level, deep within a headland. Visitable on foot (500 steps) but more impressive when entered by boat. Regular trips from quay opposite Bastione della Maddalena, a 25-km round trip.

ARZACHENA
Guarded by a massive tortoise and a gigantic mushroom – typical of contorted rock formations of Sardinia's north and north-east coasts. This once-rundown village is now the heart of the Costa Smeralda. For something different, take the track for **Li Mura**, 8 km along the Luogosanto road. It has **'giants' graves'** – a half-circle of monoliths and a corridor connecting cells where these unknown Titans were laid in the 3rdC BC.

BAIA SARDINIA
A new prestige resort, northernmost of Costa Smeralda. Immaculate hotels, villas and golf courses. Nearby **Pitrizza** and **Porto Cervo** are also custombuilt resorts with the emphasis on water-sports. Wonderfully clear sea: when you moor your yacht the anchor is plainly visible lying on the bottom. A potential mini-paradise just down the coast is Capricciola: it may escape development. Some say that for the jet set the novelty of the Costa is wearing off.

BONORVA
A town known for mineral waters and traditional crafts, especially carpets and tapestries. **Grottoes of Sant' Andrea Priu** on road to Bono (after 9 km look for signs) are man-made burial chambers known as *domus de janas* or 'witches' houses'. Solar symbols decorate the 20 tombs; a great headless bull, carved from a single block of stone, stands guard. We are in mythological country here despite Sant' Andrea's holy name.

CAPRERA
See La Maddalena, this page.

CASTELSARDO ⊨
A Genoese outpost of old, heaped up on a promontory. Superb seascapes towards Gallura mountains. Late Gothic **cathedral** teeters on brink of a cliff. Big **crafts market** and *ateliers* (palm-leaf baskets, leatherwork) testify to a healthy passing trade – as do a selection of satisfactory hotels and restaurants.

LA MADDALENA
Italian naval base. Ferry from Palau, 15 minutes. Observe a prize item for the stony menagerie snapshot collection: a huge **polar bear**, apparently transfixed by the enchanting view of sea, islands and rock pinnacles. From La Maddalena a 600-m bridge crosses to **Caprera**, a nature reserve and focus of visitor attention because here lies Garibaldi the Liberator, 'a lion in his sepulchre whose breathing makes the ocean swell' as an Italian poet wrote. His house and tomb are a museum. From La Maddalena, the metropolis of island hotels and restaurants, you can visit all the isles of the archipelago which bears its name. **Naval museum** in town.

MOLARA
And Tavolara, see Posada, page 307.

NUORO
Inland, halfway house between southern and northern Sardinia, Nuoro is strewn along a gash in the hills, shabby at first glance yet a centre of commerce and birthplace of a Nobel Prize winner, Grazia Deledda, the early 20thC novelist. Her humble cottage is now a humble **museum**. Little else to see in the town, apart from a startlingly up-to-date **folk museum**, mostly costumes, jewellery and tools. See the dashing lightweight garb of the moustachioed mountaineers and the heavy stifling cages of female attire.

A bronze statue of Christ the Redeemer on **Monte Ortobene**, over-

• *Porto Cervo,* Sardinia.

looking the town, is honoured with a feast annually (end of August). From this summit there are striking views of the impenetrable central highlands.

OLBIA ✕

This ancient port at the head of the deep Golfo Aranci has remains of a pre-Christian **necropolis** and, at 11thC **San Simplicio church**, some Roman tombs. Atte, concubine of Nero, came from Olbia. With its airport, ferry to the mainland and situation as gateway to the Costa Smeralda, the town has smartened itself up. Undeveloped shoreline along the Gulf has dense woodland – through which a tiny branch railway crawls – much wildlife and millions of tortoises.

PORTO TORRES

Earmarked by Nature for a ferry port, which it is. The summer scene gives new arrivals no clues to the sort of land they are entering: the pagan memories, strange dialects and superstitions, the shadows of the vendetta and the arbitrary control of romantic affairs (hence, very often, the vendetta) by the traditional matchmaker.

South of the port is the megalithic altar of **Monte d'Accodi**, scene of Stone Age fertility rites, with a sacrificial table on its 10-m high mound.

POSADA

One of a number of pretty coastal villages above snowy ribbons of sand, backed by pine-woods along a shore not much frequented by strangers. The hinterland is clothed in cork woods, with outcrops of grotesque granite rocks. At Posada the ruined **castle of Fava** was built for defence against the Moorish pirates.

Two delightful little adjoining villages are **La Caletta** and **San Teodoro**, the former with a characteristic harbour, the latter locked into cliffs and tiny coves. On the horizon the isles of **Molara** and **Tavolara** resemble monsters coming from the deep to join the north Sardinia bestiary of monoliths.

SACCARGIA BASILICA

See Sassari, page 308.

RECOMMENDED HOTELS

On the Costa Smeralda between Olbia and the Bonifacio Strait the transformation of a lonely shore involved commandeering whole bays and coves and enclosing them in high-ly expensive fairylands for adults. From pseudo-Moorish palaces, luxury cottages and yacht marinas to acres of costly flowers and shrubs, every-thing is immaculate and in a world of its own. Hotels compete to see who can charge most for ultra-refined relaxation. Four of the most astonish-ing, all **LLL**, all taking credit cards AE, DC, E, MC, V, are:
Cala di Volpe, tel. 078 996 083; **Romazzino**, tel. 078 996 020; **Cervo**, tel. 078 992 593; and (not quite as expensive) **Sporting**, tel. 078 934 005, at Porto Rotondo just north of Olbia.

All are closed Oct-Apr – the best time for ordinary mortals to visit the fabled shore and still find a few smart bars open.

ALGHERO
Calabona, LL; *Calabona; tel. 079 975 728; credit cards*, AE, DC, E, MC, V; *closed in winter.*

Excellent large modern sea-front hotel 0.5 km from popular resort. Terraces (roof-top and garden), pool, own beach.

CAPO TESTA
Capo Testa e Due Mari, LL; *tel.* 078 975 4333; *credit cards*, AE, DC, E, MC, V.

On the famous 'sunset' headland of Santa Teresa Gallura. Beach, pool, gardens, a more credible version of Costa Smeralda palaces.

CASTELSARDO
Riviera, L; *tel.* 079 470 143; *credit cards*, AE, MC, V.

Budget stopover on north coast road at historic fortress town. No restaurant (we recommend **Sa Feru-la, LL**, *tel.* 079 474 049), same credit cards, at Lu Bagnu – 4 km).

SINISCOLA
L'Aragosta, L; *La Caletta, 6 km from Siniscola; tel.* 078 481 0046; *credit cards*, AE, DC, E, MC, V.

Quiet location in cliff-and-estuary setting by-passed by main tourist route. An established favourite with amazing range of fish and seafood nearby, but none in the hotel despite its name ('Lobster').

SANT' ANDREA PRIU
See *Bonorva, page 306.*

SANTA TERESA GALLURA
It overlooks the Bonifacio Strait above sheer cliffs and contorted rocks. Gor-geous sunsets bring visitors here. The old village is equipped to handle their needs. Five kilometres through a multi-coloured geology is **Capo Testa** with Roman diggings still visible along the cliffs. This granite built the docks of Rome at Ostia Antica.

SAN TEODORO
See *Posada, page 307.*

SANTU ANTINE
The celebrated *nuraghe* was begun (about 15thC BC) with a three-storey stone tower to which other towers, well walks, a curtain wall, enclosed court-yard and well were gradually added. Romans came, saw, marvelled and used the place, which is thought to be the oldest citadel of the lost civilization.

SASSARI ✕
If you come to Sardinia from a north-ern European port this is your first large town – second largest in Sar-dinia, in fact. The area was at the cen-tre of early touristic developments before the Costa Smeralda was dreamed of. This north-west corner of the island, Alghero especially, has its share of visitors and Sassari has responded with a biennial **crafts fair**, encouragement of traditional crafts and permanent arts exhibitions. The **Cavalcata** (see Introduction, page 304) is one of Europe's most presti-gious folkloristic manifestations.

In other ways Sassari has more the air of a mainland town (its **Piazza Italia** is the only one in Sardinia). It was caught up in the medieval squabbles of the maritime republics and was allied with Pisa, then with Genoa. While under French influence it almost succeeded in importing the 1789 revolution. All this is reflected in the minglings of building styles round the city's hub.

The cathedral is an architectural goulash, based on 14thC foundations. The **Sanna Museum of Archaeology** has collections worthy of the region's antiquities and the **Pinacoteca** exhibits a wide range of Italian and Sardinian artists. The city's grand emblem is the **Rosello Fountain**, below Rosello Bridge as you exit for Castelsardo. It is late Renaissance, made by Genoese craftsmen and has an equestrian statue, several large masks and dolphins and symbols of the seasons. Another extraordinary

blend of old styles, this time in che-quered stonework, is the **Saccargia basilica** and separate bell-tower, set amid olives and citrus groves 16 km south-east of town on Route 597.

RECOMMENDED RESTAURANTS

ALGHERO
Lepanto, LL; *Via Carlo Alberto* 135; *tel.* 079 979 116; *credit cards*, AE, DC, E, MC, V.

Plat du jour always fish, a voyage downstream from river crayfish to oysters and from crab to striped bass and swordfish. Always a cheerful clientele here, residents and visitors alike, typical of the best restaurants along the north and north-west coasts where fish and *frutta di mare* dominate menus and you sometimes munch your *calamari* next door to an aquatic monster in the dining-room aquarium, munching his live prawns and unaware that he will be on the menu for dinner tomorrow.

OLBIA
Leone e Anna, LL; *Via Barcellona* 90; *tel.* 078 926 333; *credit cards*, AE, V; *closed* Wed.

Simple dishes – again mostly fish – superbly presented. Probably the best on the Aranci gulf, where competition is not keen.

OLIENA
Su Gologone, LL; *8 km E of Oliena*; *tel.* 078 428 7512; *credit cards*, AE, E, MC, V; *closed* Nov.

Determinedly rustic, smothered in shrubbery on fringe of wild interior mountains south-east of Nuoro. Authentic Sardinian cuisine attracts

weekenders but dining-room and pleasant courtyard can generally cope.

ORISTANO
Da Renzo, L; *at road junction, signposted 'Siamaggiore', 7 km NE of town*; *tel.* 078 333 658; *credit cards, none.*

Country restaurant away from main road. Exquisite home cooking of grills with traditional herbs. Crowds flock here on Sundays, though the town has a few quite satisfactory restaurants.

PALAU
Vecchia Gallura, L; *on Route* 133, 3 *km SW of Palau*; *tel.* 078 970 8194; *credit cards*, AE, DC, E, MC, V; *open summer only.*

A small establishment which can give points in cooking and variety to grander places along the Costa Smeralda, and at a fifth of the price. Seafood, fried fish, lamb, traditional recipes.

SASSARI
Del Giamaranto di Gianni e Amedeo, LL; *Via Alghero* 69; *tel.* 079 274 598; *credit cards*, AE, DC, E, MC, V; *closed* Mon *in summer,* Aug.

Unpretentious old-fashioned *trattoria*, atmosphere as genuine as well-cooked local dishes. Some call this the only really civilized eating-place in Sassari. At weekends you should book.

INDEX